The History of the Worshipful Company of Framework Knitters

The Art and Mystery of Framework Knitting in England and Wales

The History of the Worshipful Company of Framework Knitters

The Art and Mystery of Framework Knitting in England and Wales

Sheila A. Mason

First published in the United Kingdom in 2000 by
The Worshipful Company of Framework Knitters,
Cottage Homes,
Stoughton5 Road,
Oadby, Leicester LE2 4FQ

British Library Cataloguing in Publication Data
A catalogue record for this book is available from the British Library

ISBN 0-9538998-0-2

Typeset in 11/12pt Times New Roman by
Hands Fotoset, Woodthorpe, Nottingham

Printed and bound in Great Britain by
The Cavendish Press Limited
Whiteacres, Whetstone, Leicester

Contents

List of Plates

List of Tables

THE RIGHT HONOURABLE THE LORD MAYOR

ALDERMAN CLIVE MARTIN OBE TD DL

MANSION HOUSE · LONDON · EC4N 8BH

TELEPHONE 020 7626 2500   FACSIMILE 020 7623 9524   E-MAIL lord.mayor@corpoflondon.gov.uk

Sheila Mason's definitive history of The Worshipful Company of Framework Knitters follows the Company from its incorporation in 1657 until the end of the twentieth century. It should appeal both to historians of London as well as those of the East Midlands for it details the industrial, economic and social history of a Livery Company which was indisputably part of the City of London and yet had its roots firmly in the East Midlands.

It is a fascinating story. Even though the Framework Knitters' are a Livery Company of the City of London, providing eight Lord Mayors, as well as a number of Sheriffs and Members of Parliament and being embroiled in London's radical politics of the eighteenth and early nineteenth centuries, this book is much more than a recital of the Company's relationship with the City. Its seventeenth century Charters gave The Worshipful Company of Framework Knitters monopolistic legal control of the industry with which it is associated throughout England and Wales, and Sheila Mason's fully documented and detailed research clearly shows how the Company interacted with the development of the hosiery trade. The story of the Company's attempts to exert its powers nationwide throw new light on early industrial history and the demise of this total power and the emergence of the modern Livery Company are treated sympathetically and fully.

Preface

I should like to express my gratitude for the help and encouragement I have received from the members of the Worshipful Company of Framework Knitters, especially from the members of the Millennium Book Sub-Committee led by the Immediate Past Master Michael Turnbull. I should also like to thank the present Clerk to the Company, H. W. H. Ellis, the Deputy Clerk based in Leicester, Mrs. Anne Brown, Liveryman Henry Hurt whose practical knowledge of framework knitting is unsurpassed and Dr. David Bethel C.B.E., a member of the Court of the Company and former Director of Leicester Polytechnic, who kindly read the manuscript and made helpful suggestions and corrections. Finally my gratitude goes to my husband, Steward John Mason, my son, Liveryman Charles Mason, and the rest of my family whose practical help and patience have been infinite.

I should also like to thank the staff of the Guildhall Library of the Corporation of London, especially the Manuscripts Department, the Records Office and the Art Gallery of the Corporation of London, the Nottinghamshire Archives and the Record Office of Leicestershire, Leicester and Rutland for all their helpfulness and efficiency.

It is my regret that, other than in the appendix listing, I could not mention every member of the Art and Mystery of Framework Knitters by name and trace his, or her, relationship to the work and history of the Society, and I extend my apologies to those members, both past and present, who have taken a leading role in the Company's affairs if I have misread their prominence in the Company, and omitted their contribution to the Company's continuing success. Any misinterpretations and mistakes are entirely my own.

Sheila A. Mason
Nottingham, 2000

Introduction

Just as knitting on the frame is performed with a single continuous thread, so the history of the Worshipful Society of Framework Knitters is one of continuous involvement with the mechanical knitting industry.

The roots of the Society lie in 1589 when William Lee of Calverton, Nottinghamshire, with the help of relatives and friends, invented a method of knitting mechanically. From his machine, usually called the stocking frame, in spite of this nomenclature concealing the fact that it could also knit other products, was developed an industry that over the years gave employment to thousands throughout Great Britain, and by the time of Lee's quatercentenary in 1989 was a £20 billion worldwide industry.[1]

In 1657, just under threequarters of a century after Lee's invention, Oliver Cromwell recognised the importance of framework knitting to the country by granting a Charter to its most prominent and organised participants, giving them complete authority as 'one Body Corporate and Politic in deed and in name and shall have continuance forever by the name of Master Wardens Assistants and Society of the Art or Mystery of Framework Knitters of the City of London' within the City of London and four miles around (see Appendix 2). In 1663 a second Charter, granted by Charles II, extended the Society's absolute authority to the City of Westminster and the whole of England and Wales. By incorporating the Framework Knitters' as a Society, rather than a Company, the two rulers recognised the countrywide importance of framework knitting and through the Charters and subsequent Bye-laws gave the Society such total control of mechanical knitting that it was more powerful than any modern industrial organisation.

The Company was completely enmeshed in framework knitting through this monopolistic control of the industry throughout England and Wales. Even after the repeal of some of the powers granted to the Company in the Statute Law Revision Acts of the late 1860s and 1870s, the Society's legal authority would seem to have continued into the twenty first century, although the 1809 decision that 'the Company had no power by their Charter and Bye-laws to compel the operative Framework Knitters to be admitted members of the Company' considerably reduced the Company's overall control by confining these powers only to members of the Society.[2]

For the first century and a half working journeymen constituted the largest group within the Society of Framework Knitters. Then, as the knitting industry

1

grew increasingly complex and powered machinery mainly replaced the hand-operated frame, its Freemen came to be drawn largely from the upper echelons of the multitudinous sections of the industry; the Society became a most valuable forum for the whole trade and its members were to be found on numerous government and official bodies affecting the knitting industry.

The Framework Knitters' Society is no exception to the concept that the characteristic of Livery Companies which enabled them to survive long after they had given up any pretence of regulating a trade and gave them a sense of purpose has been their charities, and the Society's involvement in charity and education has continued since its inception.[3] When the working apprentice system administered by the Company almost died out the Company's role in technical education became less direct but nevertheless remained important.

Although its Freemen have been drawn largely from the East Midland counties of Leicestershire, Nottinghamshire and Derbyshire, the Company has taken a full part in the affairs of the City of London, providing eight Lord Mayors plus a number of Members of Parliament and Sheriffs of the City of London.

As this is a history of the Society of Framework Knitters wherever possible its documents have been used, and where their version differs from other, often later, sources the Company's manuscripts have been accepted as the contemporary report. The documents of the Society of Framework Knitters, formerly kept by the Company's Clerk, are now housed in the Guildhall Library, London. In addition there is a small collection of manuscripts relating to the Company in the Nottinghamshire Archives. Even taken together, however, these documents are not chronologically complete. The Minute books from 1657 to 1824, with the exception of a recently acquired one for 1726 to 1730, are missing, so that the period until 1825 is only partially covered by the Society's record of events.[4]

The largest number of entries in the Society's documents concern the management and distribution of the charitable funds. The most complete of the early records are the apprenticeship bindings, although these record only the name of the parties concerned and in one book whether the binding took place under the aegis of the London or Nottingham Court.[5]

It used to be believed that many documents relating to the first century of the Company's business were used by the House of Commons during the enquiries into the validity of the Company's regulations in the 1750's and, after being filed in the House, were destroyed in the fire of 1834. But, although this could be true of some, it is not a completely accurate picture, as in 1875 the then Clerk of the Company James Funston would have appeared to have consulted a number of Company records dating back to 1664 for his report of that year to the Court of Assistants on the subject of the admission of females to the Freedom of the Company. It is also known that a Wardens' Account Book from June 1664 to June 1730 and the Minutes from 1730 to 1825, rebound into two volumes in 1901, were still in the Clerk's possession in 1931. The last recorded person to have used many of these lost documents was Professor F. A. Wells of the University of Nottingham who refers to a large number of Company manuscripts of the 1700 and 1800s in his history of the hosiery industry first published in 1935.[6] On 10/11 May 1941 the Clerk's office was destroyed by enemy action and the Minute Book from 1927–1941 and other modern papers relating to the Company, including some for the Oadby Cottage Homes, the Company's corporate property and the Company's

1933 Grant of Arms, were destroyed, but there was no record that any 1700 and 1800 manuscripts were among this World War II loss, and subsequent searches by the present Clerk have failed to unearth these documents in former Clerks' offices.

The Company has also not always been fortunate in the carefulness of either its Clerks or its members when other Company possessions were left in their care. Either John Thurlby or Henry Matthews, the Clerks, took charge of the Company's effects when its Hall in Red Cross Street was mortgaged in the 1720s and, although their deposition was never fully recorded, some items were subsequently housed by the landlords of the various venues where the Company had its meetings, or were lodged with various officers of the Company, as in 1769 when the 'books, plate and other things' were removed from the White Hart to the house of Mr. Thomas Lever the Upper Warden Elect'.[7] When Prince Albert wished to establish a portrait gallery for British 'inventors, discoverers and introducers of useful arts' in 1851 the first picture he is reported to have asked for was that of William Lee painted by Balder(s)ton, who was a relative of, or was himself, the Company's 1663 Warden. It was then realised that this picture, together with other paintings and artifacts from the Hall had vanished. Enquiries by the Clerk failed to unearth any items, some, or all, of which were then thought to have been used as surety for money lent to the Company in the 1790s by Robinson, a prominent member. An engraving of the Balderton picture was then reported in various publications written at the beginning of the twentieth century as being hung in the Museum of the Patent Office at South Kensington. However, lengthy correspondence and searches of London Museums have failed to produce a copy of this engraving, so that the only existing copy of this painting is to be found on early Society documents (see Plate 1).

Moreover, as well as losing some possessions, the perceived value of others changed, and what is of inestimable value now was at other times regarded as almost valueless. The Master's Chair (see Plate C2b), given by Thomas Carwarden about 1680, is now considered important enough to be on permanent exhibition at the Museum of London but during most of the eighteenth and nineteenth century was placed in whichever venue the Company held its Courts; it spent the First World War at the Savoy Hotel, London, and most of the Second World War stored at Timson & Sons of Leicester's Removal Depot. Another example of changed values is the saga of the full length portrait of Robert Waithman MP, Master of the Company in 1815, Lord Mayor of London in 1823, and six times returned as Member of Parliament for London, which was offered unconditionally to the Company in 1901 (see Plate 2). The Court did not know what to do with such a bequest and it 'was left to the Clerk to deal with at his discretion'. After the Clerk reported that both the Library Committee of the Corporation of London and the Ward of Farringdon Without, for which Waithman had been the Alderman, had declined to accept it, it was proposed by the Court that the Clerk 'dispose of it as best he could'. No disposition had been possible by the end of 1903 when the Clerk was authorised to cut the portrait down to about five feet by three feet six inches; the cost of such alteration and framing being borne by the then Master Captain Thomas Blashill. In 1919 it was still in the Clerk's possession listed as 'oil painting of a gentleman' and eventually found its way to the Corah Hall where it now hangs.[8]

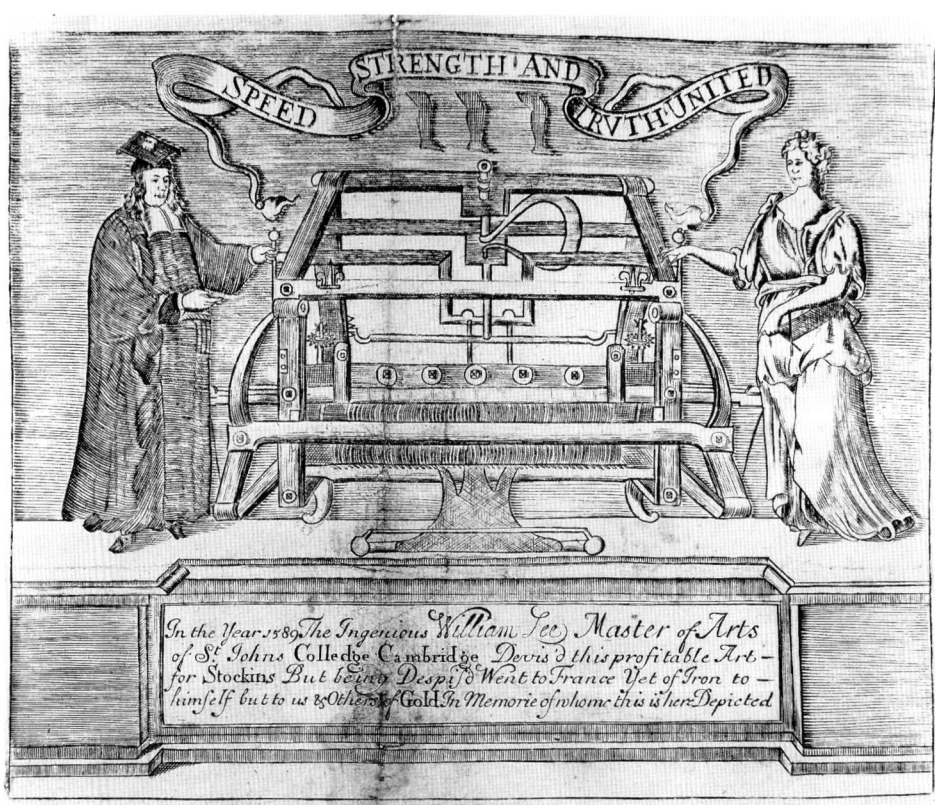

PLATE 1   *repr. with permission of Nottinghamshire Archives*

ENGRAVING OF A PAINTING BY BALDERTON OF WILLIAM LEE
AND THE KNITTING FRAME

This engraving, found on documents of the Worshipful Company of Framework Knitters, is one
of the only remaining examples of this painting. The original, which hung in the Company's
Hall, was lost by 1851. It was apparently painted by George Balderton, an Assistant of the
Company in 1657 and Warden in 1663, or by a close relative, and is the only possible near-
contemporary likeness of William Lee, who is depicted as a portly cleric on the left hand side of
the machine. Moreover, as the same engraving of the knitting frame appears on the Company's
Loving Cup of 1656, it is also the earliest known depiction of a stocking frame.

Because of this lack of care with its possessions the Society found itself
'disrespectful to civic authority' in the late 1830s. In 1837 the government enquiry
into municipal corporations reported that the Framework Knitters' Company
'declined to furnish . . . copies of their Charters or Byelaws, or to answer the
circular queries, on the grounds of expense'. Even when reasonable expenses were
offered 'no person attended on behalf of the Company at the Guildhall to produce
the Charters'. However, it would appear that this refusal on the grounds of expense
was just an excuse to cover the fact that at this time the Company did not have a
copy of the Cromwell Charter and had mislaid that of Charles II. Indeed until its
presentation to the Company in the 1890s the Cromwell Charter was not even

PLATE 2   *F.W.K. MSS.*

PAST MASTER ALDERMAN ROBERT WAITHMAN, M.P.

Robert Waithman was Master of the Company in 1815, Lord Mayor of London in 1823, and six times returned as Member of Parliament for the City of London. Presented to the Company in 1901, this portrait, in oils, now hangs in the Corah Hall at the Oadby Cottage Homes.

believed to exist. John Throsby writing in 1797 stated that 'During Cromwell's usurpation the framework knitters addressed him by petition that they might be incorporated, by charter, under the great seal of England. This request was couched in strong and manly language; but it did not succeed'. This incorrect assumption was perpetuated by succeeding writers, for Gravenor Henson, writing in 1831, felt that 'Cromwell, who was extremely ignorant in these matters, had his mind too much occupied with conspiracies and military arrangements, to interfere with trade, especially in such minute concerns as framing bodies politic', while in the 1845 *Report on Framework Knitting* it was noted that 'the petition to the Protector does not appear to have met with any attention'. The Company was a little more forthcoming to the second municipal enquiry in 1881 when it admitted that 'the date of the foundation of the Company, so far as can be discovered from public records, was, by letters patent dated 13th June 1657 . . . (but) the Company has no document in its possession which states this'.[9]

However, as the Charter granted by Cromwell in 1657, the second original of the Charter of 1663 and the Ordinances of 1664 were restored in 1898, and in 1976 the Minute Book of 1727–30 was bought from a London auction house, it is hoped that other items appertaining to the Company may still come to light.

The Charters, and the Ordinances of 1664, are the most important, and imposing, of the Company's documents.[10] In addition two copies of the Ordinances were presented to the Company by its first Clerk, John Hannis, for use at the Company's Courts; one, rebound in red leather, is now at the Guildhall Library and the other in the Nottinghamshire Archives Office (see Appendices 2, 3, 4 and Plates 3–8 and C1).

The Masters, Wardens and Assistants, including John Lee, presumably a relative of William Lee, are named in both Charters and, allowing for some exaggeration as to the state of trade, their details of events are accepted as evidence of how machine knitting and the Company started (see Appendix 8). In addition to the Charters the earliest Company books detail the registration of apprentices from 1694 in the Company's Courts at both London and Nottingham for an Orphan's Tax payable to the City of London, although not all Company apprentices are recorded; exemptions were made in the case of the placing of pauper apprentices by the parishes or where no payment changed hands, as in the case of apprenticeships within a family. There is also a detailed membership list of 1722 and odd snippets of information in various later Company papers, usually documented by the Clerk when he was searching for answers to government or Court questions. However, in spite of the lack of other Company documentation about the early years it has been possible to make significant correlations about the early history of the Company from state and government papers and by tracing the families of those named in the Charters and involved in framework knitting at this time from such documents as wills, probate inventories and various tax returns, although it is admitted that such presumptive links cannot be proved conclusively. City of London Freedom and apprentice records are not complete for this early period, the Freedoms are fragmentary before 1681, and few apprentice details are available before 1694, but those available nevertheless also form a valuable resource and make possible a more informed picture of the Company's early history.

Although dating from much later, the histories written by Gravenor Henson in 1831 and William Felkin in 1867 have also been consulted as both men came

PLATE 3   *F.W.K. MSS.*

1657 CHARTER – CROMWELL'S PORTRAIT

Executed in black ink on the first sheet of the 1657 Charter, this portrait depicts the Protector at the end of his life. The translation of this Charter is in Appendix 2.

from families associated with framework knitting from at least the 1600s (1695 – Richard Felkin bound apprentice at the Company's Nottingham Court to John Leeson of Calverton; 1696 – Henry Henson bound to Benjamin Mather at the Nottingham Court[11]), although the limitations of these histories have been taken into account wherever possible, especially in the case of Gravenor Henson who allowed his wholehearted support of the operative framework knitters at the beginning of the 1800s to inhibit accuracy in so far as the Society was concerned. His vehement attack on the Framework Knitters' Company for apeing the pomp of rich Livery Companies, such as the Goldsmiths', by building a gilt barge and

PLATE 4

1657 CHARTER – CROMWELL'S SEAL   *F.W.K. MSS.*

The seal is at the bottom of the final vellum page of the Charter. The original was unfortunately broken, presumably during the time the Charter was lost, and this example is a reproduction.

splendid carriage for the Master and Wardens, which was then repeated in government reports and elsewhere, including modern histories, would appear to owe more to his imagination and his dislike, almost hatred, of the Company than to facts.[12] No trace of the Framework Knitters' Company ever owning a barge or carriage has so far been found.

During the sixteenth, seventeenth, and into the eighteenth centuries the spelling of surnames in English and French was both idiosyncratic and fickle. To obviate lengthy explanations in each case, such as for example with the spelling of the English workmen in France or interchangeable names such as Aston or Ashton the alternative spellings, including those given by linguistic experts, will often be shown within the name or given alongside in brackets. In addition, the word hosiery refers, strictly speaking, to the dealing 'in hose and frame-knitted or woven

PLATE 5

1663 CHARTER – CHARLES II'S PORTRAIT AND THE TOP HALF OF THE FIRST PAGE

Both the portrait of Charles II (Colour Plate 1) and the borders of this Charter are skillfully painted, and depict beautiful birds and flowers. An abstract of this Charter is in Appendix 3.

PLATE 6   *F.W.K. MSS.*

1663 CHARTER – CHARLES II'S SEAL

As with the seal of Oliver Cromwell in the 1657 Charter, the original seal on this Charter is incomplete, and this too is a reproduction.

underclothing', but as in common usage it is also used to describe the knitting processes, and other garments made by these processes, it is here used in both contexts.[13] In the text the words 'Society' or 'Company' on their own will refer to the Worshipful Society of Framework Knitters. 'F.W.K. MSS.' as shown on Plate 6, means that the illustration comes from the Company's manuscripts. For those who want to convert the many historical monetary references into modern monies the equivalent values of the pound are given in Appendix 12.

There is no doubt that future research will illuminate further areas, such as the relationships between the framework knitting families who were members of the Society in London and the East Midlands in the sixteenth, seventeenth and early eighteenth centuries and the connection between these families and the participants in the disturbances in the East Midlands in the nineteenth century, but it is

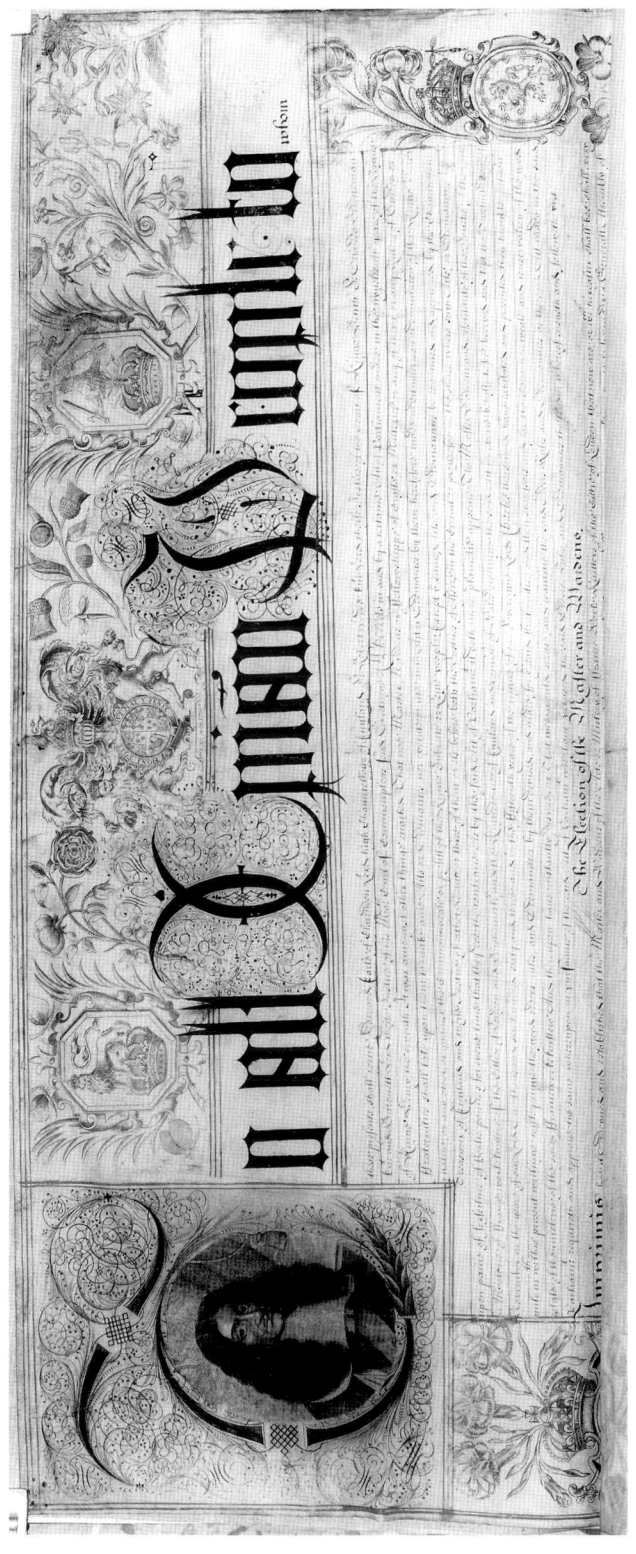

PLATE 7

1664 ORDINANCES – CHARLES II'S PORTRAIT AND THE TOP HALF OF THE FIRST PAGE

These are the first existing Bye-laws of the Society of Framework Knitters. This first page shows the rules for the Election of the Master and Wardens. As in the 1663 Charter the coloured border of these Ordinances is a work of art.

F.W.K. MSS.

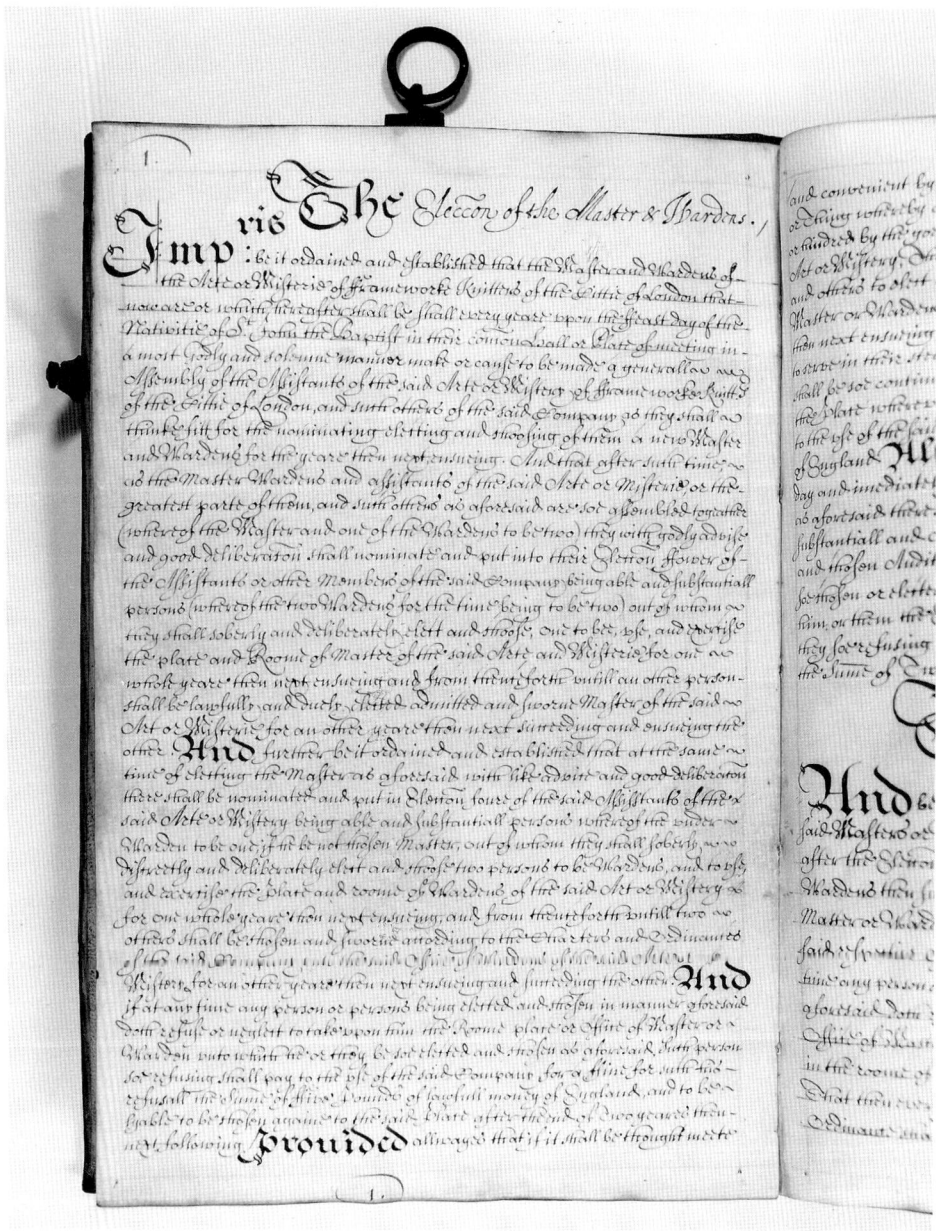

PLATE 8(a)   *repr. with permission of Nottinghamshire Archives*

A 'TRUE' COPY OF THE 1664 ORDINANCES

Made by the first Clerk of the Society of Framework Knitters, John Hannis, these illustrations show *(a)* the Bye-law for the Election of the Master and Wardens and *(b)* Hannis's declaration as to authenticity. Hannis made two copies of the Ordinances, and these illustrations are from the copy sent to the Nottingham Court. This Nottingham copy is in its original binding and illustration (a) shows at the left hand side of the page the book's original iron clasp and at the top the iron ring by which it was attached to the lectern at Company Courts.

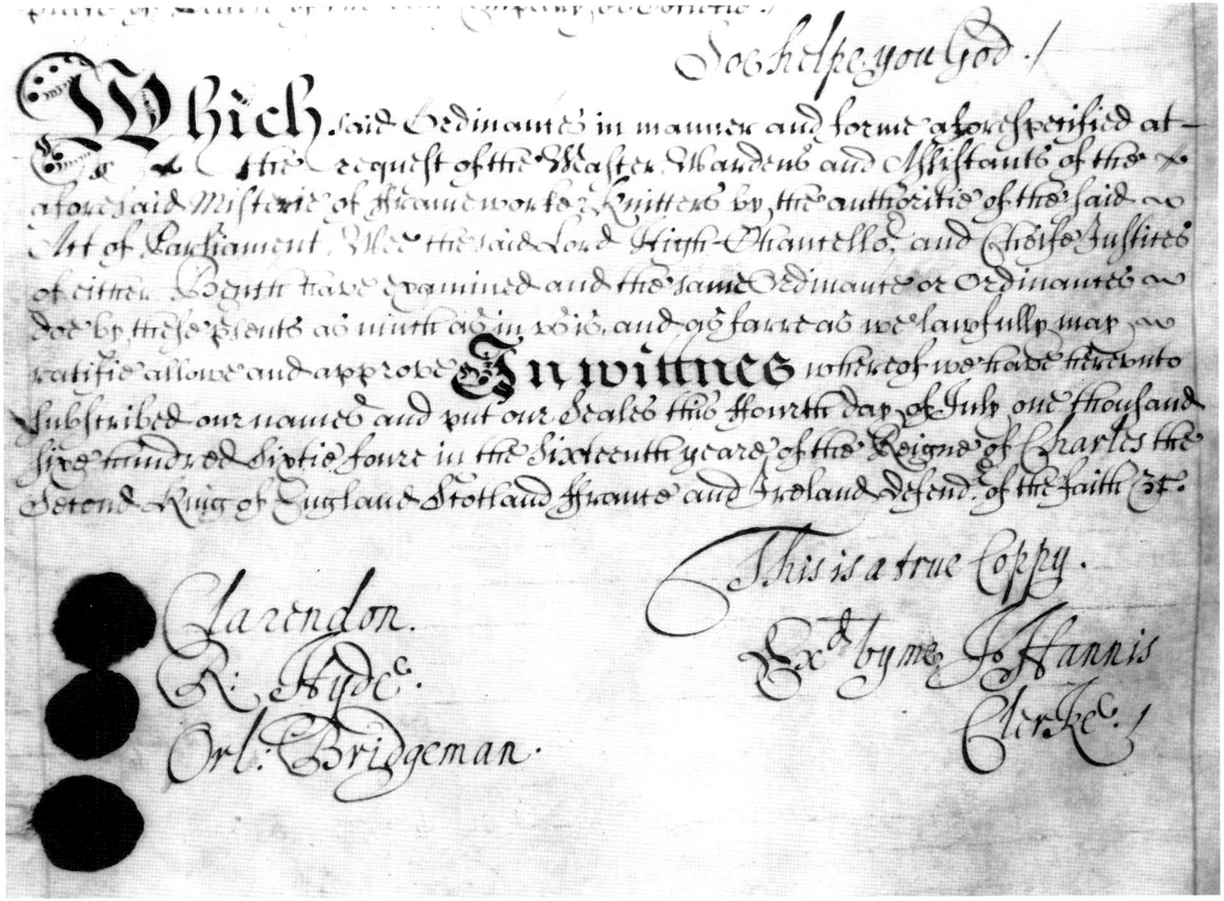
So helpe you God.

Which said Ordinances in manner and forme aforespecified at the request of the Master, Wardens and Assistants of the aforesaid Misterie of Framework Knitters by the authoritie of the said Act of Parliament, Wee the said Lord High Chancellor and Chiefe Justices of either Bench have examined and the same Ordinance or Ordinances doe by these presents as much as in us is, and so farre as wee lawfully may ratifie allowe and approve. In witness whereof wee have hereunto subscribed our names and put our Seales this fourth day of July one thousand six hundred sixtie foure in the Sixteenth yeare of the Reigne of Charles the Second King of England Scotland France and Ireland Defend. of the faith &c.

Clarendon.
R: Hyde.
Orl: Bridgeman.

This is a true Coppy.
Ex.d by me Jo: Harris Clerke.

PLATE 8(b) *repr. with permission of Nottinghamshire Archives* evident from this study of the Worshipful Society of Framework Knitters that the initial organisation of knitting manufacture in Britain, and therefore British industrial history, starts earlier, was largely funded and worked by persons native to the area around and to the north east of Nottingham, and is much more complex than has hitherto been allowed for.

References

1   Speech by Andrew Walker, Chairman of William Lee Quater-centenary Committee at Arnold, 23 September 1987.

2   C(ity of) L(ondon) G(uildhall) L(ibrary), W(orshipful) C(ompany) of F(ramework) K(nitters') MSS (L.37.), 3451/1, 24 June 1865, 11 April 1871, letter dated 12 April 1871. (As the WCFK's MSS are all housed in the CLGL, reference to it, and to the WCFK, will be omitted when referring to these MSS, but not when referring to other documents in this depositary.)

3   William F. Kahl, *The Development of London Livery Companies* (Boston: Baker Library, 1960), p. 21.

4   MSS, 16840 – *The Notes and Minutes of the Worshipful Company of Framework Knitters: February 1729 to April 1730* – was purchased at a Sotheby's auction in 1976 at a cost of £275, of which the Company paid £137.50 and the Guildhall Library paid the remainder; *Minutes*, 18 January 1977.

5   N(ottinghamshire) A(rchives) O(ffice), MSS, CA 4040.

6   MSS, 3451/1, pp. 380–86. Professor F. A. Wells, *The British Hosiery and Knitwear Industry: Its History and Organisation* (Newton Abbot: David & Charles, 1970), reprinted but first published 1935, refers to a *Court Book* of 1746, *Account Book* of 1749, *Admittance Book of Apprentices*, 1724–1786, *Minute Book* from at least 1779–1809.

7   James Funston, *Framework Knitters: A Short Story of the Company and its Work from 1840 to the present time*, 1901 pamphlet, p. 8; MSS. 3452/1, extracts from *Minute Book* of 24 June 1769.

8   MSS, 3451/2, 16 April 1901, 14 January 1902; 3452/3, 13 October 1903, 12 April 1904, 1 April 1905; 3451/4, 13 January 1919.

9   William Felkin, *A History of the Machine-Wrought Hosiery and Lace Manufactures* (London: Longmans,Green, 1867) p. 117; *Second Report of the Commissioners appointed to inquire into the Municipal Corporations in England and Wales*, House of Commons, 25 April 1837, p. 294; John Throsby, *Thoroton's History of Nottinghamshire*, II (London: B. & J. White, 1797), p. 59; *Henson's History of the Framework Knitters* (Newton Abbot: David & Charles Reprints, 1970), p. 58; *Report of the Commissioners appointed to Inquire into the Condition of the Framework Knitters*; 1845 609 (XV), p. 5; *City of London Livery Companies' Commission, Report and Appendix*, III (London: Eyre and Spottiswoode, 1884), p. 419.

10   MSS, 16865, 16866, 16868; NAO, MSS, CA 4039.

11   MSS. 3444; NAO, MSS, CA 4040.

12   Henson, pp. 91–2; Report of the Commissioners, 1845, p. 7.

13   *The Concise Oxford Dictionary* (Oxford: Clarendon Press, 1959), p. 576.

I

William Lee and the Roots of the Worshipful Company of Framework Knitters

Although the Society of Framework Knitters was not officially incorporated until 13 June 1657 and the Charter signed by Oliver Cromwell gave it jurisdiction over the art and mystery of framework knitting, its history started in 1589 when the knitting frame was invented by William Lee of Calverton, Nottinghamshire. In an age in which technology of any sort was almost unknown the invention of a machine to knit by a man who was, by all accounts, not trained in either mechanical or practical matters was a remarkable achievement. However 'the study of the history of technology shows repeatedly that it seldom if ever happens that an invention is the product of a single genius . . . (and this was also) true of the stocking frame'.[1] It was Lee's relatives, friends and workmen from Calverton and the area immediately around – the 'promoters, contrivers, and inventors of the art, mystery, or trade of framework knitting' – whose encouragement and practical help were instrumental in assisting Lee with his invention, perfecting it, organising the industry and establishing the Society of Framework Knitters.[2]

Knitting in England before William Lee

Knitting by hand is only a little older than knitting by machine. It was introduced into Britain from Europe, probably Spain, in about the first half of the fifteenth century when the former custom of the English peasantry to wear cloth caps began to give way to the wearing of the newly invented hand-knitted caps. In 1488 the price of knitted woollen caps was fixed at 2s. 8d. and between 1488 and 1563 several decrees of Parliament concerned the making, sale and wearing of hand-knitted goods. Hand knitting was carried on throughout the country and in 1563 an Act was passed which compelled every person not being possessed of twenty marks yearly rental to wear on Sundays and holidays a woollen knit cap, or pay a fine. However, although an Act of 1552 refers to knitted garments – including petticoats, gloves, and sleeves – stockings at this time, whether made of silk or wool, were not usually knitted, for until the reign of Queen Elizabeth I it was the custom of even royalty and nobility to wear woven-cloth hose; even silk cloth stockings were a luxury and usually came from abroad. Knitted stockings were not worn earlier than 1550 and Queen Elizabeth was the first English monarch to wear English-made knitted silk stockings. In about 1560 Mrs. Montague, the royal silk woman, is said to have presented the Queen with a pair of black hand-knitted silk stockings with which she was so pleased that she declared, 'Henceforth, I will wear no more cloathe stockings'. In some accounts Mrs. Montague's fine stockings are said to have taken two years to knit, in which case there was a ready market for a quicker, and cheaper, knitting process.[3]

William Lee and the invention of the Knitting Frame

Numerous accounts, many contradicting each other and some more romantic than others, abound about William Lee's invention of the stocking frame. Most would seem to be pure speculation and written long after any personal or family knowledge of the event was possible, for it was only after the frame became successful that anything other than the bare facts were printed. In their petition to Oliver Cromwell in 1655 the 'promoters, contrivers, and inventors . . . of framework-knitting, or making silk stockings, and other work in a frame, or engine', briefly stated that 'this trade of framework-knitting was never known or practised either here in England, or in any other place in the world, before it was (above fifty years past) invented and found out by one William Lee of Calverton, in the county of Nottingham, gentleman; who by himself and such of his kindred and countrymen, as he took unto him for servants, practised the same many years'. Robert Thoroton was the earliest Nottinghamshire historian to mention William Lee and his account was even briefer. In 1677 he wrote 'At Calverton was born William Lee, Master of Arts in Cambridge, and heir to a pretty freehold here; who seeing a woman knit, invented a Loom to knit, in which he, or his brother James, performed and exercised before Queen Elizabeth'.[4]

It would seem that William Lee was born about 1560 the eldest son of nine children born to William Lee in Calverton, a village about eight miles north east of Nottingham and situated on the southern edge of Sherwood Forest. The parish registers of Calverton do not begin until 1568, too late to record William's baptism, and are not continuous until after 1574, but they do record the birth of a number of his brothers and sisters, including in 1582 James, the youngest and later the brother most closely connected with William and the knitting frame.[5] Both the framework knitters' petition of 1655 and the Charters of 1657 and 1663 describe William Lee as a 'gentleman'. At this time the term 'gentleman' was not just the vague form of address it later became but denoted that, although untitled and lower that an Esquire, the person concerned was one of consequence in the social hierarchy for he was a member of the gentry and entitled to a coat of arms. Thoroton's 'pretty freehold' is confirmed by the will of his father, who in 1607 left a considerable amount of land and property to two of his sons, John and Edward. The Lee family holding has been calculated to have been of over 400 acres with, significantly, a flock of 143 sheep, presumably the source of the wool for the early experiments in knitting mechanically.[6] In addition to the Lee family in Calverton there would seem to be numerous other Lees in the immediate vicinity. In the Hearth Tax records of 1664 and 1674 Lees are shown to be living in Woodborough and a further fourteen Nottinghamshire villages; one of them, at Sutton-on-Trent, being of the same social standing as the Lees of Calverton, while the Lee family at Norwell were Esquires, one grade higher up the social scale.[7]

William Lee the inventor was not only well connected, he was also well educated. He went to Cambridge University, apparently first to Christ's College, where he matriculated in 1579, and then to St. John's, which he left about 1586. Tradition states that he was ordained and became a curate of Calverton and, although there is no record of him having taken the MA which would have allowed him to be ordained, it is possible that he acted as curate in Calverton in the two or three years during which he invented the stocking frame.[8] The only possible likeness now in existence of William Lee is the engraving on the Society's early stationery apparently taken from the picture painted by Balder(s)ton(n)(e), (also Balderstoun) (see Plate 1). The picture portrayed, on the left hand side, a stout man in academic costume pointing to the working parts of a stocking frame in the middle of the picture and addressing a woman dressed in flowing draperies, who is hand knitting on the right hand side; underneath is the inscription 'In the year 1589 The Ingenious William Lee Master of Arts of St. Johns College, Cambridge, Devis'd this profitable Art for Stockins But being Despis'd Went to France Yet of Iron to himself but to us and others of Gold In Memorie of whome this is here Depicted'.

In addition to showing the only possible likeness of William Lee this picture also incorporated how the stocking frame is believed to have been inspired. In 1677 Thoroton wrote that William Lee 'seeing a woman knit, invented a loom to knit' and from this brief description the various legends have emerged. This involvement of a handknitter is acknowledged by the female supporter of the stocking frame holding knitting needles, although whether this figure is meant to represent the shy girl in the neighbouring village of Woodborough, who is said to have hidden behind her knitting whenever Lee appeared, or the arrogant girl of Calverton, who some suppose scorned his advances by continuing to concentrate on her knitting whenever he visited, or his mother and relatives solely occupied with making a living for the family, it is impossible to say from the evidence available.[9] What is without doubt is that William Lee, with his academic education, must have been gifted with a turn for practical technology and have noted the movements of a hand knitter's fingers and the operation of the knitting needles in making the knitted fabric and, whether for love of his sweetheart, or his mother and relatives, or revenge as a scorned suitor, determined to invent a machine that would mechanically make the same mesh.

Apparently Lee started making a knitting frame in 1586 and took two or three years to produce a working model. By about 1589 Lee's stocking loom was in operation and he taught both his brother, James, and several male relations in and around Calverton to work it.

The roots of the Society of Framework Knitters

In 1590 William and James left Calverton for London accompanied by relatives and friends, leaving behind in the area around Calverton other relatives and friends who continued to work frames. These two groups were eventually to form the nucleus of the Society of Framework Knitters for, even when based in London, most of the first framework knitters' leaders had their roots firmly in the East Midlands.

William Lee and the City of London

In London the East Midlands party resided just outside the walls of the City, in Cripplegate parish through which passed the Great North Road. They settled in

Bunhill Row, then a pleasant area overlooking the open spaces of the Artillery Ground and Moor Fields, which was the medieval and Tudor equivalent of the modern West End and St. James's Park, where lived such luminaries as John Milton (see Plate 9).[10]

In view of the fact that although he was the eldest son he was only left a ring in the will of his father, William Lee had probably been permitted to use what would have been his inheritance on his invention prior to his departure and during the early days in London. If he was to advance his invention he needed an additional source of finance, and therefore must have hoped for patronage and preferably a grant from Queen Elizabeth I of 'letters patent' which would have given him a monopoly. To give patents to royal favourites was however one thing, to grant it to a member of the minor gentry for a machine which in full production would put many hundreds, perhaps thousands, of hand knitters out of work was another, and the legends that have sprung up around Lee's relationships with Queen Elizabeth indicate that she seems to have treated him in much the same way as she treated so many other questions during her reign, she prevaricated.

The Lees were apparently able to meet the Queen through the intercession of Henry Carey, Lord Hunsdon. Carey was a cousin of the Queen, Lord Chamberlain of her household and a Privy Councillor, with connections in Nottinghamshire. Moreover his grandfather had been a leading member of the Mercer's Company and a successful merchant in London, so that he came from a family well versed in the wool trade.[11] William or brother James apparently worked the frame in front of Queen Elizabeth, who was by this time nearly sixty years old and who, according to Henson writing a century and a half later, 'was excited by curiosity' and in company with Lord Hunsdon and his son 'went to inspect the frame incognito'. However, the Lees' hopes of immediate remuneration proved delusive. The Queen refused to make a grant, using the excuse that the frame invented only made thick wool stockings and, because of the threat to the employment of the hand knitters of woollen stockings, what was required were stockings of silk. These were a luxury item, usually imported, of which her Majesty was very fond – she apparently wore a new pair of silk stockings every week – and the Queen apparently encouraged William to hope 'that if he would make silk stockings he might then have hopes of a remuneration by a monopoly'.[12] Henson goes on to report that when the Lees required a guarantee for the security of the invention, 'Sir William (Carey) offered to become his apprentice. . . . Thus, the first stocking-maker's apprentice was a knight, the eldest son to a lord, who was of the blood royal'.[13] Presumably Carey, or even Elizabeth, or the family back in Calverton, continued to support Lee and his party financially for only in about 1599 was the frame finally adapted to knit silk, as John Stow recalls that in that year 'was devised and perfected the art of knitting or weaving silke stockings, wastecoates, and divers, other things by engines or steele loomes, by William Lee', who then built and worked nine frames.[14]

In 1600 the story of William Lee at last becomes more fact than guesswork, for on 6 June that year an Indenture was signed between George Brooke of London, Esquire, and William Lee of London, Gentleman, acknowledging that 'the said William Lee hath . . . invented a certeine Invention or Artificialitie beinge a very speedie manner of workinge and makinge in a loome or frame All manner of workes usually wrought by knittinge needles as stockings wastcootes and

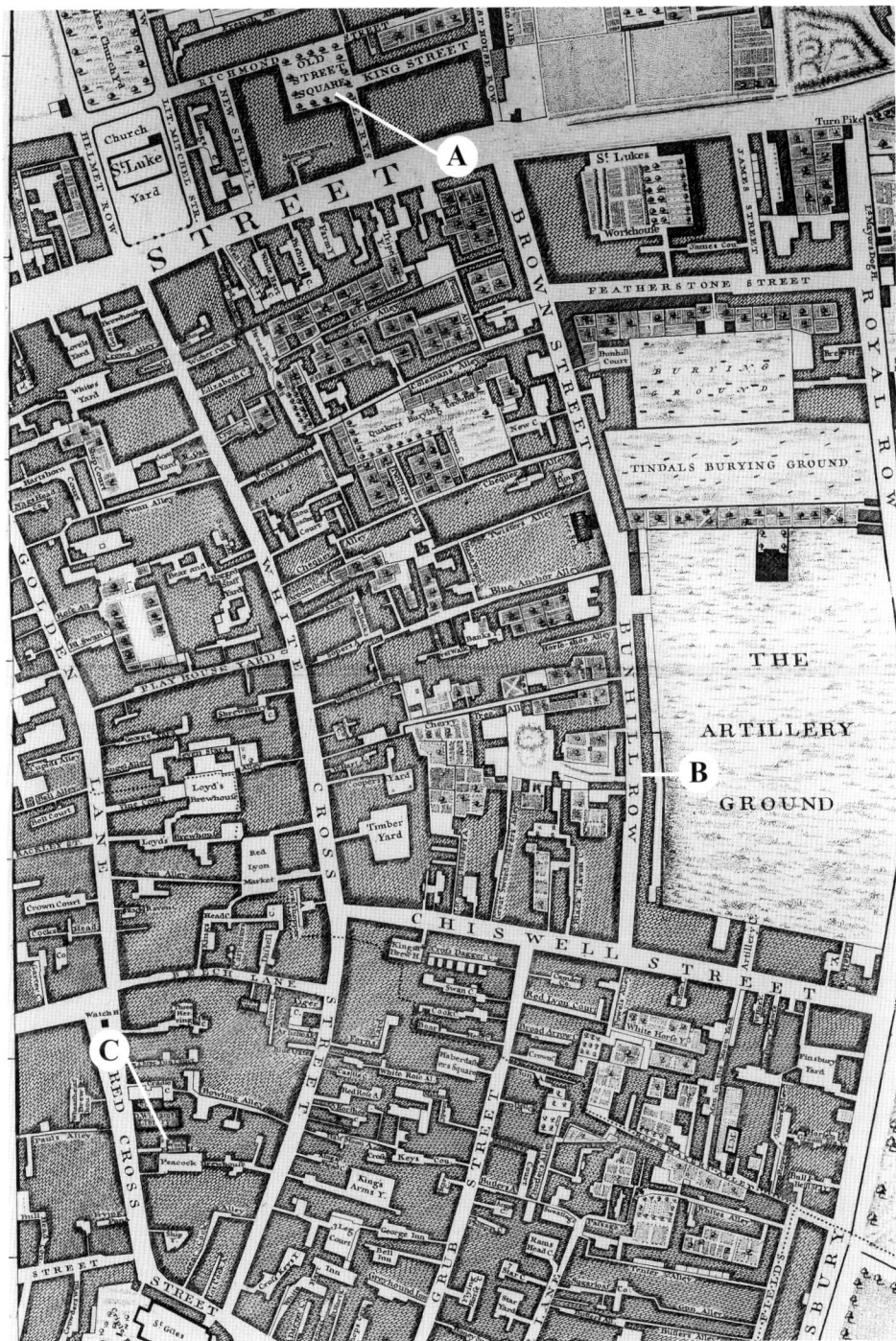

PLATE 9   *repr. with permission from the Guildhall Library, Corporation of London*

1746 MAP OF PART OF LONDON BY JOHN ROQUE

This map shows: **A**. Old Street Square; **B**. Bunhill Row; **C**. The Framework Knitters' Hall.

suchlike', and in which the pair were to become 'Coparteners' 'during the space of Twoe and Twenty yeres next'. The first £200 of profit was to go to William, subsequent profit was to be shared, although, as until this venture was established, George Brooke would not invest his £500, perhaps even now the commercial viability of the frame has not been completely validated.[15]

However, in spite of all accounts to the contrary, Elizabeth I must have offered Lee some patronage. He had been allowed to trade and to bind at least one apprentice in London, Sir William Carey, in spite of the fact that he was neither a Freeman of the City nor a member of any City of London Guild and it is unlikely that this would have been possible without some protection. After Elizabeth's death in 1603 – the death of his patron Lord Hunsdon had occurred in 1596 – it would appear that William had to start regularising his position with the arbiters of London trade, the City Aldermen, and to become both a Freeman of the City and a member of one of the City Companies if he wanted to continue to make stockings and experiment with his stocking frame, or, more importantly, bind apprentices, or take advantage of the cheap labour available in the Bridewell House of Correction on the Fleet. He applied for the Freedom of the City of London on 1 October 1605. The relevant entry in the Proceedings of the Court reads

'the petition of William Lee, Master of Arts, first inventor of an ingine to make silke stockings, made to this Court, for his freedom of the City by redemption',

and his application was referred to Sir Stephen Soames, Sir John Garrard, Sir Thomas Bennett, Sir Humphrey Welles, and Sir Thomas Romeny, for consideration.[16]

There were three ways of becoming a member of a Guild or Livery Company, by being the son of a Liveryman, by apprenticeship, or by purchase. As the first two ways were excluded, Lee had to purchase his Freedom in a Company which was permitted to sell or deal in stockings, which meant that he had a choice of three. In 1502 Henry VII had granted to the Merchant Taylors' the 'exclusive monopoly of working, cutting or making men's apparel within the City of London', including 'all types of cut and sewn stockings'. After 1530, the Drapers' also secured the right of making and selling stockings, while the Weavers' also claimed the right to make 'loom-knit' stockings. The Weavers' most nearly corresponded to the description of Lee's work and so he applied to join that Company. In the Freedom Admission Books of the Weavers' Company it is recorded that

'William Lee weaver of Silk stockings by Ingyn was the Seaventh day of March, 1608(9) admitted a forren brother for Three pounds whereof he payd Fortie shillings in hand and the rest he is to pay whensoever he shall sett up anie Loome or Sapyn to use the Art of weaving and is sworne I say for 03.00.00',

and in another folio

'William Lee. Rec. of him when he was admitted in pte. of payment the sume of 02.00.00'.

However, Lee does not feature again in the Weavers' documents and there is no record that he paid the remaining £1.[17]

William Lee and framework knitting in France

The most likely reason that William Lee did not fully take up his Freedom is that, even before he began negotiating with the City of London and the Weavers' Company, he was in talks with the French.

The other artisans in London at this time who were most interested in silk manufacture and skilled in the trades Lee required to convert his frame from a coarse gauge utilising wool into a fine gauge one making silk articles were Huguenot refugees from France, many of whom had arrived after the St. Bartholomew Day Massacre of 1572 (see Chapter II for machine details). Lee became particularly involved with the Huguenot family of de Caux, natives of Rouen in Normandy who had settled in England about 1590.[18] Situated on the Seine, Rouen had close commercial connections with England and was at this time both an important port and a commercial centre famous for its textiles, including hosiery. The hosiery industry there had been regulated and organised into a guild since at least 1450, and the master hosiers had had their own headquarters since 1489. In April 1596 the Protestant king, Henri IV, had granted further privileges to the hosiers in Rouen which were confirmed by the balliwick of Rouen in October that same year in the 'Statuts, Lettres et priviléges de l'état et métier de Marchand Bonnetier-Chapelier, et appartenance en la Ville et Banlieuë'.[19] In 1598 by the Edict of Nantes the harassing of Protestants in France was prohibited. Although no specific patent to William Lee seems to exist the fact that privileges had been granted to the Rouen hosiers and fact that the king was a Protestant must have tempted Lee.[20]

At the same time he must have increasingly despaired of help in England. First Elizabeth and then James I had feared his invention would prejudice the hand stocking knitters so that the knitting of stockings by machines was frowned upon by the authorities; indeed, the manufacture could even have been banned for, although no public notice to that affect has been found, George Carleton writing to Sir Dudley Carleton in 1611 'begs his favour for Mr. Joiner . . . who is going to Venice to practice the silk-loom stocking weaving, which is not permitted in England, for fear of ruining the knitters'. In addition, in November 1601, there was a 'Proclamation against Monopolies' which was 'for the reformation of many abuses and misdemeanours committed by Patentes of certaine Priviledges and Licences, to the generall good of all her maiesties loving Subjects', and, when monopolies were abolished by James I in 1604, Lee must have finally relinquished any hope of personal advancement in England.[21]

Contemporary reports about Lee's involvement with France are short on dates, just stating that 'Wanting due encouragement at home' Lee was 'invited over into France, upon the allurements of great rewards, privilege, and honour' and that he transposed 'himself with nine workmen, his servants with some frames unto Roan',[22] but it is possible that he had connections there as early as 1596, as William Dewick wrote to his brother Thomas Edmondes at Rouen on 28 September that year that 'we are all here as you left us; Mr. Lee no changling'.[23] Certainly by 1604 'three English apprentices and Jean Granges (John Granger), another Englishman', were working for Gédéon Langlois, a hosier and a member of a prominent

Protestant family. In view of the fact that Granger, and probably the three former apprentices, later signed agreements involving William Lee in 1611 and 1614, it would seem that Lee arranged for men trained by himself to move to France with their frames much earlier than has so far been thought.[24]

William Lee seems to have shipped his own frames and workmen to France in 1608–9 where, through the influence of Pierre de Caux, and his brother Solomon who was 'Ingénieur du Roi', he was the protégé of Henri IV's chief minister, Sully, who was so impressed with the stocking frame that he 'gave Lee the means to construct new looms'.[25] When Lee signed a first contract with Pierre de Caux is unknown, but the second one, for nineteen years, was recorded between the two men in Rouen in February 1611 'for a company to manufacture stockings of silk and of wool upon a loom to be introduced in France'. William Lee 'an English Gentleman', 'the inventor' and 'head of manufacture', agreed to supply six English workmen, Jehan Grangyer (Jean Granges/John Granger), and Jehan Stede (John Steed), both mechanics with a contract for two years, Helie Yonc for four years and François Fuleaue (Francis Foljambe), Andre Raynel (Andrew Raynor) and George Onyc (George Wye) for five years from March 25 1610. Lee had already supplied four machines, presumably worked by the journeymen named, and was to supply a further four frames, and was to teach the same number of apprentices 'as there will be looms made'. De Caux for his part was to pay 2,500 livres for the labour already performed by the five workmen. Thirty two additional frames were to be supplied 'as speedily as possible' from funds 'furnish(ed) and loan(ed) by . . . de Caux and associates'. If De Caux and his associates did not keep their part of the contract Lee and his workers were free to leave France.[26]

It now seemed as if William Lee had finally received the fiscal aid that he had always been seeking, but unfortunately it was too late. Henri IV had been assassinated in 1610, to be succeeded by his under-age son Louis XIII, for whom the Regent was his mother Marie de Medici. Sully was dismissed and the regularisation of the Protestant Lee's position and the French citizenship that had been promised in the 1611 document now had to be obtained from the staunchly Roman Catholic Marie de Medici and the new king.

Where or how Lee died is unknown. In March 1614 he was appointed to plead 'all causes and deeds . . . before the Paris Court of Parliament' on behalf of John Granger, Francis Feljambe (Foljambe), Andrew Raynar (Andrew Raynor), and Georges Wye, and it would seem that either later in 1614 or early 1615 he left Rouen and died either on the journey or in Paris. By now he was an old man of over sixty years of age, and he must have been tired of the continual struggle to get his knitting frame officially accepted, although whether his death was a natural one or suicide will never be known. Deering in 1751 wrote that 'seized with Grief, he ended his Life at Paris', which points to a possible suicide, in which case it is understandable that the facts about Lee's death were deliberately obscured by his family and friends.[27]

The return of the framework knitters to England

After Lee's death and the recommencement of the Roman Catholic persecution of Protestants, seven of the framework knitters in Rouen returned to England with their frames. Together with As(h)ton and the other knitters left in Nottinghamshire and London, these workmen were the inaugurators first of an Association of

Framework Knitters and later they, or their descendants, founded the Society of Framework Knitters.[28]

In addition to William Lee's brother, James, the returning men were presumably those named in the documents drawn up in Rouen in 1604, 1611 and 1614. Although sixteenth and seventeenth century spelling is notoriously fickle, nevertheless the names of the workmen in Rouen deciphered by the translators of the Rouen documents and the surnames of families in Nottinghamshire, principally from around the Lee's home village of Calverton, are sometimes the same. Francis Foljambe was one man named in the Rouen documents of 1611 and 1614. Foljambe is a prominent Nottinghamshire name – the family still own Osberton Hall in north Nottinghamshire – and Francis was one of the family names of the period, while a Geoffrey Foljambe was involved in land transactions in Calverton during Elizabeth's reign.[29] The John Granger of Rouen seems to have returned to London to become a member of the Clothworkers' Company before the formation of the Framework Knitters' Company but, again, there were a number of Grangers in the East Midlands and in framework knitting; a Christopher Granger was vicar of Mansfield in Queen Mary's reign while five Grangers were long serving members of the Society by 1722. Raynor too is a Nottinghamshire surname closely connected with framework knitting in the seventeenth and eighteenth centuries; Anne Rayner bound two apprentices in the Nottingham Court in 1695 and 1696 while one William Rayner was apprenticed in the same court in 1694. However, whether the Yonc in Rouen in 1611 could possibly be a contemporary French spelling of Youle and 'Helie' therefore a relative of Humfrey Youle a freeholder of Calverton in 1612 needs further research.[30]

The framework knitters returning from France first settled in Old Street Square, again just outside the walls of the City of London and not far from the William Lee's former workshop in Bunhill Row, and in the middle of the area around which framework knitting was to grow (see Plate 9).

About 1620, while the other framework knitters stayed in London, James Lee returned to Nottinghamshire where he joined As(h)ton, William's former apprentice, who had by now improved Lee's frame[31] (see Chapter II on frames). Together the two Nottinghamshire-based knitters 'quickly turned their attention to making woollen hose with facility', confirming the establishment of the East Midlands as the centre for the manufacture of mechanically knitted woollen products, although the manufacture of silk goods was also not neglected. It would seem that the Lee family and the core of framework knitters in north east Nottinghamshire kept up to date with development and, in the same way that framework knitters in London made both silk and worsted hose, the East Midlands manufacture was not just confined to coarse frames making woollen hose; the inventories, recording what happened in a household before the person's death, in the late 1600s in Nottinghamshire show that framework knitters such as John Lee of Woodborough, Richard Alcock of Calverton and Thomas Grammer of Blidworth were already silk stocking framework knitters.[32]

The Association of Framework Knitters and the spread of framework knitting

In spite of the innate caution with which people in the seventeenth century regarded the manufacture of goods by mechanical means, the numbers of framework knitters had continued to grow. The first Association of Framework Knitters was formed about 1621, in which the elite of the trade, who were mostly Lee's former apprentices and workmen, many of them his relatives, 'wore their working needles, having ornamental silver shafts, suspended from a silver chain . . . (preserving) this mark of distinction . . . so late as the reign of Queen Anne'. The Association opposed the export of frames and attempted to regulate trade affairs by issuing rules for prices, the binding of apprentices and working practices; work had to meet certain standards of production and poor dyeing, a deficiency in the number of threads the work contained, or binding edges instead of narrowing the stocking on the machine were all forbidden. By 1636 knitted silk goods, stockings especially, were so widespread that there was a petition in favour of a 'mark of distinction' so as to prevent woven silk stockings being sold as knitted silk ones, although the Association of Framework Knitters was not officially recognised as it was noted that the tradesmen 'have no corporation'.[33]

By the 1650s it was claimed that framework knitting was the livelihood of 'hundreds of poor families' and was dispersed in a number of areas in England, as well as in Ireland.

In Table 1.1 a median period has been allocated because, although the location of the frames is known, their number at this time was not assigned to a specific year by contemporaries and later writers, although using almost similar statistics, are unsure of the year to which these apply – Gravenor Henson, writing in 1831, attributing them to 1644 while in the Framework Knitters's Report of 1845 the date given is 1669. In addition, as the machines were doubled handed at this time the number of operatives has also been calculated.[34]

In the 1650s, as would be expected, the largest concentration of frames outside London was in Nottinghamshire, where two hosiers were listed in the market town in 1641, presumably acting as agents for the already considerable number of framework knitters. In Surrey and Buckinghamshire those who had served their apprenticeships in London would by now have returned to their home counties, for the first, incomplete, Freedom Register of London shows that the largest number of framework knitting apprentices bound to London Freemen came from the counties around London where framework knitting was an accepted occupation from at

Table 1.1 **Number of frames and framework knitters about the 1650s**

Location	Number of frames	Number of knitters
London (City, St. Lukes, Norton Falgate, Shoreditch)	400 (400–500)	800
Bucks. (Berkhampstead, Herts., Chesham & Tring, Bucks.)	50	100
Surrey (& Hants.)	50 (c. 25)	100
Nottingham(shire)	100	200
Leicester(shire)	50	100
Dublin	10	20
	660 (c. 650)	1320 (1220)

Sources: *Report of the Commissioners appointed to inquire into the Condition of the Framework Knitters; Part II, Nottinghamshire and Derbyshire: 1845*, 609 (XV) p.15. Henson, p. 60 (Henson's additions and alternatives to the 1845 Report figures are given in brackets).

least 1648 when Francis East was described as a framework knitter in an enrolment.[35] In Leicestershire framework knitting had gradually spread both north from London and south from Nottinghamshire so that in the town of Leicester the first frame is not believed to have been set up until about 1670 by Nicholas Alsop, and even then, because of prejudice, had to be worked in secret for some years. Yet, in Hinckley the first frame arrived before 1640, brought by William Iliffe from London where he was one of a family of framework knitters who answered to the Company's London Court. And in the area around Wanlip, just north of Leicester, it would seem that framework knitting was established before the granting of the Company's first Charter, as is shown by the close family connections of Nicholas Alsop, son of John a yeoman of Wanlip, who was apprenticed to Edward Noone, a mercer, on 11 November 1648, while Arthur Noon, previously apprenticed to the framework knitter Nicholas Alsop, became a Freeman of Leicester in 1699. Nicholas's connection to framework knitting in Wanlip is further reinforced by his binding as an apprentice framework knitter John Alsop, son of Francis Alsop of Wanlip. Nicholas continued to be described as a mercer in Leicester until at least 1687, well after the time he is alleged to have set up the stocking frame, and then as a hosier in 1692, and is not described as a framework knitter until 1698 when he is first shown as binding apprentices to the Company, so that it is probable that, before setting up his own frames, Nicholas Alsop was probably acting as a merchant hosier for the framework knitting trade in north Leicestershire, in the same way as the two hosiers in Nottingham.[36]

The framework knitters' petition of 1655

By 1655, therefore, framework knitting had expanded greatly in the sixty six years since the invention of the frame. Knitting manufacture was now widespread and more than a thousand males worked at the frame, even though in local records there are few traces of this multitude because, as until incorporation framework knitting did not officially exist as an occupation and, as under the laws of Tudor, Stuart and Commonwealth England, only Freemen could bind apprentices, early framework knitters took the Freedom and were recorded as members of their former master's Company. The product range was considerable for the frame could produce 'all commodities of knit-work, (such) as stockings, calceoons (knitted pieces for breeches and trowsers): waistcoats, and many other things . . . for the cover of the whole body'. Moreover, as it was claimed that only a seventh of the retail price of silk stockings was not 'totally clear gain to the commonwealth', the profit in knitting at this time must have been considerable, even allowing for the exaggeration necessary to emphasise the advantage to the prosperity of England the granting of a charter would bring. In addition there must also have been a large profit in the manufacture of frames as the Venetian ambassador reputedly paid £500 for Mead and his frame and Iliffe had paid £60 for his.[37]

It was, therefore, decided by the leaders of framework knitting, that the Association of those engaged in framework knitting, that had now been in existence for over a quarter of a century, needed official recognition, and on 26 December 1655 the 'promoters, contrivers, and inventors of the art, mystery, or trade of framework knitting, or making of silk stockings and other work in a frame, or engine' petitioned Oliver Cromwell for incorporation by charter.

The signatures of these 'promoters, contrivers, and inventors' of 1655 to incorporate framework knitting have not been preserved, but it can only be presumed that they are mostly the same men as those named in the first Charter – George Ashton, Thomas Phillips, Humphrey Jamson, Henry Womball, John Lee, John Crosen, Lawrence Pomfret, Gregory Fishborne, Jonathan Gramar, Richard Burnby, Joseph Tomlinson, Gabriel Brewer, Richard Read, George Baldersto(u)n, Anthony Bennett, and Samuel Knight. Many of these men, as will be seen in Chapter IV, had close connections with the East Midlands, especially in the area north east of Nottingham around Calverton; Lee's relatives and friends, or their descendants, who had been to the forefront of framework knitting since its inception and were largely responsible for organising framework knitting in the 1620s, had positions of influence within the industry which they wanted to retain.

The multi-paged petition was written 'in Language . . . with so much Strength, and giving so good an Account of the Usefulness and publick Advantage of this Manufacture' that it painted a detailed picture of the already sophisticated organisation of the trade in the middle of the seventeenth century (see Appendix 1). The suppliants were extremely skillful in their petitioning of Cromwell, carefully emphasising that they had 'made a large and competent probation of the worth of this manufacture . . . have voluntarily amongst themselves kept order in their trading, according to the duty of probationers . . . until they found themselves risen into a number not incapable of an incorporation' and they laid stress on, and asked for regulation of, the points that they knew would find favour.[38]

One of the main reasons given for the necessity of incorporation was so that the 'just right to the Invention may be preserved from Foreigners'. Emphasis was laid on the fact that, although it was 'an English invention and no part of the world has it', the threatened foreign competition had been only removed temporarily due to the failure of framesmiths abroad to develop the frames. The two workmen left behind in Rouen by James Lee had not been able to improve their frames in the forty years that they had been there. John Lee's apprentice, Henry Mead, whose unexpired apprenticeship and machine had been bought by the Venetians, 'could neither make his own needles nor sinkers, nor repair his frame, nor keep it in good condition' so that Mead and his frame had been returned to London about 1621. While one Abraham Jones who had reportedly been so harassed by the Association that he had fled to Amsterdam to set up some of Aston's improved frames had, fortuitously for the English, died of the plague in 1633 and when his frames could not be worked by the Dutch, they too had been returned to London. Although when the petition was presented, there were apparently no new frames working outside Britain, the petitioners' fear of foreign competition was justified when a year later, in 1656, Jean Hindret was sent to England from France by the minister Colbert and made twenty four technical drawings of the improved frame which became the foundation of a thriving framework knitting industry in France.[39]

In addition to playing upon English xenophobia, the petitioners emphasised that framework knitting 'hath chosen to be practised in silk', although admitting 'this manufacture may be wrought in any other materials'. They claimed that the manufacture of silk stockings was of the 'greatest advantage unto this State and Commonwealth, yielding several payments to the sue of the State . . . imported raw at cheap rates, exported ready wrought at the utmost extent of value', for between the beginning of the century and 1655 the export of silk stockings had become a

Table 1.2 **Export of silk stockings 1608–1641**

Date	Amount exported
1608	95 pairs
1618–19	581 pairs (main markets Netherlands and Hamburg)
1641	4,278 pairs (main market Netherlands)
1641	3,912 silk gloves

Source: Pauline Croft, 'The Rise of the English Stocking Export Trade', *Textile History*, XVIII, 1987, pp. 3–16, p. 13).

thriving export trade, which had the added advantage of reducing the import of these luxury items. 'Common', or hand knitting, used woollen yarn making worsted hose mainly for the home market, so, by emphasising the exportation of the silk goods knitted on the frame, it was claimed that the new manufacture would not cause unemployment for it was 'leaving the homeseale (in great part) unto the common knitters'.

It was also pointed out that the quality of production was declining as the number of knitters increased and, in order to maintain a high standard of manufacture, the promoters of the petition asked for permission to regulate officially the abuses that Pickard and the other 'intruders', who were presumably not members of the Association, had been perpetrating concerning working practices and apprenticeships when, rather than accept that entry was only to be, as was normal in other trades, through the thorough training given in apprenticeship, adults were paying to learn mechanical knitting.

Progress of the petition

The 'humble representation of the promoters, contrivers,and inventors of the art, mystery, or trade of framework knitting' in 1655 was referred first to the Lord Mayor and Aldermen of London on 1 August 1655, and then, on their favourable report in the December, to the Committee of Council and after that, in the following February to the Board of Trade.[40]

On 13 June 1657 the Worshipful Company of Framework Knitters was incorporated by charter by the Lord Protector Oliver Cromwell.

References

1 Peta Lewis, 'William Lee's Stocking Frame: Technical Evolution and Economic Viability 1589–1750', *Textile History*, 17, 1986, pp. 129–48, p. 135.
2 *Seventeenth-Century Economic Documents*, ed. Joan Thirsk and J. P. Cooper, 'The Framework Knitters Appeal for Incorporation, 1655' (Oxford: Clarendon Press, 1972), pp. 259–64; Charles Deering, *The History of Nottingham*, first published Nottingham 1751 (Nottingham: S.R. Publishers, 1970), pp. 301–8. The Deering version is given in Appendix I. The Thomason Tract E 863 used by Thirsk and Cooper is quoted here because of the significant inclusion of the word 'contrivers' in this version.
3 Henson, p. 34; John Chamberlain, *Manufacture of Knitted Footwear* (Leicester: Alfred Tacey, 1930), p. 2; W. H. Webb, F.R.Hist.S., 'The Genesis and History of the Hosier or machine-knitting trade', *The Textile Recorder*, November 15 1913, p. 212; Milton and Anna Grass, *Stockings for a Queen* (London: Heinemann, 1967), p. 102.

4 Thirsk and Cooper, p. 261; Robert Thoroton, *The Antiquities of Nottinghamshire* (London: Robert White for Henry Mortlock, 1677), p. 296.

5 Grass, p. 4; information from Mrs. E. Cupitt, Curator of the Framework Knitting Museum, Main St., Calverton, Notts.

6 Thoroton, p. 296; Grass, p. 14.

7 Other villages are Annesley, Caythorpe, East Stoke, Gedling, Hucknall Torknall, Kirkby-in-Ashfield, Lambley, Lowdham, Mansfield, Nexton uxta Shelford, Oxton, Southwell, Stoke Bardolph, Sutton-in-Asfield, and slightly further afield but still in north Nottinghamshire, Collingham, Cromwell, Kneesall, Laxton, Norton Cuckney, Ossington, Worksopp: see Thoroton, pp. 317, 342, 351, 360, 425, etc.

8 *Dictionary of National Biography*, XXXII, ed. Sidney Lee (London: Smith Elder & Co., 1892); Grass, p. 38; letter from M. G. Underwood, Archivist, St. John's College, Cambridge, 4 September 1998.

9 Thoroton, p. 297; Deering, p. 99.

10 Henson, p. 34; Deering, p. 99; Grass, p. 79; Rev. W. Denton, *Records of St. Giles' Cripplegate without* (London: George Bell & Sons, 1883), pp. 27, 31, 115, 140, 155, 157, 161.

11 Grass, p. 93; J. Orange, *History of Nottinghamshire*, 1840; *Dictionary of National Biography*; Wells, p. 219.

12 Thoroton, p. 297; Henson, pp. 43, 45; Susan Watkins, *In Public and in Private: Elizabeth I and her World* (London: Thames and Hudson, 1998), p. 75.

13 Henson, p. 46.

14 John Stow's *The Annuals of England*, ed. Edmund Howes, 1615, p. 869; Henson, p. 48.

15 Full text in E.W. Pasold, 'In Search of William Lee', *Textile History*, 1975, pp. 7–17, pp. 12–6.

16 Grass, pp. 121–2; C(ity of) L(ondon) R(ecord) O(ffice), Proceedings of the Court of Aldermen, City of London, October 1, 1605, Repertory 27, Folio 87.

17 Grass, p. 82–3; Alfred Plummer, *The London Weavers' Company: 1600–1970* (London: Routledge & Kegan Paul, 1972), pp. 169–70.

18 Grass, p. 126.

19 *Receuil des Anciennes et Nouvelles Statuts, Lettres Patentes, Divers Arrest du Conseil, et de la Cour du Parlement, Sentence et Ordonnance du Police concernant l'État du Corps des Marchands Bonnetiers de la Ville, Fauxbourg et Banlieuë de Rouen* (Rouen: Imprimerie de Prevost, 1736), pp. 3, 76, 82.

20 Thoroton, p. 297; C(alendar of) S(tate) P(apers), 1590, nos. 27 and 39, etc.

21 *Dictionary of National Biography*, p. 382; CSP, LXV, 9, 1611 4 July; ed. R.H. Tawney and Eileen Power, *Tudor Economic Documents* (London: Longmans, Green, 1924), pp. 292–5; Henson, p. 48.

22 'Roan' = Rouen; Thirsk and Cooper, p. 261.

23 CSP, CCLXIII, 33.

24 Grass, pp. 129, 141; Archives de la Seine Maritime, Rouen, *Register of Protestant Baptisms in Temple de Queilly: 1564–1604*; Joan Thirsk, 'The Fantastical Folly of Fashion', *Textile History and Economic History: Essays in Honour of Julia de Lacy Mann*, ed. N. R. Harte and K. G. Ponting (Manchester: Manchester University Press, 1973), p. 70.

25 Grass, pp. 134,139; Thirsk p. 70.

26 The names given in brackets were given by language experts who translated the documents; Grass, pp. 165–71 (Grass Appendices C & D – full transcription of the contract. In this contract is the only contemporary reference that Lee might have been married, although Grass, p. 138, thinks that the widow's 'provision was inserted . . . for future contingencies', although at age 60 this might have been unlikely).

27 Full text of 1614 agreement in K. G. Ponting, 'In Search of William Lee' *Textile History*, 9, 1978, p. 174.

28 Deering, p. 100.

29 Deering, p. 100.

30 MSS, 3446/1; Henson, p. 48; Thoroton, pp. 273, 296; Foljambe – NAO, Preface to the large collection of Foljambe papers – NAO, MSS, CA 4040, 1695 – Charles bound an apprentice at Nottingham and MSS, 3446/1 – before 1701 Charles bound three more apprentices; Granger – NAO, MSS, CA 4040, 1697, Edward apprenticed at Nottingham Court – MSS. 3444, 1722, Benjamin, John, Joshua and Robert – CLRO, MSS. 204A, between 1810 and at least 1830

William a Freeman of the Company – 1844, Mary an Almshouse inmate – There is still a Granger in the Society of Framework Knitters at the beginning of 2000; Richard Granger, son of John, is currently a Liveryman of the Company; Raynor – MSS, CA 3993 Benjamin, framework knitter of Greasley – Samuel, one of first two stewards of the Friendly Society of Framework Knitters in 1785; Youle – Thoroton, p. 296.

31 Thoroton, p. 297.
32 Henson, p. 56–7; NAO, MSS, PRSW 96/14,PRSW 102/1 and 102/8.
33 Henson, pp. 48, 54–8; Felkin, p. 61; S(tate) P(apers), DXXXVI, No 43, p. 532.
34 *Report from the Select Committee appointed to take into consideration the several Petitions which have been presented in this Session of Parliament by the Persons employed in Framework-knitting*: 1812 247 (II), John Blackner's evidence, 15 May 1812, p. 25.
35 CLRO, MSS, 204A.
36 NAO, MSS, CA 4040; John Nichols, *The History and Antiquities of Leicester: 1811* (Leicester: Leicestershire County Council/S.R. Publishers, republished 1971), II, p. 621, IV, p. 679; T. Fielding Johnson, *Glimpses of Leicester* (Leicester: Clarke and Satchell, 1906), p. 255; Henry Hartopp, *Register of the Freemen of Leicester: 1196–1770* (Leicester: Corporation of Leicester, 1927), pp. 171, 175, 181, 183, 374, etc; Deering, p. 94.
37 1665 Petition; Deering, pp. 305–6.
38 Deering p. 100; Thirsk and Cooper, pp. 259–64.
39 SP, CII, pp. 77–8; Henson, p. 54–5; Paul-M. Bonduis, *Colbert et la fabrication du bas: 1655–1683: La transformation d'une industrie par le méchinisme au XVII siècle* (Paris: Librarie des Sciences Economique et Socials, 1929), pp. 3–26.
40 SP. Dom(estic), XXV, I 76, pp. 214–16; XXV, 77, CII, No. 72; CII, I 76, pp. 440–5; CLIII, 27, 5 February 1656–7; Thirsk and Cooper, pp. 259–64, p. 259.

II

Knitting frames

Before embarking, however, on the history of the Society of Framework Knitters, to enable that history to be placed in the context of the technical developments in the industry and their connection to the Society, it would be appropriate to give a very brief description of the frame, some of its improvements, and its early powered successors, and the materials used in machine knitting, as well as the machine builders and the connections to the Society.

William Lee's frame and its development

Knitted fabric is more elastic than a woven fabric produced from warp and weft threads and conforms well to the shape of the body, hence it suitability to make hose. In its simplest form, and in the frame invented by William Lee, basically a single length of yarn is looped over needles by a sequence of movements of hand and feet to form the fabric.

Although it has been generally agreed that William Lee was a 'mechanical genius' there is disagreement as to the source of his inspiration and his materials. Legend, and some authorities, believe, as mentioned in Chapter I, that the concept for the knitting frame came directly from Lee's observations of hand knitting in which the knitter keeps one needle 'rigid and holds the knitting previously completed, while new loops are created and drawn through the loops on the rigid needle by a second needle which is moved to and fro'. Others feel that it is unbelievable that such a complicated piece of apparatus as the knitting frame could be invented without reference to a previous technical idea and that the linear peg frame is the most likely forerunner of Lee's frame. In the linear frame 'The knitting hangs from cross pieces on top of pegs. Each new row is made by placing fresh yarn across the tops of the pegs. One by one the old (top) loops are cast off over this yarn and form new loops. The knitted fabric which results hangs down in front of the pegs'.[1]

In the frame invented by William Lee (see Plates 10, 11, 12), the working parts were mounted in a wooden frame, (hence the name), which stood about five feet high and incorporated a seat for the operative (A). Lengths of wire with a hook at the end, called needles (B), were fixed horizontally in a needle bar. Mounted vertically between each needle were specially shaped steel plates called jack sinkers (D, K) which formed loops in the thread lying under the hooked ends of the needles, the hooks were closed and the previous row of loops formed were then drawn over the needles and the new loops to form a new course of knitting. The process was repeated until the required length was reached. The flat fabric hung down between the knitter and the frame. When making stockings only one was knitted at a time and the fashioning, or shaping, of the leg and heel required manual manipulation of the stitches in each row of knitting. On completion the flat, fashioned stocking, as shown on the frame in the Balderton painting and one of the Company's Coats of Arms, would be removed from the machine and the selveges seamed by hand (see Plate 1 and Front Jacket).[2]

William Lee's first frame was primitive when compared to later frames and much of the work made on it would have been inferior to that made by hand. However, even at its crudest, it was much quicker than a hand knitter as a whole row of loops was made in the time it took a hand knitter to make one stitch, and it has been estimated that 500 to 600 loops could be made per minute compared to approximately the 100 possible in hand knitting. The original frame had eight bearded needles to the inch and knitted up only woollen yarn and was too coarse to make silk stockings; such an enormous quantity of silk would have been needed that a pair of silk stockings made on this first machine would have weighed at least one pound. The fabric of an acceptable pair of silk stockings needed to be two and a half times finer than that of a woollen stocking and this was only achieved about 1599, by which time there were sixty needles to a three inch needle bar and it has been estimated that between 1,000 and 1,500 loops could be made per minute. Altogether there were over 2,000 separate parts in a stocking frame by 1655, and its construction hardly changed in the next 200 years, as Gravenor Henson counted 2,066 pieces in a twenty-four gauge silk frame fifteen inches wide in 1831. Every part of the knitting frame was hand-made and hand-assembled and, as every single piece of wood, iron and lead had to be extremely accurate to make a working whole, the occupation of a framesmith was an extremely skilled one, especially in the days before the invention of calibrated machine tools. By 1750 Nottingham framesmiths had accomplished the ultimate in precision, having succeeded in building a 38 gauge machine with three needles moulded together, almost the finest ever built, although two needles moulded together was considered to be more efficient.[3]

Over the years little changed in the work required by the frame operative, and a description written in 1845 applies as well today as it did in the 1600s, for 'The art of framework knitting is not difficult to acquire; but the best fashioned work, and all fancy work, require a quick sight, a ready hand, and retentive faculties . . . Each course (row) involves several movements of the hands, in passing the thread over the needles (as the rows of hooks is called technically), and in passing the body of the frame through four motions. The feet are required in every course to move alternatively one or two treadles, requiring a certain power to draw the jacks, whereby the loops are successively formed; and by putting down another treadle . . . to press them into the grooves, and so allow the loops last formed to pass over those in process of formation. While the hands are thus busy, and the feet moving at the rate of four feet per second, the eye must keep watch on the needles as to their soundness and position, and upon the work, that it be perfect and free from blemish'.[4]

The stocking frame never seems to have been patented, probably because it was not considered commercially viable until after 1604, the year James I abolished

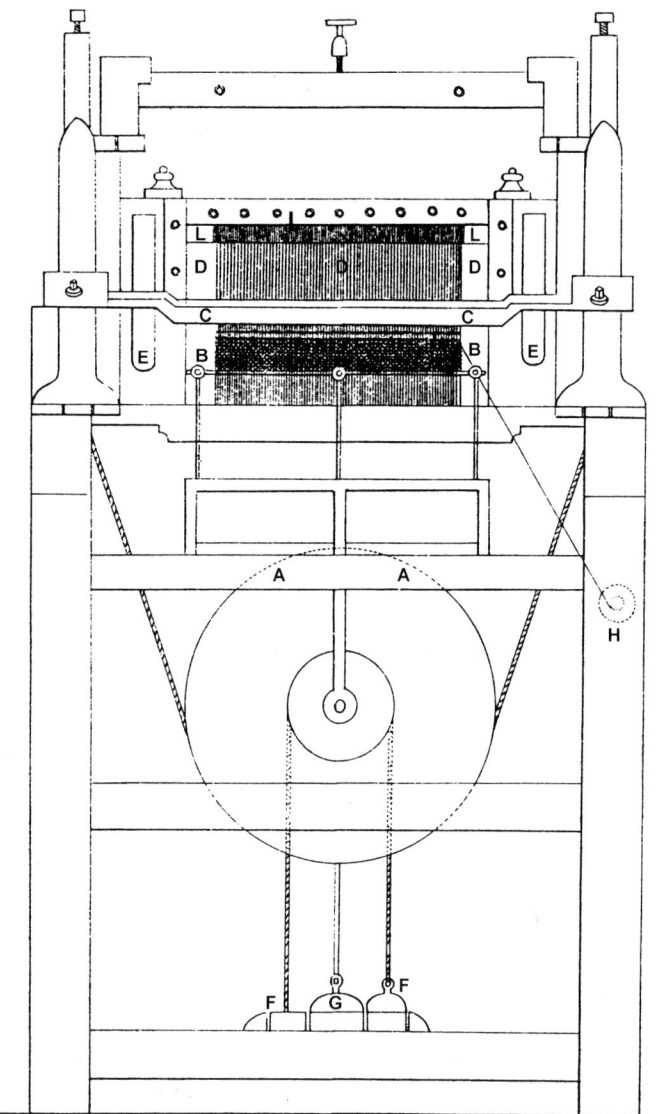

PLATE 10

Adapted from William Felkin's *History of the machine-wrought hosiery and lace manufactures* with the help of Liveryman Henry Hurt

THE KNITTING FRAME – FRONT VIEW

A. Knitter's seat.

B. Needles as hooks.

C. Presser.

D. Sinkers.

E. Frame Handles

F. Treddles for drawing Jacks.

G. Treddle to force down Presser.

H. Bobbin supplying Yarn.

K. Jacks from the cords of which Sinkers, D, are suspended.

L. Combs.

M. Spring.

N. Spring.

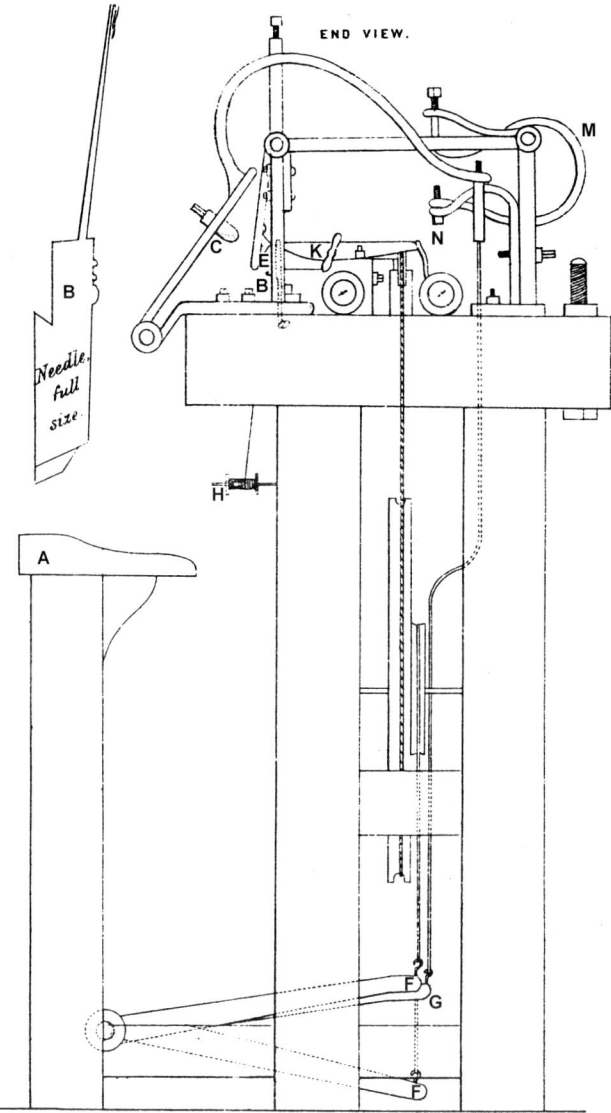

PLATE 11

Adapted from William Felkin's *History of the machine-wrought hosiery and lace manufactures* with the help of Liveryman Henry Hurt

THE KNITTING FRAME – SIDE VIEW

A. Knitter's seat.
B. Needles as hooks.
C. Presser.
D. Sinkers.
E. Frame Handles
F. Treddles for drawing Jacks.
G. Treddle to force down Presser.

H. Bobbin supplying Yarn.
K. Jacks from the cords of which
   Sinkers, D, are suspended.
L. Combs.
M. Spring.
N. Spring.

FRAME-WORK-KNITTERS Company,
London, *April* 22, 1724.

At a General Court of Assistants then held. Upon Complaint made by several Persons to the Court, that the Two By-Laws of this Company (hereafter mention'd) had not of late Years been put in Execution against Transgressors therein, to the great Prejudice of the Trade and Company; It was thereupon ORDERED, That there should be forthwith Printed and Distributed amongst the several Members of this Company, the Copies of Two Original By-Laws Established by Virtue of the Royal Charter of King *CHARLES* the Second (of Blessed Memory,) granted to the Company of FRAME-WORK-KNITTERS of the Kingdom of *England*, and Dominion of *Wales*, That all Persons and Members of this Company may be publickly Informed, and not pretend or plead Ignorance, or that they had forgot the laid Ordinances; the Company intending to Sue all Persons that shall Act contrary to the laid By-Laws, or either of them, in any Point whatsoever, *viz.*

repr. with permission of Nottinghamshire Archives

PLATE 12

THE FRAMEWORK KNITTERS' ARMS

Here used on a document of 1724 sent by the Court in London to Courts outside London. The machine parts of the Coat of Arms have been marked with letters corresponding to the key for the frame in Plates 1C and 11, so as to show where these parts fitted into the frame.

monopolies, and by the time that James Lee and Ashton had made their improvements the king had passed in 1624 another law stating that patents were only to be
granted to a 'new invention or method not known or used before'.

The first technical drawings of the stocking frame were made by the French spy
Jean Hindret in 1666, by which time a number of improvements had been made.
The original lacked, among other things, dividing sinkers. Lee's apprentice Ashton
added a second set of sinkers, which he called lead sinkers, introducing one fixed
sinker between every two movable jack sinkers. The addition of these sinkers, plus
thumb plates and lockers, and an equal number of needles meant that the gauge
of the machine could be doubled – the old twelve-gauge machines becoming
twenty four-gauge – finer work could be made and the cost of frames was
reduced. John Pa(r)giter, assisted by a framesmith called Luddington, first cast the
needles in pewter, instead of soldering them in brass. When invented the frame
needed two people to work it, but the number of hand and feet movements needed
to produce one course went unrecorded. In 1831, by which time improvements had
made it possible for the frame to be worked by one person, only eleven motions of
hand or feet were needed to make a single row of work.[5] Although there was a
continuing number of improvements the basic principle of Lee's stocking frame
was not superseded for nearly two centuries and the frame continued to make
only plain stocking stitch; fully fashioned hose could be made on the machine but
to achieve ribbing framework knitters had to remove and reverse the stitches
by hand.

Indeed it would seem that some improvements were not acceptable to at least
the section of the trade that made hose. Stockings could have been knitted mechanically much more speedily as early as the 1670s, for John Aubrey records that,
sometime after 1673, 'Sir Christopher Wren proposed to the Silke-stocking
weavers of London . . . a way to weave seven pair or nine paire of stockings (it must
be an odd Number)' and demonstrated his ideas with a model of the 'engine'.
Although Aubrey does not say to which Livery Company the 'engine' was offered,
he does record that the Company concerned, presumably the recently incorporated
Society of Framework Knitters, rejected Wren's price of £400, pleading poverty,
and that then Wren nobally, 'breakes the Modell all to pieces before their faces'. It
is not recorded how Wren's machine worked and, although Wren's price of £400 –
a considerable sum at that time – could have been the main reason for the rejection,
this decision by the Society was just as likely to have been made because the hose it
produced did not conform to the strict rules on production laid down by the Company's regulations, (see Chapter IV), and there was opposition from journeymen
to larger and more powerful machines, as the London Weavers' Riots of 1675
showed. Indeed, the introduction of new technology continued to be viewed with
suspicion by the stocking knitters for in 1773 a mob of them destroyed a frame
rumoured to be capable of making twelve stockings at a time at an exhibition at the
Leicester Exchange, while one of the main causes of the Luddite Riots in the early
1800s was the making of cheap, 'cut-up', stockings on the wide frames, previously
producing the highly profitable, knitted point net, when new frames twisting lace
net, as opposed to knitting it, were introduced.[6]

It was only in the second half of the eighteenth century that radical alterations
began to be made to the knitting frame. Before the end of the century the thread
carrier had been added, which obviated the necessity of the knitter having to lay the

thread across the needles by hand, and made wide machines easier to operate, for until its introduction most frames had remained a narrow eighteen inches or less. The possibility of knitting wide fabric on the frame meant that several stockings could be cut from a single piece without the need to narrow and widen the stocking as in the skilled, fully fashioned work; such 'bad and deceitful' cut-ups were against the Company's regulations and led to a great deal of hostility from the knitters who made the fully fashioned work. The first successful making of ribbing on the hand frame, without the necessity for time consuming manual work, was achieved by Jedediah Strutt of Derby in 1758. A patent for making fancy work in hose was taken out in Nottinghamshire in 1764. However, other technical innovations meant that the gloves and mittens previously made on the single thread knitting frame were now increasingly made on the warp knitting frame, which united the looped stitch of the stocking frame with the warp of the weaver's loom, using a separate thread for each row of vertical loops, so that the fabric was formed from vertical chains of loops. Invented about 1775 by Crane and Porter of Edmonton near London, the warp frame was improved by Ingham of Nottingham in 1785 and, although the goods it produced were still classed as hosiery, its introduction meant that framework knitters using the stocking frame lost another section of production. In addition, the manufacture of net, which had originally been the most profitable branch of framework knitting, was after 1809 increasingly made on a new type of frame which twisted together the threads rather than knitting them, and this led to the establishment of a completely separate textile industry in the East Midlands – lace making. Although by 1815 about forty five different versions of the knitting frame produced a wide variety of fabrics, the introduction of these technically different frames was to have a profound effect on the long term economic viability of ordinary framework knitting.[7]

During the first half of the nineteenth century, when technical innovations were leading to most textile manufacture being converted to steam power, it was discovered that the basic technology of the stocking frame could not be so adapted, and its motive power had to remain the hands and feet movements of the operator, so that the frame continued to be housed in the operator's home or a small workshop in close vicinity, rather than in a factory (see Plate 13). There was a long period, while steam powered knitting machines were being developed, that hand framework knitting continued on a large scale for, until the 1870s and the introduction of compulsory education, there was an adequate supply of cheap labour, which suited many employers as they could still exercise a strong control over the labour force as well as keep costs down by domestic production. Even after the general introduction of steam-powered hosiery machinery, the stocking frame continued in use; firms such as I. and R. Morley continuing for a long time to use hand-operated knitting frames for fine work. A small domestic system of hosiery production still existed in 1946 and a fair amount of glove production was still carried on in the operatives' homes. Until 1956 Allen Solly worked a shop of hand frames in Calverton and in 1960 there were still approximately fifty handframe knitters in the United Wool Shawl, Fall and Antimacassar Trade Union of Hucknall and District, which was only disbanded in 1965. Up to the present Liveryman Henry Hurt operates a plant of hand frames making fancy woollen shawls in Chilwell, Nottinghamshire.[8] However, from the 1850s the general economic viability of the hand-operated knitting frames had steadily declined.

The Art of STOCKING-FRAME-WORK-KNITTING.

Engrav'd for the Universal Magazine 1750, for J.Hinton at the Kings. Arms in S.Pauls Church Yard LONDON.

PLATE 13   *lent by Liveryman Henry Hurt*

THE ART OF FRAMEWORK KNITTING ABOUT 1750

While the male of the family is working at the frame the females are carrying out the auxiliary task of preparing the yarn.

Powered knitting machines

Two main types of powered knitting machine were developed, the flat frame, based on William Lee's manually operated machine, and the circular machine. The adaption of the flat frame to powered working meant that a number of garments, such as socks, stockings, underwear and outerwear, could be made and shaped at the same time eventually getting rid of laborious hand work. The circular frames, with the exception of the seamless hose machines, produce mostly knitted fabric, plain, rib, or a combination of the two, as well as open work, interlock, and plated fabrics. The gauges of all machines are different and each are set up to make an individualised production.

Flat frame development

Development of steam powered flat frames was slow and new inventions were only gradually disseminated through the industry. Wise took out a patent for a rotary power frame as early as 1769 and Betts invented a rotary frame with moveable needle bar in 1777, but suitable power sources were not yet available; the powered flat frame was not successfully introduced until the nineteenth century for it was not until 1828–9 that the first steam-powered rotary frames were apparently working in Loughborough. One of the more difficult problems was how to fashion garments without stopping the machine, and this was partly achieved in 1838 by Luke Barton of Arnold, Nottingham, who patented the automatic narrowing mechanism for rotary machines, while William Coltman first produced in Leicester that same year the combined ratchet wheel and screw thread which was used extensively on straight bar frames into the mid-twentieth century. In 1857 Luke Barton introduced the self-acting rotary frame and four years later Paget of Loughborough a self-acting moveable needle bar rotary frame. Nevertheless, although these machines were power driven, they were still only the width of the wider hand frames.[9]

The flat frame machine that revolutionised the industry was patented by William Cotton of Loughborough in 1864. In it Cotton changed the position of the fundamental knitting parts; Lee's bearded needles were placed vertically instead of horizontally, while the sinkers became horizontal instead of vertical, and knitting motions were reduced from nine to seven; fine gauge, wide fabric could be produced. It came to be known as Cotton's System, or 'Cotton's Patent', and even at the beginning could knit four identical articles at the same time although, because the patent was confined to the company and its licensees into the late 1870s, it was only after that date that the machine became generally available to manufacturers[10] (see Plate 14).

Circular machines
The development of the powered circular machine was as protracted as that of the powered flat frame. In 1816 Sir Marc Isambard Brunel, father of the famous engineer Isambard Kingdom Brunel, invented a circular frame using Lee's bearded needles, which he called the 'tricoteur', but this only came into use about 1845 when the Pagets established a steam powered factory in Loughborough making caps, shirts and straight-down hose. Circular knitting was only revolutionised with the invention of the tumbler needle, usually called the latch needle, by Matthew Townsend of Leicester in 1847, which made possible individual stitch selection, and therefore considerably widened the product range[11] (see Plate 14).

Products

Stockings were never the only product of the hand knitting frames for the Charter of 1657 refers to 'stockings tops waistcoats trouches (trousers/breeches) or any

---

PLATE 14 (opposite)   *repr. with permission of the Snibston Discovery Park, Leics.*

OLD KNITTING FRAMES

Housed at the Snibston Museum these five machines are representative of the many that superseded Lee's frame: *(a)* Townsend's machine; *(b)* Lamb's flat frame; *(c)* The rotary frame; *(d)* 'George' machine; *(e)* William Cotton's fully fashioned stocking machine.

(a)

(b)

(c)

(e)

(d)

other things whatsoever made or wrought by the said frames'. By the first half of eighteenth century production had altered little since the mid-1600s as Henson referred to 'considerable quantities of worsted pieces . . . made into waistcoats, trousers, and breeches, of various colours', although with the machine improvements 'the waistcoat pieces were worked in stripes' and 'another extensive manufacture of silk purses, was carried on, principally in London'.[12] With the advent of the different powered machines production widened and became more flexible, and there was always competition to bring out new lines; new sections were continually being added to the range of knitted products and production expanded. For example, when ladies' seamless hose became an important item of hosiery in the 1940s, by the end of 1950 there were more than 144 plants of this type of machinery in the United Kingdom, a very large proportion of it in the East Midlands.[13] By the twentieth century there was a plethora of specialised knitting machines on the market and the term 'hosiery', which originally referred to hose or stockings, now came to have a more general meaning and encompass more or less different trades. A firm producing knitted outerwear had little in common with one making underwear, while one producing womens' fully-fashioned nylon stockings had little in common with one producing men's or children's socks, or even with one producing women's seamless tights.

Machine builders and the Framework Knitters' Society

Specialisation in machine building emerged early, as in the Framework Knitters' petition of 1655 'smiths, joiners, and turners, for the making, erecting, and repairing of the frames, and other necessary instruments . . . and also their needlemakers' are noted as being allied to framework knitting, although framework knitters were often their own framesmiths. The development of flat frames especially was the speciality of English machine builders and many of the inventions or improvements to frames were made by people who had long family connections with the industry and the Framework Knitters' Society. After about two centuries of input into the knitting frame mainly from the Nottinghamshire and London framesmiths, the ones in Nottinghamshire increasingly developed the separate lace trade, and a number of framework knitting families from Leicestershire became more prominent in hosiery machine building. William Coltman was one of the Leicestershire inventors whose family roots were in the Framework Knitters' Society for in 1696 Thomas Coltman had been apprenticed at the Nottingham Court. Matthew Townsend was another, for in 1697 John Townsend was apprenticed at the Nottingham Court and Matthew himself was presumably the 'sworn member' who signed the petition from Leicestershire to the Court in October 1824 (see Plate 35). Other descendants of active members of the Framework Knitters' Society who constructed machines were the Paget family, for in 1732 William Paget had been the most important of the Leicestershire Deputies.[14]

After knitting and frame building became separate businesses from the 1800s machine builders did not resume an active association with the Society until the beginning of the twentieth century when directors of G. Stibbe & Company and William Bentley of Bentley Engineering, both of Leicester, became closely involved in both the Company and in education for the hosiery trade.[15]

Auxiliary trades and the Framework Knitters' Society

Alongside the development in knitting machines yarns were also improved, and often helped to determine the location in which different sections of mechanical knitting were developed. William Lee's first stockings were made of coarse, hand-spun wool, presumably from the long stapled fleece of the sheep in Sherwood Forest around his home village of Calverton. Later the even longer staple fleeces of the Leicester sheep were found to be more suitable for spinning into worsted yarn, and this was one factor that encouraged woollen knitting by machine to become centred in Leicestershire rather than Nottinghamshire. Silk too was a yarn widely used in early framework knitting. Until about 1717 it was imported as spun yarn mainly through the Port of London, thus encouraging the manufacture of silk stockings in London; after Thomas Lombe spun silk commercially at his factory on the Derwent Derby became a centre for silk yarn production. Because of its uneven and poor quality cotton yarn was not often used in knitting frames until about 1730. Even when the quality improved the London framework knitters apparently refused to work Indian spun cotton 'on account of its stubborness, when compared with silk', and the yarn was sent to Nottingham where it was made into stockings by a journeyman named Draper on a twenty-gauge silk frame. Nottingham's subsequent growth into the centre for cotton framework knitting encouraged Hargreaves and Arkwright to move to the area and further develop spinning, although the spinning jenny was only suitable for cotton and could not be used to spin wool. A machine to spin worsted yarn was not produced until 1785 but, although invented in Leicester, it could not be used there until the nineteenth century because of the opposition of the town's workers. By the mid-1800s, although there was never a rigid demarcation, it was generalised that in the East Midland counties silk knitting was carried on in Derbyshire, cotton in Nottinghamshire and wool in Leicestershire.[16]

However, until the twentieth century no member of the Company appears to have been connected with hosiery yarns. The earliest was Frederick Russell Donisthorpe, Master in 1911, who was followed by five other directors of Donisthorpes of Leicester, worsted spinners and doublers, and later knitwear manufacturers.[17] Other families of yarn agents who have also been closely connected with the Company in the twentieth century are the Morleys and the Frasers.[18]

Dyeing and finishing were also a necessary part of knitted garment production, although members of the Company only came from this section of the industry in the twentieth century, including Clarence Kershaw, Master in 1931. In 1970 the Master was the dyer Edward Russell Trotman one of whose ancestors appear to have been London members of the Company at the end of the seventeenth century when Richard Trot(t)man was apprenticed to a member of the East family. Master Trotman was typical of so many of the modern leaders of the Company who had wide interests within the hosiery trade; his experience spanned knitting in both Leicester and Nottingham and, as well as being author of two text books on dyeing and textile technology, he was also vice-president of the Textile Institute.[19]

Summary

This short outline of the tools of mechanical knitting shows that the location of frame and machine building, yarn manufacture and dyeing mirrors almost exactly the locations for membership of the Society of Framework Knitters, and shows that for most of its history these sections had a very close relationship with the Society.

References

1 Marilyn Palmer, *Framework Knitting* (Princes Risborough: Shire Publications, 1990), p. 3; pamphlet on 'Framework Knitting', Leicestershire Museum Services, Snibston, p. 1; Henson, p. 40.

2 Full description with diagrams is given in Palmer, pp. 3-6; Bill Partridge, *A possible Source of Wire for William Lee's Bearded Needles* (Nottingham: Partridge and Ruddington Framework Knitters' Museum, 1998).

3 1655 Petition; David J. Spencer, *Knitting Technology* (Pergamon Press, 1983), p. 8; Grass, pp. 109, 116; Henson, pp. 61–6; Deering, p. 101; information from Liveryman Henry Hurt.

4 W. Felkin, *An Account of the machine-wrought hosiery trade* (London: W. Strange, 1845). Detailed accounts of the evolution of the stocking frame are given by William Felkin, Gravenor Henson and Peta Lewis. Deering, pp. 364–72 gives a detailed description and illustrations of the parts of the frame.

5 Henson pp. 47, 48 (footnote), 55, 66, 86; John Blackner, *The History of Nottingham* (Nottingham: Sutton & Sons, 1815), p. 214.

6 Bruce Marsden, 'From St. Paul's to silk stockings', *History Today*, 47(11), November 1997, p. 34, quoting John Aubrey's *Natural History of Wiltshire*; Jean English, 'Framework Knitting in Leicestershire', *Leicestershire Historian*, 1, 5, 1969, pp. 159–64, p. 162; Sheila A. Mason, *Nottingham Lace: 1760s–1950s* (Cluny Lace Co. Ltd: Ilkeston, 1994), p. 74.

7 Blackner, pp. 219, 232, 244–5; Mason, pp. 9, 11, 72; Jedediah Strutt, Patent no. 772; Thomas & John Morris, hosiers of Nottingham and John & William Betts of Mansfield, Patent no. 807, 1764; *Report from the Select Committee appointed to take into consideration the several Petitions which have been presented to this House in this Session of Parliament by the Persons employed in the Framework-knitting; 1812 247 (II)*, p. 5; information Mr. Bill Partridge, Hinckley – one frame at Hinckley Museum has no thread carrier and is the oldest one in Britain.

8 Frederick Moy Thomas, *I. and R. Morley: A Record of a Hundred Years* (London: Chiswick Press, 1900), p. 28; H. A. Silverman, *Studies in Industrial Organisation* (London: Metheun, 1946), 'The Hosiery Industry', p. 9; David M. Smith, *Industrial Archaeology of the East Midlands* (Dawlish: David & Charles, 1965), p. 53; information from Liveryman Henry Hurt.

9 Felkin, pp. 490, 492; NAO, MSS, CA 4041/52.

10 Patent no. 3123, 16 December 1864: ed. S. G. Mason, *British Hosiery and Knitwear*, p. 12; Palmer, p. 27, Moy Thomas, p. 33.

11 Felkin pp. 39–40, 490–8, 500, 502; *1845 Appendix to the Report on the Condition of Framework Knitters*, pp. 404–5.

12 Henson, p. 105.

13 *Survey of Ladies' Seamless Hose Knitting Machinery in Great Britain* (Leicester: National Hosiery Manufacturers' Federation, 1951).

14 MSS. 3444; NAO, MSS. CA 4040/52; Thirsk and Cooper, p. 263; John Chamberlain, *Manufacture of Knitted Footwear* (Leicester: Alfred Tacey, 1930).

15 *G. Stibbe & Co. Ltd, Leicester: 1886–1950* (Leicester: Stibbe, 1950); G. Stibbe – Chairman of the Textile Trades Advisory Committee of the Leicester College of Technology 1918–1931; Edward Victor Stibbe – Master in 1946; Arthur Stannage Whitehead – Master in 1933; John Whitehead – Master 1978, Chairman of Governors of the Leicester Polytechnic and of Leicester De Montfort University.

16 Stephen Glover, *The History, Gazetteer, and Directory of the County of Derby* (Derby: Mozley, 1829), p. 247; Henson, pp. 164–5.

17 Shirley Ellis, *A Mill on the Soar* (Leicester: Blackfriars Press, 1978); George Ellis – Master 1926; John Ellis – Master 1928; Archibald Ellis – Master 1940; Shirley Ellis – Master 1948; Howard Ellis – Master 1985.

18 Cecil Morley – Master 1951; Peter Morley – Master 1977; Peter's daughter Anne Brown has been Deputy Clerk since 1994.

19 MSS. 3444; 16840.

III

The organisation of the Worshipful Company of Framework Knitters

The Worshipful Company of Framework Knitters' first Charter was granted on 13 June 1657 by Oliver Cromwell, the Lord Protector, and enrolled in the Chamber of London on 14 July the same year (see Appendix 2). Less than three years later, in May 1660, Charles II was restored to the throne and the Company lost little time in applying for another Charter. This was obtained at a cost of twenty marks on 19 August 1663, and was enrolled by the City of London on 24 September 1663 (see Appendix 3). Both Charters were quickly followed by Ordinances, usually called Bye-laws. Those of 1657 have vanished, but on 4 July 1664 those drawn up after the restoration Charter were ratified, and thus given legal authority, by Edward, Earl of Clarendon, Lord High Chancellor of England, Sir Robert Hyde, Lord Chief Justice of the King's Bench, and Sir Orlando Bridgeman, Lord Chief Justice of the Common Pleas (see Appendix 4). Their subsequent acceptance by the Court of Aldermen also conferred on the Company the political and administrative advantages of the City of London. Details of the Ordinances, most typically the fines, were adjusted from time to time, and in 1745 they were rewritten and signed on 22 May by Lord Hardwicke, the Lord Chancellor, Sir William Lee, the Lord Chief Justice of the King's Bench, and Sir J. Willes, the Lord Chief Justice of the Common Pleas, which meant that they again had legal authority (see Appendix 5 and Plates 15–17). It would seem that, with the exception of the laws altered or rescinded in the nineteenth century, in theory, even though probably not in practice, the Society of Framework Knitters still legally controls mechanical knitting. Although the Company is now typical of most Livery Companies of the City of London with an emphasis on its charitable and educational work, the countrywide extent of its power granted through these Charters and Ordinances gave it complete control over the whole knitting industry of England and Wales.[1]

In the precedence of Livery Companies, established in 1515, the Framework Knitters' ranks sixty fourth. It was the first Company concerned solely with the consequences of machine-made production, not a trade, and is one of only two not originally incorporated by a crowned head. Together with the Needlemakers' Company it obtained its original charter during the rule of Oliver Cromwell; the Needlemakers' in 1656, a year before the Framework Knitters'. However, except for their first Charters, which were penned by the same person and are, except for very slight variations in Cromwell's portrait, identical in design, there is no

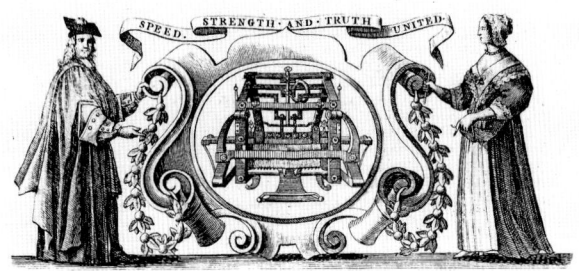

An ABSTRACT *of the Orders, Rules and Ordinances, of the Company of* FRAME-WORK-KNITTERS; *made by the Master, Wardens, and Assistants of the said Company, on the Twenty-second Day of* May, 1745. *And confirmed, pursuant to Act of Parliament, by the Right Hon.* PHILIP Lord HARDWICKE, *Lord High Chancellor of* Great Britain; *Sir* WILLIAM LEE, *Knt. Lord Chief Justice of his Majesty's Court of King's Bench, and Sir* JOHN WILLES, *Knt. Lord Chief Justice of his Majesty's Court of Common Pleas.*

1. *The Election of Master and Wardens.*	THE Court of Assistants shall yearly on *Midsummer-Day* (if it be not *Sunday*, and if it be then the Day following) choose out of the Assistants One Master and Two Wardens, for the Year ensuing.
2. *The Election of Auditors.*	THE said Court at the same Time to choose three Persons out of the Assistants to audit the Master and Wardens Accompts.
3. *To chuse others in the Place of Master and Wardens, in case of Death or Removal.*	THE said Court may choose others to serve in the Place of Master or Wardens, dying or being displaced within the Year, for the remaining Part of the Year.
4. *For Swearing the Master and Wardens.*	THE Master and Wardens Elect shall on the Day of Election, or within one Week after, be sworn into their Offices.
5. *The Election of Assistants.*	THE Court of Assistants shall, as often as they think fit, admit such Members as are free of the City, and of the Livery, to be of the Assistants; and every Person so admitted, and refusing to accept thereof (not having a reasonable Excuse) to forfeit 10 *l.*
6. *The Election of the Livery-Men.*	THE said Court may admit into the Livery so many Members of the Company as they shall think meet; and every Person so admitted, refusing to come into the Clothing (not having a reasonable Impediment, to be allowed by the Lord Mayor of *London*, or one of the Aldermen of the said City) to forfeit 20 *l.*
7. *The Choice of Deputies.*	THE said Court may elect two or more Members to be their Deputies, within such Distance from their Habitations as in their Deputations shall be limitted, to rule and govern all Persons exercising the Trade of FRAMEWORK-KNITTING, according to the Powers granted by the Charter, in the same Manner the Master, Wardens, and Assistants may do, by Virtue of the Charter.
8. *The Choice of Stewards for Midsummer-Day.*	THE said Court may yearly, on the second *Tuesday* in *April*, elect Two Members, residing within 40 Miles of *London*, to be Stewards on *Midsummer* Day; and on that Day to provide a Dinner for the Master, Wardens and Assistants: And every Person so elected, and refusing to serve, or having undertaken so to do, shall afterwards neglect it, shall forfeit 6 *l.*
9. *The Choice of Stewards for the Lord Mayor's Day.*	THE said Court may elect three Members to be Stewards on Lord Mayor's Day, to provide a Dinner for the Master, Wardens, Assistants and Livery: And every Person so elected, and refusing to serve, shall forfeit 10 *l.*
10. *The Choice of Clerk.*	THE said Court shall chuse one Person to be Clerk of the Company, and upon just Occasion may displace him.

11. *The*

PLATE 15   *repr. with permission of Nottinghamshire Archives*

1745 ORDINANCES – FIRST PAGE OF THE ABSTRACT

This Abstract was printed by the Court in London and sent to the Nottingham Court to be distributed to all framework knitters. Appendix 5 gives the Table of Orders, Rules and Ordinances.

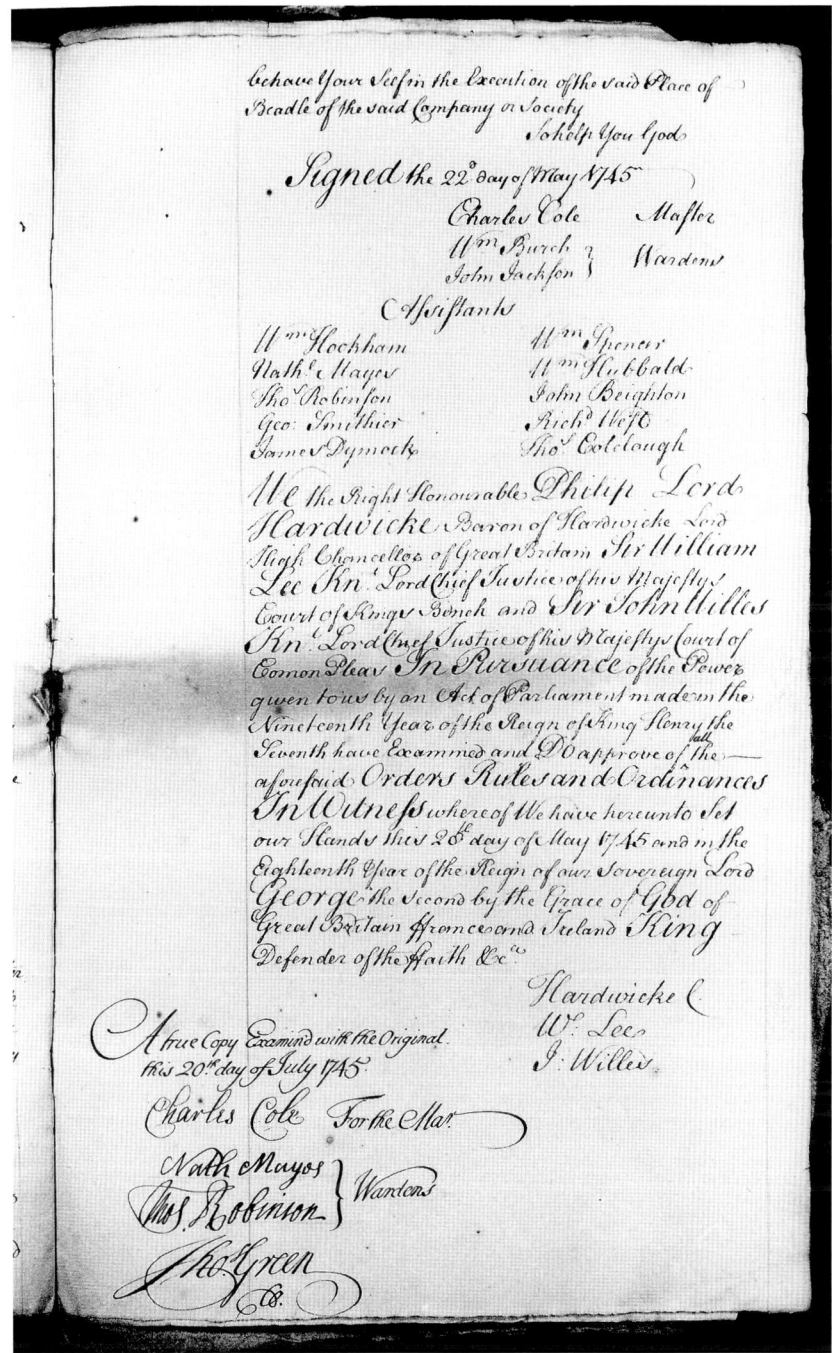

PLATE 16   *repr. with permission of Nottinghamshire Archives*

1745 ORDINANCES – THE 'TRUE', AND COMPLETE, COPY

These were certified by Charles Cole, the Master at the time these Bye-laws were passed, and Nathaniel Mayes and Thomas Robinson, the Wardens, and sent to the Nottingham Court.

A TABLE *of Fees and Fines, directed to be paid by the aforesaid Ordinances.*

	Company.	Clerk.	Beadle.	Total.
For every Perfon at his Firft Admittance ———	0 10 0	0 2 0	0 1 0	0 15 0
Stamps ———	0 2 0			
Upon the Allowance of every Workhoufe-keeper for his Proof Piece	0 10 0	0 2 0	0 1 0	0 13 0
For every Apprentice bound ———	0 3 0	0 2 0	0 1 0	0 9 0
Stamps ———	0 3 0			
And more, if the Mafter is a Freeman of *London*, to the Orphans, 2 *s*. 6 *d*.				
For the Turning over an Apprentice ———	0 2 0	0 1 0	0 0 6	0 3 6
For the Stewards Fine for Midfummer Day ———	6 0 0	0 5 0	0 2 6	6 7 6
Ditto ——— for Lord Mayor's Day	10 0 0	0 5 0	0 2 6	10 7 6
For the Livery Fine ———	10 0 0	0 10 0	0 5 0	10 15 0
For the Affiftants Fine ———	10 0 0	0 10 0	0 5 0	10 15 0
For every Perfon elected an Auditor, and not ferving ———	1 0 0	———	———	1 0 0
For every Perfon elected Mafter or Warden, and not ferving	5 0 0	———	———	5 0 0

The Oath of every Freeman of the Company of FRAME-WORK-KNITTERS, *at his firft Admittance.*

YOU do fincerely Promife and Swear, that you will be faithful and bear true Allegiance to our Sovereign Lord King GEORGE, his Heirs and Succeffors, You fhall be true to the Fellowfhip of FRAME-WORK-KNITTERS whereunto you are now admitted. You fhall not do any Thing to the Difadvantage of the faid Art or Myftery, nor ufe any Fraud in the Manufacture of FRAME-WORK-KNITTING. You fhall not difcover the lawful Counfels of this Fraternity, which you ought to keep fecret. You fhall be Contributary to all Manner of Charges in and about the Public Weal of the faid Society to your Power. You fhall obey, keep and perform all the Acts and Ordinances made and to be made for the good Order of the faid Art and Myftery. Thefe Points, and all other good Rules, you fhall maintain to your Power.   So help you GOD.

PLATE 17   *repr. with permission of Nottinghamshire Archives*

1745 ORDINANCES – FEES AND FINES

These formed part of the Abstract sent to Nottingham framework knitters.

perceiveable connection between the Companies as the 'needles' used in the stocking frame were in reality hooks manufactured by the framesmith, or even the local blacksmith, while the Needlemakers' Company concentrated on the domestic sewing needle.

Charters

For two centuries the Cromwell Charter was not thought to exist and it only returned to the public domain in 1898. It was discovered among the papers of the Hyde family by Frank Hyde during a visit to the family house in Berkshire, where he found his younger brother cutting up old parchments for jam pot covers and decided to retain as wall decorations for his study in London some manuscripts which had been put on one side as being too thick to cut easily. These manuscripts included the Cromwell Charter and a vellum copy of the Charles II Charter and a few years later, after a maid had accidentally spilt water down one of them, Mr. Hyde presented the relevant ones to the Company.[2]

This Cromwell Charter, together with two copies of the Charter of Charles II and one of the Ordinances, are now housed in the Guildhall Library in the City of London. All are penned on sheets of vellum about three feet by two-and-a-half feet, and have beautifully illustrated borders, those on the Cromwell Charter, one of the Charles II Charters and the Ordinances in black ink, while the second Charles II Charter and one of the Ordinances are exquisitely painted in colour (see Plates C1, 3–7). On the top left-hand corner of both Charters and the Ordinances is, as was usual, a head and shoulders portrait of the ruler who incorporated the Society. On the Charles II Charter the rose of England and multi-coloured tulips are among the flowers depicted in the borders, and these, together with paintings of grey parrots and other plants and birds, illustrate in allegorical form the high esteem in which the Framework Knitters' Society was regarded in this period, as well as honouring the incorporator. Tulips had only been bought into England in Elizabeth I's reign and were very popular after the Restoration. The bulbs of the multi-coloured ones cost up to five pounds each and were 'the most sought after, costly and prestigious flowers that a seventeenth-century gardener could possess'. In the portrait of the Capel family painted in 1640 the two urns behind the head of Elizabeth Lady Capel are filled with such tulips. The inclusion of the grey parrot reinforces the Society's homage to the king. From the middle ages parrots were highly prized presents for royalty and one grey parrot, belonging to a mistress of Charles II, was such a favourite that on its demise it was stuffed and is now the oldest surviving example of avian taxidermy.[3]

The Charters of Incorporation do 'not give any exclusive Right, or Privilege, to any one Person, but the Intention of the Charter(s), and the Powers thereby granted, (is) to incorporate all Frame-work Knitters in England and Wales, that so the whole Manufactory might be under general and proper Regulations'. They gave the Society a constitution and governing body, rights to sue and be sued, of having a common seal and holding landed property and, although the limitation of one hundred marks prevented the Framework Knitters' from becoming a wealthy landed Company, it was also allowed to acquire charitable estates and funds. No mention is made in the Charles II Charter of the one of Cromwell, presumably because of political niceties and the desire to unite the country, but both were granted after petitions to the ruler detailing the many deceits and abuses practised in the trade to the detriment of both the petitioners practicing the trade and to the country, and are similar in content. Cromwell's Charter permitted divers persons 'within the said City of London and four miles compass' to be a 'Body Corporate and Politic . . . by the name of Master Wardens Assistants and Society of the Art or Mystery of Framework Knitters of the City of London'. Charles II's addressed 'our well beloved subjects the Framework Knitters in our Cities of London and Westminster and our Kingdom of England and Dominion of Wales' and incorporated them into 'one fellowship and one Body Politique and Corporate in deeds and in name by the Name of the Master Wardens Assistants and Society of the Art or Mysterie of Framework Knitters in our said Cities of London and Westminster and Kingdom of England, and Dominion of Wales'. Neither Cromwell's nor Charles II's Charters made the Framework Knitters' solely a Company of the City of London and both granted the Framework Knitters the wider status of a Society, as were the Apothecaries' under James I. While twenty-four Livery Companies were restricted during the reign of Charles II to the City of London and forty-three had areas comprising the City and a stated radius of miles around, in most cases between two and ten miles, the Framework Knitters' were among a very small minority of Livery Companies, including the Tobacco Pipe Makers', which were granted a national role with complete authority over all practitioners of their trade throughout England and Wales. Even in the Cromwell Charter the Deputies were not restricted to an area around London but had 'power and authority under the common seal . . . to make search . . . in the presence of a constable or other lawful officer in all or any place or places within this Commonwealth'. Both Charters granted the strictest type of guild organisation and gave total control of the industry, at a time when it has been felt by some authorities that London's Livery Companies were already in decline, to a Court appointed for life, 'with power to name their successors; to make laws and enforce them by fines; to levy fees, and to dispose of fines and fees at their pleasure'. They were also 'empowered to choose their members from the body of citizens, whether frame-work-knitters or not', but all persons working at framework knitting in England and Wales had to become members of the Society and none but those who had served apprenticeships and become masters, on the production of a master piece, were allowed to take apprentices. The 'search' was the quality control of framework knitting, whereby the Society was given powers to destroy any 'unworkmanlike wrought . . . bad and deceitful stuff . . . to be cut in pieces and defaced', wherever it was found, while the knitters concerned were to be punished by 'fines and penalties according to the ordinances orders and bye-laws'. 'Mayors, sheriffs, bailiffs, constables, and officers, were commanded to assist the Company according to the laws of the realm', premises could be searched and, as well as faulty merchandise, frames intended for export could also be seized. The fine for exporting any frame or frame parts was £10 'for the only use and benefit of the said Society'.[4]

Ordinances

The Ordinances signed by the Chancellor and the Chief Justices were effective in law and were the day-to-day rules which regulated the whole of framework knitting and laid down the punishment of offenders. As has already been stated, their acceptance by the Court of Aldermen conferred on the Company the avantages of the City of London. The first existing Bye-laws of the Society date from 1664 and were rewritten in 1745 (see Appendices 4 and 5).[5]

The 1663 Clerk, John Hannis, presented to the Society copies of the signed Ordinances bound, together with subsequent regulations, into two volumes to be used at the Company's Courts or to reinforce the authority of the searchers for fraudulent and illegal work or workers. One such volume, rebound in the 1930s, is housed with the Company's manuscripts in London and another, in Nottingham, has its original binding and clasps. Attached to the volume in Nottingham is the metal ring by which it was attached to a lectern when the Ordinances were read out, as ordered, at the Courts outside London or to the saddle when the Deputies took it to the various Courts or went out on searches and needed proof of their authority (see Plate 8a).[6]

Details within the organisation of the Society have changed in the last three centuries, sometimes considerably and sometimes unknowingly or because of contemporary pressure and, together with the basics established by the Charters and Ordinances, are outlined hereafter.

Freedom of the Society

To become a member of the Society, now usually entitled the Worshipful Company of Framework Knitters, the Freedom of the Company has to be taken up, which meant that until 1809 everyone working as a framework knitter should have been a member. From the beginning restrictive rules governed the Freemen. No-one was to be admitted to the Company under the age of twenty four. Members had to appear before the Master, Wardens or Deputies when summoned; the fine for needing to be summonsed was 10s. to the Court of Assistants, and non-appearance brought a fine of sixpence due to the Beadle and after three summons the offence was to be looked upon as contempt of the Court of the Framework Knitters' and was severely dealt with. Even the 'custom of London', whereby since 1614 a Freeman of the City of London was allowed to belong to any Livery Company regardless of which trade he followed, was abrogated in the case of the Framework Knitters', for both Charters ruled that 'as the Framework Knitters are now dispersed amongst divers Companies of London and elsewhere . . . all persons as well freemen as foreigners who now do or hereafter shall use or exercise the Art Trade or Mystery of Framework Knitting . . . shall be . . . one body Corporate and Politic'; Freemen of other Companies, therefore, who were working at framework knitting at the date of incorporation had to translate to the new Company. This requirement was first made compulsory for all practising the trade within a four mile circle around the City of London in 1657, and was extended in 1663 to cover the whole of England and Wales, when everyone within twenty miles of London was required to enrol in the Company within three months, and those living further away within six months, or otherwise face a fine of £5 a week.

Theory and practice do not, however, always go hand in hand and from the beginning a number of framework knitters never became members of the Society and, as the years went on, the number of dissidents increased.

The usual cost in most Companies in the City of London to those being granted their Freedom in the seventeenth century was a breakfast for the Master and Wardens, but 'to avoid greater charges' in the case of the Framework Knitters this was commuted to a silver spoon of at least ten shillings in value, as well two shillings to the Clerk and one shilling to the Beadle. This fine (fee) of a silver spoon was changed to a monetary one before the end of the seventeenth century.[7]

However, although every framework knitter was required to become a Freeman of the Society, there was no stipulation that every such member had also to become a Freeman of the City of London, and in the early years of compulsory membership most never progressed beyond taking up the Freedom of the Company. The Framework Knitters' Company would appear, therefore, to be among a minority of City of London Livery Companies in that from the beginning 'Persons free of their Trade (of framework knitting) are not obliged to be free of the City of London'. Members who were only free of the Company were, in the early documents, usually identified in the Company's books as 'foreign brother' – 'forr' for short – to distinguish them from the 'citizen', – or 'cit' – who was also a Freeman of the City of London. Moreover, the label 'foreign brother' does not mean that the member concerned necessarily lived outside the City of London. A comparison of the Framework Knitter's manuscripts and the Freedom registers of the City of London show that those who are listed in the Framework Knitters' quarterage book of 1722 as 'forr' do not appear in the registers of the City dating back to the 1680s. Other Company papers also make this distinction. Lawrence Pomfrett, either the 1657 Assistant, or a descendant of the same name, who took Samuel Roe as apprentice in 1710, is described as 'citizen and FWK of London' on the indenture documents while foreign brother(s) such as Joseph Garton and Charles Villiers are identified as 'foreign brother(s) of the Company of Framework Knitters of the City of London' (see Plates 18 and 19).[8] At least a third of the Framework Knitters' Company came under the 'forr' category for, of the 3,248 whose status was recorded among the 4,925 framework knitters listed in 1722, 1,354 were categorised as foreign brothers, with 1,894 Citizens and Freemen of the City of London.

However, it was both Cromwell's and Charles II's intention that only those who were also Freemen of London were to be subject to the government of City of London; the 'foreign brother' had none of the privileges or benefits that the additional Freedom of the City of London secured, including becoming a Liveryman of the Company.[9]

It was only after 1809, when it was decreed that the rules of the Company only applied to its members, that the term 'foreign brother' was generally replaced in favour of the more accurate 'Freeman'. During the nineteenth century the number of foreign brothers decreased for, although in 1840 there were still about seventy such Freemen, by 1884 it was reported 'that the freedom of the City of London is a condition subsequent of membership. There are not any members of the Company who are not free of the City of London to the knowledge of the Company'.[10] This category of membership, allowing the taking up the Freedom of the Company only, was reintroduced in 1999 'to broaden the appeal of the Company and to make it more accessible to a wider range of applicant'.[11] In the intervening century all Freemen of the Company had been expected to become also Freemen of the City of London.

However, as the following Oaths show, the new Freeman's loyalty was expected to be to the Company. Before becoming Freemen in the 1690s it was required of framework knitters that

> 'You shall swear to be true to the Fellowship of Frame-work Knitters; you shall not disobey the Summons of the Company, but you shall be Obedient at all times; every Apprentice you shall cause to be Enrolled in London within the first year of his term, as the Custom asketh; you shall be at all time be Contributary to all manner of Charges done, or to be done by the Company, in, and about the Weal of the said Mystery to your power; and also well and truly you shall in all things obey and keep all the Acts and Ordinances made, or herein after to be made, for the Governance and Orders of the same Mystery, and confirmed according to the Laws of the Kingdom: These Points, and all other good Rules and Ordinances made and to be made, not repealed and reversed, you shall obey, keep and maintain to your power, so help you God'.[12]

and between the 1700s and at least the 1870s the new Freeman promised that

> 'You do sincerely declare that you will be faithful and bear true allegiance to our Sovereign (Lady Queen Victoria her) Heirs and Successors, you will be

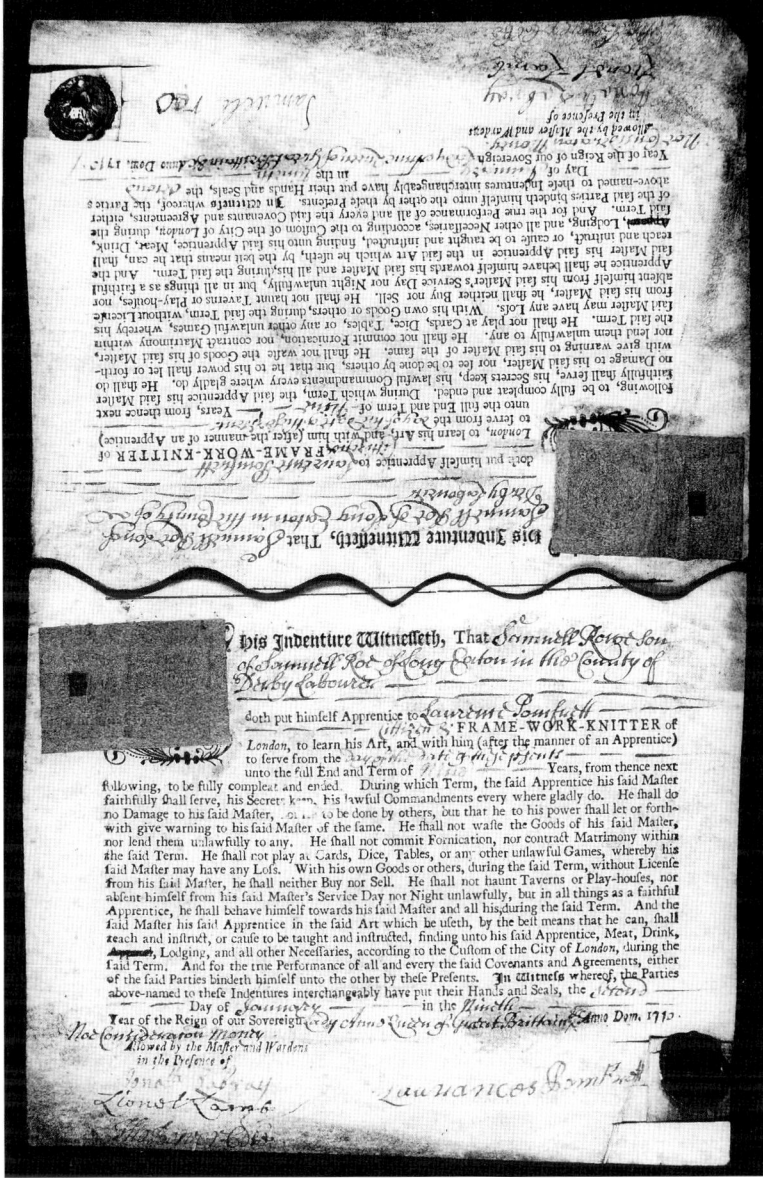

PLATE 18   *repr. with permission of Nottinghamshire Archives*

1710 APPRENTICE INDENTURE

This 1710 binding of Samuel Roe of Long Eaton, Derbyshire, to Lawrence Pomfret, Citizen and Framework Knitter of London, took place at the Nottingham Court; the signatures of the Nottingham Deputies Jonathan Labray and Lionel Lamb, are in the bottom left hand corner of the document. It is extremely rare to have a both parts of a pair of back-to-back indentures like these; the apprentice signed one half and the master the other and then the pair were cut through the middle, as the wavy black line shows; one half was handed to each signatory. The master, Lawrence Pomfret, was either the Assistant of the 1663 Charter or, more probably, his son.

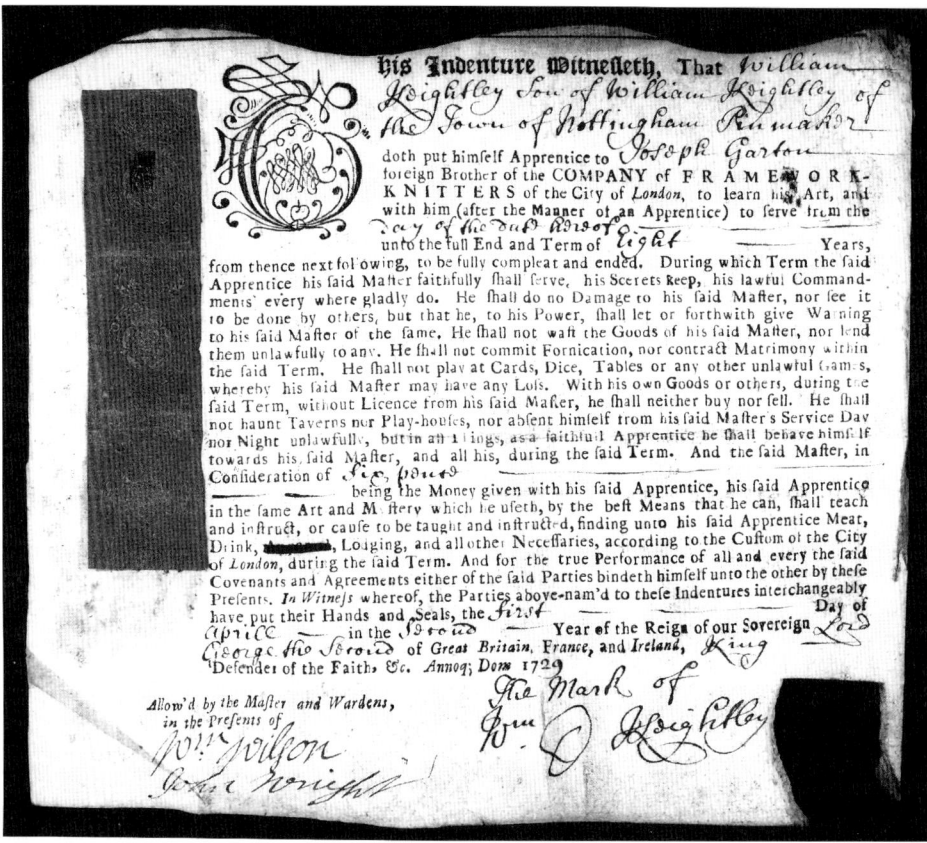

PLATES 19a and 19b (opposite)   *repr. with permission of Nottinghamshire Archives*

APPRENTICE INDENTURES OF 1729 AND 1752

Both these documents also come from the Nottingham Court and while *(a)* the 1729 indenture between William Keightley of Nottingham to Joseph Garton, foreign brother of the Company of Framework Knitters, is part of a batch on which 'foreign brother' was printed in *(b)*, the 1752 indenture between William Dearman of Wakefield, Yorkshire, to Charles Villiers, also foreign brother of the Company of Framework Knitters, the 'foreign brother' has had to be written in. Moreover, while the Deputies Wilson and Wright witnessed the 1729 indenture, by 1752 the Company is taking less interest in its apprentices and the place for signatures has been left blank.

true to the Fellowship of Framework Knitters whereunto you are now admitted, you will not do anything to the disadvantage of the said Art or Mystery, nor use any Fraud in the manufacture of Framework Knitting you will not discover the lawful councils of this Fraternity which you ought to keep secret, you will be contributory to all manner of charges in and about the Public Weal of the said Society to your power, you will obey keep and perform all the Acts and Ordinances made and to be made for the good order of the said Art and Mystery. These points and all other good Rules you will maintain to your power'.[13] (See Plates 17 and 28).

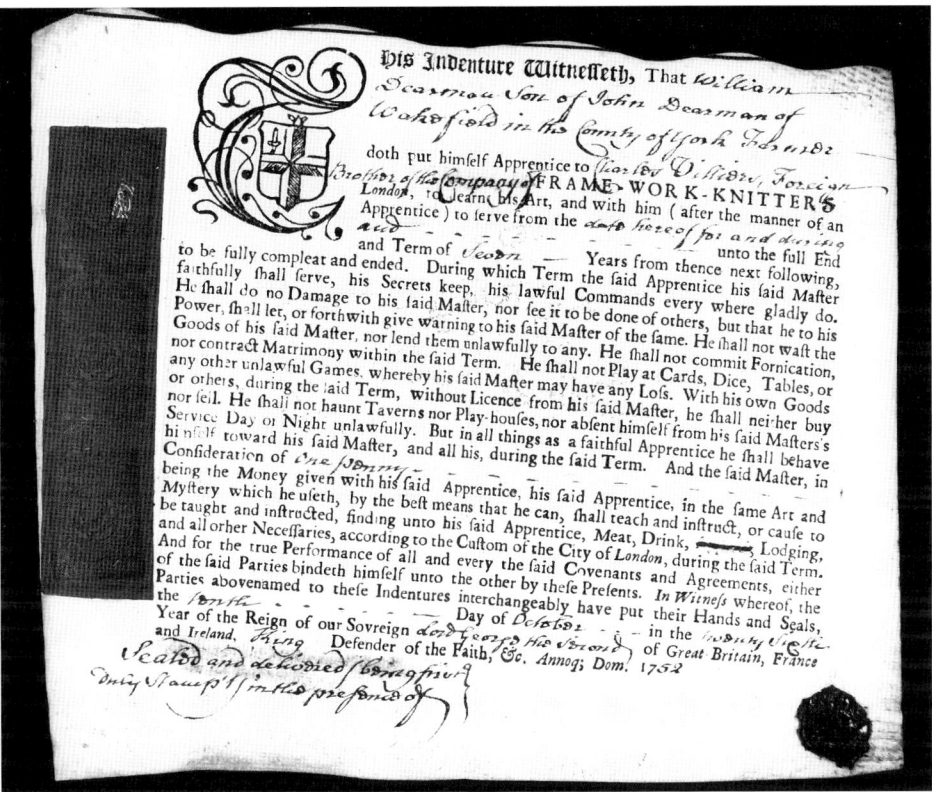

PLATE 19b   *repr. with permission of Nottinghamshire Archives*

Initially, the only way to enter the Company was to transfer from another Company, but after the first few years this changed. Soon admittance required either apprenticeship to a Freeman of the Company for a minimum of seven years, or to be the child of a Freeman, and these two methods – 'by Servitude' and 'by Patrimony' – still exist, although the majority of members have not entered by these ways since the Society's control of the industry was diminished; they were granted without application to the Court, the Clerk being satisfied of the applicants' rights by searches of the Company's books. The third method of gaining admission to the Company is 'by Redemption', in which the Freedom is purchased and for which, unless the Master gave special leave, permission of the Court was necessary.[14] A further alteration was made to the Freedom regulations during the Second World War when, on advice from the City, the Freedom of the Company was restricted to 'Natural Born British Subjects'. This has now been rescinded and the nationality restrictions relaxed.[15]

Females were not barred from being Free of the Society of Framework Knitters. The Bye-laws of 1664 provide 'That Widdowes of any Freeman of the said Company shall during their Widowhood continue in the use of the Art . . . they being lawfully admitted as members of the Company', and the 'daughter born of a Freeman has a right to her Freedom of the Company by patrimony as well as a son'.

Admitted females are called 'Free Sisters'. However, until the twentieth century married women were not allowed to take up the Freedom, and it would appear that the Sisters' Freedom was limited to that of the Company as no record of any female framework knitters also being Free of the City of London has been found for the previous centuries. By 1698 there were at least twenty four female framework knitting masters under the jurisdiction of the Nottingham Court and sixteen in London, all of whom had registered apprentices since 1694. When the Bye-laws were revised in 1745 the admission of women to the Freedom was retained, and in 1748 Mary Stear, widow of Joseph Stear, Almsman, and Ann Walker, daughter of Samuel Walker, Almsman, were admitted. Altogether about 130 spinsters and widows were admitted to the Freedom of the Society between 1675 and 1874.[16]

On 12 January 1875 the rules were amended when it was unanimously resolved 'that no female be admitted to the Freedom of the Company without the special authority of the Court given at one of the Quarterly meetings'. This tightening up regarding female election to the Freedom had been caused by Isabelle Stephenson who, after purchasing her Freedom, almost immediately petitioned for the Almshouse place to which as a Free Sister she was entitled and, although the Court tried to find some way to prevent it, she also had eventually to be awarded a Company pension. The new ruling achieved its aim of preventing further entry into the Almshouses by this method for in October 1875 the petition for the Freedom by purchase of a Miss Burford was turned down. Females were subsequently only admitted to the Company in the nineteenth century to enable residents already in the London Almshouses to receive a Company pension. In the last five years of the 1880s Mary Archer, Mary and Ann Page and Mary Simmons were admitted by Patrimony, a 'stranger', Susannah Dover, was admitted by Redemption, and Elizabeth Smith and Mary Dawes were admitted as the widows of Freemen.[17]

Other than these Almspersons no further females seem to have been admitted to the Company until 1946 when on 31 October Sara Frances and Fiona Rosemary Henderson, daughters of Liveryman Clive Henderson, were enrolled as apprentices to take up their Freedom by Patrimony in 1963 and 1967 respectively; to be joined in the following year by Cynthia Kay, daughter of Under Warden Shirley Ellis, who was enrolled to take up her Freedom by Patrimony in 1955.[18]

Honorary Freedoms of the Company were only started in the second half of the nineteenth century (see page 142). In 1943 the Duke of Portland accepted such an award but then failed to take it up. Then in 1950 W. T. Rowlett accepted an Honorary Freedom awarded in recognition of his two years work for the industry in translating a treatise on the technology of knitting from German, while in 1972 the Beadle John William Barker was presented with an Honorary Freedom in recognition of over twenty-one years service to the Society. Previous to this in 1920, although not strictly honorary, Alderman Jabez Chaplin, Mayor of Leicester and Secretary of the Leicester Amalgamated Hosiery Union, was admitted to the Freedom and to the Livery of the Company without personally paying fines; Past Master Rowley paid both the City of London and Clerk's fees and the stamp duty.[19]

Freedom of the City of London

It was ordered in the Cromwell Charter that No 'person or persons' could be 'admitted to the place of Master Warden or Wardens or Assistant or Assistants or

Deputies . . . unless he or they shall be a freeman or freemen of the said City of London'. However not all who should have taken up the Freedom of London before taking office always did so. Although the earlier Deputies appear to have been Freemen of the City, by the 1750s this stipulation had been forgotten for at least two of the Deputies, Thomas Twells and Humphrey Cox, were recorded as 'foreign brothers'. In addition, it would also seem that the Court of Aldermen were reluctant to admit as Freemen of London framework knitters who were eligible, but were not living in London, for in 1730 the Court of the Framework Knitters' Society had to take up the case of a number of members living in Hampshire who were eligible to take up the Freedom of the City by Servitude.[20]

The Freedom of the City of London is obtained in the same way as that of the Freedom of the Company, by Servitude, by Patrimony, or by Redemption. In addition to allowing a member of the Company to become an Assistant and hold office in the Company, as well as to vote for members to the Court of Aldermen and, at the annual meeting of Common Hall, the right to elect the Sheriffs on Midsummer Day and to designate two Aldermen, who had previously served as Sheriffs, as nominees for the Lord Mayor who was elected on Michaelmas Day, it also initially conferred the right to work and trade in the City, as well as the right to vote for the Members of Parliament for the City. Even though some of the advantages conferred by the Freedom of the City of London have now gone – the economic benefits were whittled away in the 1700s and the political ones went with the abolition of the Liveryman's right to vote for the City's parliamentary candidates in 1918 and with the abolition of the business qualification in 1948 – nevertheless every member of the Company has to take up this Freedom before he can become a Liveryman.

Livery

The Livery had to be elected from those Freemen of the Company who were also Freemen of the City of London by the Court of the Company, and from its ranks the Master, Wardens and Court were chosen. Included in all the City rights conferred by the Freedom this elite also had the right to wear the Livery gown of the Company, in which they paraded at Lord Mayor's processions or other city and state occasions.

In addition to being Freemen of the City of London early Liverymen of the Framework Knitters' also had to be wealthy, for by an Act of the Court of Aldermen of July 1697 no one was 'allowed to take upon himself the clothing of . . . the inferior Companies unless he have an estate of £500'. Later this qualification was reduced to £50, although even this amount was beyond many framework knitters, who, if then elected to the Livery and unable to join, had to swear to the Lord Mayor of London that they were not worth £50, as did John Smithier in 1729.[21]

The Company's right to possess a Livery came from incorporation and from the consent of the Lord Mayor and Aldermen. In 1664 it was ruled that the Livery was to be chosen by the Master, Wardens and Assistants from the qualified Freemen as they thought fit and convenient and found needful, and no limit was put on the number allowed. Only on 9 June 1713 did the City rule that this was not to exceed sixty. This permission to have sixty in the Livery shows that the

Framework Knitters' were regarded as one of the more prominent Companies as the Livery granted to the Needlemakers' the previous year had been restricted to fifty, while other Companies were never granted a Livery.[22]

The permitted maximum for the Framework Knitters' Livery remained at sixty until the end of the nineteenth century and during the middle of the 1800s it had difficulty in reaching even half this number. Only with the revival of the Company in the 1880s did the Livery approach the permitted maximum, and in 1887 the Company was allowed by the Court of Aldermen to increase the number of Liverymen to 100 and six years later this was raised to 125. These extra twenty five vacancies were not filled quickly for in 1903 there were only ninety nine Livery-men on the books of the Company, for eight of whom the Company had no recorded address. By the end of the First World War there were so many vacancies that candidates were enrolled as Freemen of London and Liverymen almost before taking up the Freedom of the Company.[23]

It was not until 1925, when the Livery had reached 122 out of the possible 125, that the Court of Aldermen was petitioned to grant an increase to 175; this was granted in 1926. Numbers in the Livery finally reached 175 in 1933 and a year later the permitted number was raised to the 225 at which it still stands. By end of November 1945 the Livery only numbered 207, but then climbed so rapidly to 221 a year later that the investiture of three candidates already elected as Freemen had to be held over to enable vacancies to be kept 'so that there would always be a vacancy either for a son of a member of the Court or for any candidate who was specially distinguished in the industry'. From the beginning of January 1948 it had been agreed that 'future candidates for the Freedom and Livery of the Company must be proposed and seconded by members of the Court', and the number was allowed to hover between 210 and 220 – in 1952 it numbered 220. One feature of selection to the Livery in the nineteen fifties and sixties was that a number of directors of some of the prominent firms in the hosiery trade, such as Corah or Wolsey, were often elected simultaneously, possibly at a time of change in the Company's hierarchy. Such was the number of applications for admissions in the 1960s and early 1970s that now there was often a considerable gap between admission to the Freedom and admission to the Livery; Willoughby Potter was put on the waiting list in June 1971 but only became a member of the Livery the following June.[24]

However, by the mid-1970s the position had changed again. A number of deaths meant that there were two vacancies on the Livery for which there were no applicants, and on the resolution of Assistant Barrie Byford, seconded by Assistant Howard Russell Ellis, the admission of ladies to the Livery was passed by fifteen votes to eleven in January 1976. In the following year two ladies, Mrs. Jill Morse, daughter of Past Master Gerald Holland, and Mrs Anne White, daughter of Past Master John Foister, were chosen.[25]

In the second half of the twentieth century the Court decided to bring some of the Society's practices up-to-date, and in 1957 the ceremony of admission of Livery-men to the Freedom by Redemption, Patrimony or Servitude, plus binding of apprentices, were modernised. In 1998, after it was felt that the Court and the Livery were too remote from each other, a Liverymen's committee consisting of the Master and Wardens, Liverymen Matthew Ellis and Peter Corah and Assistant Clerk Anne Brown was formed to rectify the problem.[26]

The Court of Assistants

The Court is the governing body of the Company and was already the universal form of administration for Livery Companies by the time of Cromwell. The Assistants were named in both the first and second Charters (Appendix 8).[27] In the case of the Framework Knitters' the Court comprises the Master and two Wardens, elected annually, and Assistants who serve for life, or until resignation. Both the annual elections of officers and the selection of future Assistants is carried out by the Court. The Court, therefore, has complete judicial, administrative and legislative control and ordinary members, including Liverymen, have little input into the affairs of the Company. It is no wonder that under such oligarchal government conflict arose soon after incorporation between ordinary framework knitters, who were compelled to join the Society, and the Court in London and that the whole question of the monopoly of the Company was called increasingly into question during the eighteenth century.

Unlike the Livery the size of the Court of the Society of Framework Knitters was never regulated by the Alderman of the City of London but depended upon the decision of the Court itself. It is therefore difficult to ascertain exactly how many Assistants there were at any one time as the numbers attending Court meetings were by no means the total number of Assistants in the Company; as Court members sat until they either resigned or died many were often too old or too ill to attend meetings for years.[28]

Cromwell's Charter appointed thirteen Assistants, in addition to the Master and Wardens, all of whom were to 'continue in their said offices of Assistants during their natural lives'. In Charles II's Charter the Company was allowed 'fifteen or more' Assistants and twenty were named as the 'first and present Assistants' elected for life in 1663. In 1696 nineteen Assistants signed the Association Oath Rolls for the City of London. Forty seven Assistants were named in the quarterage records of 1722 and in June 1766 there were apparently fifty three – eighteen of whom were Past Masters – although numbers attending Court meetings had fluctuated between twenty one on 24 June 1748 to thirty five on 24 June 1766. On 24 June 1781 it was resolved that no further Assistants were to be elected until the total number had been reduced by natural wastage to thirty five. This number was increased to forty in January 1788, then decreased in June 1801 to thirty one. For the next eighty five years thirty one was the maximum number allowed, although this figure seems to have been wildly over-optimistic, for as the nineteenth century progressed the number of Assistants fell. In 1851 there were twenty four, of whom only Benjamin Ponsonby Tennant, resident in Liverpool, had not been Master, and by 1887/8, there were only eight active Assistants. In January 1899 Court membership was officially set at twenty five, with a temporary increase to thirty while five Past Masters were unable to attend Court Meetings, for reasons ranging from infirmity or residence outside England, and there were several others who were seldom in London. The temporary resolution was changed to a permanent Court of thirty on 20 November 1906. In 1931 the Clerk felt that a Court of thirty was against the Constitution of the Company and tried, unsuccessfully, to reduce the number to twenty, so that the number of Assistants remained at thirty until 1969. In 1969 its composition was again increased to thirty five because some members of the Livery complained that they had waited too long to become Assistants, even though by now it was often difficult to get anyone to serve on the Court. In 1969 the chosen candidates, two each from Nottinghamshire and Leicestershire, declined to serve and in the following year all seven candidates refused. The expense of Mastership being advanced as one reason for these refusals it was agreed in 1970 that the Society should pay for the music at the Livery, Court and Ladies' dinners and also for the Master to have two guests at each of the dinners, which was later altered to a total of twelve.[29]

In October 1964 there was unanimous acceptance of the proposal by Past Master Donald Byford that any Past Master or Assistant who had resigned, or would in future resign, through ill health or advancing years could be elected an Honorary Member of the Court, entitled to attend all Court Dinners or other functions as the guest of the Court and be allowed to invite guests on the same terms as Members of the Court, although they were not be entitled to attend Court meetings or vote on any resolution before the Court. No quarterage was to be paid by these Honorary Assistants. The first to be asked to join under this proposal was Sir John Corah who had given fifty four years service to the Company.[30] The name of this position has now been changed to Past Master Emeritus and in 2000 there are six holders of this title.

All decisions about who should serve on the Court or become Master or Wardens are taken by the Court. Between 1657 and the 1880s the progression from Assistant to Warden to Master was not automatic. The Master would be elected from either the Wardens or Assistants, while the Wardens would be chosen from among the Assistants, and a number of nominations were put forward for each of the three positions on which members of the Court present voted. On 24 June 1728 Michael Mitchell was elected Master from a list of four candidates, although George Grimes had been Senior Warden the previous year; Michael Mitchell had been Warden back in 1724, and had previously been a candidate for the Mastership in 1727. In the same year, 1728, there were also four candidates for the two Wardens' positions – Timothy Smart being elected Upper Warden and Samuel Gourd Under Warden – four candidates for the three positions of Auditors and five nominations for the two Stewards for Michaelmas Day. In 1729 Joseph Rossell, a Quaker, was elected Master, and not Timothy Smart the Senior Warden of 1728. In September 1728, in addition to the nine nominees for six places on the Livery, there were eight nominees for four vacancies among the Assistants of which only one of those elected, Thomas Robinson, was eventually to become Master (see Plate 20).[31]

Since the revival of the Society in the 1880s both admission to the Court and the annual elections for the Master and Wardens have been more of a formality and taken in order of seniority in the Company. If the next most senior Assistant declined to take up the Wardenship it then went to the most senior person after him, as occurred in 1902 when Mr. Makower requested to be passed over and the position of Junior Warden went to F. Dyer, and again in 1903 when Walter Slack and Henry Fletcher requested to be passed over and John Arthur Corah was voted in as Junior Warden.[32]

Only since 1942 has admission to the Court been decided by a Selection Committee and not completely by seniority in the Livery. Liverymen were canvassed as to whether they would be willing to go forward to take up the offices of the Company and vacancies were filled as they occurred from the willing candidates.

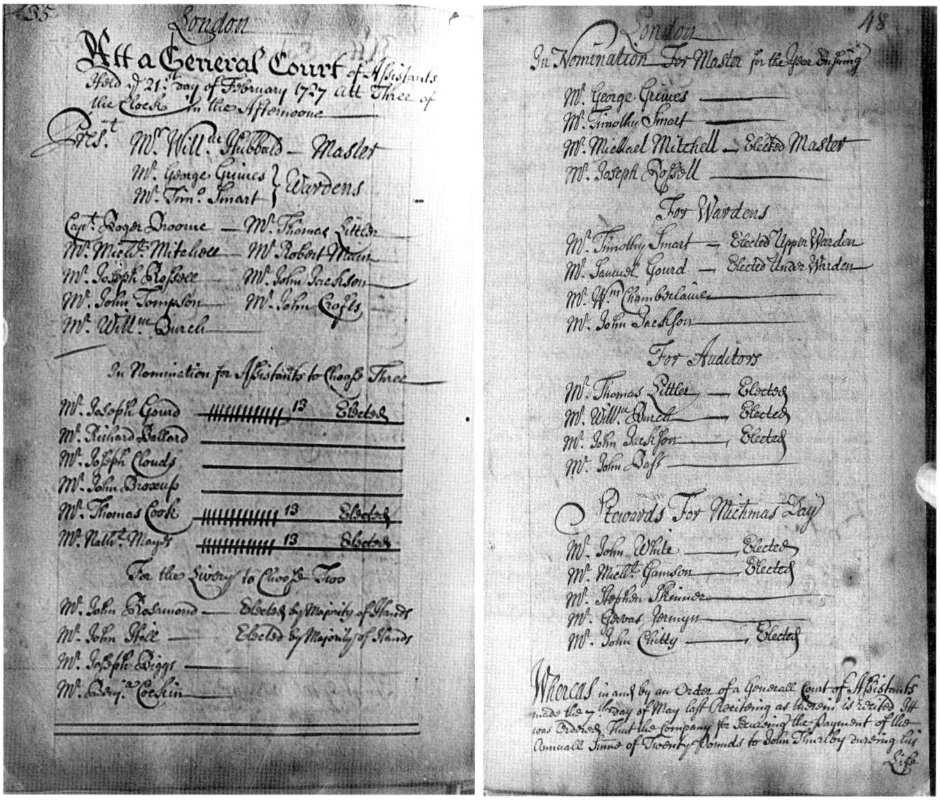
London

Att a Generall Court of Assistants Held ye 21st day of February 1727 att Three of the Clock in the Afternoone

Prest. Mr. Willm. Hubbald – Master

Mr. George Grimes }
Mr. Tim: Smart } Wardens

Capt. Roger Broome – Mr. Thomas Littler
Mr. Michl. Mitchell – Mr. Robert Martin
Mr. Joseph Rossell – Mr. John Jackson
Mr. John Tompson – Mr. John Crofts
Mr. Willm. Burch

In Nomination for Assistants to Choose Three

Mr. Joseph Gourd 13 Elected
Mr. Richard Stafford
Mr. Joseph Cloudy
Mr. John Broxup
Mr. Thomas Cook 13 Elected
Mr. Nathl. Mayes 13 Elected

For the Livery to Choose Two

Mr. John Rosamond — Elected by Majority of Hands
Mr. John Hill — Elected by Majority of Hands
Mr. Joseph Biggs
Mr. Benja. Cockin

London 48

In Nomination For Master for the Year Ensuing

Mr. George Grimes
Mr. Timothy Smart
Mr. Michael Mitchell – Elected Master
Mr. Joseph Rossell

For Wardens

Mr. Timothy Smart – Elected Upper Warden
Mr. Samuel Gourd – Elected Under Warden
Mr. Wm. Chamberlaine
Mr. John Jackson

For Auditors

Mr. Thomas Littler – Elected
Mr. Willm. Burch – Elected
Mr. John Jackson – Elected
Mr. John Dass

Stewards For Michmas Day

Mr. John White – Elected
Mr. Matth. Gamson – Elected
Mr. Stephen Skinner
Mr. Edward Jennings
Mr. John Chitty – Elected

Whereas in and by an Order of a Generall Court of Assistants made the 7th day of May last (Reciting as therein is Recited) It was Ordered That the Company ... for Securing the Payment of the Annuall Summe of Twenty Pounds to John Thurloy during his Life

PLATE 20

1727 AND 1728 FRAMEWORK KNITTERS' COMPANY ELECTIONS *F.W.K. MSS.*

These pages from the Company's earliest known Minute Book show the elections for vacancies among Assistants and in the Livery in 1727 and for the Master, Wardens, Auditors and Stewards in 1728.

At the same time those Assistants who were unable or unwilling to go forward to become Under Warden were asked to resign from the Court.[33]

The duties of the officers of the Company changed considerably over the years. Early duties included the trade searches for bad work and to prevent the export of frames, as well as looking after apprentices' and Almspersons's welfare, and, while this latter duty was to continue into the twentieth century, firms in both the nineteenth and twentieth centuries would have been extremely annoyed if the Company had continued to scrutinise working arrangements or inhibit the export of machinery.

One duty that did not change until the twentieth century and the appointment of a separate Treasurer was the control of the Company's finances by the Renter, or Upper, Warden who produced annual accounts for acceptance by the Court. To prevent fraud, before taking up office each year the Renter Warden was required to produce a bond naming his sponsors and their places of abode so that enquiries could be made about the circumstances and financial probity of all parties. When he became Renter Warden in 1728 a £600 security bond was required from Timothy

Smart, citizen and framework knitter, for which William Al(l)cock, framesmith of Bethnall Green, and Arthur Ginn, victualler of St. Giles-without-Cripplegate, stood surety. The Deputies who acted as Treasurers at Courts outside London were also required to provide the Company with security bonds.[34]

Until well into the twentieth century Assistants were paid for attendance at Court. The amounts varied, although it was originally usually five shillings, and could be totally suspended in times of austerity such as 1727, or partially, as happened a hundred years later when it was agreed that no payment would be made at Special Courts. In 1856 it was resolved that unless an Assistant was present before the Master took the chair he would not be paid and that the number of those entitled to the fee of five shillings should be limited to the first sixteen attending. An order of 1878 directed that the amount to be paid to these first sixteen should be increased to ten shillings, but this was altered again in January 1912 so that the ten shillings was only paid to members attending the Quarterly Courts but not to those attending Special Courts, and it would seem that this system lasted until sometime between the two World Wars.[35]

The Society of Framework Knitters of England and Wales was one of very few Companies possessing the right to hold Courts anywhere outside London. From 1657 until the mid-eighteenth century synchronised Courts were regularly held in both London, at the Company's Hall, and Nottingham, originally at Mrs. Theobald's or The Feathers in Wheelergate, and usually on the first Tuesday in each month. Also, when ordered by London, Courts could be called at any other location; Leicester and Hinckley were regular venues in the first half of the eighteenth century, while Derby, Northampton, Godalming and Odiham are among a number of other places recorded as having Courts, albeit often short-lived ones and often for a single agenda. The complaints of framework knitters during the eighteenth century that a former apprentice had to take up his Freedom in London is not born out by the existing books of the Company, as only apprentices of Citizens of London had to do this, while former apprentices of foreign brothers could take up their Freedom in their local Court. There was a gap of eighty years from 1814 when no Courts were held outside London and then, in 1894, these were resumed, although no longer in Nottingham, but in Leicester. All Courts outside London were properly constituted with either Court members or Deputies, as well as Clerks and Beadles, in attendance.[36]

Deputies

The Deputies were the Company's representative outside London where they ran the Company's business, including the Courts. Cromwell's Charter had decreed that two or more of the Society 'shall have power and authority by writing under the Common Seal . . . as Deputies of the said Master Wardens and Assistants to make search in the presence of a constable or other lawful officer in all or any place or places within this Commonwealth', and these powers were extended by the Charter and Ordinances of Charles II. While the Society of Framework Knitters controlled framework knitting the Deputies enjoyed a high degree of operational autonomy acting as, and often being called, 'Deputy Masters'.[37]

Although in theory the Deputies could be sworn in or dismissed whenever the London Court wished, in practice they were re-elected annually at the same time as the Master and Wardens. Differing numbers of Deputies in various locations were chosen at any one time, although Nottingham remained the most regular Court venue outside London into the nineteenth century. During the seventeenth and early eighteenth centuries there were a number of different Deputies for the Nottingham Court, including Jonathan Labray, George Eaton, Lionel Lamb, William Rawson, Francis Godfrey, Charles Villiers and Thomas Bower, although the number appointed to serve at any one time is unknown. In 1718 the number of Deputies sitting in Nottingham for the East Midland counties of Nottinghamshire, Derby-shire and Leicestershire was seven – William Wilson, John Wright, John Gil(l)man, William Robinson, John Stephenson acting in the first two counties named and William Hurst and William Paget(t) in Leicestershire; these gentlemen continued sitting during the 1720's. In 1727 six Deputies were elected to the Nottingham Court which by now only covered Nottinghamshire and Derbyshire – Samuel Spray, who was then elected Treasurer, George Eaton, John Wright, who later became Treasurer, and John Gilman, all of whom lived in Nottingham, were prin-cipally responsible for that town, while William Wilson covered Mansfield and John Bloodworth Derby; Francis Godfrey, an attorney, was the Deputy Clerk and Nathaniel Birkhead the Deputy Beadle. The four Leicestershire Deputies were Samuel Spray and George Eaton of the Nottingham Court, together with John Wood, who was also Treasurer and lived in Hinckley, and Michael Wire of Mountsorrel; John Foster, an attorney at Hinckley, was the Deputy Clerk and Conyers White of Leicester the Deputy Beadle. In 1751 at least six East Midland Deputies were officially appointed, for working in Nottingham were John Killingley, John Wright, Thomas Twells, Humphrey Cox, Thomas Haywood, and in Leicester George Iliffe.[38]

The Courts outside London were expected to be financially independent. The Deputies' salaries of £3, plus those of the Clerks and Beadles, and the expenses, were deducted from the fines collected locally before the remainder of the money was despatched to the London Court. Auditing was carried out in London and was often a source of conflict, for in September 1725 London complained that Francis Godfrey, the Clerk at Nottingham, had not sent in his accounts. By the late 1720s the Courts outside London often did not pay their way so that little or no money was despatched to London, as in 1727 when the expenses of the Nottingham Court amounted to £13 12s. 10d., leaving only £5 12s. 8d. for London. Sometimes the local officials even went unpaid for in October 1726 John Wood, the Leicester and Hinckley Deputy and Treasurer, wrote that he was 'some pounds out of pocket' and other Leicestershire Deputies were complaining that their last year's salaries had not been paid.[39]

Between 1730 and 1751 the position of the Deputies was precarious for Courts outside London were held only intermittently. After 1751, although it would seem that a number of the former Deputies continued for a time to be consulted spas-modically by the Court in London and the provincial positions were resurrected at the very beginning of the 1800s during the Court case against Payne, for the most part the official position of Deputy was suspended and after 1809 fell into disuse.[40]

Clerks and Beadles

Both are salaried officials of the Company whose appointment was provided for in the Charters. Since its incorporation the Company has only had twenty-four Clerks in London.

The Clerk is the chief administrative officer answerable to the Court and traditionally, although not always, the position has been occupied by a lawyer. While the Society of Framework Knitters controlled an industry the Clerk would seem to have worked only for the Company but since the mid-nineteenth century they engaged in additional work, including acting as Clerk to other Livery Companies; Dr. Ernest Ebblewhite, the Clerk between 1931 and 1937, was also in the service of the Gardeners' Company, while the Company's present Clerk was previously also Clerk to the Farriers' Company.[41]

The name of the first appointee to the post is not recorded but was probably John Hannis, the Clerk appointed for life in the 1663 Charter. Subsequently the position was a Court appointment and, being a prestigious one, there was usually no shortage of applicants. In 1787 Charles Bicknell of Lamb's Conduit Street and Mr. Foskett of Red Cross Street lost the election to Thomas Lodington, also of Lamb's Conduit Street. The Clerk was often appointed from within the Society. Lodington's successor, former Assistant Thomas Wood, held the Clerkship for almost ten years, only resigning to become first an Alderman, and in 1838 Sheriff; on resigning the Clerkship he was also reappointed an Assistant and was Master of the Company in 1837. Thomas Bless Pugh, Clerk between 1834 and 1846, was the son of John Pugh, Master in 1799, and brother of Robert, Master in 1830. In October 1854 James Funston was admitted to the Freedom of the Company and elected Beadle, the position he held until he became Clerk in 1874. On James Funston's death at the end of 1902 two Liverymen, Edward Lyon Shelton and John Woodhouse, vied for the Clerkship, which was won by the latter.[42]

Until the first decade of the nineteenth century Deputy Clerks, and Deputy Beadles, administered the Company's affairs in the Courts outside London. They were answerable to the Deputies, in particular the local Treasurer, and in practice their positions were usually confirmed annually at the same time as those of the Deputies, although in theory they could be removed at any time. From at least 1725 until 1728 Francis Godfrey held the Deputy Clerkship for Nottingham and Derby. He was removed from the position in the October and followed by Richard Smith, while John Foster continued to cover Leicestershire, Hinckley and Warwickshire until 1729 when the Courts at Leicester were discontinued. The position fell into abeyance in the early nineteenth century but was revived in 1979 after the Company had experienced difficulty in finding a Clerk to replace Mr. Weale. It had been suggested a year earlier that Harry Weale continue as Clerk and an Assistant Clerk be appointed in Leicester to do most of the administrative work but the idea was abandoned in favour of appointing a single Clerk, Ian Williamson, who was also Clerk to the Poulters'. The original idea was only followed when Williamson relinquished the Clerkship after a year; Harry Weale was reappointed Clerk and Arthur Scrimshaw was appointed Assistant Clerk in Leicester. The present Assistant Clerk, Mrs. Anne Brown, was appointed in October 1994.[43]

Although the first Clerk was appointed for life the first known Beadle, William Patrick, was appointed subject to the Court's 'pleasure'; and subsequently few records have been kept naming those who held this office either in or outside London. During at least part of the early 1700s William Paine was the Beadle in London, while Nathaniel Birkhead was the Deputy Beadle in Nottingham and Conyers White that in Leicester. From 1754 until well into the 1800s the Simmons, George and his son Edward, were the Beadles in London. Prior to its sale, a furnished house, valued at £6 6s. yearly and attached to the Company's Hall in Red Cross Street, was provided for the Beadle and his family, and he attended the Master at official functions such as Common Hall, City processions or to the Courts outside London, dressed in Company robes and carrying the Company mace. The Beadle was, after the Company lost its Hall, also required to move the Master's Chair and Company plate from the Clerk's office to wherever Court meetings were being held.[44]

The position has continued to the present day. John Barker was the Beadle between 1952 and 1979 and in 1972 was granted the Honorary Freedom of the Company in recognition of over twenty-one years service, as well as being given a cheque for £150. He was succeeded by Arthur Seaman. The present Beadle is James Wallis.[45]

From incorporation the Clerks' and Beadles' remuneration was a small salary and a percentage of each fee collected. In 1727 in London these were respectively £20 and £10, paid quarterly, plus the allocated percentage of the fees, which for an apprentice turned over was one shilling to the Clerk and sixpence to the Beadle. This arrangement continued into the twentieth century for from October 1912 the Clerk was to be paid eighty guineas per annum plus the appropriate fees, and only sometime in the twenties or thirties was this changed to an inclusive rate. In 1964 the Clerk's annual salary was advertised at £700, and by 1978 it was £2,500. By 1974 the Beadle was paid £63. Outside London the arrangement was different, for prior to 1745 the remuneration of the Deputy Clerks and Beadles would seem to have been one third of the appropriate fees collected in the Courts under their control, which was raised in 1745 to three quarters of the fees.[46]

Apprentices and Masters

In the sixteenth and seventeenth centuries apprenticeship was the normal method of training young persons in craftsmanship before the days of universal schooling, and the rules governing apprenticeship within a Company controlled the number of persons entering a trade. It provided the most usual entry into commerce and industry and the Livery Companies. The Framework Knitters' Society was no exception to these conventions and detailed regulations for apprenticeship were laid down in the Charters and Ordinances.

The Cromwell Charter ruled that 'no person . . . shall exercise the said Art Trade or Mystery of a Framework Knitter unless he or they shall have served as apprentice or apprentices for the term . . . of seven years at least by covenant of indenture unto some person lawfully using and exercising the same trade', and even apprentices working in the frame for members of another society or guild were to be bound a member and, at the end of their apprenticeship, be enrolled in the Framework Knitters' Society. These rules were ratified by the City of London by an Act of Common Council passed on 1 July 1658 which decreed that the apprentices of all persons practising framework knitting, even if they themselves were free of other companies, were to be bound to the Company.[47]

This strict regulation of apprentices entering framework knitting continued in the restoration Charter. In the 1664 Ordnances only a person Free of the Company was permitted to become a framework knitter and he was not allowed to bind an apprentice until his masterpiece was approved; this masterpiece was to be made in the presence of the Master and Wardens, or a person appointed by them, and was originally a pair of silk stockings or other item wrought in the frame, although this was, very soon, commuted to a fine of ten shilling to the Company, two shillings to the Clerk and one shilling to the Beadle; the fine for not following this rule was £5. However, after this initial regulation about the masterpiece, there were different versions of the Bye-laws for London and outside London. The Ordinances written on parchment and in the book presented by Clerk Hannis to the London Court, and presumably following the custom of London, differed considerably from the book Hannis presented to the Nottingham Court and, although not mentioned among the grievances later cited to Parliament, must have created much animosity between London and those members outside London who were aware of the different inter-pretations of the Bye-laws. In London a master only had to be Free of the Company for one year and a workhouse keeper before taking an apprentice, outside London the master had to be an accepted workhouse keeper for two years before the first apprentice could be bound. A second apprentice could be taken in London after four years while outside London it was after seven years. Only members of the Court or Livery could bind a third apprentice. A new apprentice could, however, be bound in all cases in the last six months of service of the previous indentured apprentice. The fine for teaching anyone other than bound apprentices was an astronomical £50. Sons of framework knitters, who did not have to be bound, were the only exception to these regulations. In addition, only the widows of framework knitters who had not remarried could become female master framework knitters and bind apprentices.[48]

Further, the legislation laid down that apprentices were not to be bound under the age of fourteen and for a period of usually seven years, although in a few cases this was up to nine years. In addition, before binding an apprentice a master was required to be up-to-date with his membership dues, so that in the recording of a binding in the Society's books back-dated quarterage, as well as the admission charge, Orphan's Tax and fees to the Clerk and Beadle, are included. Binding an apprentice under Company regulations was an expensive business.

Indentures were drawn up according to the practices established in the City of London and, though at first glance, these seem especially hard on the apprentice – among other things he was not allowed to get married or drunk during his service – they also bound masters to an agreed and acceptable code of behaviour monitored by the Company. In 1710 the Nottingham Court refused to allow Richard Gibson to bind an apprentice because he was so poor he was 'no housekeeper' and had no permanent address. The Company also controlled, and charged a fee, for the turnover of an apprentice, which was usually caused by the illness or death of the first master although, again, if a master renaged on his side of the contract he was investigated by the Society and his appentice could be taken away. In 1725, when the father of an apprentice in Godalming asked permission to turn his son over to a second master as the first had allegedly beaten the boy and kicked him down the stairs, the master in question, James Toft, was summoned to London to interviewed by the Company's lawyer.[49]

Between 1694 and 1861 an Orphans' Tax was imposed by the City of London on apprentice bindings drawn up according to the custom of London, with exceptions made only in the case of pauper apprentices bound by a parish and where no payment was made, as was often the case with family members. The Framework

Knitters' documents recording these transactions are, however, essentially fiscal records and note only the apprentice's name, the date of binding, the 2s. 6d. paid to the Chamberlain of London and, for the years until the end of the seventeenth century, in which of the Society's Courts the binding took place. From the eighteenth century the books are divided into 'L'(ondon) and 'C'(ountry) bindings, and as by now a number of places in addition to Nottingham held Courts from time to time it is unknown where these took place. In addition, although the Orphan's tax was originally paid by all framework knitters, by 1745 only masters who were also Free of the City of London paid this tax.[50]

A pair of apprenticeship indentures, recording the contract between the master and the parent or guardian of the apprentice, were drawn up, and one section was retained by each party to the agreement. Under the Society's apprenticeship system pairs of these printed indentures, made out for either 'Citizens' or 'foreign brothers', had the tax printed on them by the Company in London and were sent to the outside Courts as required. On 28 February 1727–8 Warden Grimes stamped seven pairs of indentures for 'foreign brothers' and on 2 March six pairs were despatched to Samuel Spray, the Treasurer at Nottingham, and in July a further thirty, out of the sixty seven stamped, were sent to the same town (see Plates 18 and 19).[51]

A comparison of the names of the apprentices in the Orphan's Tax records and those known to be Free of the Company suggest that there was either a large and early drop out of apprentices or, as the Tables show that there was a continual increase in the number of framework knitters and, as the Company rules covered all of England and Wales, then many of even the earliest apprentices did not take up the Freedom of the Society and few took up the Freedom of the City of London. This situation continued, and grew worse, for the Company was physically unable to enforce its Ordinances and hundreds became framework knitters without ever having served an indentured apprenticeship, so that by 1809 the binding of apprentices by the Company was largely discontinued. In spite of the regulations, it was often considered that the taking of a trade apprentice 'would be taking a dead-weight' and that 'regular apprenticeship (was) a thing of the past'. From the middle of the eighteenth century it would seem that most of those who were apprenticed to the Company usually had connections with members of the Court and/or London and wanted the advantages membership of a City Livery Company could bring.[52]

Although from the 1800s an increasing number took up the Freedom of the Company by Patrimony or Redemption, nevertheless indentured apprenticeship continued as an option for entry to the Company, and since the 1930s at least thirteen apprentices have been bound to the Company. Olga Lindsay Rouse completed her apprenticeship in 1937, while in 1945 David Percy Bussens took up his Freedom by Servitude during the year his father was Master.[53] At the beginning of 2000 the Company has four indentured apprentices. In 1958 the format for binding of apprentices was updated and a bible embossed with the Arms of the Company was presented to an applicant at this time. Then from 1999, providing that the Worshipful Company of Framework Knitters is a Liveryman's Mother Company, restrictions were removed on the number of apprentices which can be bound to a relative for a period of between four and eight years providing that the young person is above the age of fourteen and below the age of twenty one when bound. The fine for each binding is £15, and it enables the apprentice to be admitted to the Freedom of the Company and Livery by Servitude for a reduced fee.[54]

Framework Knitters' Arms/Colours

The Coat of Arms of the Society of Framework Knitters and its motto, 'Speed Strength and Truth United', were adopted at their first incorporation in 1657. The colours of the Company are red and white.[55]

One original armorial bearing showed the working parts of the first machines and directly represented the activities of the Company (see back cover and Plate 12). They are described as 'On a chevron between two combs, and as many leads of needles in chief, and an iron Jack; lead sinker in Base; a main spring between two small springs'. The shield was surmounted by a lamb. These arms are on the head of the Beadle's mace and were used on Company documents into the 1920s. Both the ceremonial shields and banners of the Company showed these arms and colours and, originally housed in the Society's Hall, they were taken down to be used in London processions that the Company joined. When the Society hired barges the shields were hung along the sides of the barges while the banners flew from the mast heads.

In addition to using arms depicting the working tools of framework knitting the Company also used a reproduction of the painting by Balderton. In the middle of this picture are the working parts of the frame without the woodwork, with the knitting hanging from it divided at the heel, and this is depicted on the Company's 1656 silver goblet (see Plate C2a). In all Company depictions the frame has never changed and it is, therefore, the oldest existing representation of a knitting frame, as it predated Hindret's drawings by at least ten years.[56]

However, the supporters of both the frame and shield have differed considerably in build, age and dress over the centuries. The stout male in academic dress on the left hand side and the woman in a long flowing gown with uncovered hair, who was holding a piece of knitting and two needles in one hand and had her other hand resting on the frame on her right hand side, in the Balderton picture are replaced by very different figures in the engraving above the abstract of the 1745 Bye-laws; William Lee is now much slimmer and more handsome while the female, now wearing a plainly styled, although ornamented, gown with her hair concealed under a cap, holds three knitting needles. Another couple appears in Felkin's *History* while on a printed sheet of paper stuck in the front of one of the Society's books there is a subtle elaboration of the costumes of the two supporters, who again differ from either of the previous couples, although in both cases the female is holding three needles (see Plates 1, 15, 21). In 1881 the Clerk altered the costume of the male supporter from the period of Charles II to that of Elizabeth I and the Coat of Arms granted to the Company in 1933 was copied from this (see front cover).[57]

Even though apparently lacking the necessary authority to bear arms until 1933, the Company paid one guinea fee annually for its armorial bearings during the eighteenth and nineteenth centuries. In addition an annual rent of four nobles, (£1 6s. 8d. in 1859), was paid to the Crown for the Charles II Charter, until in 1858 the Society was notified that if the 'Rent is not purchased . . . before 31 March 1859' the Charter would be sold at public auction. The Company was forced to sell some annuities to pay this charge of £41 6s. 8d. to keep its own Charter.[58]

Surprisingly the Company received its first patent for a Coat of Arms only in 1933. Since 1910 it had gradually become apparent that neither of the Company's distinctive logos, both of which had been used since the founding of the Company,

a   *F.W.K. MSS.*

b   William Felkin: *History of the Machine-Wrought Hosiery and Lace Manufactures*

PLATE 21

SUPPORTERS AND VARIATIONS ON THE FRAMEWORK KNITTERS' ARMS

had been registered with the College of Arms, in spite of being required to pay the armorial bearings tax. In 1932 Thomas Rowley proposed that Letters Patent should be obtained and twenty six members of the Court each subscribed five guineas towards the cost of applying for this. The Patent was granted to the then Master, William Moore, in 1933 and the original, showing the frame and supporters, was hung in the Corah Hall.[59]

Corporate property and accounts – fees, fines, feasts and religion

As the Society's corporate property was limited by both the Cromwell and Charles II Charters to a 'yearly value of one hundred pounds', the Company came first to rely on the 'fines' established by the Bye-laws and then a combination of the invested monies raised by the sale of the Hall plus the 'fines' to keep itself functioning.[60] As many of these fines, or fees, were only paid once by any particular member the income of the corporate account fluctuated annually. No figures exist for the early years when membership was compulsory although, if collected efficiently, the income must have been considerable and was estimated by one hostile section of the trade at the end of the seventeenth century to be about £200 per annum, while Gravenor Henson, in 1831, reported a surplus of £10,000 by 1720. But, by the time figures area available, between 1839 and 1846 total fees received for admissions were only £130 18s. 6d., from 1848 to 1874, £460 13s., and between 1874 and 1879, £627 19s. 6d. The corporate accounts were produced annually and those kept throughout much of the Company's history still exist. However, when looking at these accounts it should be borne in mind that they are not strictly profit-and-loss accounts, nor balance sheets, nor even a day-to-day financial records as their aim was to show and justify the Wardens' handling of monies entrusted to them so that they could obtain a discharge at the annual audit meetings of the Court.[61]

The two fines paid by all members were for admission and annual membership. In 1664 the admission fee was collected in the form of a silver spoon, although this would appear to have been replaced before the end of the seventeenth century by a monetary one, which in 1727 was twelve shillings and by 1745 fifteen shillings. The membership fee due from all members, whether Freemen of the City of London or just foreign brothers, was originally paid four times a year on the Quarter Days – hence the name quarterage. It was set at twelvepence a quarter in the Charter of 1657 and reduced by the 1745 Bye-laws to sixpence a quarter for masters and threepence a quarter for journeymen, with a fine of 6s. 8d. for those who refused to pay. However, the organisation required to collect this annual subscription from a large and scattered membership was enormous and its levy continued to be spasmodic into the twentieth century. In spite of the attempt from 1722 to trace and collect quarterage from every member of the Company, for most of the eighteenth century it was only levied when members came to the attention of the Court, usually when a new apprentice was bound or a Freeman joined the Livery or became an officer. Another attempt was made to bring quarterage up-to-date in 1826 when it was decided that a Liveryman could not partake of the Lord Mayor's Day dinner until he had paid; the Beadle was instructed to collect the fine for the five preceding years, and, as an inducement, was allowed to keep fourpence in the pound instead of the twopence previously permitted. However, even this effort soon faded away. In 1909 quarterage was still only four shillings a year and was collected only from members of the Court because of concern as to its legality, with the result that in 1910/11 only £4 12s. was collected. In 1942 the quarterage formerly paid by Court members was merged into an annual subscription of two guineas, except for those admitted prior to 1932. Quarterage was not made universally compulsory again until 1981, and then only for Liverymen joining after 1 January that year, while for those admitted prior to 31 December 1980 the fee was voluntary. In 1999 the quarterage fee was £12.[62]

In addition to the fees for admission and quarterage there were a large number of other fines which were levied at certain periods of a member's career within the Company or for infringements of the Company's Bye-laws. Until the 1809 ruling that the Bye-laws only applied to its members these were so complicated and numerous that it would have been difficult for a framework knitter not to have transgressed sometime during his working life. First set out in the Ordinances of 4 July 1664, they were periodically altered, especially when the Bye-laws were rewritten in 1745.

Table 3.1 **Some rules and fines – 1664 and 1745 compared where possible**

Rules	Fines	
	1664	*1745*
Master and Wardens – refusal to serve	£5	
Chosen in the place of officers dead or removed – refusal	£2	
For swearing of the Master and Wardens	5s.	
Assistants	£2	£10
1745 Refusing to or not attending meetings –	1st(time) 1s.; 2nd 2s.; 3+ 5s.	
Election to the Livery	£20	
1745 – refusal		£20
Hindering the Deputies	£5	
Steward		
1664	cost of dinner	
1745 – refusing to provide £12 dinner at midsummer		£6
1745 – refusing to provide £21 dinner on Lord Mayor's Day		£7
Omitting to Keep Quarter Days and pay Quarterage	6s. 8d.	6s. 8d.
Bad Work	£1	>10s.
1745 – obstructing searchers		£5
1745 – for search		4d.
1745 – for refusing to pay for search		3s. 4d.
For hiring Frames to non-members	1s. per week	1s. per week
For teaching non-indentured apprentices	£50.00.00	£50.00.00
Person taking Apprentice before Masterpiece approved and		
permitted to be a Workhouse Keeper	£5.00.00	£5.00.00
For refusing to become a member	£1 10. 00	£1 10. 00
For keeping incorrect number of apprentices	£5 per month	£5 per month
Employment of foreigners	£40	£10
Incorrect presentation of apprentices	£2.00.00	£2.00.00
1745 – Freeman of London binding app. to another Company		£5
Incorrect binding of apprentice	£2	
Failure to enrol apprentice within one year	£1	£2
Incorrect turnover or buying or selling of apprentices	£3	£2
Frequent abuse in turning over apprentices	£50	
Incorrect indentures	£1	
Departure of journeyman without month's warning	£5.00.00	£5.00.00
Master not giving month's notice to journeyman		£5
Enticement of apprentice out of service	£3	
Working with non-members	£3	£1
Setting to work non-members	£5.00.00	£5.00.00
Daily penalty for officers not bringing in accounts	£1	
Despising the Master, Wardens, Assistants or Deputies	6s. 8d.	6s. 8d.
Rebuking another before the Master and Wardens	1s.	
Proportional contributions towards the defraying of necessary		
charges fixed by Court	Double the sum	Double the sum

Comparison of the fines detailed for 1664 and 1745 in Table 3.1 show clearly that, during the time the Company was still all powerful in the industry, it was prepared to make few concession to the rank and file of framework knitters, even though the tide of opinion was turning against monopolistic Companies by the mid-eighteenth century. In 1745 apprenticeship was still regarded as important as a century earlier, although the laws concerning journeymen were no longer as biased on the side of the master, as one month's notice had to be given by both sides, and not just by the journeyman. In addition, the increase in the number of knitters not taking up the Freedom of the Company in 1745 is recognised by a reduction in the fine for working alongside unregistered labour from £3 to £1, and for employing foreigners from £40 to £10, although the employment of non-members in a Society workshop was still punishable by a £5 fine. Between 1664 and 1745, however, these fees and fines of the Society were the cause of continual ill feeling between the Court and the ordinary member, although in the petitions to Parliament the permission for the Court to pick whom they wanted as Stewards to provide feasts for the Court and Livery, and the provision of Court dinners at the Livery's and ordinary members' expense were especially singled out.

After the 1809 ruling that only members were bound by its rules the Society no longer embraced all sections of the trade and the type, number and amount of the fines changed considerably, and were altered piecemeal; fines applicable when the Company controlled an industry were abandoned and, as can be seen in Table 3.2, a much shorter list of fees applicable to the modernised Livery Company came to be applied. Some fines were still, however, imposed on the instruction of the City of London for the Company was only permitted an increase in the number of Livery-men to 100 in 1888 on the condition that the Livery fine was not less than £27. Fines, or fees of honour, to be paid by the Master and Wardens during their years in office were adopted in 1921, being set initially at £21 for each Warden and £42 for the Master.[63]

By 2000 the nature of the fees and fines had altered almost completely from those of 1664, as a comparison of Tables 3.1 and 3.3 illustrate.

The largest expense on the corporate account were Court meetings and dinners. Feasting is a fraternal tradition Livery Companies inherited from the medieval guilds, but it raised the ire of the ordinary members as the, often considerable, cost

Table 3.2 **Fees imposed between 1870 and 1999** (individual years in brackets)

	Period		
Description of Fees	*1870–1900*	*1900–50*	*1951–2000*
Freedom by Patrimony & Servitude	£4.16s.(70)		£15 (75)
Freedom by Purchase	£6.16s.(70)		£30 (83)
Freedom			£25 (99)
Livery	£20 (79)	£31.6.6 (26)	£150 (75)
Freedom & Livery (taken same day)	£25 (79)		
Assistant £21 10s.(70)	£52 10s.(79)	£105(23)	£125 (56)
Court annual subscription		£5 5s. (23)	£21 (56)
Warden annual subscription		£21 (21)	£50 (56)
Master annual subscription		£42 (21)	£50 (56)
Turnover of apprentice			£10 (83)

Table 3.3 **Fees, Fines and Quarterage – April 2000**

Fees

Admission to the Freedom and Livery by Redemption	£575
Admission to the Freedom and Livery for the Son or Daughter of a Liveryman	
by Redemption	£450
Admission to the Freedom and Livery by Patrimony or Servitude	£275
Admission to Membership of the Company limited to the Freedom	£25

Fines

On Election to the Court as an Assistant	£250
On Election as Under Warden, Upper Warden and Master	£125
On Registration of a Minor for Admission by Patrimony	£25
On Binding an Apprentice	£15

Quarterage – (payable on 6 April)

Mandatory Quarterage for a Liveryman admitted after 1 January 1981	£70.50
Voluntary Quarterage for a Liveryman admitted prior to 31 December 1980	£60
Mandatory Quarterage for Membership limited to the Freedom	£12

Deeds of Covenant

In addition, each Liveryman must make a Deed of Covenant for either or both of	
the Company's Almshouse or Education Charities	£50

was met from their fines, and yet they received no benefit. When the custom of charging annually elected Stewards for the Court feasts at midsummer and on Lord Mayor's days ceased, all dinners were charged to the corporate account which led to a shortfall in the accounts by the twentieth century. By 1947 ordinary expenditure exceeded income by £609, largely due to the increase in the cost of the dinners. By 1967 the annual Livery subscription of £21 did not cover the £23 1s. 2d. cost of the year's dinners, nor did the guest's charges of £4 14s. 6d. cover the costs of their dinners either. From June 1968 guest and Livery dining fees for functions had to be periodically increased so that costs were more fully covered, although into the 1980s the corporate account continued to pay for Court events. It was not until the late 1980s that events attended were paid for in full, for in both 1977 and 1983 amendments that the subscriptions should cover expenses were defeated.[64]

Another, and recent, call on the corporate fund has been some of the Masters' expenses for it was only in 1981 that, realising that the cost of office was inhibiting many Liverymen from joining the Court, the system was changed. From henceforth the cost of entertaining the Masters of other Livery Companies and their wives up to a total of six persons, as well as the Lord Mayor, Sheriffs, Household Officer and visiting speakers and their wives at Company dinners was borne by the corporate fund while the cost of the lunch and half the cost of the presents given to the residents in the Cottage Homes at Christmas were to be borne by the charitable account.[65]

Along with feasting, religion too was a reminder of Livery Companies' medieval origins. The Court of the Framework Knitters' Society, joined by those Liverymen who were able, were expected to attend a special Church of England service annually. Between the founding of the Company and 1925 the annual service was

PLATE 22

ST. GILES'S CHURCH, CRIPPLEGATE, IN 1830   *lent by S. A. Mason*

St. Giles's was the Church of the Framework Knitters' Company until the twentieth century. It is now within the Barbican Centre, having been gutted by fire in the Second World War.

held at St. Giles, Cripplegate, the Chaplain to the Company being the Vicar of that parish (see Plate 22). Then from 1925 the service has been held in May each year in the Parish Church of Oadby, Leicestershire, when members of the Court and their wives form the procession into the Church; the Honorary Chaplain being for the most part the Vicar of the parish (see Plate 23).[66]

Summary

The Charters and Bye-laws are the framework within which the Worshipful Company of Framework Knitters operated from its incorporation to the present day, as will be shown in the following, chronologically arranged, chapters.

References

1 MSS, 16868; 18116; NAO, MSS, CA 4039; C. R. H. Cooper, 'The Archives of the City of London Livery Companies and related organisations', *Archives*, 16, no. 72, October 1984, pp. 323–53.
2 MSS, 3451/2, 11 October 1898; 3451/4, 27 June 1916; 3452/9 – letter from Frank Hyde Esq., 26 April 1916; *Report of the Framework Knitters*, 1844, p. 4.

PLATE 23   *repr. with permission of Mr. Martin Sharp*

OADBY CHURCH, LEICESTERSHIRE

The Vicar of Oadby is the Honorary Chaplin of the Worshipful Company of Framework Knitters, and the Company holds an annual service in this Church which commences with a procession of the Master and Wardens.

3 Anna Pavord, *The Tulip* (London: Bloomsbury Publishing plc., 1999), pp. 75, 103, 110, 112, 117, 121–2, 153; Martin Skinner, *The Proper Care of Parrots* (Neptune City, NJ: T.F.H. Publications, Inc., 1992), pp. 11–12.

4 Cromwell Charter; B(ritish)M(useum), MSS, SPR. 357.d.41; *C(ity) P(ress)*, 25 November 1949; Cooper, *Archives*, pp. 323–53, p. 349; Mark Knight, 'A City Revolution: The Remodelling of the London Livery Companies in the 1680s', *English Historical Review*, 112, November 1997, pp. 1141–78, p. 1143; Felkin, p. 71.

5 MSS, 16868; 18116;

6 MSS, 16865–8; NAO, MSS, CA 4039.

7 NAO, MSS, 4039.

8 NAO, MSS, 4041/21 &/22.

9 MSS, 16,840; 3444; 3445; NAO, MSS, 4041/37.

10 James Funston, 1901, p. 7; *City of London Livery Companies' Commission, Report and Appendix*, III, 1884, p. 423.

11 MSS, WCFK, *Newsletter*, 6, April 1999.

12 BM, MSS, 816.m.12.(105).

13 MSS, 3452.

14 MSS, 3451/1, p. 385.

15 MSS, 3451/5, 11 May 1944.

16 MSS, 3446/1; 3451/1, p. 384; 3452/3, p. 55; NAO, MSS, CA 4040.

17 MSS, 3451/1, pp. 379, 391; 3452/3, p. 55; Funston, 'Report on the Distribution of the Charitable Fund', 1886, pp. 4–7.

18 MSS, 3451/5, 31 October 1946, 13 February 1947.
19 MSS, 3451/4, 27 January 1920; 3451/5, 15 October 1943, 25 January 1944, 5 May, 27 June 1950; *Minutes*, 27 June 1972. (Rowlett's freedom grant now hangs in the Corah Hall, Oadby).
20 MSS, 16840, 5 March 1729/30; NAO, MSS, CA 4041/17.
21 MSS, 16840, 27 August, 1729; W. Carew Hazlitt, *The Livery Companies of the City of London* (New York/London: Benjamin Blom, 1969), p. 77.
22 NAO, MSS, CA 4039, 'Tables of Orders Rules and Ordinances, 4 July 1664; CLRO, Misc MSS, 1/18, ibn 244; Rep. Hoare No, 117, fo. 147; *Trade Directory of the City of London*, 1740, Society of Genealogists access no. 20988.
23 MSS, 3451/3, p. 11; 3451/2, 10 January 1888, 25 June 1894; 3452/3, 13 October 1903; CLRO, MSS, Companies 2.30.
24 MSS, 3451/4, 21 April 1925, 19 April 1926, 24 July 1933; 3451/5, 19 November 1945, 16 January 1948; 3451/6, – 22 January 1952, 24 April 1959 – Corah 2 directors; 28 October 1959 – Byford 2 directors, 27 January 1961 – Wolsey 2 directors; 8 October 1968 – Wolsey 2 directors; *Minutes*, 29 June 1971, 27 June 1972.
25 MSS, *Minutes*, 13 January 1976.
26 MSS, 3451/6, 22 January 1957. Appendix 7 gives a list of the members of the present Company.
27 George Unwin, *The Gilds and Companies of London* (London: Methuen & Co, 1925), p. 302.
28 MSS, 3451/5, 3 November 1942.
29 MSS, 3444; 3451/2, 11 October 1898; 3451/3, 20 November 1906; 3451/6, 25 January, 17 May, 28 August 1946, 26 June, 23 October 1969, 14 April, 24 June 1970; 3452/14, 'Memoir of Ernest A. Ebblewhite', 9 October 1931; Minutes, 14 April 1972; CLRO, MSS, P.D. 142.5.
30 MSS, 3451/6, 21 January 1945, 21 October 1964.
31 MSS, 16840, 24 June 1727, 24 June, 6 September 1728, 24 June 1729.
32 MSS, 3451/3,, 24 June 1902, 24 June 1903.
33 MSS, 3451/5, 3 November 1942; 3451/6, 2 May 1957 – Mr. Edmonds was an example.
34 MSS, 3450 *Renter Wardens' Accounts 1786–1905*; 16840, 6 August, 6 September 1728, September 1729.
35 MSS, 3442, 21 June 1727; 3451/1, p 27, 14 October 1856; 3451/3, 10 October 1911, 23 January 1912.
36 MSS, 3446/1; NAO, MSS, 4039; Henson, p. 92.
37 NMSS, 3446/1.
38 MSS, 16840, 24 June 1727; NAO, MSS, CA 4041 18–41; DDR 127 1–20; Henson, p. 136.
39 MSS, 16840, 24 June, 7 November 1727; 3442 June 1725, 10 October 1726; NAO, MSS, CA 4041/53.
40 MSS, 3445; 3447; 3451, 1805–09.
41 *CP*, 5 November 1937.
42 MSS, 3451/3, 13 January, 21 April 1903; *The Times*, 8 November 1787.
43 MSS, 16840, pp. 92–4, 24 June, 29 October 1728, 7 January 1728/9, 29 June 1729; *Minutes*, 20 January, 27 June 1978, 23 October 1979.
44 MSS, 3442, 29 January 1725; 16840, 24 June 1727, 6 Sept 1728; 3452/1, 1 March 1790; 3452/13.
45 MSS, Minutes, 27 June 1972, 23 October 1979.
46 MSS, 16840; 3442, 20 June 1745; 3451/3, 25 April 1913; 3451/6, 21 October 1964; *Minutes*, 8 January 1974, 20 January, 27 June 1978; NAO, MSS, CA 4041/53.
47 MSS, 3442, p. 183.
48 MSS, 16868: NAO, MSS, CA 4039; 1745 Bye-laws.
49 MSS, 3442, 18 October 1725; NAO, MSS, CA 4041/51; William F. Kahl, 'Apprenticeship and the Freedom of the London Livery Companies, 1690–1750', *Guildhall Miscellany*, VII, August 1956, pp. 17–20, p. 17.
50 NAO, MSS, CA 4041/53, 22 July 1745; Cooper, *Archives*, p 343; Cliff Webb, 'City of London apprenticeship and livery company records', *Genealogists' Magazine*, XXVI, March 1998, pp. 1–4, p 1.
51 MSS, 16840.
52 MSS, 3446/3, etc.; *Minutes of evidence to the Report of the Select Committee appointed to inquire into the Grievances . . . of Hosiers and Framework Knitters in the Woollen Manufactory of the town and county of Leicester . . . 1 April 1819*, evidence of Thomas Hitchcock, p. 33, evidence of Jackson, p. 40.

53 MSS, 3451/5, 19 January 1943, 25 October 1945.
54 MSS.3451/6, 24 June, 16 October 1959; WCFK, *Newsletter*, 6, April 1999.
55 Felkin, p. 45.
56 MSS, 3450 4 May 1800; 3451/1, frontpiece; 3452/4 photograph of mace; 3452/7.
57 MSS, 3450, 1 April 1798; 3451/1, 9 April 1872; 3452/2, p. 2, Clerk's Accounts, 14 February 1872; NAO, MSS, CA 4041/5 and 10.
58 MSS, 3451/1, 12 October 1858, 11 January 1859, etc.; 3452/3, 10 October 1
59 MSS, 3450, *Renter Warden's accounts 1797–1800*; 3451/6, 4 May 1962; 3452/9, letter 9 August 1910; 3452/15.
60 The 1664 Bye-laws and early Minute books use the word 'fine' for all monies due irrespective of whether these were the 'sums payable to a public officer', 'entrance money' or 'due as a penalty'.
62 MSS, 3451/1, 24 June 1880; BM, MSS, 816.m.12.(105); Cooper, *Archives*, p. 339.
62 MSS, 16840, 6 June 1727, 8 August 1728 etc.; 3444; 3451/1, 24 June, 10 October 1826; 3451/5, 28 January 1942; 3452/3, 10 October 1911; 3452/7, 6 July 1909; WCFK *Newsletter*, 6, April 1999; *Report of the Commissioners*, 1845, p. 9.
63 MSS, 3451/2, 10 January 1888; 3451/4, 20 April 1921.
64 MSS, 3451/5, Cooper Bros. letter 6 January 1947; 3451/6, 27 June 1967, 25 June 1968, 14 January 1969; *Minutes*, 27 June 1972, 26 June 1973, 25 April 1980, 14 April 1983; Kahl, p. 7.
65 MSS, *Minutes*, 30 April 1981.
66 MSS, *Minutes*, 18 June 1977.

IV

From the incorporation of the Company to the end of the seventeenth century

Between 1657 and 1710 the Society of Framework Knitters was at its most powerful. Through the Charters and Bye-laws the Court of the Company was legally authorised to enrol and control all framework knitters and it had, therefore, complete regulation of a sophisticated industrial operation long before the Industrial Revolution is considered to have started.

Location of frames and yarns

By the 1650s it was claimed that framework knitting was the livelihood of 'hundreds of poor families' and, as was seen in Table 1.1, was widely located across England. London was the most important centre of machine knitting, not only because it contained the largest number of frames but, because it was the hub of fashion, held 'much of the finishing trades' and 'accounted for some two-thirds of all cloth exported overseas', it was the marketing centre for a large part of framework knitting. Nottinghamshire contained the second largest number of frames, with a subsidiary marketing centre in the county town.[1]

Three fifths of the total number of frames knitted up silk goods, with most of the remainder making worsted items, and there seems to have been little specialisation as to the type of yarn used in any one area, for Pickard's 'underfashioned and unsound' silk and worsted hose production in London was one of the reasons for the petition for incorporation, while in the East Midlands both worsted and silk hosiery production had been developed, with frames working silk appearing in probate inventories by the middle of the century.[2]

Incorporations and the development of the Company

As the 1655 petition claimed that the profits of the industry were 'diffused among merchants, owners of ships, hosiers, dyers, winders, throwsters', in addition to the 'promoters, contrivers, and inventors', there would appear to have been a great deal of specialisation within the industrial organisation of framework knitting by the middle of the seventeenth century. However, the Society of Framework Knitters was incorporated solely to regulate the frame, the fabric it produced and its workforce.

By 1657 'Cromwell's successive efforts to govern with and through parliament (had) failed, and failed abjectly' so that, by the time he granted the Framework Knitters' Charter on 13 June 1657, he was probably willing to grant control of this burgeoning and important industry to anyone who could impose strong leadership, inhibit overmanning, overproduction and poor workmanship, and prevent what was acknowledged to be an English invention from enriching foreign countries through the export of frames.[3]

The Bye-laws of 1658 have disappeared, but reference was made to them on 1 July 1658 when a Common Council, held in the Guildhall in London and attended by the Lord Mayor, six Aldermen, the Sheriffs and more than forty commoners, reinforced Charter and Bye-laws with the powers of the City (see Plate 24). They were probably very similar to those ratified in 1664.[4]

With the accession of Charles II the Framework Knitters' Society was in a difficult position for, as one of only two Companies incorporated by Cromwell, it could have been argued that its Charter was invalid. Some members of the trade obviously took this view, for in November 1660 a petition was presented from William Savill and John Chettle, engineers, and forty nine other men connected with framework knitting for 'making void the corporation granted to the stocking weavers in 1658 . . . and for grant to the petitioners who have much improved the art, of power to correct abuses in frames and work'. Except for George Massey, who became an Assistant of the Society of Framework Knitters in 1663, the fate of this petition and its signatories is unknown. However, the members of the Society incorporated by Cromwell also wasted little time in trying to engage the interest of the new king and his most technically-minded confidant in framework knitting. On 23 April 1660/1 Charles II was crowned and on 3 May 1660/1 John Evelyn, who was a founding member of the Royal Society, as well as a Commissioner 'for reforming the buildings, ways streets, and encumbrances', and also for Charitable Uses dealing with the City and the Mercers' Company, 'went with Monsieur Zili-chem (another member of the Royal Society), to see the wonderful engine for weaving silk stockings'. A petition to grant a new Charter was made to the king in March the following year. The Society was (re)incorporated on 19 August 1663, with jurisdiction over England and Wales in all matters relating to framework knitting, and it was enrolled at the Guildhall on 24 September 1663.[5]

Although it might have been expected that the founders of an organisation incorporated by Cromwell might have been rejected by Charles II, there is a surprising continuity between the commonwealth and restoration Charters, and many of the Assistants appointed in 1657 continued to govern the Society after 1663. All the main points, such as membership, apprenticeship and the exportation of frames, received comparable treatment in both Charters and in both instances Bye-laws were swiftly drawn up and both Charters and Ordinances were endorsed by the City of London.

The first recorded meeting of the Society under the second Charter was on 30 June 1664, and new Bye-laws, signed by Edward, Earl of Clarendon, the Lord High Chancellor, Sir Robert Hyde, Lord Chief Justice, and Sir Orlando Bridgeman, Lord Chief Justice of the Common Pleas, were ratified on 4 July 1664. By now a sophisticated, industry-wide, organisation was in place and the leaders of the Company were closely involved with all aspects of framework knitting. Courts established in London and Nottingham were held in both locations on the same day and there was a considerable trade in knitted items between Nottingham and

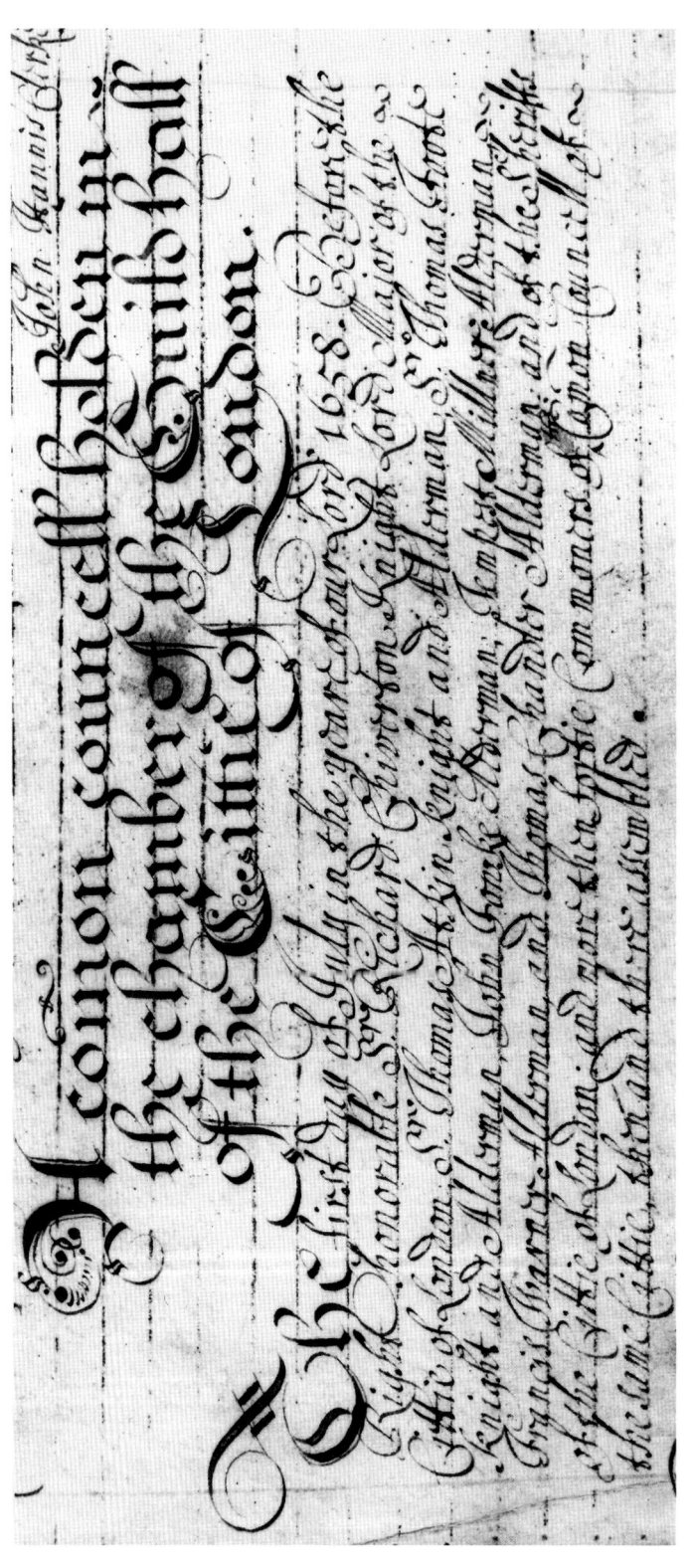

PLATE 24

1658 REPORT OF THE CITY OF LONDON COMMON COUNCIL

This report, copied by John Hannis, shows the acceptance by the City of London of the Society of Framework Knitters.

London, as is illustrated in the 1681 inventory of the framework knitter William Brookes of Mansfield, who was owed at his death £29 3s. 7d. by the London merchant Richard Oakley.[6]

Twenty years after incorporation by Charles II the Framework Knitters', together with most other Livery Companies, were compelled to surrender their Charters, because, as new ones cost between £200 and £300, the issuing of such documents was a useful source of revenue for the crown. The Framework Knitters' surrendered their Charter on 5 May 1684, at the same time as the Cordwainers' and Bricklayers', but, although there is a record of the reincorporation of a number of other Companies, such as the Clothworkers' and Fishmongers', there is no indication that the Framework Knitters' either sought, or received, a third Charter. As the most commonly granted privilege under these latest Charters was a further extension of a Company's jurisdiction into the London suburbs, perhaps the Framework Knitters' felt that they had no need of a third Charter as they already had complete control over their trade throughout England and Wales, or perhaps they either did not have, or were unwilling to meet, the required cost, and decided to keep a low profile and just comply with the requirements of the Corporation Act applicable to the Livery Companies. Whatever the reason, the Framework Knitters' Society of England and Wales does not seem to have obtained a new Charter at this time, although in 1686 James II had incorporated a Framework Knitters' Company in Ireland with a Charter similar to that granted to the English by Charles II, and, before it needed to reconsider its position, the Crown's policy on Livery Companies was reversed. On 2 October 1688 James II, as a mark of his confidence in the City of London, restored its ancient Charters and privileges, and a few days later issued a proclamation restoring their ancient Charters to the Corporations; in the following weeks the Companies, including the Framework Knitters', received back their original Charters.[7]

Membership of the Society

By order of both Cromwell's and Charles II's Charters framework knitters, whether or not they were already members of other Companies, were required to join the Society. Under the 1663 Charter those living within twenty miles of London were required to join within three months and the remainder within six months. Framework knitters in London transferred from a variety of other Companies, not all of which were connected with textiles. A number of the first Assistants were, like William Lee, originally in the Weavers' Company, including George Massey, William Pargetter, (Pa(r)git(t)er), Joseph Tomlinson and Thomas Stevenson, while among the transferring ordinary members was Philip Knight and William Wright. Another Company that sheltered many framework knitters before incorporation was the Clothworkers', of which James Lee, and the Assistants John Lee, Jonathan and William Grammar, John Bennet(t), Gabriel Brewer, Francis East and William Rigson were originally Freemen, together with John Granger and Thomas Rayner, who presumably had some connection with the workmen in Rouen, and James Birch, an ancestor of Thomas, the Master of the Company in 1771. A number of other Companies also contributed some of the first Framework Knitters'; John Cros(s)on, (Crossin), was originally a Merchant Taylor, John Pa(r)giter was a Grocer, while John and Edward Needham, whose descendants were prominent among later framework knitters, were originally Habersdashers'. Even some of the more unlikely Companies provided some of the first members of the Framework Knitters', Thomas East had previously been a Sadler and Thomas Cawardin(e), (Carwarden), Master in either 1678 or 1681, a Girdler.[8]

In 1671, by which time the period allowed to the framework knitters to transfer into their own Society had expired, 'Rules and directions . . . for every person in the Art of Framework knitting to observe that all may be without excuse, and none plead ignorance' were drawn up from the 'heads of several byelaws, ordinances and orders' of the Company. From this date 'no persons but admitted members, the spouses of such members or their apprentices duly bound by the said company shall henceforth work in the Art of Framework knitting'.[9]

Even before the Company was incorporated knowledge about the commercial success of the new trade must have spread for young men migrated from all over the country to London to learn it and to become Freemen. One came from as far north as Cheshire while others, instead of staying in their own frameworking areas, such as Anstey in Leicestershire, also moved to London. William Coster and Samuel Sheppard, who were later prominent in the Company, originated from Oxfordshire and Northamptonshire respectively, while Anthony Russell, probably the master of 1696, came from Bedfordshire, the county which, together with Buckinghamshire, provided the London knitters with the most recruits. Between 1681 and 1700 376 framework knitters became Freemen of the City of London. The vast majority were enrolled by Servitude, for few could yet claim to be second generation framework knitters, and only nineteen claimed by Patrimony. Of these nineteen four, John Burton, Thomas Lupton, Thomas Marshall and Thomas Towers, had fathers who had originally been members of the Clothworkers' Company, another's father had been a Weaver and another a Salter. Only one, Thomas Grimes, came from a family which ever became prominent in the Framework Knitters' Society for in 1696 Thomas Grimes was an Assistant and in 1766 another Thomas Grimes was Master. Only two men purchased their Freedom by Redemption, William Iliffe in 1682 and Robert Cleater in 1692, which refutes Gravenor Henson's 1831 slur that at this time the Company was full of persons 'of all trades and occupations . . . who had bought their livery for the sake of the vote'.[10]

However, as many framework knitters who joined the Company were 'foreign brothers' and therefore not entered in the London Freedom registers, the number of early East Midlands members is unknown, nor is there any record of the East Midlands framework knitters who transferred from other guilds. Nevertheless, it would appear that after corporation a high proportion of knitters within easy reach of the Nottingham Court did join the Society, although further south, in the area around Leicester, the picture is more obscure. In Leicester the corporation had a vested interest in not encouraging the Society for, as a petition of 1674 explained, it employed hosiers to set the poor to work handknitting and the burgesses fought a case, (outcome not found), for the right of framework knitters to bind their apprentices only with the town and not with the Company. That there were a number of stocking framework knitters in Leicester well before the end of the seventeenth century is without doubt, for in 1695 when they, together with the jersey combers, petitioned parliament against the jobbers engrossing nearly all the wool in the county and the aulnagers charging whatever they liked for sealing the stockings, they pointed out that for the past ten years they had employed nearly all the poorer sort of people with the work of their trades. It is this local authority opposition which could, perhaps, explain why only twenty seven framework knitters have been found in the marriage licences between 1660 and 1699 in Leicestershire, while there were 234 in Nottinghamshire, and why it would seem that although the Alsops and other families were involved in framework knitting in Leicestershire from at least the middle of the century, most continued to be recorded in other trades, such as mercers, until the end of the seventeenth century.[11]

Membership/composition of the Court in 1657 and 1663

A number of the officers appointed under both the Charters were either the same person or came from the same families. Out of the thirty Court members nine – George Balderton, Gabriel Brewer, John Croson, Jonathan Grammar, Samuel Knight, John Lee, Thomas Phillips, Richard Read and Joseph Tomlinson, served on both Courts, as did members of the Ben(n)et family, while a second member of the Gram(m)ar family was appointed in 1663. However, only one of the three officers of 1657, Thomas Phillips, was still on the Court in 1663, while all three of the officers of 1663, John Croson, the Master, and George Balderton and Jonathan Grammar, the Wardens, had been Assistants in 1657 (see Appendix 8).

Relationship between Assistants and Freemen

As membership of the Society of Framework Knitters was compulsory, the potential for conflict between the self-perpetuating oligarchy of a Court and the Freemen was always present, but would seem to have been minimised, at least until the end of the seventeenth century. Although William Lee had died about forty years previously, it was acknowledged in the petition of 1655 that his workmen, relatives and friends still controlled the trade, thus giving many of the officers appointed in the Charters ties to the East Midlands region, especially to the Nottinghamshire villages around Calverton. In the absence of the Framework Knitters' records of this period it is difficult to prove this conclusively, but allowing for the notoriously fickle spelling of names in Tudor and Stuart times, in which the same person could have his surname spelt differently in the same documents only a few years apart, searches of contemporary documents, such as hearth tax, militia records, poll books, church registers and wills, in all the East Midland counties and in London, confirm this premise (see Plate 25).

'Aston' is given by Thoroton as the name of the William Lee's Nottinghamshire apprentice; George Ashton was the first Master of the Society. As the surnames 'Ashton' and 'Aston' are regarded as interchangeable by those transcribing the hearth tax into modern English and were also interchangeable in the registers of many of the villages north and east of Nottingham, especially in Calverton and the neighbouring village of Woodborough where the family belonged, like Lee, to the minor gentry, it would seem that it was either William Lee's apprentice, by now an old man and too old to continue under the 1663 Charter, or that apprentice's London-based son who was the leader of the Association of Framework Knitters and the chief petitioner of 1655, and was subsequently honoured by being appointed the first Master of the Society of Framework Knitters. Moreover, when one of the

PLATE 25

lent by S. A. Mason

SIGNIFICANT LOCATIONS IN THE HISTORY OF THE WORSHIPFUL COMPANY OF FRAMEWORK KNITTERS IN NOTTINGHAMSHIRE, LEICESTERSHIRE AND DERBYSHIRE

Ashton family died in Calverton in 1719 his will showed that he was linked to the Lees by marriage.[12]

At least three of the Wardens and many of the Assistants named in the Charters had connections with both London and the East Midlands. Humphrey Jamson, presumably the Warden of 1657 or, again, his son, owned in 1681 a substantial house at Greasley Castle with four 'chambers' and a garret which contained four stocking frames with appurtenances, worth £28 10s., as well a 'house at London in the Spittle Yard . . . divided into 100 tenements'. Both Wardens of 1663 would seem to have come from Nottinghamshire families. Although Grammars were to be found in many of the villages north east of Nottingham Jonathan was probably from Calverton, where in 1688 at least three family members, Thomas who had died the previous year owning two frames, Richard and James are all described as 'silk storking framework knitters'; while George Balderton would seem to be descended from a Nottingham smith. At least nine other Assistants, John Lee, the Pargiters, Henry Womball, Joseph Tomlinson, Thomas Stevenson, Francis East, Lawrence Pomfret and William Rigson (Rixon), would also seem to have Nottinghamshire connections, while as Knights too can be found scattered all over north east Nottinghamshire in the late 1600s, perhaps Samuel Knight also came from the area. Because of the commonness of the name Smith it is not known where Osmond originated from, although it could be significant that a James Smith from Calverton paid 8s. subsidy tax in 1689.[13]

Other Assistants are less easy to trace and the Assistants Anthony and John Bennet(t) and Richard Read could have had connections with both Nottinghamshire and London. There were a number of Bennets in Nottinghamshire, including one William who married in Calverton in 1594, but the most important was Sir Thomas Bennet, the Alderman of London who signed William Lee's application to the Weavers' Company, who bought the manor of Shelton in Nottinghamshire and whose relatives would appear to have been involved with the Deputy of the Company Jonathan Labray. There were Reads too scattered around a number of parishes in east Nottinghamshire but, as there were Richard Reads prominent in both Nottinghamshire and London at this time, it is impossible to know which part of the country provided the Framework Knitters' Assistant. In 1653 one Richard Read was elected an Alderman of London – interestingly no Company was named in the record of election, contrary to almost every other Alderman listed, although it was guessed that he was a member of the Merchant Taylors' – while another Richard Read(e) was a mercer and Alderman of Newark, who died in 1706.[14]

Another Nottinghamshire family that was influential in the Framework Knitters' Society from the beginning until well into the eighteenth century were the Robinsons descended from William Robinson, Archdeacon of Nottingham in 1665. John Robinson, William's eldest son, was extremely influential at the royal court and in the City. He was knighted on Charles II restoration in 1660, Master of the Clothworkers' Company in 1656, the Member of Parliament for the City of London in 1660 and during 1662, when the Framework Knitters' second Charter was being considered, was Lord Mayor of London (see Plate C3). As only Freemen of the twelve 'Great Companies, which included the Clothworkers', could at this time be Lord Mayor this is probably the reason why he was not himself prominent in the Framework Knitters' Company, although it would seem his son, also called John, was a member of the Company in 1696, and his descendants were Masters in 1746,

1765 and 1781. It was believed by some within the Company that it was a Robinson who, sometime prior to 1851, on lending the Company money took as security some of the treasures, including the Balderton picture of William Lee.[15]

Only one member of the first two named Courts might have come from one of the Leicestershire villages later closely connected with framework knitting. John Crossin, as he is named in the first Charter, would at first glance appear to be of possible French extraction, but Cros(s)on, as his name is spelt in the second Charter and in a petition to Parliament in 1658 points to this possible origin in Leicestershire. The name does not appear in the records of Nottinghamshire, but in the probate records of Leicestershire ten Crosons are recorded in the seventeenth century, including a John Croson, husbandman of Hathern, who died in 1645 leaving an estate of £101 10s.[16]

The one Assistant whose surname could only be found in London documents was Owen Lavender.[17]

Nowhere are the complex and close relationships between various families in the hierarchy of the Society at the turn of the seventeenth century, as well as their importance, more clearly shown than in the affairs of the Nottingham Deputy Jonathan Labray. Labray was born in Calverton, to a family who were freeholders in 1612. In December 1697 Joseph Hoe, framework knitter of London, appointed Jonathan Labray, hosier of Nottingham, to recover money due to him, possibly frame rents. By 1706 Jonathan himself was hiring out frames and two years later Samuel Wardlow, a Nottingham framework knitter, owed Labray, Edward Benet, gent of London, and Elizabeth Benet, spinster of Nottingham, £17. In March 1709 Jonathan Labray drew up an agreement with John Hoe, mercer of Beverley, Yorkshire, for a bond of £100 which was in the hands of Thomas Smith, presumably the ancestor of the founder of Smith's Bank but here described as a mercer of Nottingham; if John Hoe died before he reached Barbados, West Indies, then the bond was Labray's, if Hoe reached the West Indies the money stayed with Smith. Then in September 1709 Edward Benet, gent, now of Stamford, Lincolnshire, and one of the executors of John Hoe's will, was party to a partnership agreement for three years whereby Ann Hoe, John's widow, and Jonathan Labray were to buy, make and sell worsted frame-wrought hose and yarn and thread and cotton frame-wrought hose, with a joint stock of £1,800. By 1711 Jonathan Labray, now also described as a 'gent', was a witness, Richard Knight another, to the turnover of the apprentice John Hoe, nephew of framework knitter and Alderman of Nottingham John Hoe, to Anthony Johnson, (a possible modernisation of Jamson).[18]

The Company's entrepreneurs/hosiers

Members of the oligarchy who controlled the Framework Knitters' Company thought to establish themselves as the chief entrepreneurs of the mechanical knitting industry. By the end of the century these entrepreneurs of framework knitting were called 'hosiers', but, as in the mid-1600s this title would seem to have been applied only to those who traded in hand-knitted stockings, those dealing in machine-made knitting were labelled 'promoters', as in the petition of 1655. They were based in both London and the East Midlands, with the Deputies, as well as members of the Court, playing an important entrepreneurial role at this stage in the Company's development. One function they carried out was arranging for the making and collection of production from the provincial frames and its marketing through London. Either the Society's Hall and the adjacent Company-owned hostelry and stables could have been used after construction in 1678 as warehousing – the Hall was certainly used for just such a function when it was the head quarters of the Company's Joint Stock Company at the beginning of the following century – or Wood Street in the City of London, where in 1638 Mr. Aston had a large house and shop, might have been a centre of framework knitting warehousing at a much earlier date than has hitherto been thought.[19]

In addition to organising the sale of hosiery, the Society also controlled the hiring out of frames, for through the Ordinances of 1664 it was made illegal to hire frames from anyone other than a member of the Company, and the fine for 'Hiring Frames of Strangers' was an astronomical one shilling a week. As the biggest capital expense to becoming established as a framework knitter was the frame, the cost of which in 1640 was about £60 for a new frame falling to about £10 for an old one, it was more than a journeyman framework knitter setting up on his own account without capital could afford, with the result that the entrepreneurs in charge of the Company could at the same time both control manufacture and become wealthy.[20]

This entrepreneurial involvement of the inner circle of the Company is again clearly illustrated by the career of Deputy Jonathan Labray. As a hosier with close connections to other members of the Company's hierarchy he hired out frames – one rented in Beeston to Henry Wright, the former apprentice of Richard Alcock of Calverton, in 1706 earned Labray fifty shillings a year – but even more significant in the organisation of the Society and of framework knitting before the end of the seventeenth century, is that there is no indication that Labray himself worked frames, or even had his own workshop. It was stated that only workmen took apprentices, not hosiers, and nowhere is there any indication that apprentices were bound to Jonathan Labray, as would have been expected of one in such a prominent position in the Company if, in addition to being a hosier, he ever worked as a framework knitter or had a workshop with working frames. This, therefore, suggests that Labray always worked solely as a hosier and was responsible for the Company's total organisation of framework knitting, including marketing, in the East Midlands. It is pertinent to this argument that Jonathan Labray died a wealthy man and in his will of 1718 left enough money to build six almshouses for 'poor and aged framework knitters' on Chapel Bar in Nottingham and provide the inmates with a weekly allowance of one shilling, as well as give £10 per annum to support a schoolmaster to teach poor children in Calverton free of charge.[21] The seeds of the conflict between the entrepreneurs within the Company and those outside, which surfaced increasingly during the seventeenth century, were laid during these early years of the Company. However, when hosiers, such as Jonathan Labray, were members of the Framework Knitters' Company, there was little conflict between manufacturing and marketing. Even when hosiers, such as John Sutton of Leicester, began to market both hand- and frame-knitted articles there was still minimal conflict of interest. But, as soon as they began to expand into owning frames, buying yarn and generally employing journeymen, the hosiers inevitably came into conflict with the Company with its jurisdiction over the whole knitting process. By the end of the seventeenth century, and increasingly in the eighteenth, many hosiers engaged in the framework knitting trade had neither been brought up in the trade nor apprenticed to it, nor were they members of the Company. In the eyes of the Company they were interlopers into the industry, yet because they had not, and did not work, frames there was little that the Company could do to compel them to join. Long after the Framework Knitters' Company was incorporated to control everyone working the knitting frame hosiers were to be found in other Companies, such as the Broderers', in which William Saunders, hosier, was made a Freeman in 1752, Robert Brewin, hosier, was made a Freeman in 1795 and Samuel Cooper, hosier, was made a Freeman in 1784.[22]

Search and the export of frames

As well as ensuring that the leading families of the East Midlands and London controlled entrepreneurial activities within the industry the Court was also empowered by the Charters and Bye-laws to regulate, through searches, all aspects of the trade. Such rights of search had become increasingly controversial so that other Companies had given them up before the end of the seventeenth century, almost before those of the Framework Knitters' started. The Society's clauses authorising the searches included ones to prevent frames from being exported and others to maintain quality control through the regulation of masters and apprentices. The searches were to be made quarterly, and were not confined just to premises where framework knitting was made, for anyone found with bad work could be fined and the work defaced.[23]

In order to safeguard the home industry Cromwell's Charter had made it a penal offence to export knitting frames. Unfortunately the Charter alone was insufficient to halt this trade and in 1658 a further petition to Parliament requested that frames be seized by customs officials until Bye-laws had been passed prohibiting exportation as an Englishman was proposing to introduce knitting frames to Genoa and, as John Croson and Jonathan Grammar from the Society testified, 'one Burdina, an Italian merchant, hath bespoke thirty or forty frames . . . with an intention of transporting beyond the seas'. A year later another petition from the Framework Knitters' asked for impounded frames to be taken to the Customs House in London to await arrangements being made for their disposal; this was considered necessary to prevent the ones seized the previous year, which were still in the hands of the searcher at Deal, being bought back cheaply by the exporter. Reference was also made to other frames waiting at Shoreham for shipment to France, and the necessary order was passed on 14 June and forty frames were seized.[24]

The 1663 Charter again dealt with the question of illegally exported frames, for 'no person, whether freeman or foreigner, denizen or alien, shall presume to carry, or cause to be carried, any frames used for making silk stockings, or used in Framework Knitting, beyond the seas, upon any pretense whatsoever'. In January 1665 another proclamation was issued 'prohibiting the transportation of frames for knitting'. The Court and Deputies were to be informed about the movement of all frames, and, with the help of government and local officials, were given further powers to search for and seize any frames or pieces of frames considered illegal.[25]

However, in spite of the threat of being prosecuted with the 'utmost severity of the law', frames still went abroad. In 1665 a workshop of stocking frames was set up at Schloss Walpersdorf, Austria, and in 1666 yet another proclamation prohibited the export of frames. Again this was not completely effective.[26]

The frantic activities of the Company in the search for frames thought to be destined for export can be glimpsed in the State Papers of the period. In 1666, when searchers arrived at a house in London in which frames bound for Portugal were thought to be hidden, it was found that most had already been removed to Somerset House, although at least one was thought to be in the house of the former Ambassador of Portugal. One miscreant, John Herbert of Stepney was arrested, but no effective action was taken against him or, Countess Panerna, the principal in this attempt to send frames abroad, for in 1678 Herbert made another attempt. In August that year Osmond Smith and Simon Sumner, Assistants of the Society, reported that Herbert was helping Haggett, a tailor, and 'Mirrell' to buy at least three silk stocking frames for export to Portugal, as well as recruiting members of the Company to go abroad to work these frames. A warrant was issued to bring Herbert, Haggett and Mirrell, plus the frames, before Secretary Sir J. Williamson, but again the frames had gone to Somerset House and to the former Portuguese Ambassador's residence, where the Ambassador's secretary, one Marueil, (presumably the 'Mirrel' of the warrant) was found; whereupon the authorities issued instructions that there was to be no search of either Somerset House or St. James. In September that same year Henry Ragnall, a smith, was taken before Secretary Williamson, on information from the framework knitter Joseph Roode, and charged with having taken a silk stocking frame to his own house without having informed the Company, and having ordered 'several thousand needles, which makes it suspicious as if he designed to transport the said frames beyond seas'. Such was the importance attached to these searches that those who refused to assist in them, when required to do so, were ordered to be detained, as happened to Plant, a coffeeman of the Strand, when he refused to help the government messenger George Pierce in the execution of a search warrant for silk stocking frames suspected of being destined for export.[27]

On 24 October 1686, the second year of James II's reign, a further proclamation ordered that no frames should be 'bought, sold or removed' without notifying the Framework Knitters' Company, and required civil and military authorities to assist in searches and seize all frames destined for abroad (see Plate 26). But again the order was not completely effective and in 1692 the House of Commons reiterated that because of mechanical improvements it was necessary to prevent the exports of frames, and a further proclamation against the export of frames was published in 1693. Up to the mid-1690s the Company's biggest worry had been the export of frames making silk goods, but by 1697 the production of woollen stockings on the frame was also so important that the Company petitioned the House of Commons to ban the export of woollen frames too, and a further proclamation was issued by William III.[28]

Even though the stream of proclamations prohibiting the export of frames may have prevented the dissemination of some of the more important improvements, the Framework Knitters' Company was unable to prevent all exportation. Altogether between 1670 and 1695 not less than 400 frames went abroad. The twenty-four technical drawings made by Jean Hindret in 1656 had led to a thriving industry in France and by 1669 silk stockings were mechanically knitted at factories in Paris and Lyons and worsted stockings in more than thirty French towns. In Italy knitting by machine was widespread by the second half of the seventeenth century. Tommaso Harnaggi had proposed to introduce the knitting frame to

By the King,
A PROCLAMATION

For Prohibiting the Transportation of Frames for Knitting and Making of Silk-Stockings, and other Wearing Neceffaries.

JAMES R.

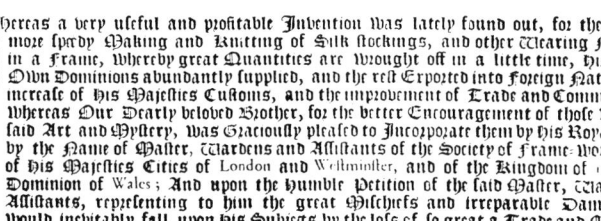

Whereas a very useful and profitable Invention was lately found out, for the better and more speedy Making and Knitting of Silk stockings, and other Wearing Neceffaries, in a frame, whereby great Quantities are wrought off in a little time, His Majesties Own Dominions abundantly supplied, and the rest Exported into Foreign Nations, to the increase of His Majesties Customs, and the improvement of Trade and Commerce: And Whereas Our Dearly beloved Brother, for the better Encouragement of those who use the said Art and Mystery, was Graciously pleased to Incorporate them by His Royal Charter, by the Name of Master, Wardens and Affiftants of the Society of Frame-Work knitters of His Majesties Cities of London and Weftminfter, and of the Kingdom of England and Dominion of Wales; And upon the humble Petition of the said Master, Wardens and Affiftants, reprefenting to him the great Mifchiefs and irreparable Damage which would inevitably fall upon His Subjects by the lofs of fo great a Trade and Myftery, by reafon that feveral Merchant-Strangers and Foreigners were labouring to Purchafe frames to convey them to fecret places near the Sea Coaft, for their better and more eafie Tranfportation, His faid Majefty, by His Royal Proclamation, bearing date the Fifteenth day of January in the Seventeenth year of His Reign, did ftrictly prohibit Tranfportation of the faid New Invented Frames, or any parcel thereof beyond the Seas; And We being informed thereof by the humble Petition of the faid Master, Wardens and Affiftants, praying that We would be Gracioufly pleafed, for prefervation of fo Confiderable a Trade and Myftery within this Our Kingdom, to iffue forth Our Royal Proclamation for the fame purpofes; We, by the Advice of Our Privy Council, have thought fit to declare Our Royal Will and Pleafure to be, and We do hereby ftraightly Charge and Command all and every of Our Subjects, as well Natives as Foreigners, that they prefume not to Tranfport or caufe to be Tranfported any of the faid New Invented Frames, or any pieces or parcels of frames, nor to be Aiding or Affifting to any Perfon or Perfons who fhall endeavour to Tranfport the fame, as they will anfwer the contrary at their utmoft Perils. And, for the better hindrance and prevention of the Tranfportation of fuch frames, and pieces or parcels of frames, We do further hereby ftraightly Charge and Command, That no Frames or pieces or parcels of frames, fhall be bought, fold, or removed by any Perfon or Perfons whatfoever, from place to place, without information thereof be firft given to the Mafter, Wardens and Affiftants of the faid Company of Frame-Work knitters, or any three of them, or their Deputies, to the intent they may take Cognizance where and in whofe hands they be. And, that Our Will and Pleafure herein declared, may be the better obferved and executed, We do further ftraightly Charge and Command all Cuftomers, Comptrollers, Searchers, Waiters, and other Officers and Minifters whatfoever, attending in any of Our Ports, that they do from time to time caufe diligent and ftrict Search and Enquiry to be made for all fuch frames, and pieces and parcels of frames, as fhall be endeavoured to be Tranfported, and the fame to feize and detein, under pain of forfeiting their refpective places and Imployments, in cafe they fhould be found negligent or remifs in the execution of thefe Our Commands. And We do further Charge and Command all Mayors, Sheriffs, Juftices of the Peace, Conftables, and all other Officers, Civil and Military whatfoever, that they be Aiding and Affifting from time to time unto the faid Mafter, Wardens, and Affiftants, or their Deputies, in the Searching for all fuch frames, and pieces and parcels of fuch frames, as fhall be endeavoured to be Tranfported, or fhall be brought unto any place near the Sea Coafts, with intention to Tranfport the fame, or fhall be removed from place to place contrary to Our Pleafure herein before declared, and in caufing the fame to be feized and deteined: And that they do from time to time Certifie unto the Lords of Our Privy Council, the Names of all fuch Perfons whom they fhall find to be Offenders againft this Our Proclamation, to the End that there may be fuch further Proceedings againft them, as fhall be agreeable to the utmoft Severity of the Law in fuch Cafes.

Given at Our Court at Whitehall the Twenty fourth Day of October 1686. in the Second Year of Our Reign.

GOD SAVE THE KING.

London, Printed by Charles Bill, Henry Hills, and Thomas Newcomb, Printers to the Kings moft Excellent Majefty. 1686.

PLATE 26   *repr. with permission from the Guildhall Library, Corporation of London*

1686 PROCLAMATION PROHIBITING THE TRANSPORTATION OF FRAMES

The provenance of this document in the Guildhall Library is unrecorded, but as the same Proclamation was purchased by the Librarian on behalf of Master Sidney Pears for the Society of Framework Knitters in January 1943, it is wondered if this was originally the Company's copy.

Genoa in 1658, and in 1662 a ten year monopoly was granted to G. F. Ghersi. John Hanford was granted a monopoly for fifteen years and started the manufacture of silk stockings in Milan in 1663, where there were at least nine frames in three different shops by 1686; while Turin must have had frames before 1667 as in that year another Englishman, Richard Shuberg, proposed to transport his frames from that town to Genoa. By 1690 the Framework Knitters' Guild in Venice numbered ninety-four persons.[29]

At the same time as trying to prevent frames from being smuggled abroad, at home the Company was seriously concerned with the effect that poor workman-ship and the growing number of frames and workmen was having on standards in England and Wales. After incorporation the Framework Knitters' Society drew up further rules prohibiting poor workmanship and regulating the knitting of hose. In 1671, while prices were 'so low', overtime was frowned upon and the minimum width of men's hose was fixed at thirteen inches and women's at twelve inches. On March 28, 1674, 'the making of articles upon the frame of 'bad silk, thread, hair or worsted' was forbidden and work had to be 'good and merchantable'. A few years later further regulations were introduced for the making of men's and women's stockings; now the top of men's silk stockings were not to be less than twelve and a quarter inches wide, and those of women not less than seven inches, while the measurement from heel to toe for women's stockings was to be a minimum of eight inches, with men's nine inches.[30]

Workhouse keepers

Poor workmanship was further controlled by the Bye-laws which allowed no-one to become a master, or, as it was termed, a 'work-house keeper' and bind an apprentice until he had presented his master piece to the Court. The thousands of masters named in the apprentice registers and the 1722 quarterage book had gone through this process before working on their own account. One of the most notable of the earliest work-house keepers of the seventeenth century was Lord Robert Carey, Earl of Hunsdon, a descendant of William Lee's apprentice Sir William Carey, who was admitted to the Company on 25 June 1666, and in 1667 was accepted as a workhouse keeper and bound William Pope as an apprentice.[31]

Apprentices

After its initial incorporation the Company lost little time in securing the co-operation of the City of London in putting into operation its rules on apprentice-ship. On 1 July 1658 Common Council decreed that apprentices of framework knitters in other Companies should be bound 'unto the Master or one of the Wardens or Assistants of the said Company . . . to the intent that, at the expiration of the said term the same Apprentice or Apprentices may be made free of the said Company of Framework Knitters'. The fine for not binding apprentices in this way was £20, payable to the Chamberlain of the City of London, half to go to the City and the other £10 to whoever made the complaint, in most cases, presumably, the Framework Knitters' Company. In addition, the Chamberlain of the City was empowered to admit any Apprentice or son of a Freeman who had used the frame for seven years into the Company upon witness testimony that he had served the required period. A number of former apprentices engaged in framework knitting applied for their Freedoms through the 1657 Assistant Gregory Fishborn(e), and it was noted in the London Freedom Register that they had faithfully completed their term as framework knitters with the said Gregory and their master who had been a framework knitting member of another Company, such as John Lee, Clothworker, or John Pargiter, Grocer.[32] Until the 1690s information about apprentices to the Company is confined to the thirty-two who are known to have become Free of the City of London through the Framework Knitters' Company. However, even with this sparse information, it is interesting to see the type of recruit to the Company. The fathers of these early apprentices were of the 'middling' classes, with occupations varying from gentleman to farmer, yeoman, grocer and inn holder. They originated from as far north as Stretton, Cheshire, through Nottinghamshire and Leicestershire, to Towcester, Northamptonshire, and Alton, Hampshire, showing that by the end of the seventeenth century the knowledge that framework knitting offered an acceptable and well regulated apprenticeship was widely disseminated.

Moreover, although apprenticeship details before 1694, when the City of London Orphan's Tax began, are no longer available they must have been substantial owing to the large number of framework knitting masters who are recorded as binding apprentices from 1694, all of whom had served apprenticeships before becoming workhouse keepers. Unfortunately, the surviving Framework Knitters Apprentice Registers list only those bindings for which the 2s. 6d. London Orphans' Tax was due, so that children apprenticed by the parish and family members are omitted; in addition, and in contrast to many other Companies, the Framework Knitters' books only record the name of the apprentice and the master, the term of apprenticeship – which is usually seven years – and the Court – either London or Nottingham – in which the apprenticeship was recorded. The name and occupation of the father and the place of abode, from which it would have been possible to learn about the social and geographical origins of the apprentices after the Company had been established for about forty years, are missing. Nevertheless, it can be clearly seen, that the numbers learning knitting were higher in the East Midlands than in London. In the period between June 1694 and December 1699 London bound 407 apprentices and Nottingham 645. Only in two six-month periods, July to December 1697 and 1698, did London enrol more apprentices than Nottingham – twenty-nine to nineteen and sixty-seven to sixty-five respectively – while in 1699 Nottingham enrolled 228 compared to London's ninety-four. During this period 285 masters are named for Nottingham, 19.3 per cent of them with more than one apprentice, with 239 in London, 18.4 per cent with more than one apprentice. It is also noticeable from the apprenticeship registers that by the end of the seventeenth century there were more female framework knitters who were masters in the East Midlands than there were in London – twenty four with thirty two apprentices in the Nottingham Court as compared to thirteen with eighteen apprentices in London. Four of the widows of framework knitters binding at the Nottingham Court, including Anne Rayner and Ann Hoe, bound two apprentices, while Dorothy Lamb(e) and Anne Roebuck each bound three, while in London only five widows bound two apprentices, and none had more than two. All a clear indication that the East Midlands had always been at least equal with London, and could even have produced more than London at an earlier date than previously realised.[33]

The Company's Hall and possessions

Although a number of the Companies of the City of London, such as the Needle-makers', never built a Hall, in 1677 the Society of Framework Knitters purchased a block of land between Red Cross and White Cross Streets with monies accumulated from income. The site was planned on a medieval layout. The street frontage was developed as an inn, the Golden Hind, which was rented out for revenue, and the Hall was one of a number of buildings, including stables, grouped around an inner courtyard behind the inn and reached by a passage from Red Cross Street (see Plates 9 and 27). Built between 1678 and 1680, the Hall measured about sixty feet by about forty feet and was used for all the Company's business. As it was the custom at this period for a Master to make a present to the Company on assuming office, such as a silver cup, painting, or article of furniture, the Hall would have been largely furnished with these gifts, together with the Company's banners and shields. The painting of William Lee by a Balderton would seem to have been presented to the Company in this way – George Balderton being Warden in 1663, and probably Master the following year.[34]

The Master's Chair (see Plate C2b), now in the Museum of London, is the only one of the Company's early possessions which has remained in its ownership to the present day since it was, together with his portrait, presented to the Company by Thomas Ca(r)warden, probably in 1681. Thomas Cawarden was Upper Warden in 1677, Treasurer in 1678, and it is believed that he was Master in 1678 or 1681. Unsupported tradition within the Company believed that this Chair originated from either the House of Essex or Leicester and had been used by Queen Elizabeth I, and that the Cawarden Coat of Arms on the back were only inserted after his purchase. Tradition also has it that the Chair was sat upon by Charles II when he visited the Company's Hall, although no record of this visit has been found.[35]

Unless a great deal disappeared prior to the sale in 1861 the Company never seems to have been particularly rich in silver, in spite of the fact that every Freeman was supposed to present to the Company a silver spoon valued at at least ten shillings on Admission. In addition to the gift of the chair from Thomas, John Cawarden presented the Company with a large silver cup with a cover. There was also a two-handled silver cup and cover the gift of Robert Summer, and another, dated 1664, the gift of W. Richardson. Although their date is unknown, presumably the large silver cup engraved with the arms of the Company and another with a cover and weighing 33 ozs. 10 dwts., entered in the inventory as the 'gift of a well wisher', plus the silver tankard and cover which was the gift of J. Margrave, together with most of the twelve silver salts, three table spoons with buttons at the end and eight 'old fashioned' table spoons, catalogued in the 1850s, also date from the seventeenth century.[36]

No evidence has been found to corroborate the idea promulgated by the Nottinghamshire writers, Charles Deering in 1751 and Gravenor Henson in 1831, that from the beginning the Company was profligate and, apeing the pomp of the rich Livery Companies, built a gilt barge, 'rowed by twenty watermen, in splendid liveries, accompanied by a numerous band of music, and adorned with magnificent flags, having the arms of the company emblazoned', plus a 'splendid carriage for the master and wardens', while 'carriages and horses were hired for the clerk and assistants', and the officials of the Company were clothed in liveries covered with

PLATE 27   *repr. with permission from the Guildhall Library, Corporation of London*

THE FRONTAGE OF THE FRAMEWORK KNITTERS' HALL – RED CROSS STREET

This illustration is housed in the Corporation of London's Guildhall Library Print Room. However, as the Coat of Arms over the door is not that of the Framework Knitters', and as the fenestration would seem to be out of character for the small Hall built by the Framework Knitters' Company by 1680 down an alleyway behind the Golden Hind Alehouse, this would seem to be more an illustration showing how the Company would have wished its Hall to look, rather than the actual Hall.

gold lace. Such blatent extravagances would surely have been complained about in the various petitions to Parliament, starting in 1693; and no reference can be found to any barge belonging to the Worshipful Company of Framework Knitters in either the Lord Mayors' or Royal Processions. Moreover the Company would have had very few years in which to enjoy the luxuries of a barge or a state coach. In 1702 the great pageants on the Thames and through the streets of the City were discontinued as being too costly and, although each Company generally contributed to its trade pageant on the mayorality of a member, until 1742 the Lord Mayor of London was only appointed from one of the twelve 'Great Companies', among which the Framework Knitters' was not included. The inescapable conclusion in the light of the available evidence is that, although the Company built a Hall in which the Court feasted, it is unlikely to have owned either a barge or a carriage in the seventeenth century and, if it had required such items, it would have hired or shared with other Companies, as it did in later centuries.[37]

The end of the 1600s

After three-quarters of a century of organisation the composition of the Society was changing, and by the end of the century the Company was entering a new phase in its development. There was a decreasing reliance on officers who had direct connections with the founders of the Company and with the East Midlands. In 1696 no Assistant of 1657 and only Osmond Smith of 1663 still remained on the Court, while only one other of the original families still remained represented – John East presumably being a relative of Francis, Assistant in 1663. Anthony Ruslye, (Russell/Rossell), was Master and the Wardens were Thomas Pilkington, whose family was to become prominent in Company affairs in the 1700s, and Sampson Colclough, an apprentice of George Balderton, whose descendant Thomas Colcough was an Assistant and trustee of the Company's Almshouses in the 1740s. Two future Masters, Thomas Grimes and William Portress, were also already Assistants. Altogether 243 members of the Company based in, or connected closely with, London signed the Association Oath Roll in 1696 and while there were a few ordinary members, such as Charles Bennett, Thomas Brewer and William Ashton, whose forbears were closely connected with the beginning of the Company others, such as Henry Whitehead, Edward and James Morley, John and Benjamin Gardner, Benjamin and Samuel Cole, Richard Trotman, Edward Painter, and Samuel Ne(e)dham belonged to families whose descendants later featured prominently in the Company or the industry, often in both.[38]

Split as framework knitting was between London and the provinces there must always have been some degree of antipathy from knitters outside London for the Court, but until the final decade of the seventeenth century such feelings remained largely hidden. Then, in the last decade of the seventeenth century this conflict between the monopolistic powers of the oligarchal Court in London and the ordinary members, who came mostly from the manufacturing elements of the Company and who were increasingly aided and abetted by hosiers who were not members of the Company and were pursuing their own interests, was first brought into the open. In December 1693 the Masters, Wardens and Assistants of the Company petitioned the House of Commons to be allowed to regulate further the abuses of the exportation of frames and the standard of knitted products, as it was admitted several members of the Company had lately fallen into the habit of making substandard work in order to undersell the rest of the Company. A counter-petition in the following January from framework knitters in and about Nottingham complained about the hardships caused by Bye-laws imposed by a Court whose members were 'living constantly in London'. No references was made to the abuses previously highlighted by the Master and Wardens, instead these petitioners complained about the heavy expenses occurred in taking up their Freedom and the cost of being appointed a Company Steward, and it was felt that the £200 estimated to be raised each year by the fines, from which the petitioners got no benefit, would be better spent on the numerous poor in the trade.[39]

The outcome of these petitions was not recorded, so presumably they were lost in the Parliamentary process, and the direct agitation died down. Nevertheless, this hostility between the Court and members was to increase in the eighteenth century.

References

1   Peter Earle, *The Making of the English Middle Class: Business, Society and Family Life in London 1660–1730* (London: Methuen, 1989), p. 21; Nicholls, Leicester, II, p. 621; IV, p. 679; Henson, p. 58, 168; Felkin, p. 62; information from Mr. Bill Partridge, Hinckley.

2   Henson, pp. 56, 57, 60; NAO, MSS, PRSW 78/9 – inventory of Thomas Butterworth of Farnsfield valued three silk stocking frames and implements at £90.

3   Slingsby Bethel, *The World's Mistake in Oliver Cromwell* (tract pub. 1668, details supplied by Assistant Dr. David Bethel); H. R. Trevor-Roper, 'Oliver Cromwell and his Parliaments', in *Essays presented to Sir Lewis Namier*, ed. by Richard Pares and A. J. P. Taylor, (London: Macmillan & Co. Ltd., 1956), pp. 1–48, p. 45.

4   NAO, MSS, CA 4039.

5   SP 29/22, p. 155; XXII, p. 373; XXXII, p. 532; P(ublic) R(ecord) O(ffice), MSS, CO 389/1; *Diary and Correspondence of John Evelyn, FRS.*, ed. William Bray Esq., 1854, 3 May 1662 – closeness to Charles II, shown 13 September, 1, 3 October 1661, 14 April 1662, 14 August 1662, 29 October 1662 etc. – Royal Society, 21, 29 August 1662, 17 September 1662, 30 November 1663.

6   MSS. 3446; 16840, p. 25; 3451/1, p. 381; NAO, MSS, CA 4039; MSS, PRMW 26/2b, inventory January 1681

7   SP Dom, Entry Book 55, p. 349, Entry Book 335, p. 243; *L(ondon) G(azette)*, 1688; Knights, pp. 1151, 1152, 1174.

8   CLGL, Weaver's MSS. L37. 4657A/1 & 2; CLRO. MSS. 204A, Calendar of Register of Freedom Admissions, pp. 25, 33, 35, 38, 47, 78, 110, 119, 134, 148, 159, 245.

9   NAO, MSS, CA 4039.

10 CLRO, MSS, PD 142.5; 204A, pp. 47, 51, 57, 78, 90, 109, 110, 157; Henson, p. 91.

11 *J(ournal of the) H(ouse of) C(ommons)*, XI, 28 February 1695/6; Collin Ellis, *History in Leicester: 55BC – AD1976* (Leicester: Information Bureau, 1976), p. 75; David L. Wykes, 'The Origins and Development of the Leicestershire Hosiery Trade', *Textile History*, 23, 1992, pp. 23–54, p. 30; Hartopp. pp. 181, 374, MSS 3444 – recorded as no. B143 'Abraham Ward apprentice to Nicholas Alsop'.

12 MSS, 3444; Thoroton, pp. 257, 297, 298, 350, 413, 421, 480; Nottinghamshire Hearth Tax, 1664: 1674, ed. W.F. Webster, *Thoroton Society Record Series*, Vol XXXVII; Beryl Cobbing, *William Lee and the Stocking Frame* (Calverton Preservation Society pamphlet, 1991), p. 9; The surname 'Ashton' appears for the first time in the Calverton registers in 1589 with the baptism of a daughter of William Ashton. In 1627 Margaret Ashton of Calverton married Francis Leeson of St. Mary's parish, Nottingham (NRO, MSS, PR 22,914), Margaret also being the name of the wife of John Aston, gentleman, who had died in 1582. Edward Aston, late of Calverton, inventory 1639 (photostat Calverton FWK Museum).

13 NAO, MSS, CA 4040 – Charles Wombell bound apprentices at the Nottingham Court in 1694 and 1698 PRNW; PRSW 102/8c; 1605 inventory of Giles Balderston included crossbows, swords, and daggers and a book called the 'French Academye'; *Nottinghamshire Subsidies*

1689, Nottinghamshire Family History Society Records Series, XXIV (Marshall), Part I; *Nottinghamshire Marriage Index up to 1699*, Part I, Nottinghamshire Family History Society Record Series Vol 84 – 1668 Henry Jamson's daughter Mary married Daniel Sulley in Greasly; Thoroton, pp. 142, 221, 250, 283; Wombells in places such as Ollerton and Rufford: Tomlinsons in Gunthorpe; Easts were congregated in Gunthorpe and Lambley.

14 NAO, MSS, PRNW, PR 22,914; Bennets also lived in the Granby, Hucknall and other villages around, and if the family christian names were perpetuated then Anthony a cutler by profession of Nottingham who died in 1795 had stocking frames; Thoroton, p. 168; Alfred B. Beavan, *The Aldermen of the City of London*, II (London: Eden, Fisher, 1913), p. 81.

15 Major J. B. Whitmore, *London Aldermen* (Typescript for the Society of Genealogists, 1961); John James Baddeley, *The Aldermen of Cripplegate Ward* (London: Baddeley, 1900), p. 72.

16 SP 18/184, no 34; R(ecord) O(ffice of) L(eicestershire) L(eicester and) R(utland), MSS, PR/I/47/12, PR/1/103/22; Hartopp, p. 183.

17 CLGL, MSS. Dept., Card Index.

18 NAO, MSS, DDAC 5/1 –9, 14–7, 20, 51.

19 PRO, Wills/inventories of 'hosiers'; T. C. Dale, *The Inhabitants of London: 1638*, Ms.p. 300 – Mr. Ashton, rent £20.

20 NAO, MSS, PRSW 102/1b 8 August 1689; PR103/3, 31 July 1691; LLRRO, MSS.,PR/I/93/1/40, 26 March 1690; Nichols, IV, p. 679.

21 MSS. 3446/1–3; 3444; NAO, MSS. CA 4041/12; PRSW/102/1a; DDAC 5/1/14; *Minutes of evidence . . . Leicester*, 1819, Watt's evidence, p. 35; Alan Wilkinson, *Labrays: portrait of a village school: 1718–1973* (Calverton, 1973); Blackner, p. 154–5.

22 LLRRO, MSS, PR/1/103/121; *Minutes of evidence . . . Leicester*, 1819, Watt's evidence, p. 35; for details about the growth of framework knitting in Leicestershire see David L. Wykes, 'The Origins and Development of the Leicestershire Hosiery Trade', *Textile History*, 23, Spring 1992, pp. 23–54; Christopher Holford, *A Chat about the Broderers Company*, 1910.

23 NAO, MSS, CA 4039, March 28 1674; Unwin, p. 344.

24 S. P. Dom. 1658, CLXXXIV, p. 215; S.P. CCXX, item 53, March 1659; S.P. 18/184, 1658, no. 34; Carlo Marco Belfanti, 'Fashion and Innovation: The Origins of the Italian Hosiery Industry in the Sixteenth and Seventeenth Centuries', *Textile History*, 27, 1996, pp. 132–47, p. 139; Felkin, p. 31.

25 NAO, MSS, CA 4039; *FWK Report*, 1845, p. 6.

26 SP, CXLV, p 205; E.W. Pasold, 'In Search of William Lee', *Textile History*, 6, 1975, pp. 7–17, p. 9.

27 S.P. CXLV, pp. 205, 206, 375, 396, 399.

28 *BM, MSS, SPP. 357.d.41*; *JHC*, XI, 1692, p. 27, 27 March 1696/7;*Collection of Proclamations* (London: Charles Bull, Henry Hills and Thomas Newcomb).

29 Henson, p. 88; Bondois, p. 26; Belfanti, p. 136–9.

30 NAO, MSS, CA 4039.

31 MSS, 3446/1; 3447, 3452/1.

32 NAO, MSS, CA 4039; CLRO, MSS, 204A, pp. 33, 45, 97.

33 MSS, 3446/1.

34 MSS, 3446/1; 3447/1, p. 394; 3450; 3451/1, pp. 394, 448; 16840, 5 August, 1729; *JHC*, 6 April 1699/1700; *The Builder*, 15 June 1917, p. 385; *Trade Directory of the City of London*, 1752, p. 97 (Society of Genealogists' access number 990).

35 MSS, 3451/1, p. 393–4; 3451/2 p. 209. Appendix 11, 1999 appraisal of The Master's Chair arranged by Liveryman David Little.

36 MSS, 3451/1, endpages – The engraving on the 1656 cup could have been executed later than the hall mark.(letter Hickleton & Phillips, 20 April 1956); NAO, MSS, CA 4039, 4 July 1664.

37 *JHC*, XXVI, 19 April 1753; Henson, pp. 91–2; Knight, p. 155; John Gough Nichols, *London Pageants* (London: Nichols, 1831), pp. 80–3, 87, 88, 91; Sir Walter Sherburne Prideaux, *Memorials of the Goldsmiths' Company* (London: Eyre & Spottiswoode, 1896), pp. 105–7, 312; Kenneth Nicholls Palmer, *Ceremonial Barges on the River Thames* (London: Unicorn Press, 1997), pp. 70, 142–4; Programme for the Master's lunch on Lord Mayor's Day at Bakers' Hall, 9 November 1996.It should not be forgotten that in the Luddite Riots of the early 1800s Gravenor Henson championed the frameworker, and was even suspected of being King Ludd.

38 MSS, 3444; 18116; 3452/1; CLRO, MSS, PD142.5.

39 *BM, MSS, 816.m.12.(105)*; *JHC*, XI, 11 December 1693, 9 January 1693/4.

V

The Company in the
first half of the
eighteenth century

During the first half of the eighteenth century the Worshipful Company of Frame-work Knitters continued to retain total control of a trade that increased annually and became larger and more dispersed than many modern industries. However, these growing numbers caused problems because, in the age of the horse and cart, the Company was never able to enforce completely its widespread monopoly, and a disastrous financial venture between 1720 and 1730 compounded the difficulty by leaving the Company permanently short of money. The growing groundswell of opposition to its monopolistic powers meant that the regulations legally imposed by the seventeenth century Charters and Bye-laws were increasingly ignored, especially in the under-regulated country districts, and, although revised Ordinances were introduced in 1745 to try to reimpose discipline on the industry, these were swiftly challenged.

State of trade

With no census of production in the eighteenth century there are considerable differences about the number of frames and frameworkers; although, whichever figures are accepted, all agree that there was an extension of the acknowledged centres of production and an enormous increase in the number of frames from the 1650s. By the end of the first quarter of the eighteenth century the number of frames totalled about 8,600, with between 2,500 and 3,500 of these in the East Midlands, and in the following twenty-five years these nearly doubled again. London and the south east declined steadily during the first half of the eighteenth century as a centre of framework knitting because the fashion of wearing stockings in the same colour as clothes died out and, with this decline in demand for instantly fashionable knitted items, merchants and hosiers in London found that they could often get cheaper work done in the country, especially in the East Midlands. Moreover, in addition to the locations named in Table 5.1 by the historians, the Framework Knitters' records show that at this period there were also frames in Lincolnshire, Essex, Cheshire, Yorkshire, Huntingdonshire, Cambridgeshire, Worcestershire, Berkshire, Hampshire and Oxfordshire.[1]

Even though most frames were worked single-handedly by the eighteenth century, alongside the increase in the number of frames there had been a corresponding increase in the number of framework knitters, who would also have numbered

Table 5.1 **Number and location of recorded frames between about 1714 and 1750**

Location	c. 1714 No. of Frames	c.1750 No. of Frames
London	2,500	1,000
Surrey	between 500 and 700(H)	350
Leicester	600, (between 500 and 700)(H)	1,000
Nottingham	400, (not more than 400)(H)	1,500
Mansfield	(30–40)(H)	
Sutton-in-Ashfield	(40+)(H)	
Derby	50 (VCH), (30–40)(H)	200
Elsewhere in Midlands		7,300
Herts & Bucks	declined rather than increased(H)	
Towcester, Northants	new manufactory of 150 frames (H)	
Odiham, Reading and Neighbourhood	100+ frames (H)	
Tewkesbury, Glos.	between 50 and 70(H)	
Elsewhere in England and Scotland		1,850
Ireland		1,400
Total	8,600	14,000

Source: Felkin, *History*, p. 76; Felkin, *1845*, p. 4; Henson [shown as (H)], p. 106: Victoria County History [shown as (VCH)]: *Derbyshire*, p. 367.

about 8,600 in the 1720s and 14,000 in the 1750s. At the same time the number of families, not only the immediate ones of the knitters, who performed auxiliary tasks in the home such as spinning and seaming, but also all the other trades necessary to mechanical knitting, such as needlemakers, sinkermakers, frame-smiths, dyers, sizers, carriers and merchants, which relied on framework knitting for their livelihood had increased, as had the number of hosiers dealing in machine-made knitting and hiring out frames. The cost of frames was still above the means of most journeyman, but offered a good return on investment both for the capitalist hosier and for other owners, some completely divorced from framework knitting, thus leading to overproduction and shoddy work made by poorly paid labourers, who were not part of the Company of Framework Knitters, underselling the knitted goods made to agreed specifications by Company members. This manufacture of 'fraudulent' goods, plus the use of 'colts' (not bound apprentices), were two among a growing number of complaints about the unregulated knitters, hosiers, and bagmen made by those who had taken up the Freedom of the Company and had to pay the cost of membership.[2]

The Company 1700–1720

Against this background of the enormous increase in framework knitting, the changes in frame ownership, and the gradual removal of much framework knitting from London, the Court of the Worshipful Company of Framework Knitters, ruling by Ordinances drawn up when industrial mechanisation was in its infancy, had to try to control from its London Hall a growing, widely dispersed, and increasingly hostile trade in the first half of the eighteenth century (see Plate 28).

   Opposition to the Company had continued from the seventeenth century and in

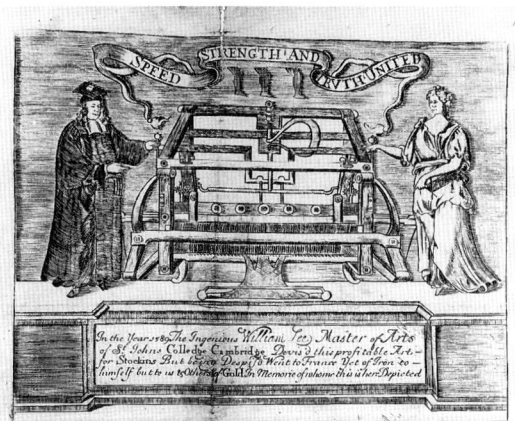

By the Master of the Company of Frame=Work=Knittets.

THESE Rules and Directions are publifhed for every Perfon ufing the Art of *Frame Work Knitting* to obferve, that all may be without Excufe, and none plead Ignorance therein ; being the Heads of feveral By-Laws, Orders, and Ordinances of the faid Company, as now are eftablifhed by the Court of Affiftants : Alfo the Contents of the Oath taken by every Member at their firft Admittance.

Imprimis, That no Perfons, but admitted Members, the Sons of fuch Members, or their Apprentices duly bound, fhall henceforth work in the Art of *Frame-Work-Knitting.*

2. That every Perfon having ferved by Indenture, fhall within one Month after the Expiration, take his Admittance, his Mafter or fome other Member by him appointed, teftifying for his Service ; that the Sons of admitted Members imployed in the faid Art fhall not, under the Age of Twenty One Years, take their Admittance.

that no Member fo admitted fhall bind or keep an Apprentice, till he be by the Mafter, Wardens, or their Deputies, allowed a Work-houfe, and as aforefaid two Years, and not to bind or keep two, till he hath been admitted full feven Years.

are Perfon in the faid Art, but his Male Children and Apprentices duly bound, except Boys upon Tryal.

at none on the faid Company, nor inftruct or teach Boys upon Tryal longer than one before they them to the Mafter, Wardens, or their Deputies, that fuch a Perfon is an admitted Member.

6. That none fhall bind any Boys under the Age of fourteen Years, and that none above that Age fha

7. That none fhall turn over any Apprentice before the Chamberlain, or elfewhere, nor none fhall receive any Turn-o for the Mafter, Wardens, or their Deputies, for their turning over as aforefaid.

8. That none contract with his Apprentice, or any other Perfon, for the Term of his Indenture, nor bind an Apprentice intentionally to ferve another Man.

9. That none conceal any Foreigners, nor imploy in the faid Art any Perfon as Journey-man, unlefs it fhall appear by a Certificate under the Hands of the Mafter, Wardens, or their Deputies, that fuch a Perfon is an admitted Member.

10. That none entice any Member's Servant out of his Service, nor no Journey-man to depart his Service without a Month's Warning, except it be otherwife agreed, and then to perform the Contract, and pay what fhall be juftly due ; and in cafe of Difference between Mafter and Servant, upon Complaint made to the Mafter, Wardens, or their Deputies, the Wronged fhall be relieved, and the Offender punifhed according to his Crime.

11. That no Member fhall employ another Man's Journey-man or Servant, till there be a lawful Departing, as aforefaid, efpecially after Notice given, that the Departing was not lawful.

12. That no Member, as Journey-man, fhall work with any other than admitted Members of this Society.

13. That no Perfon whatfoever fhall remove any Frame from one Houfe or Place to another, but fhall within two Months after fuch Removal, give Notice in Writing to the Mafter, Wardens, or their Deputies, of the Time when, the Place from whence, and the Place whither fuch Frame was removed.

14. That none fhall defpife or difobey the Mafter, Wardens, or their Deputies, in the Execution of their Office.

15. That none fhall refufe the Search, nor to pay their Quarteridge, Fines, or Arrears, to the Mafter, Wardens, or their Deputies, whenfoever by them demanded.

16. That none fhall contemn nor difobey the Summons of the Mafter, Wardens, or their Deputies, every Offender appearing at the firft Summons, fhall, upon their Submiffion and Reformation, be favourably dealt with ; but for their Non-appearance, for every Summons after, they fhall pay Six-pence to the Beadle ; and whofoever appears not at the third Summons, fhall be look'd upon as a Contemner of the Court, and profecuted according to the By-Law in that Cafe provided.

17. That no Member fhall have a Court of Affiftance fummoned upon his particular Account, but fhall pay ten Shillings, to be divided amongft the Officers, for their Attendance and Charge therein.

18. That the Widows and Children of thofe that are not admitted, fhall have no Right to the Trade ; and the Widows of thofe that are admitted, Marrying out of the Trade, fhall lofe their Benefit : Every Widow having Servants, and Marrying in the Trade, thofe Servants are thereby her Huf-band's, and fhe may not bind any more till their Times are near expired.

19. Every Member that defires to be further fatisfied concerning thefe feveral Penalties due upon the Breach of thefe By-Laws, may in the Morning of the firft *Tuefday* of the next Month after Quarter-Day, at the Company's Hall or Meeting Place, hear them openly and fully read ; at which Time all Members are to pay their Quarteridge.

Note, Every Perfon having a Right to the Freedom of the City of *London*, fhall, at the Prefentation of their firft Apprentice, produce a Copy of their Freedom, or they will be denied the Benefit of Binding.

The *OATH* of every *Free-Man*, at his firft Admittance into the Society of *Frame-Work-Knitters.*

YOU do fincerely promife and Swear, That you will be faithful, and bear true Allegiance to His Majefty King GEORGE, His Heirs or Succeffors ; You fhall be true to the Fellowfhip of Frame Work Knitters, whereinto you are now admitted : You fhall be obedient to the Mafter and Wardens for the Time being : You fhall obey their lawful Summons : You fhall not difcover the lawful Councils of this Fraternity, which you ought to keep fecret within your felf : You fhall not conceal any Foreigner, whereby the faid Fraternity may be prejudiced : You fhall not take any Foreigner into your Service, nor other, but fuch as have well and truly ferved as Apprentices, for Seven Years within the Kingdom of England ; or Dominion of Wales, or elfe Apprentices duly bound ; or the Sons of admitted Members : You fhall caufe your Apprentices to be Enroll'd, as the Cuftom of this City requireth : You fhall not entice any Man's Apprentice, or Covenant-Servant, till reafonable Departing be made between the Mafter and the Servant : You fhall be contributary to all Manner of Charges in, or about the publick Weal of the faid Society, to your Power : You fhall obey, keep, and perform all the Acts and Ordinances made and to be made for the good Order of the faid Art and Myftery. Thefe Points, and all other good Rules, you fhall maintain to your Power.

So Help you God, &c.

PLATE 28   *repr. with permission of Nottinghamshire Archives*

ABSTRACT OF THE FRAMEWORK KNITTERS' COMPANY'S REGULATIONS IN THE EARLY EIGHTEENTH CENTURY

This Abstract of the Ordinances was sent from the London Court to Nottingham early in the eighteenth century. In addition to reiterating the Company's basic rules, this Abstract is headed by the Balderton picture, instead of the more usual shield showing parts of the frame, and also includes the contemporary Oath for the Freeman's Admission to the Company.

January 1699/1700 framework knitters in Leicestershire, Nottinghamshire and Derbyshire again petitioned the House of Commons. In their petition they complained, mostly inaccurately, that the governing body, living constantly in London, imposed severe penalties on any poor framework knitter who did not comply with the many Bye-laws. Two that were anathema to the East Midlands knitters were the necessity to travel to London to obtain their Freedoms and the £1 2s. 6d. cost of binding apprentices, and they claimed that the compulsory visit to London, costing an estimated £5, beggared the poorer knitters; one Trueman complained that he had been unable to return north because of the expense, while James Shaw stated that he had had to work for a whole year to recoup costs. Another complaint made to the Commons was that, claiming that the Court of Common Pleas had declared illegal the Bye-law requiring the Stewards chosen by the Court either to pay for the Company's feasts or be fined £10, the Company had continued with the practice and sued the chosen Steward if the fine was not paid; Thomas Godfrey had been imprisoned when he had not paid the Steward's fine and £14 damages and only a collection among fellow framework knitters had saved him, while Benjamin Green's costs had been £50. Other petitioners objected to the payment of the sixpence quarterage, claiming that they had 'no manner of Benefit' from this or other fines and there was no 'rendering (of) any Account'. The Company argued in reply that through the Charter granted by Charles II it was entitled 'to rule and govern all Persons using the said Art', and under the Bye-laws it had the power to appoint two country members to be Stewards on Michaelmas Day, and to fine them if they refused, and that, moreover, it thought that '6d. a Quarterage very moderate'. It pointed out that some of the journeymen's claims were inaccurate as only former apprentices of Freemen of the City of London, and not those of foreign brothers, were required to journey to London to be admitted to the Company and the cost was fifteen shillings, (ten shillings to the Company in lieu of the silver spoon, two shillings each to the Clerk and the King, and one shilling to the Beadle), and that the £1 2s. 6d. quoted by the opposition comprised ten shillings to the Company in lieu of the master piece, a further two shillings and sixpence to the Company under a Statute of Henry VIII, three shillings and sixpence to the Clerk, one shilling to the Beadle, sixpence for parchment and then two shillings and sixpence each for the King's Duty and the City of London Orphan's tax.[3]

As the matter was adjourned on 6 April and does not feature again in the House of Commons' papers, it was presumably allowed to drop; nevertheless, it shows that opposition to the Company was growing.[4]

Open conflict in the industry was not recorded again until about 1710 when, owing to poor trade, many journeymen framework knitters in London were out of work. A case against a number of masters who had contravened the Bye-law restricting the number of apprentices to a maximum of three, was thrown out by a magistrate in Spitalfields, much to the dismay of ordinary framework knitting members of the Company. It was felt that a first meeting of the Court of Assistants and Livery failed to address this issue effectively and at a subsequent meeting at the Cock Inn in Old Street Square tempers, fuelled probably by the amount of liquor drunk, ran so high that in the evening attendant journeymen attacked a frameshop in the opposite corner of the square owned by a knitter called Nicholson, who had provoked the delegates by making his illegal number of apprentices work throughout the meeting. Nicholson and his apprentices were 'soundly beaten, and his frames broken and thrown out of the windows'. Frame breaking then continued for a further forty eight hours in the parishes of St. Luke, Cripplegate and Shoreditch and almost a hundred frames were destroyed. Although not initiated by the Company this orgy of framebreaking strengthened its position, for many London masters, fearing that their workshops would also be destroyed, accepted the Company's rules on apprentices; although some, including Samuel Fellows who was reported to have forty nine apprentices, and Cartwright who took 'no less than twenty-three', while momentarily appearing to accept the Company's rules, decided, together with other hosiers, to move their machines out of London.[4]

Even while these disputes were going on, however, the ordinary business of the Company continued. The Court of Aldermen of the City of London granted the Company a Livery of not more than sixty on 13 June 1713, which by 1724 numbered fifty eight. Moreover, although the Company rarely attended the Lord Mayor's parade it did so in 1718; full details of this participation are, however, sadly lacking, although it is wondered if the first mortgage of the Hall in 1717 helped to pay for this outing.[5]

In 1719 the position of the Company was strengthened further by a law pro-hibiting the exportation of machinery and workmen, the draconian clauses of which apparently inhibited framework knitting in Europe for 'more than a century'. A fine of £300 and a minimum of two years' imprisonment was imposed for the export of machinery, while anyone enticing a workman abroad was fined £500 for the first offence and £1,000 for the second, plus two years imprisonment. A workman already abroad who did not return home within six months of receiving notice from the British Ambassador lost his citizenship and was prohibited from inheriting property, voting, and forfeited any possessions in England.[6]

While both journeymen and masters seemed to welcome the Society's regulations on maintaining standards of work and its attempts to prohibit the export of machinery those relating to apprentices were widely resented, not only by individuals but also by many town authorities, such as those of Leicester which declared 'that when and as often as any Framework Knitter Inhabiteing within this Corporacion being treemen are sued by the Company of Framework Knitters . . . the Corporacion at their Charge will defend the said prosecucion'. In 1715 the Company, as part of an attempt to enforce control over all framework knitting in the East Midlands, brought an action against two framework knitters of Leicester, Thomas Derbyshire and William Browne, who had bound and made free their apprentices before the Mayor of Leicester instead of before the Company's Deputies. Derbyshire and Brown were defended by the Leicester town solicitor Mr. Noble, who was instructed that, even if the Company declined to bring the matter to trial, he was to sue for costs, and to ensure that Derbyshire and Brown did not submit to the Company's claims they had to give a bond of £100 to Leicester Corporation. The Company seems to have dropped the prosecution, although whether it had to pay costs is unrecorded, but as all other framework knitters in the borough were treated in the same way by the civic authority the Society's recruitment in Leicester was severely restricted.[7]

Joint Stock Company 1720

In 1720 the Company tried to enforce its monopoly and get rid of the independent hosiery entrepreneurs, as well as absorbing surplus labour and keep up and equalise wages, by investing in a self-administered Joint Stock Company to make silk and worsted stockings and other knitted goods the substantial sum of money accumulated from fees and fines; this sum could have amounted to up to £12,600, and is calculated by Henson at £10,000.[8]

On 7 June 1720 a general Court ordered 'That a Joint Stock of Two Million be raised by Subscription, by the Members of this Company, and others, for the carrying on the Trade of making Silk and Worsted Stockings, and other goods, in Frames, to the utmost Extent and Advantage of the Traders in general, and of the Company in particular'. An order book for shares of denominations between one thousand and ten thousand pounds was opened on 15 June. Each subscriber paid to Renter Warden Richard Austin twenty five shillings for each thousand pounds of stock ordered. The promoter, and attorney, of the scheme was William Pocklington to whom the Company gave £200 out of the subscription money and who was allowed to take up to ten thousand pounds worth of stock without paying a deposit. Renter Warden Austin was bought 'a piece of plate' to the value of ten guineas for his 'extraordinary trouble' and the Clerk of the Company was paid sixpence for each certificate he produced.

The scheme was run initially by Mr. Pocklington, advised by a committee consisting of the Master, Wardens, and Captain Whitehand, Captain Portress, Mr. Hart, Mr. Edgloy and Mr. Brandreth, or any three of them. On 15 June, having reserved £1,600,000 which was not to be subscribed for, the remaining stock was divided equally between Mr. Pocklington, the Clerk and the Court of Assistants. On 18 June it was decided that Assistants did not have to pay a deposit for their stock, thus in effect giving the officials of the Company a present, or, as Henson put it, defrauding the subscribers, of £18,000. Members of the Company could bring in their goods to the Company's warehouse, which would seem to have been within the curtilage of the Company's property between Red Cross and White Cross Streets, to be 'paid as the Court shall think fit'. By August thirty one people had been chosen from among the subscribers to manage the Joint Stock Company, its draft articles had been settled by counsel and were engrossed and sealed with the Company's seal.[9]

Initially the scheme was popular. An amount of £1,890 was soon raised in subscriptions, and for a time shares traded at a premium – a bond for £1,000, on which twenty-five shillings had been paid, was sold for £15 15s. in Change Alley – and wages rose in a number of the southern knitting areas. However, by the end of August 1720, some subscribers were already having doubts about the legality of the scheme, for the sub-committee of the Company had invested some of the money raised in Sword Blade Bonds, and Serjeant Darnell and Counsellor Lutwich were asked to rule as to its validity. In 1719 it had been enacted that joint stock companies had to be regularised by an Act of Parliament, with fines levied on persons running unregulated companies, and Lutwich and Darnell advised that such an act was required if the Framework Knitters' wished to continue with their Joint Stock Company. On 31 October 1721 the three members present at a committee meeting decided to apply for the appropriate Act, and this decision was endorsed by a general committee meeting held on 4 December 1721, with the proviso that 'they shall proceed to carry on the Trade with a Joint Stock, according to their first Undertaking, so far as they can do it with Safety'. In January the following year the eighteen receipts for the £1000 bonds, on which it had originally been decided that no deposits were to be paid, were called in. No Act was obtained, but meetings continued to be held in the Framework Knitters' Hall, the expenses of which were paid for by the Company, until finally, on 8 May 1730, it was decided that the treasurer of the Joint Stock Company, Richard Austin, should make up the accounts and that 'such Part of the Monies . . . as now remains . . . doth belong to this Company, and others, and ought to be accounted for, and applied . . . for their Use'. The Joint Stock Company had failed.[10]

Consequences of the Joint Stock Company

The Joint Stock Company was not the completely scatter-brained scheme it appears in hindsight because the powers that the Livery Companies had acquired to exploit their legal monopoly made them specially advantageous channels for investment of capital, and a number of them had already formed successful joint-stock enterprises; but in the case of the Framework Knitters' it did not achieve its objectives, and the loss of about £10,000 was to have a lasting effect on the Company.[11]

Whether the Court of the Company had seen it as a means of enriching themselves at the expense of the ordinary members, as some, such as Gravenor Henson in hindsight, believed, or were just gullible men unskilled in commercial and financial affairs is open to interpretation, but it would seem that commercial and financial incompetence is the more likely explanation. This was a period of numerous speculative companies in which many people eventually lost a great deal of money. At the time that the Worshipful Company of Framework Knitters inaugurated its Joint Stock Company the South Sea Company 'bubble' had not burst and the report on this, the most notorious of these schemes, was not presented to the House of Commons until two years later. Completely unscrupulous men would not have made swingeing cutbacks, even before the scheme was wound up in 1730, and would have been unlikely to have mortgaged the Hall or have deprived themselves of the perks of office, and would certainly not have lent the Company money.[12]

That the Company was short of money long before 1730 is well documented. In 1726 the London Orphan's tax was owed for 320 apprentices but only 150 bindings were paid for; the amount owed for the other 170 remained on the books until October 1728. Also in 1726 the Master, Thomas Bourne, lent the Company £10, while Deputy Master Captain Roger Broome, Renter Warden Joseph Rossell and Under Warden John Thompson, together with twelve Assistants, each lent the Company £5 for eighteen months. Two years later it employed as Clerk Henry Matthews and promptly borrowed from him £103 18s. The Company had always expected its Deputies outside London to be financially self-supporting, with the fees received at the East Midlands Courts, from such items as admissions and apprenticeship bindings, covering the salaries and expenses of the local officials, with the surplus being dispatched to the Clerk in London. Yet the accounts of Conyers White, the Deputy Beadle in Leicestershire, show that although he travelled widely in the Midlands and the north of England, from Grimsby to Hinckley, carrying out the Company's business, and his expenses between 29 June 1724 and 7 July 1725 came to £4 17s. 5d., he was still owed £2 6s. 3d. in August 1726 (see Plates 25, 29). The Deputy at Mountsorrel, Michael Wire, had a similar problem. By May 1727 things were in such parlous state, due to the 'present Badness of Trade and Company's affairs and their several Law suits', that Deputy

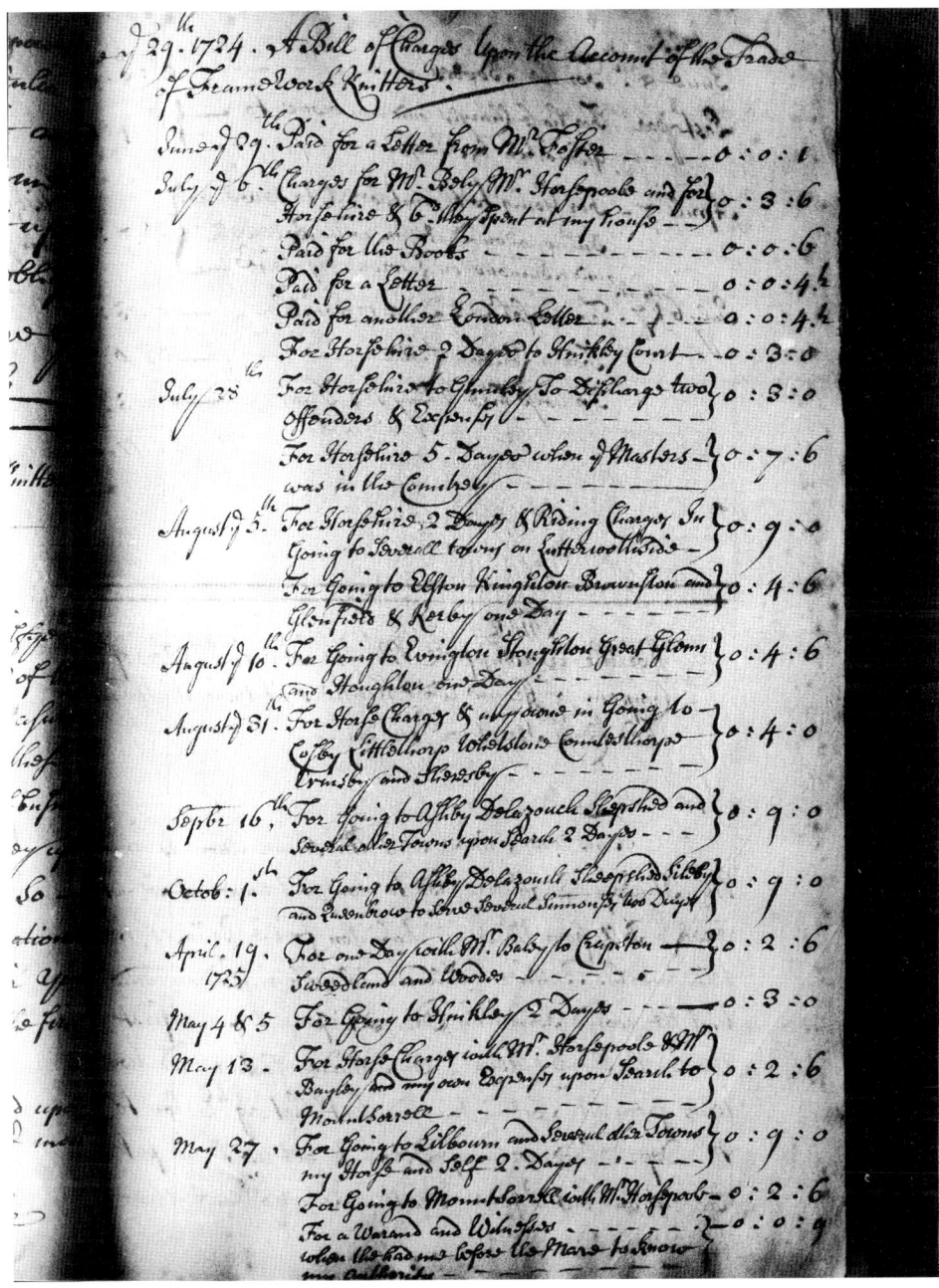

PLATE 29   *F.W.K. MSS.*

1724 ACCOUNTS OF THE DEPUTY BEADLE CONYERS WHITE

These accounts are clearly indicative of the wide spread of Company business. On 6 July the Deputy Beadle hired a horse for two days for the Hinckley Court. On 28 July he had to hire another horse to go to Grimsby, while 10 August he went to the south east of Leicester, to Evington, Stoughton, Great Glen and Houghton.

Master Roger Broome wrote to the Deputies at Nottingham and Hinckley asking them to 'doe the Affairs of the Company without any Charge or Expenses'; and, to show that London was also curtailing expenses, Nottingham and Hinckley were sent a copy of the May 1727 edict that no 'dinner, drink or provision whatsoever' was to be provided at the Hall or in any other place the Company did business. This total prohibition was replaced on 3 April 1729 with one forbidding the Renter Warden to spend a total of more than £3 per dinner at each of the two general quarterly Courts and no more than £1 5s. at the private monthly Court which only six Assistants, in addition to the Master and Wardens, were allowed to attend; if more was spent the Renter Warden was personally responsible for the deficiency.[13]

Far more serious than the loss of dinners and non-payment of officials, however, was the fact that the depletion of the accumulated funds hindered the Company in its chartered work – the regulation of framework knitting – at a time when general public opinion was turning against restrictive trade practices and hosiers and other influential people throughout the country, as well as unadmitted framework knitters, were actively opposing the complete regulation of such an important and widespread manufacturing industry by an oligarchy in London.

The methods the Court pursued to replenish its coffers, although perfectly within its Charter rights, fuelled the trade's resentment for it was probably the first time that many framework knitters realised just how all-encompassing the powers of the Company were. In 1722, when it tried to put its administration in order and regularise the payment of the membership fees owed by all frameworkers, only 4,297 members were listed of whom only a very small minority were up-to-date with quarterage. Ninety-nine men owed twenty or more years membership dues – (£2. 0. 0. plus) – with Thomas Rimmington owing back to 1694, and at a Court held in Godalming, Surrey, in August 1729 forty nine knitters were required to pay back dues of 6s. (3 years), or more.[14]

Just as the Company had been slack in collecting membership fees from the knitters it had also been remiss in pursuing transgressors of the Bye-laws; the Court at London blamed the provincial Courts for the contraventions, while the Deputies blamed London. There were, apparently, offenders in nearly every town and village in the country in which framework knitting was carried on and it was calculated that there were over 200 offenders in the East Midlands alone, although no-one could agree on which was the most heinous crime. The Deputy Clerk at Hinckley, John Foster, felt that two of the worst problems were Freemen teaching the trade to unbound persons for money and those who were out of their apprenticeship taking apprentices before they were admitted to the Company, contrary to Bye-laws 16 and 17; while elsewhere it was thought that women working frames was one of the worst offences. Although London assured the Hinckley Clerk and others that 'a considerable number of each sort of the same summons printed blank . . . lye ready at the Hall to be filled up', officers in the East Midlands and Surrey, as well as ordinary members, such as John Stanley and John Drayton, stewards of a club of framework knitters in Nottingham, were wondering why, if no-one was prosecuted, they did not save money by leaving the Company. However, it would seem that, as well as being so overwhelmed by the number of offenders that it dithered over which cases could be brought to the most successful conclusion, much of this procrastination was caused by the shortage of money, so that the Company could not always pay lawyers to prosecute cases.[15]

Even when the Company did eventually bring cases to trial they were rejected by the courts. In the prosecution against Blacknall of Calverton in 1726 the Company was nonsuited, even though Lord Chief Justice Eyre declared the Charter and Bye-laws were 'good and reasonable', because in the Charter Pa(r)giter was spelt without an 'r' while in the Declaration he was spelt with an 'r'. After this set-back the Clerk was forced to write to Samuel Spray, a Deputy at Nottingham, instructing him to assure the East Midlands that 'upon the encouragement from the Lord Chief Justice the Master and Wardens have given directions for Writts to be sent down against some other offenders the next week'.[16]

Usually the Company seems to have become so tangled up in lengthy consultations that most prosecutions took so long that few achieved their objective. Because some of the worst offenders against the Bye-laws were in Leicestershire, in 1727 a case was prepared to prosecute Thomas Gregory of Leicester who, after serving his apprenticeship, was working as a framework knitter without having taken up his Freedom, and who had also 'publically affronted' Captain Broome the Master, 'in ill language'. This prosecution dragged on for about two years and when, eventually, summoned to appear before the Master and Wardens in Red Cross Street Gregory did not turn up, the Company appears to have just dropped the case.[17]

However, a few times the threat of prosecution brought submissions to the Company. After the abortive attempt to prosecute Blacknall his two sons joined in 1726, and following the serving of a writ by the Derbyshire Deputy, John Bloodworth, Josiah Harvey of Ashbourne regularised his position in 1729.[18]

By 1728 some of the Deputies in the East Midlands felt that they received so little help from London that they had become disillusioned with the Company and could see little point in continuing in office. In September 1728 Samuel Spray refused to go on acting as Treasurer of the Nottingham Court and in the same month the Courts held at Leicester and Hinckley were cancelled and the Deputies dismissed. In June 1729 this discontinuation was advertised locally and all members were told to report to Nottingham as formerly, with the Nottingham-based Deputies instructed by London to cover Leicestershire and Warwickshire as well as Nottinghamshire and Derbyshire. Then in June 1730 London changed its mind, the Leicester and Hinckley Courts were reinstated and three new Deputies, John Stephenson of Hinckley, William Hurst of Leicester and William Pagett of Leicester were appointed, together with the same Deputy Clerk and Beadle as previously.[19]

While procedures were being sorted out in the East Midlands, the London Court joined with Nottingham members in a petition to Parliament on 29 October 1728 against journeymen 'embezzling and selling goods and for punishing offenders and redressing other Grievances'. At a cost of four guineas Serjeant Darnell advised the Company that, as it did not have sufficient powers to control the trade, it had reasonable grounds to apply to Parliament. He also made the suggestion, not taken up by the Court, that corporal punishment rather than fines would 'bring the poorer sort (of framework knitters) . . . under greater subjection'. A list of required regulations were drawn up by both London and Nottingham, and in this instance the Company was supported in Nottingham by a number of prominent local figures and leading masters in the trade, including the Mayor and four Aldermen of Nottingham, plus Sir Thomas Parkyns of Bunny and Mr. Musters.[20]

Although on 20 January the following year London suspended work on the petition to Parliament, the Court continued to exercise its authority and pursue transgressors of the Bye-laws; an irregular workhouse and unqualified apprentices in Farnham were investigated, two framework knitters working at the trade without being members of the Company were sued, another who had been a bound apprentice, but who had not been admitted as a Freeman, was accused of binding apprentices, and yet another was charged with apprenticing his daughter to the trade. In April 1729 the Master, Michael Mitchell, had written to former Deputy Bayley in Leicester 'It is the resolution of several . . . of our Court to try the point with respect to compelling persons exercising the trade and keeping workshops to be admitted, and first to begin with some unadmitted members in the town of Leicester . . . desiring you'll fix on some responsible person who hath served his apprenticeship to an admitted member and now keeps a workshop and carries on the trade, not being admitted, and if you can fix on a person who hath apprentices at work with him not regularly bound . . . so much the better'. Less than a month later a similar request went to the Deputies at Nottingham, when Master Mitchell also pointed out the futility of ridding London of unlawful workers because 'the evil is not removed; but only shifted' if the Deputies did not also do their job. However, although the Nottingham Courts continued to operate, and in the first half of 1729 bound forty apprentices, no action on either the petition or the Master's requests had been taken by either Nottingham or Leicester by the December. Matters between the East Midlands and London had now reached such a low ebb that on 15 December the East Midland Deputies refused to set up any fund before seeing an Abstract of the proposed Bill and, to show that their intentions were serious, the London Court each had to subscribe £1 11s. 6d. of the money required to obtain an Act of Parliament.[21]

Eventually in 1730 the Company decided to take action against two of the most notorious offenders against the apprentice Bye-laws. Although there is considerable confusion about the subsequent course of events between Gravenor Henson, William Felkin and John Blackner, all writing in the nineteenth century, and the Company's contemporary, but incomplete, documents, it would seem that it was decided that these Bye-laws should be enforced against Cartwright and Fellows, both of whom had migrated from London to Nottingham after the 1710 framebreaking. The fines owing from Cartwright apparently amounted to £150, and from Fellows £400, and, when those of the former were not paid, the Deputy Beadle was instructed to enter Cartwright's premises to seize and sell his goods and frames as directed in the Bye-laws. Because of the former dilatoriness of the Company it had become the custom to employ too many unbound apprentices, many of them paupers, who, when their time expired, were discharged in favour of other parish apprentices for whom the master was paid £5, and the Nottingham civic authorities, fearing that one method of cheaply getting rid of paupers would vanish, supported Cartwright when he brought an action for trespass against Deputy Wright. It was proposed by the Company's opponents that Cartwright should bind an apprentice, Charles Wood, and then bring one action against the Company's local Treasurer for demanding more fees than were allowed by a current Act of Parliament, and another for excessively high Admittance Fees. The threat of these actions so frightened the Nottingham Deputies that they asked the London Court for indemnity. When the case was eventually heard the following February, the Company was again nonsuited; the Judge not accepting the legality of the Bye-laws, even though they had been signed by the Lord Chancellor and two Judges. The Company threatened to take the whole matter before the King's Bench, but again seem not to have followed through, partly because of cost and partly because the Court now admitted privately that it would seem that 'the unadmitted are not compellable to be admitted by virtue of any by-laws . . . that must be done by authority of Parliament'.[22]

New Company Bye-laws were therefore proposed by the London Court and copies sent to the Deputies in the East Midlands for comment. The Nottingham Deputies 'compared them with the old ones and upon considerate perusal approve them and think them very reasonable', while the Leicestershire Deputies, Stephenson, Hurst and Pagett, made detailed comments, especially on those which applied to the general membership. However, even while these deliberations were going on, the London Court showed its weakness and suspended the pursuit of other Bye-law offenders, with the result that relationships between the Company and the Deputies deteriorated further. In November 1731 the four Nottingham Deputies, John Wright, William Wilson, John Bloodworth and William Robinson, complained that the London Court 'makes us look very little, and discovers a great Mistrust of us' and reported that 'Our Business is very small at Present. We have had but Two bound Today, and Two last Court, and none the Court before that'. In the December all seven Deputies queried 'whether it is proper for us to hold Courts any longer, to take and exact Money from such few poor honest Neighbours, as wish well to the Court, whilst almost all others refuse to obey any Summons, and bid open Defiance to the Court, . . . we are unanimous in our Resolution to act as Deputies no longer than next Court Day, which finish the Half Year . . . (although) we shall be ready to advise and assist to the best of our Power, in our respective Neighbourhoods'.[23]

Although the East Midlands Deputies seem to have continued the promised individual contact with London and to discuss the Bye-law proposals, no Courts were held in Nottingham, Leicester or Hinckley between 1732 and 1745 and no Freedom enrolments are recorded for the years 1731 to 1744. Framework knitting in the East Midlands was therefore not controlled during these years by the rules of the Company and more than 1,600 frames were apparently taken from London to the East Midlands during this period, thus establishing a large, unregulated, trade. In the south London held a Court in Godalming in 1734 where it brought actions against two persons, but as 'the known invalidity of their Bye-laws strengthened resistance' it was no more successful there than it had been up north, and no further Courts were held in Godalming until 1751.[24]

The 1745 Bye-laws

The discussions which had occupied the Company's time since the late 1720s came to an end in January 1744 when draft Bye-laws were finally approved by a Court of Assistants held at The White Hart Tavern, Bishopsgate, and sent to the Law Lords for their approval (see Plate 30).

On 19 June 1745, at a Court held at the Paul's Head Tavern, the Court was informed that Lord Chancellor Hardwick and the Chief Justice of the King's Bench, Sir William Lee, and of the Court of Common Pleas, Sir John Willes, had approved and confirmed the new Bye-laws, making them valid in law. An Abstract

PLATE 30   *lent by S. A. Mason*

THE WHITE HART TAVERN, BISHOPSGATE

This inn was one of many in the City of London used for Court meetings after the Framework
Knitters' leased out their Hall. The revised Ordinances of the Company were accepted by the
Court in this tavern in 1745.

was immediately printed and distributed to members of the Company (Appendix 5
gives the 1745 Table of Orders, Rules and Ordinances).[25]
    Although the number of clauses was shortened from forty to thirty one, these
Bye-laws of 1745 are remarkably similar to those of 1664. Most of the Company's
most restrictive legal powers, including the power to search premises to prove all
framework knitted goods, (Clause 14), and the confining of hiring out of frames to
members of the Company, (Clause 15), were retained. Nevertheless some grievances were addressed. Stewards providing at their own expense the Company's
feasts on Michaelmas Day were now no longer drawn from anywhere in England
and Wales but had to come from within a forty mile radius of London (Clause 8).
Some fines were reduced, so that the employment of foreigners or aliens now cost
only £10, instead of £40, (Clause 19) and the turning over of apprentices was
reduced from £3 to £2. (Clause 21) Most significantly the payment of quarterage
was altered, masters continuing to pay 6d. a quarter, while journeymen were to pay
only 3d. (Clause 26).

Post-1745 Bye-laws

After engrossment the Company began to take steps to put the revised Bye-laws into
operation, starting in London against Hollingworth of Spitalfields who was sum-

moned to take up his Freedom in October 1746. When he refused the Company, although hindered by the permanent shortage of money, instituted proceedings against him and four other masters for the offence of not taking up their Freedoms, proceeded against other masters for keeping 'unlawful workers', while another was told he was not allowed to have any frames. In January 1749/50 a general order was given to the Clerk to prosecute all offenders in the London area if they did not answer their summons. This so frightened one of the offenders, Jacobs, who had purchased frames and set himself up as a master stockinger using 'little other than embezzled materials', that he immediately took up his Freedom. Fortunately for the Company, 'his example was followed by the whole of the dissentient parties in London', although it would seem that little was done to collect quarterage, for in the ten years before 1753 the total was 'considerably short of One Hundred Pounds'.[26]

The Company also set up a committee consisting of the Master, Wardens, and Assistants West, Robinson, Spencer, Cole and Al(l)cock to prosecute offenders against the Bye-laws outside London and, although the rebellion of 1745 hindered this for a short time, in the early fifties they journeyed to Towcester. The 'trade in Northamptonshire gave them no trouble' for in 1751 ten took up their Freedoms in Towcester and nine in Northampton. Then the Master, now Richard West, together with Wardens and Assistants, held Courts in several towns in Hampshire, Buckinghamshire, Sussex and in Godalming, Surrey, to enrol knitters and to demand back payment of quarterage. No Court had been held in Godalming since 1734 and, although framework knitting there was extensive, there were now few members. However, here the payment of back-dated quarterage was resisted by the poorly paid journeymen and few joined, with the result that, after meeting little opposition to their demands at other Courts in Odiham, Oakingham, Reading and Berkhamstead, the officers on their return to London decided to proceed against two journeymen members of Godalming, John Toft and Henry Moore, although to do so they had to borrow £50 from members of the Court. This prosecution so angered many in the Godalming area, including parish officials who feared that the Company might prevent their apprenticing paupers, that it was decided to raise a public subscription to defend the actions. This opposition caused the Company to follow its practice of earlier in the century and suspend proceedings with the excuse that it did not have all the necessary proofs, although in fact shortage of money would again seem to have been the major reason.[27]

Some contact had been maintained by the London Court with the East Midlands where, since 1732, many local hosiers had become worried about London retail hosiers establishing unregulated shops of frames run by journeymen. On 20 June 1745, the day after the new Bye-laws were approved, James Dymock, an Assistant of the Company with trading connections with Nottingham, was sent by the Court to invite William Seagrave, an attorney connected with the Calverton/Oxton area north east of Nottingham, to be the Deputy Clerk at Nottingham to cover Derbyshire, Leicestershire and Warwickshire, and to 'consult proper persons' to be the Deputies in Nottinghamshire and Derbyshire and to recommend Deputies for Leicestershire and Warwickshire. In the July John Wright, who had previously been a Deputy, Samuel Fellows, who had in 1730 been attacked for having too many apprentices, Thomas Cox and Thomas Haywood were appointed to the Nottingham positions, while Samuel Robinson, the brother of Warden Thomas Robinson, became the Deputy Beadle. London recommended that the Crown Inn on Long Row be used for holding Court 'as the Young Man is a Son of a framework knitter and intends to be admitted himself', and requested that after the business of the first meeting was over the principal employers should be invited to a collation.[28]

The chosen Deputies were obviously reluctant to act for the Company as Seagrave, writing in 1750, stated that he did not find 'any of the Gentlemen here are so well disposed towards the Regulation, as they were some Years ago', and the East Midland officials often changed. In May 1751 John Wright, Thomas Haywood, Humphrey Cox, Thomas Twells and Samuel Fellows were appointed Deputies in Nottingham, by September Fellows had been replaced by John Killingley, and George Iliffe of Leicester added to the list. There was difficulty in finding more Deputies willing to serve in Leicestershire, Warwickshire and Derbyshire and in September 1751 it would appear that there was only the one Deputy in Leicester, and Thomas Haywood, one of the Deputies for Nottinghamshire, agreed to act for Derby 'until you can get one regularly'. Although the normal business of binding apprentices and admitting members continued Seagrave felt that it was not carried on with enthusiasm, and to encourage the Deputies it was agreed in October 1751 that each should be paid five shillings for attendance at the monthly provincial Courts. He also wanted the London Court to visit Nottingham to inspire the Deputies, and to strengthen the team by appointing a framesmith, Mr. Stamford, as a Deputy.[29]

The Master, Wardens and Assistants arrived in Nottingham in August 1752 and on the fifteenth published an address to all East Midlands framework knitters. At a crowded meeting at the Crown Inn the Company was vehemently opposed by the hosiers. On the urging of the local Deputies, the Court then tried to win over the journeymen through remission of the ten shillings admission fee and allow anyone hiring frames 'of an Employer' to be admitted to the Company for only five shillings – two shillings stamp duty, the Clerk's fee of two shillings and the Beadle's fee of one shilling. The journeymen were also assured that, although quarterage was 'but threepence' under the new Bye-laws, this fee would be rescinded for 'any of the poor men' as it was 'thought sufficient to call on those who keep frames or apprentices'.

However, in spite of the exhortations of journeymen members of the Company, such as Villiers and Holland, to form a trade community to fight for improvements in working conditions and pay within the industry, the Company had little success. Most ordinary framework knitters were convinced that the Company regarded them as a source of revenue while doing nothing to stem the abuses in the trade, and only nineteen took up their Freedom, which included five who had served apprenticeships. Many knitters now felt that it was not worth either joining or continuing in the Company as it could give them little or no support against the entrepreneurs who controlled production, for to secure work knitters with their own frames now had to pay 'rent' to hosiers or bagmen. Under the Ordinances frames were only to be hired out by and from members of the Company, but with the growth in the number of hosiers and bagmen this rule was almost universally flouted, which led to a great deal of ill feeling for which the ordinary framework knitter, incorrectly, blamed the Company.[30]

Opposition to the new Bye-laws

The Bye-laws engrossed in 1745 aroused such fury among the entrepreneurs, who objected to the limitations these placed on their businesses, and the gentry, who would suffer financially if the poor could not be put to work and poor rates were to rise, that by 1753 they had very effectively organised countrywide almost simultaneous opposition to the Company and vociferously petitioned the House of Commons. On 15 February three petitions against the Company bombarded the House from persons employed in the business of framework knitting in Nottingham, Godalming, Guildford and other places in Surrey, plus several gentlemen and inhabitants of Surrey; on 20 February the 'principal freeholders and several tradesmen of diverse occupations' in Nottingham sent in their petition attacking the Company, followed on 27 February by 'the Frame-work Knitters, or Dealers in the Trade and Business of working Hose, and other Commodities, upon Stocking-frames' of Nottinghamshire, and several hosiers and knitters of the Cities of London and Westminster. The petitions against the Company from the area around Mansfield and from persons 'employed and concerned in the Manufactures of Wool, Thread, Silk, and Cotton' of Leicestershire arrived on 1 and 2 March respectively. All the petitions were written in similar inflammatory language and complained about the Company's 'pernicious schemes', and the arbitrary nature of the new Bye-laws. Nottingham argued that these were 'against all reason, and contrary to the general Liberty of the subjects of Great Britain' which would 'greatly affect the trade of this kingdom, unless the poor manufacturers meet with the protection and assistance of the House', while Godalming referred to 'the decay of the said manufactury' and 'greater burthens on the . . . parishes'. On 15 February, the same day as the first three petitions were received, a Committee of the House of Commons was formed consisting of sixty four 'impartial' Members of Parliament, plus others from all the counties connected with knitting – Nottingham, York, Surrey, Leicester, Gloucester, Norfolk, Northampton, Warwick, Westmorland, Wiltshire, Derby, Worcester, Dorset, Middlesex, Somerset, and Wales.[31]

The Master, Wardens, Assistants and backers from the City of London counter-petitioned the House of Commons on 20 February and were supported by frame-work knitters from Nottingham on 26 February. The Company stated that its Bye-laws were 'best calculated to advance and improve the said Manufactory' and that as it was 'of the utmost Importance to the Trade of this Kingdom . . . some further Regulations are necessary to be made therein for restoring the Credit thereof' and asking that 'the House would be pleased to give Leave, That a bill may be brought in for regulating the said Trade, in such manner as to the House shall seem meet'. While the journeymen of Nottingham argued that they knew of no Bye-laws 'that have tended to the Discouragement of the said Trade . . . or oppress or injure the said Manufacture', and wanted several of the Bye-laws, especially those pertaining to apprentices, 'to be more strictly enforced'.[32]

This small amount of support for the Company was counteracted by the vast amount of evidence attacking it and its Bye-laws for being a restraint on trade. It was argued that 'the more any Trade is laid open, the better it is for that Trade, and for the Nation in general', and 'to shew that the Company have endeavoured to introduce and establish a Monopoly' the 1720s Joint Stock Company's affairs were rehashed. In addition the Minute and Letter Books of the Company were used extensively in such a way that the Company was made its own prosecutor for many of the extracts quoted showed the Company recognising its own limitations and not enforcing the Bye-laws. A letter written by the Clerk of the Company on the instructions of the Master and a committee in 1732 was used to show 'that the Company themselves have been of the Opinion, that the By-laws, by them made, cannot affect any but their own Members'. The Company's officials were also attacked, in many cases for not observing the Bye-laws. The stocking-making Deputies of Nottingham were accused of employing persons 'not free of the Company', including women and children, and further criticised for admitting to the Company anyone who paid to the Company, whether or not they had served an apprenticeship.[33]

After hearing all the evidence the Committee of the House of Commons reached six resolutions.

'1st. That it is the opinion of this Committee, that the several persons employed in frame-work-knitting in the town of Nottingham, who have petitioned against the Company of Frame-Work-Knitters, have fully proved the allegations of their petition.

'2nd. That the petitioners from Surrey have fully proved the allegations in their petition.

'3rd. That it is the opinion of this Committee, that the bye-laws of the Company of Frame-Work-Knitters, incorporated by a charter, bearing the date 19th August in the 15th year of the reign of Charles II, are injurious and vexatious to the manufacturers, and tend to the discouragement of the industry, and to the decay of the said manufacture.

'4th. That it is the opinion of this Committee, that many of the said bye-laws are illegal, and contrary to the liberty of the subject.

'5th. That it is the opinion of this Committee, that the powers granted by the said charter are hurtful to the trade, and tend to a monopoly.

'6th. That it is the opinion of this Committee, that the carrying on vexatious prosecutions against any person, male or female, for exercising the art and mystery of frame-work-knitting, is hurtful to the manufacturer, and destructive to the trade of the kingdom'.[34]

On 19 April the House of Commons agreed to the first, second, third, fifth and sixth resolutions but, even after a second reading, postponed the decision on the fourth resolution. The legal status of the Bye-laws remained, although the wording of the other resolutions deprived the Company of almost any expectation of reinforcing its authority over the industry in the future.

Composition of the Company 1700–1753

During the first half of the eighteenth century continuity still remained from beginning of the industry and the establishment of the Company. A number of families still had connections in both London and Nottingham. Joseph Rossell, the Master in 1729 and 1730, was one to whom this applied for in the 1690s/early 1700s Rossells were masters and apprentices in both cities. However, the previously close relationship between Nottinghamshire and London framework knitting families was growing weaker in most instances. By the middle of the century it was often no longer immediate family – brother, son, father or first cousins – who were involved in framework knitting and the Company's affairs in both London and the East Midlands; even when the same surnames reoccur persons would seem to be often only distantly related.[35]

The Court

During this period, when the opponents of the Company increasingly portrayed its hierarchy as a self-perpetuating oligarchy, 'more intent upon feasting and obtaining money' than in the good of the trade, it should not be forgotten that the leaders of the Society were, in the main, still working master framework knitters, who were themselves fighting for survival at a time when fashion had turned against the principal knitted product of London – knitting dyed to match fashionable garments – and frames were being taken away from London. Gravenor Henson claimed that by about 1703 the Assistants were 'composed part of framework-knitters and the remainder of persons who had bought their livery for the sake of the vote', but, although this might be a more accurate description of the Livery in 1831 when he wrote, this assertion is not borne out by the known occupations of the forty seven Assistants listed in the Company's quarterage records of 1722. All would appear to have been members of families originally connected with framework knitting and in all known cases were themselves apprenticed as framework knitters, although it is not impossible that by 1722 some were following other occupations. The same is true of the known Masters of the first half of the eighteenth century, and some still went back to the beginning of the industry. John Thompson, the Master in 1731 claimed one ancestor who had been Warden in 1694 and another who had been journeyman to William Lee, while Thomas Bourne, the Master of 1726 whose legacy paid for the Company's Almshouses, had had as grandfather, or father, Francis Bourne one of whose apprentices had been the son of Thomas Stevenson, Assistant in 1663 (see Plate 20 and Appendix 8).[36]

Freemen

The Company's overall governance of framework knitting during this period was not helped by the fact that, in spite of the monopolistic rules, not all framework knitters were members of the Company, and as the eighteenth century advanced the percentage who did not take up the Freedom increased. If the figures are nearly accurate for 1714 (Table 5.1), then by 1722, when only 4,295 Freemen are listed for quarterage, about half of the framework knitters in the country were not members of the Company. Most of these unregulated knitters would seem to come from outside London. Of the 3,248 whose status within the Company is recorded in 1722 1,894 were Freemen of the City of London and 1,354, only about a third of the total, were foreign brothers when this should have been the largest category, so that it would seem that the Company was subject to the indifference, even if not active opposition, of a large percentage of framework knitters outside London within the first quarter of the eighteenth century; as can be seen from Tables 5.1 and 5.2, many of the counties accepted by the House of Commons in 1753 as having frames had no members of the Society at all.

Yet in spite of this underlying dissatisfaction recruitment to the Company continued both in London and the East Midlands between 1712 and 1731, as can be seen from Table 5.2. Up to 1731 by far the largest recruitment occurred in Nottingham where in 1717 and part of 1718 only 17 per cent of masters were recorded as 'Citizens', while 71 per cent were 'foreign brothers'. The year 1722, when the Company was trying to sort out its administration, was the year with the highest number of admissions; Nottingham enrolled fifty-four, Hinckley twenty and Leicester two. After 1744, when few Courts were held outside London, the

***Table 5.2* Number and place of recorded enrolments as Freemen of the Framework Knitters'
         Company: 1712–1752**

	1712–1731	*1733–1744*	*1745–1752*
London –	4		69
Nottingham –	868	N	4
Leicester –	93		1
Hinckley –	60	O	0
Derby –	39		0
Ashby-de-la-Zouch	2	N	0
Southampton			1
Northampton		E	14
Hants.			1
Bucks.			1

Source MSS. 3447.

small number of Freedoms taken up were mostly sworn in London. So little money was raised by the Company after 1731 that in 1742 the Court of Assistants resolved to give a guinea to any member who could persuade anyone to take up the Freedom of the Company although, as the figures show, even this inducement had little effect.[37]

Apprentices

As well as most Freemen coming from Nottingham in the opening years of the century the largest number of apprentices also came from there. Between January 1699/1700 and June 1705, 849 apprentices were bound at Nottingham compared to 397 in London.[38]

The records are then missing until 1718 when there is also a change in format; there now being no indication of where the apprentices were bound except for an 'L' and a 'C' in the margin, which would seem to represent those in London and those bound in the rest of the country respectively. There were 323 in 'L' and 168 in 'C' who were bound between 2 March 1718 and 20 July 1725 suggesting that few framework knitters outside London were now registering apprentices with the Company. In the period 1727–30, of the 217 boys bound apprentice forty-eight came from the East Midlands while possibly up to 124 came from the London area even though knitting in London was on the decrease; there were no known apprentices from Leicestershire. By 1744 apprentices in Nottinghamshire were also not being bound through the Framework Knitters' Company for when William Wilson was apprenticed to the framework knitter Thomas Allen of Arnold, the binding was not recorded on a Company form and taxes were paid directly to the stamp office at 8 Lincoln's Inn, London.[39]

The Company paid for 270 apprentices between 8 November 1749 and 18 June 1787, but as many of the details in the apprenticeship manuscripts appear to have been written retrospectively to satisfy the spasmodic collection of the Orphan's Tax, it is uncertain how accurate these figures are.[40]

Almshouses

Although the first half of the eighteenth century saw the Company's control of framework knitting diminishing, it also saw the foundation of the Company's most permanent monument – its Almshouses (see Plates 31 and 32). Although almshouses for six poor framework knitters were provided in Nottingham by Deputy Jonathan Labray his charity was not administered by the Company, nor were his houses completed until two years after those for the Company in London were started.[41]

In his will, proved in 1729, Thomas Bourne, the Master of 1726, left £3,000 for erecting, building and maintaining Almshouses within five miles of London for twelve poor Freemen, or Widows of Freemen, of the Worshipful Company of Framework Knitters, to be chosen by the Court. The purchase price of the ground was not to exceed £1,000, with the residue of the money being invested for maintenance and to provide a pension for the residents. On 14 February 1732 a Chancery Suit, instituted in 1729, finally directed the Charity to be carried into effect, although it was another two years before action was taken.

The Company sited its Almshouses on the east side of Kingsland Road, Hoxton, in an area of gardens and open fields favoured by other Companies for their own Almshouses. Immediately to the south of the Framework Knitters' were the Almshouses of the Ironmongers' Company built in 1712, (which can still be seen), while nearer London were the ones erected in 1713 by the Drapers' Company (see Plate 31).

On 29 June 1734 freehold land costing £145 'containing in length, from south to north, fronting the said road, two hundred feet, and in depth from west to east one hundred feet, adjoining north on certain almshouses belonging to the Company of Ironmongers', was sold to the Framework Knitters' Company Trustees of Bourne's Charity. Originally these trustees were Richard Austin, Roger Broome, John Thompson, Samuel Gourd, Thomas Robinson, John Withrington and Richard West. By 1745 only Thomas Robinson and Richard West remained of the original trustees and they were joined by Charles Cole, William Spencer, William Hubbald, Thomas Beighton and James Dymock. Eventually, in December 1740, Thomas Bourne's bequest was completed when £2,009 16s. 9d. of the remaining £2,223 7s. 6d., was invested in Old South Sea Annuities.[42]

The Almshouses were built in sections, for when Richard Horwood surveyed the area in 1799 the two most southerly dwellings were not depicted, and eventually consisted of twelve cottages, each of one storey plus basement forming three sides of a rectangle. The space between the Almshouses and Kingsland Road was occupied by a communal garden, with allotment gardens at the rear. The cottages were built of red brick, with gaged brick dressings and a moulded deal medallion cornice to the eaves, and were covered with a tile roof. The two central cottages were slightly advanced to form a projection in the façade and formed the central feature under a low-pitched pediment containing a commemorative panel. An elliptical-arched passageway through the centre gave access down a flight of steps to the allotments, which being at a lower level than the front, gave light and access to the basement of the main block. The north and south wings obtained light for their basements from front windows placed high up in the room and overlooking the gardens. At the time of building all would seem to have had two rooms on the ground floor, with a staircase leading to the wash-house in the basement; later, except for Numbers 1 and 12, these two rooms were converted into one large room. Numbers 6 and 10 also had attics with dormer windows in the rear.[43]

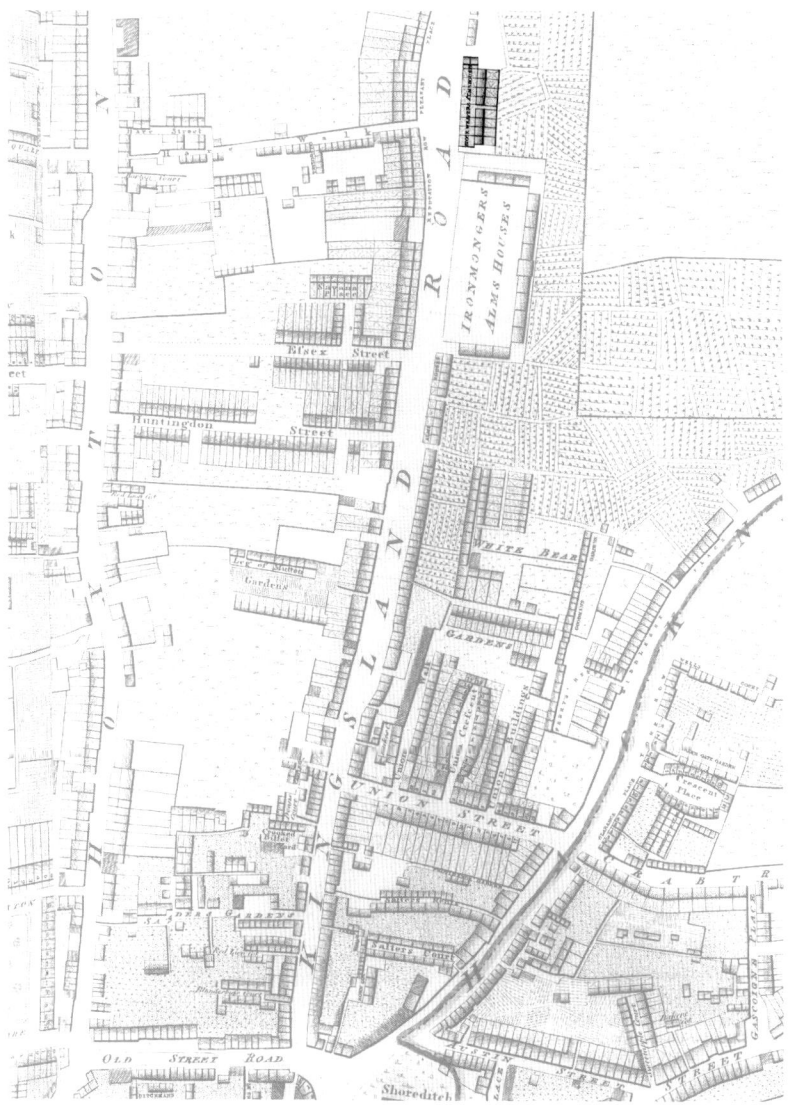

repr. with permission from the Guildhall Library, Corporation of London

PLATE 31

1799 MAP OF LONDON BY RICHARD HORWOOD SHOWING THE LONDON ALMSHOUSES

This map shows ten of the twelve Framework Knitters' Almshouses on the east side of Kingsland Road, immediately to the north of the Ironmongers' Almshouses, built in an area of gardens and open fields.

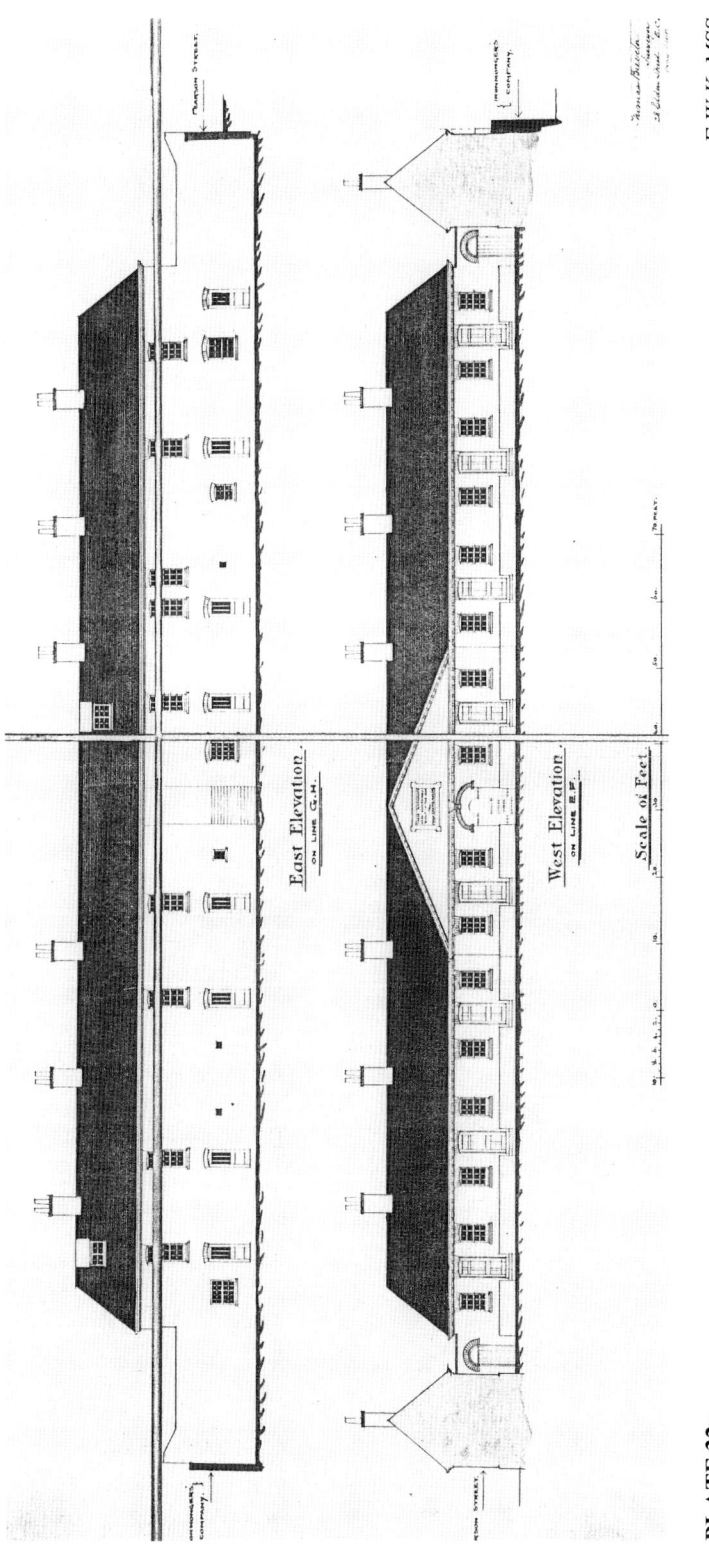

F. W. K. MSS.

PLATE 32a

THE LONDON ALMSHOUSES

(*a*) These drawings show the single storey, (west), elevation facing Kingsland Road, which incorporates the plaque giving details of construction, and the two storey elevation, (east), overlooking the rear gardens.

F.W.K. MSS.

PLATE 32b

THE LONDON ALMSHOUSES

A drawing of the front (west), of the London Almshouses presented to the Company by Sir John Peel.

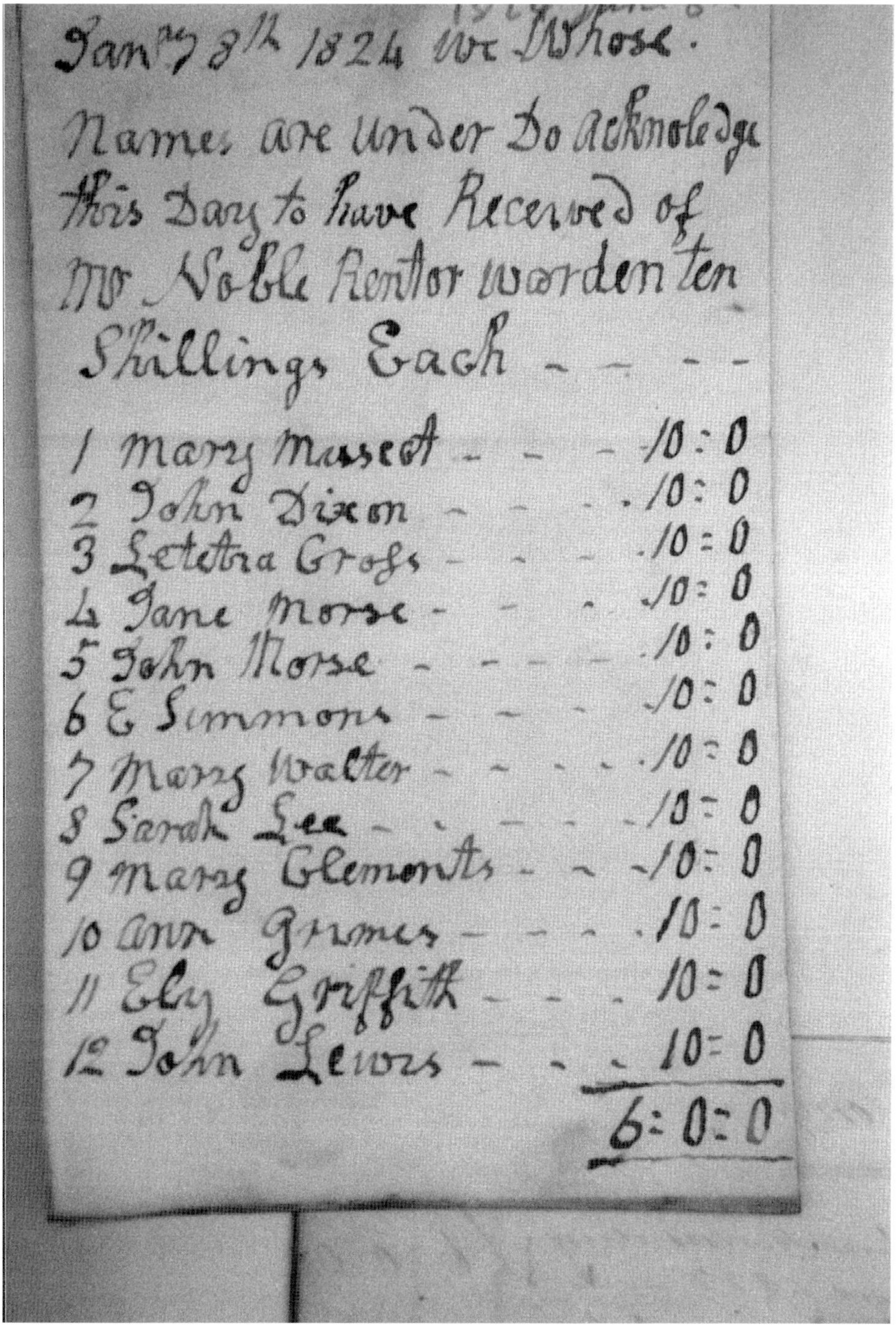

Jan'y 8th 1824 We Whose:

Names are under Do Acknoledge
this Day to have Recewed of
Mr Noble Rentor warden ten
Shillings Each — — — —

1 Mary Mascot — — —	10 : 0
2 John Dixon — — —	10 : 0
3 Letetia Gross — — —	10 : 0
4 Jane Morse — — —	10 : 0
5 John Morse — — —	10 : 0
6 E Simmons — — —	10 : 0
7 Mary Walter — — —	10 : 0
8 Sarah Lee — — —	10 : 0
9 Mary Clemonts — —	10 : 0
10 Ann Grimes — — —	10 : 0
11 Ely Griffith — —	10 : 0
12 John Lewis — — —	10 : 0
	6 : 0 : 0

PLATE 32c   *F.W.K. MSS.*

THE LONDON ALMSHOUSES

1824 receipt for pensions for the Almshouse inhabitants – including Sarah Lee.

On a tablet set into the front wall of the middle cottages was the following inscription:

"Thomas Bourne Esq., late Citizen and Framework Knitter of London having by Will given 3,000l. for the benefit of 12 poor Freemen of the Company of Framework Knitters in the City of London or of 12 poor persons part Freemen and part Widows of Freemen of the same Company to wit 1,000l. for Building and 2,000l. for Endowment. These Almshouses were accordingly built in the year 1734. Mr. John Crofts Master, Mr. John Withrington, Mr. Charles Kendall Wardens."[44]

The Hall

Although the Company continued to use the Hall after it was first mortgaged in 1717, and would seem to have hoped to redeem the pledge, it was never again free of encumbrance. The 1717 mortgage for ninety-nine years for £500, with annual interest of £50, was held by Peter Sharp, of St. Mary Magdalene, Whitechapel. After Sharp's death, Charles Jackson, an apothecary, was granted a mortgage on 16 February 1726 of £200, plus £20 interest, to be repaid by the Company on 16 February 1728. However, by February 1728 the Company had debts of £440 and John Medley, the son-in-law of Past Master William Hubbald, offered to lend the Company £500 on security of the Hall and the surrounding property, including the stables and the Golden Hind Tavern. The money raised was used to pay off all the debts, including those to William Pocklington and to John Foster the Deputy Clerk at Hinckley, with the remainder being retained in the Renter Wardens' accounts. Finances remained tight, however, for when the kitchen at the end of the garden and the passages leading from the street were repaired and the Hall painted in 1729 the work was to be carried out 'in the best and the cheapest manner'.[45]

From 1732 the Company's books show no further meetings in the Hall and from this time meetings were held in various of the City's taverns or in the Clerks' offices.[46]

Lord Mayor's parade 1729

One exception to the general restrictions on expenditure after 1720 was the participation in the Lord Mayor's parade in 1729 which cost the Society £7 19s. 6d., although no reason was given as to why it was decided that the Company should participate in this particular year. The Company had not paraded since 1718 and, although it did not take a stand, Master Joseph Rossell, Wardens Samuel Gourd and John Jackson, nineteen Assistants and fourteen Liverymen 'in their gowns with trophies, flags, streamers, standard bearers, and other officers', marched up Red Cross Street, through the Barbican and along Aldersgate Street, St. Martin le Grand, Newgate Street, and the Old Bailey, to Ludgate Hill, where Frederick, Prince of Wales viewed 'the several Company's passing and repassing and to whom this Company in their return up the hill paid their duty and compliments by loud huzzars having their hats off and shaking them in their hands with which his Royal Highness seemed well pleased'. The Company then continued through Ludgate Street, St. Paul's Church Yard, Cheapside, King Street, Lad Lane and

Wood Street 'to their Hall where they had a very elegant dinner and plenty of everything provided for them' by the Stewards for the day, Samuel Cupitt and Samuel Clouds. 'That which added much to the grandeur of their procession was the generous and costly gift of the two present wardens being a staff for the use of the Company's Beadle upon the top of which is fixed a large silver ball with an oval plate of silver standing thereon richly embossed and where is curiously engraved or wrought the figure of the frame with its supporters taken from the impression thereof made on the paper of the Company's ByLaws . . . the noble gift must not be forgot of the present master's kind benefaction of a purple gown to his Beadle'. Accompanying the Masters, Wardens, Assistants and Livery in the procession were eight whifflers and nine sidesmen, who were either apprentice or journeymen members of the Company and who were each paid 2s. 6d. A further £1 9s. 6d. was paid out to the streamer bearers, the Company carrying a great streamer, the kings', city's and union flags', and 'tailboards'.[47]

Summary

During the first half of the eighteenth century changes in political and economic thinking, in which influential opinions were increasingly swinging away from monopolies to more free trade, were beginning to outmanoeuvre the ability of the Company to control the industry, and although the debacle of the Joint Stock Company did not directly cause the eventual loss of the Company's complete control over framework knitting it certainly probably accelerated it.

References

 1 MSS, 3446.
 2 Deering, pp. 100–1.
 3 *JHC*, XIII, 19 January, 6 April 1699/1700.
 4 Henson, pp. 93–6, 98, 137.
 5 CLRO, Misc Mss. 1/18; *JHC*, XXVI, 19 April 1753; Hazlitt, p. 507.
 6 Henson, p. 97–8.
 7 *Records of the Borough of Leicester*, V, ed. by G. A. Chinnery (Leicester University Press: Leicester, 1965), p. 76.
 8 Henson, pp. 142–8; Felkin, 1845, p. 37; Felkin, p. 73.
 9 *JHC*, XXVI, 19 April 1753; Henson, p. 143.
10 MSS, 16840, 2 March 1726/27; *JHC*, 19 April 1753; Felkin, p. 74; Henson, p. 145.
11 Unwin, pp. 302–3.
12 *The Report from the Trustees of the South Sea Company to the Honourable House of Commons January 25th 1722* (London: Jacob Tomon, Bernard Lintot, William Taylor, 1724); Henson, p. 144.
13 MSS, 3446/2; 16840, pp. 5, 15–6, 114–6; 3442, pp. 23–4, 67–8, 72, 105.
14 MSS, 3444; 16840, 15 August 1729.
15 MSS, 3442, pp. 3, 4, 6–8, 15, 25–7, 52, 86, etc.; 16840, p. 86, 14 Feb. 1728/29.
16 MSS, 3442, 28 May 1726, pp. 48–51.
17 MSS, 3442, pp. 52, 79, 98, 104; 16840, 4 April 1727, pp. 12, 91.
18 MSS, 3442, 10 August 1726, 18 January 1728/29, p. 138.
19 MSS, 16840, 6 and 30 September 1728, 27 August 1729; 3442, 25 June 1730.
20 MSS, 16840, pp. 80, 85, 113; 3442, pp. 130–2, 155.
21 MSS, 16840, pp. 64, 112–5, 119–23, 156, 161, 163; 3442, pp. 163–5.
22 MSS, 3442, 14 October 1730, 25 February 1730/31, 4 December 1731, 20 May 1732/33; Felkin, p. 74; Henson, p. 96–8; Blackner, p. 216, has the case set it in 1734, Henson has it in

1723. In addition Henson's account is much more dramatic for he has the Beadle seizing the goods of both Cartwright and Fellows. However, it would seem unlikely that the Company would in 1750 appoint Samuel Fellows a Deputy of the Company, or for Fellows to accept that position, if the Company had taken such action against him in the 1730s.

23 MSS, 16840, p. 198; 3442, pp. 191, 198–200; *JHC*, XXVI, 19 April 1753.

24 MSS, 3442, pp. 202, 205; 3447; *JHC*, XXVI, 19 April 1753; Henson, p. 169; Felkin, p. 76.

25 *JHC*, XXVI, 19 April 1753.

26 Henson, pp. 181–2.

27 MSS, 3452/1, Brief in 1809 case WCFK v. Payne; 3445/2; 3447; Henson, pp. 182, 184–6.

28 MSS. 18116; 3442, 20 June, 22 July 1745; 3443, 22 July, 20 August 1745; 3444; NAO, MSS, 4041/17; DD 65 9–10; CA 4041/53; Henson, p. 186; Felkin, p. 83.

29 NAO, MSS, 4041/15 and 17; *JHC*, XXVI, 19 April 1753; Henson, p. 189.

30 NAO, MSS, CA 4041/17; *N(ottingham) W(eekly) C(ourant)*, 14, 19 October 1752; Henson, pp. 189, 190–2.

31 *JHC*, XXVI, pp. 593, 604, 606, 620, 624.

32 *JHC*, pp. 606, 615.

33 *JHC*, XXVI, pp. 781, 783, 785–7.

34 Felkin, p. 80.

35 MSS, 3446/1; CLGL, MSS, Weavers' 4657A/2; Henson, p. 137; Thoroton, pp. 142, 295.

36 MSS, 3444; 3446/1; Henson, pp. 90–91, 93.

37 MSS,. 3445; 3447; Henson, p. 186.

38 MSS, 3446/1.

39 MSS, 3446/2; 16840; NAO, MSS, DD 1933/1.

40 MSS, 3446/2.

41 MSS. 3451/ p. 406; 3452/5, 1900.

42 MSS, 3452/1; 3452/3, p. 52. *Old and New London*, V, part 2 (London: Cassell & Co., ?1883), p. 525.

43 MSS, 3452 – J. Funston, Clerk , 'Report on the distribution of the Charitable Fund', 1886, p. 4; John Woodhouse, Clerk, 'Report on Bourne's Charity', 24 June 1905; London County Council, *Survey of London*, VIII (London: B.T. Batsford, 1922), p. 132.

44 MSS, 3451/2, endpaper.

45 MSS, 16840 p. 101–3, 133.

46 John Timbs, *Curiosities of London* (London: Virtue, 1877), p. 422; P. H. Ditchfield, *The City Companies of London* (London: J. M. Dent, 1904), p. 261.

47 MSS, 16840, pp. 133, 150–2.

VI

The eclipse of the Company's total involvement in framework knitting: 1753–1809

The 1753 pronouncement by the House of Commons that the Bye-laws of the Worshipful Company of Framework Knitters were 'injurious and vexatious to the manufacturers' deprived the Company of any immediate idea of trying again to enforce its authority for, although not abandoning all involvement with the industry, it no longer actively enrolled members, and it was not until after the end of the century that it again embarked on a lawsuit.

Organisation of framework knitting

The years after the 1753 restrictions on Company activities saw a further large expansion in framework knitting in the East Midlands and Tewkesbury and another decrease in the number of frames in London and the south east. By 1782 the number of frames in the whole country amounted to some 20,000, three quarters of which were in the Midlands (see Table 6.1). Of the ten principal towns, listed by Deering as the main source of knitted production, Leicester was now noted chiefly for its woollen hosiery and made the largest quantity of goods, Derby was famous for silk and Nottingham for fine, mainly cotton, goods; London's expertise was in novelties for 'theatrical and other bizarre orders'. The occupation of hosier was now widespread and in Nottingham alone there were fifty hosiers and bagmen who traded directly to London, and others who dealt only with Leicester.[1]

Table 6.1 **The location and estimated number of frames in 1782**

Location	Number
Three Midland Counties (Leicestershire, Nottinghamshire, Derbyshire)	17,350
London	500
Surrey	200
Tewkesbury	650
Northamptonshire	300
Scotland	a few

Source: Felkin, *History*, p. 117.

Ireland

The number of frames in Ireland during the second half of the eighteenth century also increased considerably. In 1753 there were 500 and by 1782 about 1,500, with an estimated 700 in Dublin and another 300 in Cork. However, very few framework knitters living in Ireland continued to be members of the English and Welsh Company for now most belonged to the Irish Company incorporated by James II where, in stark contrast to the restrictions surrounding the English Company, they could bind an unlimited number of apprentices and were described as still making 'what laws they please for the Regulation of Trade and establishment of prices' in 1785.[2]

Enrolment in the Company 1753–1809

As can be seen in Table 6.2, during this half century of expansion of framework knitting there was a serious decline in the number entering the Company, either as Freemen or apprentices. After 1744 Courts were not held on a regular basis outside London and in most instances new members became both Freemen of the Company and of the City of London; few foreign brothers were enrolled.[3]

Only at the beginning of the 1800s, in the years immediately preceding Payne's trial, did the Company make a renewed effort to enrol more Freemen outside London and bind more apprentices. Between July 1802 to April 1806 sixteen were admitted as foreign brothers and thirteen apprentices were bound and at the end of July 1806 to mid-summer 1807, in the run-up to Payne's case, ninety two men from the East Midlands were admitted. In 1808 an additional thirty were admitted from Leicester and twenty from Loughborough.[4]

Table 6.2   **Number of enrolments as Freemen of the Framework Knitters' Company and Citizens of London: 1753–1809**

	1753–1799	*1800–1809*
London	329	44
Nottingham	2	
Berks.		1
Unrecorded	75	4

Source: Ms. 3447.

The Company and the industry after 1753

The admonitions by the House of Commons in 1753 destroyed the influence of the Company on working practices in framework knitting and mostly left the journeymen to fend for themselves. The situation was not improved by the almost continual shortage of money. When in 1768 £180 was needed urgently to pay three bills – Mrs. Love's annuity, Mr. Jones's interest and the Clerk – several of the Court again lent money without interest and, until the subscribed amount was paid off, only dinners paid for by the Stewards for Lord Mayor's Day and Midsummer Day were provided.[5]

However, in spite of its difficulties, the Company continued to have some Deputies in the East Midlands and be involved in issues affecting the hosiery trade. In 1765 it supported the British manufacturers of silk goods, including the hosiers of Nottingham, in successfully petitioning Parliament to protect the home manufacture of knitted silk goods by taking action against the large quantities of silk stockings, gloves and mitts coming in from abroad.[6]

Effect of the Company's curtailment of power

The journeymen realising that the Framework Knitters' Society could no longer act effectively on their behalf began to form their own organisations, often providing their members with documents which at first glance could have been produced by the Company (see Plate 33). In the mid-1770s an attempt was made to improve conditions by the formation in the East Midlands of the Stocking-makers' Association for Mutual Protection, also called the Amicable Association of Framework Knitters, which tried to emulate the Worshipful Company of Framework Knitters by endeavouring to enforce bye-laws, induce journeymen to take up the freedom of the Association and opposing anyone who had not served an apprenticeship.[7]

Although the Company's Court in London would seem to have given up any hope of a successful prosecution of an offender against its rules, it continued to support journeymen who were agitating to improve their conditions. In the election procession of 1778 in Nottingham two Assistants, Deputies, and Reynolds the Clerk of the Framework Knitters' Company, marched with the Association behind its sponsored candidate, Mr. Abel Smith, who was duly elected.[8]

Remuneration in the now unregulated industry had been falling steadily – decreasing between 1771 and 1778 from nine shillings per week to five shillings and sixpence – and the success of the Nottingham election prompted framework knitters throughout England to petition the House of Commons to bring in a bill to 'settle and regulate wages' arguing that, although they had served regular apprenticeships, they were unable to provide the common necessities of life due to low wages and the necessity to pay frame rent. Unfortunately for the journeymen less than a month later the hosiers counter-petitioned and their bill was lost.[9]

At this stage the Framework Knitters' Company was given a chance to act as a mediator between journeymen and hosiers and even revive the Charter. In May 1778 a leader of the journeymen's association, William Hallam, invited the Clerk of the Worshipful Company to come to Nottingham to make journeymen Free of the Company, but by August Reynolds, pleading business in Ireland, had still not arrived. After a meeting of journeymen on Nottingham's Forest Race Course, at which it was again decided to petition Parliament, Hallam travelled to London and with the leader of the London knitters, Rodgers, approached Reynolds, who informed them that the Freedom of the Company could not be taken up for less than five shillings a member (2s. stamp duty, 2s. for Reynolds as Clerk and 1s. for Simmons the Beadle). Eventually Hallam and Rodgers agreed to give Reynolds £50 and Simmons £20 so that the journeymen could be granted their Freedoms for half price. However, as the records of the Company show that only a single Freedom was granted in Nottingham in 1778 and none between 1779 and 1785, and there was only a total of sixty one Freedoms granted in London in 1778–9, it would

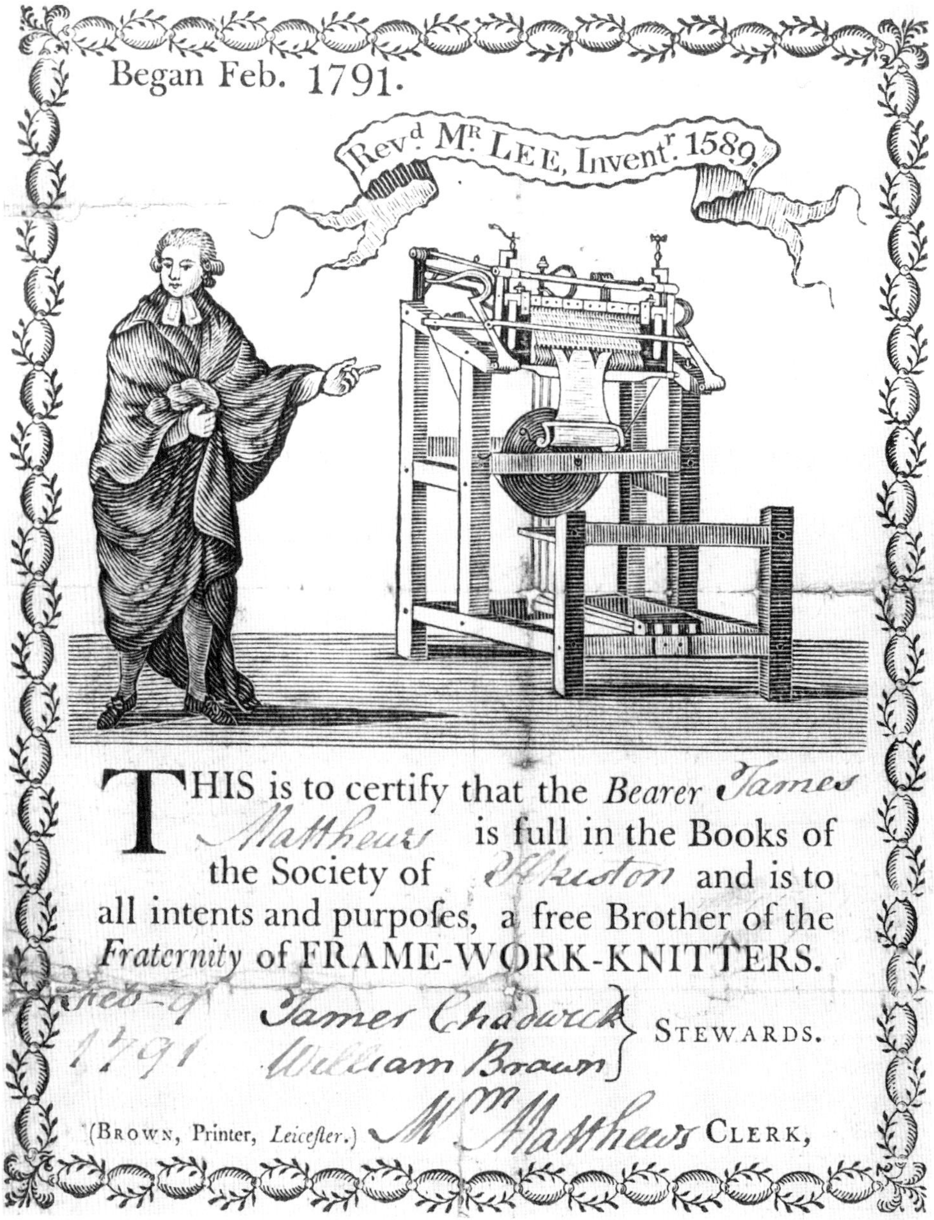

PLATE 33

repr. with permission from the Record Office of
Leicestershire, Leicester and Rutland

MEMBERSHIP CERTIFICATE OF THE ILKESTON FRATERNITY OF FRAME-WORK-KNITTERS

This illustrates how closely the independent framework knitting unions followed the precedents set by the Worshipful Company of Framework Knitters. At first glance, this certificate, with the signature of the Clerk and Stewards and the supporter pointing to the stocking frame, could have come from the Society.

seem that this proposal had only a modest effect in raising the profile of the Company. The Company had had ample opportunity to reinstate itself in the forefront of the framework knitting industry on the side of the journeymen, but failed to do so, and any further action taken by the journeymen against the hosiers was without the help of the Company. In 1779 another petition initiated from within the industry, and not by the Company, asked for protection against the hosiers and sought to end the abuses in the trade, especially the use of non-apprenticed workers ; a further bill was introduced, but a combination of the hosiers and 'venal Cornish members' defeated this journeymen's bill.[10]

The journeymen were not the only section of framework knitting that now worked with little, or no, help from the Company. Previously the Company had pursued apprentices when they absconded from their masters, even to the extent of writing to the Irish Company of Framework Knitters when the apprentice of Past Master Captain Portress was reported to be working as a journeyman in Dublin in 1726. By the 1760s, however, the Company took no part in searching for runaway apprentices. A number of masters meeting at Mr. Joseph Scott's at the Sign of the Eight Bells in Nottingham raised a standing fund to prosecute anyone harbouring or employing an absconding knitting apprentice and offered a five shilling reward for information. Leicester had a similar organisation and fund.[11]

The years 1800 to 1809

By the beginning of the 1800s conditions for the framework knitters had declined further and they again pressed for action against the surplus of workpeople in the trade caused by masters who employed large numbers of unbound apprentices – at Hinckley two masters had one hundred apprentices between them – and taught both boys and adults for payment, both contrary to the Company's Bye-laws. On again petitioning Parliament for an act to regulate the trade the journeymen took the advice of Alderman Sawbridge, a former Master of the Company and a Member of Parliament, and sought help from the Company, for, in spite of the lack of effective action in 1778–9, they continued to hope that it could act as a regulator for the industry.[12]

In mid-1805 journeymen from the East Midlands contacted the Company in London and on 16 October their delegates visited the Master John Patton 'desirous of assistance'. They wanted to come under the Company's protection and offered to pay £20 annually towards each Deputy appointed, so that, as all the former Deputies were now dead, the Court appointed two new ones each for Nottingham and Leicester and one each for Mansfield, Sutton in Ashfield, Leake, Loughborough and Hinckley. The journeymen also wanted to prosecute a hosier who was not observing the Company's Bye-laws and at a special Court on 17 October, at which the delegates were advised to take the legal advice of the Company's Clerk, it was agreed that the journeymen were to raise the money to pursue a case.

For a year many meetings took place both in London and in the East Midlands, and the Clerk assiduously took counsels' advice about the Charter and Bye-laws. On 14 October 1806 framework knitters from Nottinghamshire, Derbyshire and Leicestershire attended a general meeting of the Company in London, where it was decided that the Bye-laws should be put in place because the manner in which framework knitting had been conducted for many years past 'was highly injurious to trade and destructive to the Regular bred Frame Work Knitters and . . . that great Frauds and abuses had crept into the Manufacture since 1734 owing to want of regulation of the trade'.

As since incorporation most of the Company's East Midlands business had been conducted through Nottingham it might have been expected that this state of affairs would have continued but, although Marshall, the Secretary of the Framework Knitters' Committee in Nottingham, was involved in the approaches to the Company in 1805 and 1806, support from that area remained muted. Since the middle of the 1700s the most adroit journeymen of Nottinghamshire had largely turned their attention away from knitting stockings and other goods on narrow frames and concentrated on knitting point net lace on wide frames. In addition, the warp knitting frame invented by Crane and Porter of Edmonton near London in 1775 had been converted to make lace net by Ingham of Nottingham in about 1785, and others were experimenting with various new machines to make a fast lace mesh, so that well before the end of the century an alternative occupation to knitting on the stocking frame was emerging for frame workers. By the first decade of the 1800s the concerns of the Nottingham knitters were focussing on their declining trade, due to the over-supply of 2,300 frames knitting lace, not on the Framework Knitters' Company and implementation of its Bye-laws.[13]

Although from the Clerk's bill it would seem that at least two other prosecutions by the Company were considered – against the hosiers Gamble and Toulton – as most support for the Company now came from Leicestershire, the Deputies from Leicester and Hinckley were determined to prosecute someone from their own area. Originally they had thought to bring cases against either Hardisty, a drover's assistant, or one Fairbanks, but these were dropped in favour of the case against William Payne of Burbage near Hinckley.[14]

A letter, dated 16 February 1807, from Thomas Scott and John Warburton in Leicester to the Clerk makes it obvious that Lodington and the legal advisers tried to dissuade the Deputies from prosecuting Payne, as it was felt doubtful if many of the existing Bye-laws would stand up in a court of law in view of recent similar cases, such as that of the Feltmakers' Company against Davis. It was therefore made clear to the Deputies that the Society would take no responsibility for the expense of a Trial upon any questions relating to the Bye-laws. Nevertheless, the Deputies from Leicester determined to push on with a prosecution, writing that 'It is our wish and it is the Wish of the Trade and positive determination that a trial should be had . . . you should proceed with all possible Dispatch . . . Whatever money you may want for the purpose We will cheerfully provide, and give the Company any Indemnity you wish'. The Deputies of Leicester, (Scott and Warburton), and Hinckley, (Lee and Elliott), further stated that 'Payne is a man of some property, and the Deputies are determined to prosecute him'.

Payne had first been visited by the Deputies in December 1806 and between then and the following May he had attended all their meetings but made no application to join the Company, only 'railed against it'. On 16 February 1807 he had made an agreement, without the consent of the Company, to teach framework knitting to Thomas, the son of William Main, for three years at a charge of one shilling a week for the first two years and sixpence an week for the final year. When challenged Payne 'declared that he would continue to instruct persons in any manner he might think proper'. On 17 August 1807 William Payne was summonsed to appear in person before John Warburton and Thomas Scott of the Company of Framework-knitters at the house of Mr. John Judd, Black Lyon, Leicester, on 17 November to take up his Freedom and become a member of the Company (see Plate 34a). After Payne failed to appear at the 17 November meeting the Leicester and Hinckley Deputies continually pestered Clerk Lodington to take action.[15]

Payne was prosecuted by the Company for breaching the Bye-laws, for which £61 was asked for in fines, and the case finally went to Court on 20 August 1808. Although the judge was opposed to the Company's rights the jury found for the plantiffs and, in imposing £53 damages on the defendant, reconfirmed the Company's control of framework knitting.

During the proceedings Lodington had ran up a considerable bill in consulting a number of prominent counsel – Serjeants Sheppard, Jones and Manley, and Messers Copley, Holroyd, Gouldsmith and Tidd all received fees from the Company – and although in October 1808 the Deputies had indemnified the Master and Wardens of the Society for the sum of £440, in fact it would seem that the Company, not the Deputies shouldered the largest proportion of the costs of the case. Apparently £191 19s. 10d. was returned to the Deputies out of their £440 bond and, out of Lodington's bill of £256, £150 was paid by the Master and Wardens.[16]

However, the Company's pleasure at this confirmation of its authority over framework knitting was shortlived. Payne's counsel, Serjeant Williams, stated that he had taken a note at the time of the trial that the judge had given permission for the defendant to move for a nonsuit, and when this same note also apparently appeared in the Judges' Officers' Book the case had to be reheard (see Plate 34b). On 13 February 1809 'the entry of final judgement was stayed'. As in the case against Cartwright in 1731 the Charter and Bye-laws were found to be valid in law, but it was now decided that they were restricted to members of the Company, allowing non-members of the Company to practise framework knitting for their own profit without supervision of the Company's officers.

The Worshipful Company of Framework Knitters' total control of framework knitting had been broken for 'This Action in its result affirmed the principle of free trade, and destroyed the influence of the Company over the manufactures by the framework knitting machines'. As will be seen in the succeeding chapter, in spite of the continuing radical sympathies of many of the Court, later in the nineteenth century the Company refused to act again for the journeymen.[17]

Composition of the Company

This distancing of the Company from any further action on behalf of the frame-work knitters is not completely surprising, for in the last twenty years of the eighteenth century the connection of some of the Court with framework knitting was becoming tenuous.

There were at least seven Masters, those of 1784 and 1785, 1792–95, and 1799, for whom no connections with knitting can be found; Matthew Hilback (1793) was a silversmith, John Styles (1795) a packer and John Pugh (1799) a surgeon, while the occupations of the others went unrecorded. And, while some, such as Nathaniel Mayes in 1748, whose father Theophilus was a master framework knitter at the Nottingham Court in 1703, still maintained direct connections with the industry

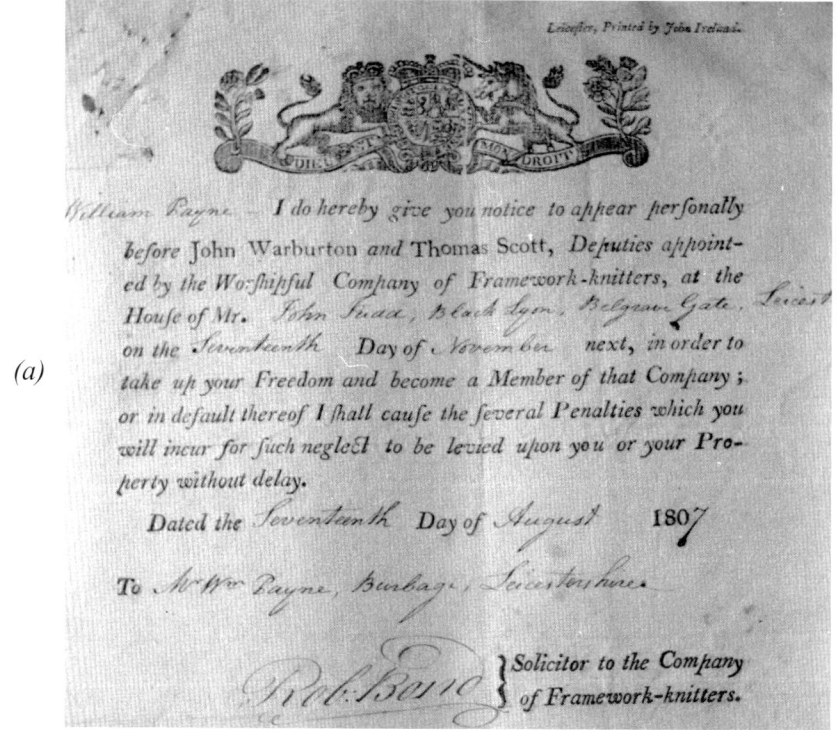

PLATE 34

F.W.K. MSS.

THE WORSHIPFUL COMPANY OF FRAMEWORK KNITTERS VERSUS WILLIAM PAYNE

(a) 1807 notice to Payne to appear before the Leicestershire Deputies on 17 August;
(b) 1809 copy of the summons to answer the application for a nonsuit.

and with the East Midlands, the connections of others had become remote. Master Thomas Hayward, (1789), belonged to a family which had been involved in framework knitting since the late 1600s and was apprenticed in the 1750s to Richard West, Master in 1750, but was himself 'Messenger to the Commissioners of Sewers and Lamps at the Guildhall'. Alderman John Sawbridge, Master of the Company in 1770, was a member of the landed gentry, Lord Mayor of London in 1775 and the Whig Member of Parliament for London between 1774 and 1795, and also had only distant ties with framework knitting, for one Joseph Sawbridge, framework knitter, had been admitted to both the Company and Livery on the 4 July 1727. The Flower family, which provided the Master in 1754 and at the beginning of the nineteenth century, were cheesemongers and provision merchants in London, although they came from a family already in framework knitting in the East Midlands by 1695 when Stephen was apprenticed to Thomas Cooke, while the two Robinsons, Thomas in 1746 and William in 1765, also had similar connections but were themselves financiers.[18]

However, probably more important than those reaching back to the past were the Masters who influenced the Company in the future. Samuel Arthur Vardon who by the time he became Master in 1823 was working as an auctioneer, had in the 1790s been apprenticed to John Duffield, a framework knitter and Master in 1745, while an apprentice of Thomas Barnfather, Master in 1755, was William Rowley, possibly an ancestor of Robert Rowley, Master in 1907.[19]

The Company and the City of London

Framework Knitters and the Radicals

The Common Hall of the City of London Livery Companies was a strong supporter of the radical movement, the most prominent representative of which for much of the later part of the eighteenth century was John Wilkes. Wilkes's voting strength in the City depended largely on Liverymen of the lesser Companies such as the Framework Knitters'. At least seven Framework Knitters voted for Wilkes in 1768, and in the City elections in the 1770s and 1780s a majority, often substantial, of the Company continued to vote for radical candidates. The two most prominent members of the Company closely involved with the radicals in the eighteenth century were the Masters of 1770 and 1784, John Sawbridge and Luke Staveley. John Sawbridge was a protege of the radical Lord Mayor of London, William Beckford, and a close friend, as well as supporter, of John Wilkes (see Plate C4). He was active in Parliament as the Whig Member for Hythe between 1768 and 1774 and the Member for London between 1774 and 1795. Luke Staveley was also for a time an enthusiastic supporter of Wilkes, and Heaton Wilkes, Master in 1788, was one of the Wardens during Staveley's Mastership. Staveley represented Bread Street Ward on the Common Council for seven years from 1770, resigning probably for economic reasons, and, even when no longer a supporter of Wilkes, continued to support radical candidates. In addition to the two Masters known to have taken an active part in radical politics at least one other family prominent in the Framework Knitters' Company in both the eighteenth and nineteenth centuries would appear to have been connected with the radicals, although the precise family relationship between Stephen Flower, Master in 1754, and Sir Charles Flower, Master in 1801, with the radical Benjamin Flower, who supported the French

Revolution and was an important opponent of the government issues at the close of the eighteenth century, is untraced.[20]

City Officers

Company members held various City offices and, as well as being ward councillors, two became Lord Mayor of London. In the minor positions Luke Staveley was one of the two auditors of the Chamber of the Bridgehouse in 1774 and 1775, and Henry Hardy, who voted for Wilkes in 1768, was one of the City's Aleconners, (Surveyors of Beer), between 1780 and 1784. In 1769 John Sawbridge became a Sheriff and in 1774 and 1775 George Grieve unsuccessfully attempted to be elected to the same position.[21]

Until 1742 the Lord Mayor of London had to belong to one of the twelve 'Great' Companies, and only in 1775 did John Sawbridge become the Worshipful Company of Framework Knitters first Lord Mayor of London. On this occasion a large number of the Company led the Lord Mayor's procession with an excellent band and new flags made specially for the occasion, among which was one with the Lord Mayor's arms and the motto 'Liberty and Law'. The Company was followed by the city marshalls on horseback and their attendants, and then the new Lord Mayor in the state coach drawn by six fine grey horses adorned with blue and light pink ribbons, and the rest of the procession. The Lord Mayor 'was dressed in light green, sprigged with gold flowers, and ornamented with fine garnets'. The Master and other members of the Court later attended the banquet in the afternoon and in the evening there was a banquet and ball for over 600 people in the Guildhall at which Sawbridge ensured that 'no expense was spared to make it as elegant an entertainment as was ever given upon the like occasion'. The ball was opened at nine o'clock by the Lady Mayoress and the Marquis of Granby and went on until nearly one.[22] In the final year of the century the Company again provided London's Sheriff when Charles Flower was elected to the position. He invited sixteen persons from the Company to be present at his swearing in and later to partake of the entertainment he and his co-Sheriff provided. The Company decided that because of financial circumstances it should not be put to any 'unreasonable expense' and the Clerk was told to inform Mr. Flower that the cost of the music, barge, coaches, robes, music, brandy and cakes should largely be defrayed by himself. Alderman Flower paid £50 out of a total bill of £69 4s. 5d.; the barge being borrowed from the Ironmongers' Company. On September 28 the Master, Wardens and twelve Assistants breakfasted at the London Tavern and then went to the Guildhall where they stood on the right of the Musicians', the Company of the second Sheriff. On 30 September, after a second breakfast at the London Tavern, the Company again went to the Guildhall and then proceeded to the waterside and, this time taking the left hand side of the Musicians' on board the borrowed barge, sailed to Westminster Hall, and then returned to the City for dinner. Variously described as a provision merchant and a cheesemonger, Sir Charles Flower was Master to the Company in 1801 and 1802, and in 1808, when he was Lord Mayor, the Framework Knitters again took part in the processions on both land and water on 10 November. Although the Company's records of this year are missing, presumably Sir Charles again had to pay the Company's expenses and, as befitting a grocer, his dinner 'was extremely well served including every delicacy in season'.[23]

Almshouses

No records exist detailing events in the Almshouses during the second half of the eighteenth century, but by a codicil of 1759, Ann Staunton, the daughter of Thomas Bourne, willed the interest of £300 to buy bread and coals annually in perpetuity for the inmates of the Almshouses established under her father's will.[24]

Company property – The Hall and its contents

When about 1759 the Company leased its Hall to the brewer Seward the Peacock Brewery was already a part of the curtilage of the court between Red Cross and White Cross Streets of which the Company-owned Hall and the Golden Hind alehouse formed a part. Until its compulsory purchase in the next century the Company's property was to remain in a brewer's hands, for from 1794 it was rented out to the brewer Calvert. In 1787 the yearly rent for the Hall and the Hind was £24 for each property, of which £1 7s. 6d. had to be paid in tax.[25]

With the Company no longer using the Hall its possessions began their perambulations around London. The landlord of the Duck Tavern, Garlic Street, for a time around 1753 controlled the plate and other chattels of the Company. Then sometime in the next fourteen years the Company regained possession of these and they were moved to the White Hart Tavern in Bishopsgate, a frequent meeting place for the Company, and in 1761 the banners and furniture, at least, were apparently moved to the Ship Tavern in Threadneedle Street where they remained for some years. In June 1769 the paintings were moved again, to the house of Thomas Lever, Upper Warden elect of the Company and son of the Master of 1722, and it is thought that it was probably soon after this that some, if not all of these, including the Balderton picture of William Lee, were used as security for money lent to the Company by Mr. Robinson of Threadneedle Street.[26]

By 1780s some of the Company's silver could also have disappeared, as on 13 October 1789 an inventory listed only twelve silver salts, seventeen silver spoons, one cup with cover, one cup without cover, one large two handled cup with cover, one large two-handled cup without cover, a silver porringer, a small silver flagon and a silver missal with double silver chain. The Company had very few spoons for one whose admission fee at incorporation had been a silver spoon, for, although it is recognised that this fee had been commuted to a monetary one by the end of the seventeenth century, it would seem unlikely that this would have happened after only seventeen admissions.[27]

Summary

Among Livery Companies the Worshipful Company of Framework Knitters was late to loose control of its industry. The Broderers' Company had lost control of its craft in 1710 and in 1725 the Vintner's Company had lost the right of search throughout England, while the Framework Knitters' retained all its rights after 1809, even though they were now restricted to Freemen of the Company. However, from 1753 the Court largely opted out of the day-to-day affairs of framework knitting and it was much against the inclination of many Assistants that the Company advised and supported the journeymen of Leicester and Hinckley in the first decade of the nineteenth century. Although the legality of the Bye-laws were still in place after the case against Payne in 1809 the Court completely lost the will to fight for its position in the industry, and was to take took no part in the numerous enquiries into framework knitting in the nineteenth century.[28]

References

1   Felkin, p. 117; Deering, pp. 100–1.
2   CLGL, MSS. 7.156 'To the Hosiers and Framework Knitters of Great Britain when the Commercial Treaty of Ireland was brought first under the consideration of Parliament', p. iii; Henson, pp. 87, 418, 237.
3   MSS, 3447.
4   MSS, 3450.
5   MSS, 3452/1, extracts from *Minute Book*, White Hart Tavern, 24 June 1768.
6   *JHC*, XXX, pp. 87, 121, 377.
7   Felkin, p. 115; Henson, pp. 383, 389.
8   Henson, p. 383; Felkin, p. 115.
9   *JHC*, XXXVI, pp. 635, 728; Henson pp. 387, 390.
10 MSS, 3447, 1778; Henson, pp. 393– 409; Felkin, p. 116.
11 MSS, 16840, 4 October 1726, 21 January 1726/7; *L(eicester and) N(ottingham) J(ournal)*, 3, 27 May, 8 December 1760, 15 August 1761.
12 Felkin, pp. 435–6.
13 *N(ottingham) J(ournal)*, 5, 19 August, 9, 30 September, 7, 14 October, 4 November 1809; Mason, p. 13.
14 MSS. 3452/1, Clerk's bill 1805–1809 plus case notes and other notes; Felkin, p. 435; Wells, pp. 92–94. As already noted in the 'Introduction' Professor F. A. Wells used the Company's manuscripts. As these manuscripts are no longer available Professor Well's interpretation of events at this point have sometimes had to be used, even though his dating does not always agree with the few documents remaining with the Worshipful Company of Framework Knitters.
15 MSS, 3452/1, bundles of documents including a letter from Robert Bond, solicitor, Leicester, 13 June 1807.
16 MSS, 3452/1; Wells, p. 93 referring to *Minute Book*, 18 October 1808, p. 44 referring to minute 14 June 1809.
17 *City of London Livery Companies' Commission, 1884, Report and Appendix*, III, p. 421.
18 MSS, 16840, pp. 23, 170; 3444; NAO, MSS, CA 4040; James Funston, *The Worshipful Company of Framework Knitters; A List of Masters*, plus various other Framework Knitters' Company manuscripts; Bevan, XI, p. 134.
19 MSS, 3446.
20 CLGL, MSS, B'side 26.25; Lucy S. Sutherland, *The City of London and the opposition to Government 1768–1774*, The Creighton Lecture in History 1958 (London: Athlone Press, 1959), pp. 17, 20; *Biographical Dictionary of Modern British Radicals: I: 1770–1830*, ed. Joseph O.Baylen and Norbert J. Grossman (Sussex: Harvester Press, 1979), pp. 173–5, 464–6. I am indebted to Peter Staveley of Middlesex for drawing to my attention the radical connections of his ancestor Luke Staveley, and for awakening me to this aspect of the Framework Knitters' history. CLRO – unfortunately the relevant poll books were 'unfit for consultation'.
21 CLRO, *Common Hall Minutes*, 8, pp. 146, 182, 225, 260.
22 *LNJ*, 18 November 1775; LG, 9 November 1775; *L(ondon) C(hronicle)*, 11 November 1775; *St. James's Chronicle*, 7–9, 9–11 November 1775; Palmer, p. 70; Bevan, p. 134.
23 MSS, 3450, 1809–1810; 3452/1; *LC*, 10 November 1808; *The Times*, 11 November 1808.
24 Funston, Charitable Fund Report, p. 4.
25 MSS, 3451/14; 3456.
26 MSS, 3452/1; 3452/14, Clerk's letter 26 November 1931; Henry B. Wheatley, *London Past and Present* (London: John Murray, 1891), p. 497; Ditchfield, p. 261.
27 MSS, 3452/1; BM, MSS, 816.m.12.(105).
28 Palmer, pp. 60, 128.

PLATE C1   *F.W.K. MSS.*

PORTRAIT OF CHARLES II FROM THE 1663 CHARTER

PLATE C2b

THE MASTER'S CHAIR

PLATE C2a

THE WORSHIPFUL COMPANY OF
FRAMEWORK KNITTERS' LOVING CUP OF ⁻656

PLATE C3 *repr. with permission from the Guildhall Library, Corporation of London*

SIR JOHN ROBINSON, LORD MAYOR OF LONDON IN 1662

Sir John was the son of Archdeacon William Robinson of Nottingham, his son John was a member of the Worshipful Company of Framework Knitters.

PLATE C4   *repr. with permission from the Guildhall Library, Corporation of London*

ALDERMAN JOHN SAWBRIDGE, THE WORSHIPFUL COMPANY OF FRAMEWORK
KNITTERS' FIRST LORD MAYOR OF LONDON

In this painting by William Miller of *The Ceremony of Swearing In Alderman Nathaniel
Newnham* in November 1782 (part of which is illustrated here), John Sawbridge, the
Worshipful Company of Framework Knitters' first Lord Mayor of London, is sitting in the
forefront, with his leg stretched out across the aisle.

PLATE C5   *F.W.K. MSS.*

COTTAGE HOMES AT OADBY, LEICESTERSHIRE

(Top) Corah Hall and a cottage
(Bottom) Corah House before alterations

PLATE C6

OPENING OF CORAH HOUSE ON 22 JUNE 1991

The opening ceremony was performed by Timothy Brooks, Esq., Lord Lieutenant of Leicestershire. *From left to right*: Master Michael Chapman; Mr. Timothy Brooks, Lord Lieutenant of Leicestershire; Mrs. T. Brooks; The Upper Warden, Mr. J. A. Ridge; The Under Warden, Mr. R. A. Wessel; The Rev. Canon Eric Devenport, Bishop of Dunwich.

F.W.K. MSS.

PLATE C7

repr. with permission of Neville Chadwick Photography, Wigston, Leics.

OPENING OF THE EXTENSIONS TO CORAH HOUSE ON 4 MARCH, 2000, BY MRS. PAULINE HALLIDAY, SHERIFF OF THE CITY OF LONDON

From left to right: Mr. Peter Swift, Mayor of Oadby; Mrs. Pauline Halliday; Warden Mr. Jonathan Dean; Clerk Mr. Howard Ellis; Mrs. Alison Wilson, High Sheriff of Leicestershire; Mr. Timothy Brooks, Lord Lieutenant of Leicestershire; Master Mr. Michael Turnbull.

PLATE C8

THE COURT OF THE WORSHIPFUL COMPANY OF FRAMEWORK KNITTERS
7 APRIL, 2000

repr. with permission of Gerald Sharp Photographers, Ilford, Essex.

From left to right, back row: The Beadle, Mr. J. M. Wa lis; Assistant The Rt. Hon. The Lord Sanderson of Bowden; Assistant Mr. J. Ashton; The Hon. Treasurer, Assistant Mr. H. C. Stevenson; Assistant Mr. G. D. Johnson; Steward Mr. J. B. Mason; Assistant Mrs. S. K. Murray; Assistant Mr. J. C. Strange; Assistant Mr. R. T. S. Kempton; Past Master Mr. P. C. Osborne; Past Master Mr. R. A. Wessel; Past Master Mr. A. J. W. Lewis; Past Master Mr. T. M. Fraser; Assistant Mr. A. J. Glover; Assistant Mrs. S. F. Richards; Assistant Mr. D. A. Buswell; Assistant Dr. D. P. Bethel; Assistant Mr. P. W. Tasker; The Assistant Clerk Mrs. A. Brown; The Clerk Mr. H. W. H. Ellis. *Front row:* Past Master Mr. J. A. Ridge; Past Master Mr. G. N. Corah; Past Master Mr. R. F. Stevenson; Past Master Mr. J. M. S. Whitehead; The Upper Warden Mr. J. M. Dean; The Master Mr. M. D. P. Turnbull; The Under Warden Mr. B. A. F. Smith; The Immediate Past Master Mr. D. J. Goodenday; Past Master Mr. C. B. Byford; Past Master Mr. G. M. Taylor; Past Master Mr. A. M. Chapman.

VII

From 1810 to the end of the nineteenth century

In theory the Company retained its monopolistic powers over the hosiery industry even after laws relating to the right of search and the export of machinery were repealed later in the century, but in practice the freeing of the framework knitters outside the Company from observance of its Bye-laws in 1809 meant that its jurisdiction and influence over in the industry had been destroyed. As the Charters and Bye-laws were now only applicable to members of the Worshipful Company of Framework Knitters the Company was powerless to act on behalf of operative framework knitters, even though framework knitting was the subject of numerous government enquiries in the 1800s and for the next seventy years, and while the manufacture of most hosiery was being transferred from handframe knitting to power operated machines, the Company stepped back from the industry, and concentrated on its London affairs and its Almshouses, largely restricting its activities to what has been described as 'the honourable retirement of a City livery company'. Then, from the 1880s, the number of mostly London-based members from outside the knitting industry declined and by the end of the century a growing number of powerful and dynamic newcomers from the East Midlands, most especially from within the Leicester hosiery trade, became influential and the Company turned back to the industry from which it took its name.[1]

Developments in frame working in the nineteenth century

The year 1809 was not only a watershed for the Worshipful Company of Framework Knitters it was also one within frame working. Although there was an enormous increase in the number of hand-operated knitting frames at work throughout the first half of the nineteenth century (see Table 7.1), from 1809 technical changes led to the most profitable product, lace net, being decreasingly made on that type of frame.

Knitted lace net had been made on the stocking frame since the middle of the eighteenth century but in 1809 John Heathcoat invented in Loughborough, Leicestershire, a hand-operated frame which by twisting together threads produced a more reliable, fast lace net. This led to a completely new industry and in the following ten years, hundreds of wide knitting frames, especially from Nottinghamshire which had previously been the centre for knitted lace net, were converted to making other, less profitable and less skilled, knitted products. Skilled

Table 7.1 **Numbers of knitting frames in Great Britain in the first half of the nineteenth century**

Location	1812	1844
Leicestershire	11,183	16,382
Nottinghamshire	9,285	20,861
Derbyshire	4,700	6,797
Middlesex, Essex, Kent	137	178
Gloucestershire	970	936
Ireland	976	265
Scotland	11,049	2,605
Total in Britain and Ireland	29,583	48,482

Source: Blackner, 1812, pp. 238–43; Felkin, 1845, pp. 9–18.

framework knitters, many bearing surnames long associated with the Worshipful Company of Framework Knitters such as Copestake, Felkin and Wallis, soon appeared among those working in the new lace trade.[2]

Moreover, in spite of innovations in knitting machinery and the introduction of steam powered working, for much of the century many hosiers saw little economic sense in investing in new technology because the putting-out system kept over-heads low, for framework knitters working in their own homes were forced to compete economically with factory production. Skilled framework knitters in Nottinghamshire and elsewhere in the East Midlands, who had been among the most vociferous opponents of the Worshipful Company of Framework Knitters in the later half of the eighteenth century, were now forced to take a reduction, often considerable, in wages or be unemployed.

Factory working in the knitting industry only spread rapidly after 1874 when hosiers were forbidden to charge frame rent and the Education Acts made it increasingly difficult for framework knitters to operate economically when their children were hindered by schooling from carrying out the necessary auxiliary tasks.

The Company 1809–1850

Although Courts were held spasmodically in the East Midlands until 1814 the Company by then retained little or no influence in the region. From being an enemy of the employing hosiers and the ally of the artisan framework knitters in the previous century, when it had tried to enforce the Bye-laws restricting the number of apprentices and enforcing quality control, for a time at the beginning of the nineteenth century the Worshipful Company came to be regarded by many of the rank and file of frameworkers as allied to the employers in the trade – the 'Persons denominated Hosiers and Lace Manufacturers'. A scathing attack was written by Thomas Large, one of the Nottingham men's leaders, about the family hosiery shop of Robert Romanis, who was to be Master of the Company in 1842 and 1860, which sold 'the damed'ist Rubbish of Framework goods we ever saw'.[3]

Realising that the Company had lost hope of effectively defending its Bye-laws and supporting journeymen, many framework knitters, again from families long associated with the Framework Knitters' Company such as Henson, Brandreth and

Towle, again decided to form their own associations. A combination of 1812 called itself the United Committee of Framework Knitters, while one in Leicester in 1820s was the Framework Knitters' Society. However, in contrast to the associations of the previous century, the new unions would seem to have had no direct connection with the Company, and indeed the one of 1812 hoped that it could itself 'be incorporated, the same as the Cutlers' at Sheffield', with a Charter' ratify'd by Act of Parliament'.[4]

However, in spite of anti-Company feeling and the growth of these associations, some who were already members of the Framework Knitters' Society continued to hope that it could protect them from the 'manifold deceptions and abuses practiced . . . to the great injury of the regular workmen, by glutting the markets with goods of the basest texture'. In October 1824 twenty four 'sworn' members resident in Leicester, including 'Matt Townsend', 'Thos Rowlett', and 'Thos Wood', plus fourteen members from the county, six from Wigston, four from Whetstone and one each from Ratby, Thrussington, Syston, and Anstey humbly petitioned the Master, Wardens and Assistant of the Worshipful Company of Framework Knitters

'to grant them a Deputation to restrain such practices'

and they begged

'leave to observe that should they (the Master and Wardens) at any time take out a writ or commence an Action against Offenders . . . they will indemnify the Company as on former occasions when the Deputations were granted in the year of our Lord 1806' (see Plate 35).[5]

However, scorned by most of the operative framework knitters whom it felt that it had previously tried to protect, the Court took no more notice of this petition than it took of the Luddite, Pentrich, and other disturbances, disputes and hardships of framework knitting during the first half of the nineteenth century. William Booth might have been inspired to found the Salvation Army by the degradation and helpless misery of the poor stockingers of his native Nottingham, but the few records remaining of the Worshipful Company of Framework Knitters for this time are concerned not with the momentous issues affecting framework knitting but with the day to day running of the Company – the Almshouses, audits of accounts, elections to the Livery and of the Masters, Wardens and Assistants, and instructions for such Company matters as the dinners taken at the King's Head Tavern in Poultry, which were to be 'on Table at Five o'Clock precisely', and thanks in 1843 'for the ability and urbanity' with which Robert Romanis 'discharged his duties as Master'.[6]

By 1843 conditions within framework knitting were generally so appalling – few in work were paid a living wage – that the Company's former control of the trade on such matters as apprenticeships and fraudulent work was now regarded by many journeymen as the golden age of framework knitting. A petition signed by more than 25,000 knitters, mostly from the East Midlands centred in Nottingham, and presented to the House of Commons asking for a Commission of Enquiry, referred to the Charter 'granted for the protection of the Framework Knitters of these realms in the year One thousand and sixty-three' and prayed to the 'Honourable House to revive those protections'.[7]

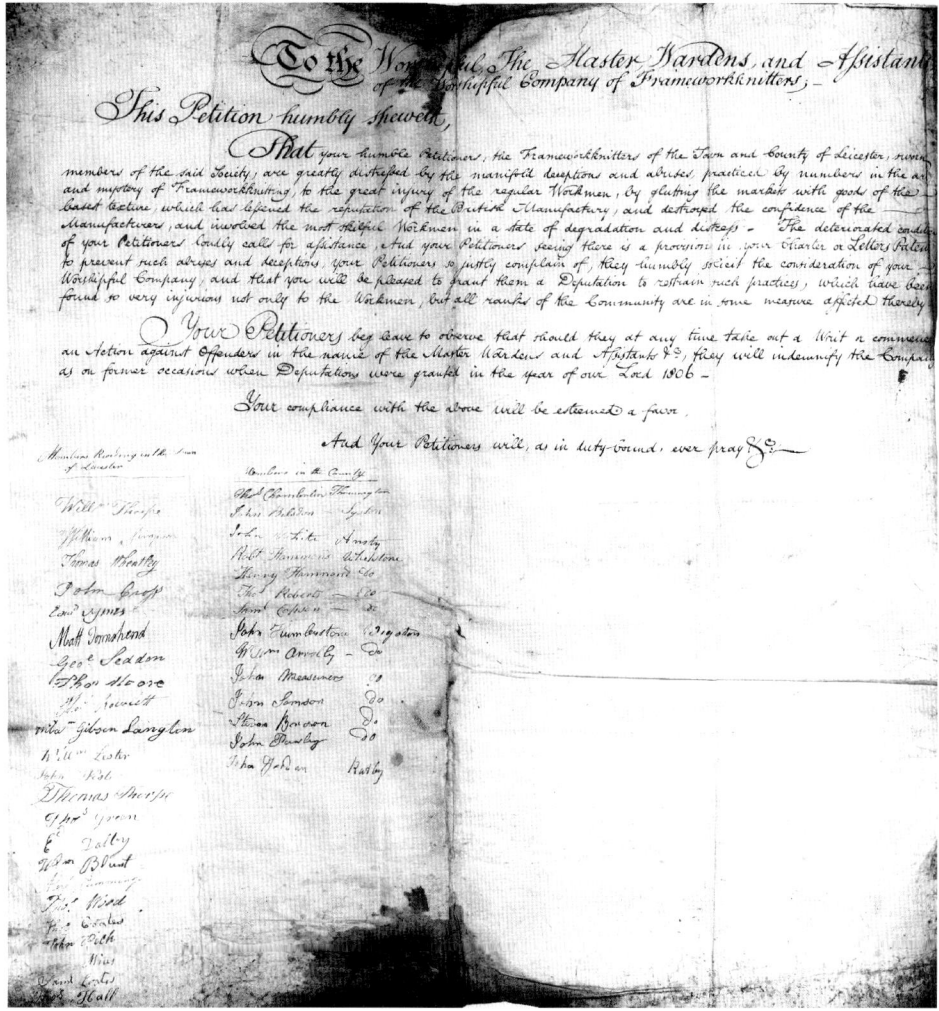

PLATE 35   *F.W.K. MSS.*

1824 PETITION FROM FRAMEWORK KNITTERS IN LEICESTERSHIRE TO THE
COMPANY

This petition was signed by twenty four 'sworn' members of the Company resident in Leicester,
including Matt. Townsend, Thos. Rowlett and Thos. Wood, and fourteen members from the
county, six from Wigston, four from Whetstone and one each from Ratby, Thrussington, Syston
and Anstey.

In addition the petitioners approached the Company for support. After their July
1843 meeting in Nottingham the operative framework knitters of Nottinghamshire, Leicestershire and Derbyshire wrote to the 'Masters Wardens Officers
Livery and Freemen of the Worshipful Company of Frame Work Knitters'

'That your Memorialists being in the most depressed state owing to the want
of protections and whereas a Charter was granted in the year 1663, for such

purpose but from some cause or causes has ceased to be of that use for which it was first intended and whereas the FrameWork Knitters consider it to be the duty of your Worshipful Company to render them assistance in matters affecting their Trade . . . (and) . . . beg to be favoured with a copy of the Bye Laws of your Worshipful Company in order thereby to give information to this important body of Workmen consisting in the whole to nearly Forty thousand. We trust therefore that no scruple will be made to this our request in the full expectation that when such information is obtained we may be enabled to raise the importance of your Worshipful Company amongst the Charted Bodies of this Queendom to what it was first intended to be and which it now only bears the name . . .'.[8]

However, after the previous rebuffs, the Company did not treat this memorial with any urgency, only considering it on 10 October at a Court attended by the Master, William Morris, the Wardens, Arthur Vardon and Robert Strachan, and twelve Liverymen, all but one of them Past Masters. Swayed neither by the threats nor the promises it contained, the Court washed its hands of the whole matter, paying the Clerk 12s. 6d. to reply that

'It was resolved unanimously
    That as it appears to this Court that in the year 1809, upon the suggestion and for the protection and benefit of the Freemen and Foreign Brothers of the Counties of Nottingham, Leicester and Derby, an Action at Law was commenced in the Court of Common Pleas by the Company against one William Payne . . . for the recovery of penalties alleged to have been incurred by his breach of the Bye Laws of the Company and thereby virtually to compel their future observance and the Company having been defeated in such Action . . . the Company and also the Freemen and Foreign Brothers were satisfied that the Company possessed no powers to assist the Trade and thereupon the Freemen and Foreign Brothers ceased to have further connection with the Company and from that period down to the present time the subject has never been agitated or revived this Court must decline acceding to the request of the Memorialists and the more especially as this Court is fully sensible of the increased and increasing feeling of the times and of the Courts of Law against all Bye Laws and Regulations which savour of monopoly and restrictive privileges.
    That this Court deeply regrets that the Trade is in the depressed condition represented in the foregoing Memorial and laments its inability to afford . . . any aid or suggest any course by which the Company could render . . . any assistance . . .'.[9]

In October 1845 a request from Thomas Winter, the secretary of the Leicestershire framework knitters, for 'a copy of the original Charter, copies of the Bye Laws and copies of the Lists of Courts of Assistants, etc.' met with the intransigent response that 'the Court resolved unanimously that the request contained therein could not be complied with'.[10]

By the middle of the century the Court had not only completely divorced itself from the upheavals in framework knitting it was not interested in recruiting further Freemen from those of journeymen status, even when approached directly. An enquiry in 1848 from Thomas Withers, a framework knitter of Leicestershire 'now living in London', as to 'whether I can become a Member of the above Company – if so, what will be the cost and the necessary qualification – or if not could you furnish me with any Papers such as the Charter . . . (and) the names and addresses of the present Officers for which I will willingly pay the cost', met with the terse reply 'that no party can claim the Right of becoming a Freeman of the Company but by Patrimony or Servitude.[11]

The Company from 1850 to 1900

Although by the middle of the nineteenth century about ninety per cent of stocking frames were in the East Midlands, the Worshipful Company, considered 'as useless as powerless for any trade purposes', remained centred around London where its Court continued to show little interest in framework knitting. In the late 1860s and early 1870s, when Parliament decided to tidy up a number of what were considered legislative anomalies and approached the Company for its observations on rescinding two acts passed in George's reign, one to prevent the fraudulent making of frame-work knitted pieces and stockings and the other for the protection of stocking frames, it only made the comment that both had long been disregarded; both were repealed in the subsequent Statute Law Revision Acts.[12]

No further interest was shown in the hosiery industry until the 1880s when the London solicitor William Bohm decided that the Company needed reviving if it was not to fold. Bohm had only entered the Company in 1878 but was Senior Warden when the Framework Knitters' replied to the Royal Commission on Livery Companies in 1881, becoming Master in June of that year, and he reassociated the Company with the trade whose name it bore, involving it in technical education for the hosiery industry as well as ensuring that the Company took a prominent role in the International Health Exhibition in South Kensington in 1884.[13]

Under Bohm's leadership the Company arranged their exhibit at South Kensington to interest 'the general public in the practical work of one of the great industries of the Country'. The ground floor of the display was arranged in two sections. In one Cooper, Corah and Company of Leicester demonstrated three machines making woollen hose – a 'one at once' and a 'two at once' and the 'smallest circular machine which ever made woollen hose' – while in the other section seventeenth century frames, lent by Past Master Bohm, J. & R. Morley and Liveryman F. W. Mart, who had helped to arrange the exhibit, made silk hose. Upstairs a room arranged in the period of William Lee exhibited both the Company's Master's Chair (see Plate 2b) and a number of antique hose, including a pair of hand-knitted silk hose worn by Queen Elizabeth I, lent by the Marquis of Salisbury, some gossamer-fine silk hose made by Morleys which had won a gold medal in the Universal Exhibition in Hyde Park in 1851, and a coarse pair of stockings worn by Ross's Antarctic Expedition.[14]

Once reinvigorated the Company's profile expanded during the final years of the nineteenth century and continued into the twentieth century.

Masters' and Officers' Jewels
One consequence of the 1880's revival was an improvement to the Company's image. The Court decided to follow the custom of a number of other Companies

and a jewel costing £48 was designed for wear by Past Masters to commemorate their year in office, the first one of which was presented in 1882 to Past Master A. R. Capel. On the obverse were the Arms of the Company and on the reverse the name of the Master concerned and the date.[15]

The Master's chain, to be worn during the year in office, was presented by Master J. H. Cooper in 1894. In 1897 Past Master Wolf Harris presented the badges to be worn by the Senior and Junior Wardens during their year of office and in 1899 a badge to be worn by the Honorary Treasurer of the Charitable Funds.[16]

Composition and internal organisation during the nineteenth century

Freemen

As operative framework knitters were no longer required, or encouraged, to become members, until the last fifteen years of the nineteenth century recruitment was slow. The Company was centred around London and between 1800 to 1886 nearly three-quarters of the 289 new recruits came from the capital. In twenty seven of these years, most notably the period between 1852 and 1864, there were no enrolments at all, so that by the 1880s there had been a serious decline in numbers. In 1809 there were sixty three Freemen, in 1852 these numbered eighty-six, but by 1875 there were only thirty-three, including four in the Almshouses.[17]

Few connected with textiles joined the Company and although in the period immediately after 1809 it would still appear to have been thought advisable for the partner running a London warehouse to join the Company, by the middle years of the century this was not considered necessary even for hosiers based in the London. The brothers Richard and John Morley had started together as hosiers towards the end of the eighteenth century in a warehouse in Greyhound Yard, Nottingham, and, when John went up to London in 1799 to establish a warehouse in Wood Street, Richard stayed in Nottingham. John Morley became a Freeman of the Society on 13 November 1818 and was a Liveryman until at least 1827, but neither Richard, nor any of his sons, nor even the eventual head of what became a very large business, John's third son Samuel, ever joined. Between 1825 and the 1880s only three men taking up the Freedom were hosiers – Robert Romanis, Richard Blatherwick, and Benjamin Cox who had been apprenticed to Robert Romanis – and only

Table 7.2 **Freedoms between 1800 and 1886**

Location	Number	Location	Number
London	261	Hants	1
Leicester	5	Yorks	1
Nottingham	4	Essex	1
Hinckley	2	Berks	1
Kent	2	Suffolk	1
Surrey	2	Cape of Good Hope	1
Cambs	1	unrecorded	6

Source: MSS. 3444.

three others, silk weavers connected to the Clements family, were involved with textiles, and all six seem to have been based in London. Most new members of the Company in the middle years of the century came from a variety of different London-based occupations, such as solicitors, stock brokers, wine merchants, lightermen and tobacconists.[18]

Only from the 1880s when a number of the prominent hosiery and lace manufacturers of Leicestershire and Nottinghamshire began to join the Company do textile connections reappear, although even in this period it is not always possible to tell what connections a new Freeman had outside London because, if there was a London warehouse, then that address was used. When the Leicester hosiery manufacturer Alfred Corah was admitted by Redemption at the Leicester Court on 26 September 1894 his given address was 122 Wood Street, while in 1885 that of Richard Birkin, the Nottingham lace manufacturer, had been recorded as Watling Street.[19]

The turnaround in the Company's membership from the end of the 1870s was organised by William Bohm and, in contrast to earlier years, those now joining the Company were from the upper echelons of society, not journeymen. Bohm was already a member of the Loriners' Company when he joined the Framework Knitters' in 1878, and in the next few years he encouraged several members of the Loriners' and Spectacle Makers' Companies onto the Livery of the Framework Knitters', including Thomas Loveridge and William Creasey. He also persuaded members of the Honourable Artillery Company to join, including Henry Pocock, W. H. Whiteway Wilkinson, Alfred Durrant and Thomas Blashill, as well as persons engaged in commerce with South Africa, including George Reid and John Paddon. The first of the East Midlands manufacturers to purchase his Freedom, and be admitted to the Livery on 13 January 1880, was Joseph Griffin Ward, a Leicester boot and shoe manufacturer. The Company's exhibition at the International Health Exhibition in South Kensington in 1884 was aimed to 'attract the manufacturers and actual workers in the industry . . . and touch hands again with the two great centres of such industry, viz., "Nottingham and Leicester",' and to foster this aim William Bohm, with the help of Liveryman Ward, involved J. H. Cooper of Cooper, Corah & Co, a hosiery manufacturer of St. Margaret's Works, Leicester, in the project. Mr. Cooper immediately became a member of the Company and was followed by a number of other prominent Leicester and Nottingham textile manufacturers. In 1884 Thomas King and William Rowlett, both connected with the Leicestershire hosiery trade, joined, to be followed by the wool spinner William Barfoot in 1888. The first of these new Freemen connected with the Nottingham lace trade was Charles James Cox, who took up his Freedom in 1885, followed by John Piggin Fearfield in 1886 and Arthur Butler in 1887. Messrs. Ward, Cooper, Butler and Rowlett subsequently became Assistants.[20]

In 1887 the Freedom of the Company was awarded to James Henry Quilter, a former mature student of the Leicester Technical School, who was closely involved with framework knitting, and in 1894 had arranged the gathering of 500 old stockingers on the occasion of the Lord Mayor of London's visit. This inspired honour was to cement close relations between the School and the Company for many years for in 1887, when awarded, Quilter had just taken over as head of the textile department, a position he was to hold until 1918, as well as being a founder of the magazine *Knitting International*. In 1892 the Honorary Freedom of the Company was conferred upon Sir James Whitehead, the Liberal Member of

Parliament for Leicester and a former Lord Mayor of London, in recognition of his valuable service to the Volunteer Force and for his continuing opposition to the high freight charges which so affected the hosiery industry.[21]

Livery

With the paucity in numbers taking up the Freedom of the Company there was a shortfall in the number of Liverymen for much of the century. In 1810 there was still the full complement, but the number had fallen to fifty in 1831, and down to twenty four in 1851; by 1873 the number had dropped to six. Numbers finally reached the permitted sixty in 1887, whereupon the Company immediately applied to the Court of Alderman of the City of London for an increase to 100, although by 1891 numbers had only crept up to ninety three out of the 100 allowed.[22]

For most of the century few Liverymen could be recruited from the long-term Freemen of the Company for those aspiring to become also Freemen of the City of London were required to be £10 householders, and by the middle of the century few existing ordinary members of the Company came into this category; although short of Liverymen in 1852, eighty six Freemen of the Company, nearly all long-serving members as only five had joined in the previous seven years, were not Liverymen. Even the advantages of being a Freeman of the City was not enough to entice persons living in London to join the Company as the number of members of the Company entitled to vote in the elections of the City declined from thirty seven in 1845 to fifteen in 1873.[23]

For suitable applicants, therefore, admission to the Freedom and the Livery often occurred on the same day. This happened on 10 January 1832 to Robert Strachan, who was already a Freeman of the Goldsmiths' Company and was to be Master of the Framework Knitters' Company in 1845 and 1866, and on 21 April 1881 to James Slater, silk manufacturer, Frank Price, tobacco manufacturer, Thomas Blashill, architect, George Bell, merchant, Thomas Donne, clothing manufacturer, and John Scholes, carrier. To encourage further the recruitment of new members for a time a special fee of £25 for the combined induction of Freedom and Livery was instituted, and in 1877 the 1848 charge of one guinea for inviting a friend to one of the Company's dinners was rescinded, and there was to be no charge for up to four visitors as the number in the Company had grown so small.[24]

During the Company's re-establishment in the 1880s two titled gentlemen accepted its Freedom and Livery. In June 1881 Lord Elcho was honoured for his 'patriotic services to the nation' and then, on 22 February 1884, a Special Court was held in the Sadlers' Hall in Cheapside to install as Liveryman John William Arthur Charles James Cavendish Bentinck, the Duke of Portland and Lieutenant Colonel commanding the Honourable Artillery Company of the City of London, in which several members of the Framework Knitters' Company already served. After his installation Lord Elcho does not feature again in the Company's records but, just as previous Dukes of Portland had taken an interest in the plight of the framework knitters, so this new Liveryman helped the Company with the Health Exhibition of 1884 and until 1915 annually presented each inhabitant of the Alms-houses with a fowl at Christmas.[25]

The Court

Between 1814 and 1894 no Court was held outside London and meetings were held in a number of inns in the City. From 1825 to 1844 the most frequented tavern was the King's Head in the Poultry, then from 1844 until its demolition in 1876 it was the London Tavern in Bishopsgate, which was a favoured meeting place for Livery Companies without halls of their own. From 24 June 1876 into the twentieth century the Albion Tavern, Aldersgate, then became the most frequent Court venue.[26]

It was a struggle to fill vacancies on the Court of Assistants, especially during the middle years of the century. Between 1809 and 1831 the number of Assistants was about thirty one, but by 1873, when the Livery numbered six, the Court of Assistants only had sixteen members. Moreover most Assistants did not turn up for meetings, and to try to encourage better attendance in 1878 the 1821 payment, of five shillings to the first sixteen to attend Court, was increased to ten shillings.[27]

During much of the century a suitable candidate could purchase his Freedom, and be clothed in the Livery and admitted to the Court of Assistants in one or two days. This occurred as early as 1812 when Robert Waithman was admitted to the Company, the Livery and to the Stewardship on same day, but it also happened on a number of other occasions, as in 1868 when on 13/14 January James Kingdom, a solicitor, who became Master in 1875, was admitted and on 13/14 April when John King, a wholesale stationer, who became Master in 1876, received the same treatment, and again on 9 April 1878 when William Bohm was admitted.[28]

The shortfall in the number of Assistants also meant that there was a scarcity in the number of different men able to serve as Masters. In 1831 twenty members of the thirty one strong Court had already served as Master. By 1854 this number had risen to twenty two out of the twenty four Assistants and by 1873 eleven Assistants had been Master twice and another one had served once; by 1877 Thomas Capel was embarking on his third term as Master.[29]

At the beginning of the century some members of the Court were still involved in framework knitting. The Masters of 1810, 1812, 1814, 1816 and 1821 – John Tyrell, Robert Morrell, Jonathan Stirtevant, John Garton and John Stirtevant respectively – were all hosiers, with the Stirtevants still connected with William Lee's village of Calverton. Then between 1821 and 1894 only further one Master, Robert Romanis in 1842 and 1864, was a hosier.[30]

Most Masters in the nineteenth century came from occupations with no connections to textiles. These included a number who were wine merchants – Richard Noble (1809), William Sampson (1824), Henry Fearon (1833), Henry Capel (1836 and 1860) and Joseph Hannah (1847 and 1868) – or were connected with occupations associated with the City of London such as stockbrokers – Robert Manning (1818 and 1851), William Smallbone (1827 and 1853), James Capel (1828), John Norbury (1829 and 1856), Stephen Cundy (1835), Robert Henry Manning (1840, 1862 and 1877), Arthur Vardon (1844 and 1865), Sidney Vardon (1848, 1869 and 1879), Joseph Withers (1850 and 1871) – or bankers – Thomas Richardson (1822).

One family which played a major part on the Court during the nineteenth century was the Capels. James Capel, Master 1828 and 1854, and his stockbroking partner James Norbury, were for many years involved in all aspects of the Company's work, including acting as Honorary Treasurers of the Company's charitable funds, and they were succeeded in this position by Arthur Risdon Capel, Master in 1849, 1870 and 1880, who was a tea broker. In addition to these two Capels and Henry the wine merchant, there was also Thomas, Master in 1841, 1863 and 1878, who was a coal merchant supplying the Company's Almshouses.[31]

By the end of the century the composition of the Court began to revert to the pattern of the seventeenth and eighteenth centuries when members from the East Midlands and from the hosiery trade again becoming influential. John Cooper in 1894 was the first of the Leicester Masters, followed by Joseph Ward in 1897 who was the first of four members of his family to hold this office. Moreover, after a break of only seventy years, it was decided to hold Courts again outside London, although these were now to be in Leicester, rather than in Nottingham as previously.[32]

The Court held in Leicester on 24 September 1894 was a very lavish affair and celebrated publically both the resurgence of the Company and 'the connection of the Craft with the Company', for Master Cooper's object was to 'afford not only to the civic dignataries but also the court of the company an opportunity of making themselves conversant with the conditions under which the industry with which the guild is associated is carried on'. The day's proceedings were reported in full in the press and in the Company's Minutes, from which this account is taken, and show how quickly the Company's prestige had been revived since the low ebb of 1873 (see Plates 36 and 37).[33]

PLATE 36   *F.W.K. MSS./DAILY GRAPHIC*

24 SEPTEMBER 1894 COURT MEETING IN LEICESTER

PLATE 37   *F.W.K. MSS.*

24 SEPTEMBER 1894 COURT MEETING IN LEICESTER, GROUP PHOTOGRAPH

Front Row: Sir Israel Hart, Mayor of Leicester; the Mayor of Nottingham; Sir J. V. Moore, Sheriff of London; Sir M. Tyler, Lord Mayor of London; Sir J. Dimsdale, Sheriff of London; Master Mr. J. H. Cooper; Past Master Mr. Thomas Loveridge; the Mayor of Hinckley.
Second Row: Clerk Mr. James Funston; Beadle Mr. Lovell; Assistant Mr. J. A. Corah; Past Master Mr. H. J. Dowden; Past Master Mr. D. W. Bell; Past Master Mr. W. Bohm; Past Master Mr. Deputy W. Creasey; Assistant Mr. E. Terry; Warden Mr. Wolf Harris; Assistant Mr. A. Pringle.
Third row: Assistant Mr. A. Corah; Alderman Barfoot of Leicester; Assistant Mr. J. G. Ward; Assistant Mr. Tertius Rowlett; Past Master Mr. W. H. Whiteway Wilkinson; Assistant Mr. H. Pocock; Assistant Mr. F. V. Nichols.
(It would seem that the identification written in the Company's documents was inserted later as two are not named on the second and one on the third rows.)

Just before noon on Monday, 24 September, the Master, J. H. Cooper

'proceeded from his factory St. Margaret's Works to the Midland Railway Station accompanied by the Clerk and Beadle Lovell, Past Masters Bohm, Whiteway-Wilkinson, Assistants Wolf Harris and J. G. Ward, and Liverymen J. L. Ward, W. Barfoot, J. A. Corah and others and there met the Lord Mayors of Leicester, Nottingham and Hinckley . . . Upon arrival of the train from London they welcomed the Right Hon the Lord Mayor, Sir Robert Tyler, and the Sheriffs of London Aldermen Sir J. V. Moore and Sir Joseph Dimsdale (who) were accompanied from St. Pancras Station by Past Masters Dowden, Creasey, Loveridge, Bell and Paddon and Assistants Nicholls, Pocock and Pringle and Liveryman Terry.

The Lord Mayor, Sheriffs, and the Mayors of Leicester, Nottingham and Hinckley then robed, and wearing their gold chains and badges, the Wardens their gowns, the Past Masters their Jewels, and the Assistants and Livery the Colours of the Company proceeded in Carriages in due order to the Town Hall. The procession was headed by mounted police and mounted police brought up the rear. The Streets were decorated with flags – the Church bells were rung and the crowds of people heartily cheered the procession on its way.

At the Town Hall the Lord Mayor and Sheriffs were introduced to the Town Council while the Master proceeded to hold a Court, at which he presented to the Company the Master's Chain he was wearing and admitted as a Freeman of the Company Alfred Corah. At the conclusion of the Court the procession reformed and proceeded to the Assembly Rooms where the Master entertained at luncheon . . . guests numbering more than 200.

At the conclusion of the luncheon the procession was again formed and . . . went to St. Margaret's Works . . .

The workpeople about 2000 employed at these works then assembled in the great yard . . . and presented . . . an illuminated address of Congratulations to the Master . . . the Lord Mayor addressed this great concourse . . . in appropriate and happy terms.

After refreshments . . . the procession was again formed and leaving the works proceeded amidst crowds of enthusiastic citizens to the Museum in New Walk. In the Lecture Hall were assembled about 500 old Stockingers none under 67 years of age while 80 of them were upwards of eighty years and one of them had reached the advanced age of 95. . . . At this Meeting the Master presided and addressed briefly those assembled – the Lord Mayor also made a short speech . . . presenting each of the old people with a new shilling . . . the Master then announced that the Mayor of Leicester, Mr. John Cook of Cook's excursion tours, the Master's partners at St. Margaret's Works, and Past Master John Paddon would each contribute an additional shilling.

The Lord Mayor and Sheriffs having to leave for London the Master attended by the Court proceeded to the Railway Station and the Lord Mayor and Sheriffs left Leicester by the 7.30 train.

The Master and the Court then returned to the Museum where a Concert was given . . . and about 11 o'clock pm. the proceedings of a most delightful day ended.

It is noteworthy of remark that the day was in weather most brilliant. That many thousands of persons assembled in the various lines of route and the welcome was marked by a display of flags and mural decorations most liberally provided by the Citizens – No hitch or awkward circumstance disturbed the days festivity and as far as was known no accident occurred even to a sightseer'.

The loving cups used in the ceremonies at Leicester were the Jubilee, Creasey and Birkin cups.[34]

Apprentices

In addition to the low number of Freemen enrolled, few apprentices were registered during the nineteenth century and most of these were bound to members of the Court outside the hosiery trade. In 1810 bindings only numbered seven, and the total number of apprentices bound between the beginning of the century and 1861, when the Orphan's Tax was abolished, was only 108.[35]

The Company and their Ladies

The first reference to ladies attending any function connected with the Company was in 1873 when the Master F. W. Cosens and his wife attended the ball and supper given at the Guildhall by the Lord Mayor in honour of the Shah of Persia. The first time that ladies dined with the Company was at a Court dinner on 20 May 1890 at the Savoy Hotel when 'wives or other Lady nominees' were invited at Master Thomas Bell's expense and he presented each lady with a specially knitted shawl. A Ladies' dinner did not, however, become an annual event until the next century for, although the subject was discussed again in 1898, the Court left further decisions to the Master and Wardens. However in 1899, in addition to bearing the costs of the Company's participation in the Lord Mayor's show, Master Henry Pocock entertained twenty members of the Court and their wives to an outing on the Thames between Henley and Maidenhead by electric launch; the nine ladies present receiving from the Master a gold bracelet as a souvenir.[36]

The Company and the City of London

During the first half of the nineteenth century many members still espoused radical ideas and the Company continued to take an active part in politics in the City of London. Following in the footsteps of the linen draper Master, Luke Staveley, one of the most prominent of the Company's radicals of the nineteenth century was another linen draper, Alderman Robert Waithman, Master in 1815, who, together with Matthew Wood, probably a relative of Thomas Wood the Master of 1837, was credited with reviving Whig politics in the City. In addition to his City interests Waithman was also a Member of Parliament, voting for a number of radical measures in the 1820s and 1830s, including the Reform Bill of 1832 (see Plate 2).[37]

The Company often participated in City events during this century. Even though it regretted its inability to pay its respects to Queen Victoria at the opening of the Coal Exchange in 1849 due to the lack of a Company barge, Past Master Dowden, the Clerk and Beadle took their place with the other Livery Companies in a procession from the Guildhall to St. Paul's Cathedral on the occasion of the Queen's Jubilee in 1887, and ten years later members of the Court attended the Diamond Jubilee Service in the same cathedral. Contact was also maintained with other City Companies and in addition to dining regularly with the Lord Mayor – Master John Edwards had this privilege when feasting with other City Companies in 1846 – the Company also provided at least one Master of another Company during the century when in 1847 its Clerk John Bless Pugh resigned to become the Master of the Merchant Taylors' Company. It also contributed to City charities and gave a grant of £26 5s. to be paid in five annual instalments to the City's Volunteer Patriotic Fund and in 1897 a ten guineas donation was made to the Prince of Wales Hospital Fund.[38]

During the nineteenth century, and including Sir Charles Flower, the Framework Knitters' provided London with four Lord Mayors who had previously served as Sheriffs and one Sheriff who did not become Lord Mayor. When Alderman Robert Waithman was elected Sheriff in 1820 sixteen members of the Court and the Company's Clerk partook of the entertainment and transportation he and his fellow Sheriff, Mr. Williams of the Goldsmiths' Company, provided; the barge, presumably that of the Goldsmiths' Company, and the coaches used by the Company being paid for by Alderman Waithman. When he became Lord Mayor in 1823 Robert Waithman this time made no direct payment to the Company's accounts, which show expenses of £83 7s. 6d., including one for £31 10s. to Mr. Searle for the hire of a barge, plus the annual cost of the Company's dinner on Lord Mayor's Day, which this year came to £70 14s.[39]

Another member of the hierarchy of the Company actively involved in both Company and City affairs in the first half of the nineteenth century was Thomas Wood. A former Assistant, he was appointed Clerk to the Company in 1826, retiring from this position in 1835 to become an Alderman of the City of London, whereupon he was immediately reinstated in the Company as Under Warden. Master in 1837, he was appointed Junior Sheriff of London in 1838 when it was agreed that the 'Coaches, Gowns and Rosettes' were to be provided at the expense of the Company, while the Sheriffs, Alderman Wood and Alderman Johnson of the Coopers' Company, provided the barge. In the ensuing processions the Framework Knitters', as the Company of the Junior Sheriff, went first and took the left hand of the Lord Mayor. In 1840 when Alderman Wood became the Senior Sheriff the Master, Wardens and fourteen Assistants breakfasted at the London Tavern with the Sheriffs, and then went to the Guildhall where the officers were sworn in, but there is no indication that the Company took part in any procession.[40]

Half a century then passed before the Company, in consecutive years, next provided holders of the highest City offices. In 1892 Alderman Sir Alfred James Newton, Master in 1895, was appointed Sheriff, to be succeeded by Alderman Sir John Voce Moore, a member of the Company who was never Master. In both years the Company decided not to take part in the Lord Mayor's procession, although it contributed £5 towards Moore's chain of office and enthusiastically entertained the Lord Mayor in Leicester the following September.[41]

When Sir James Whitehead was Lord Mayor in 1888 he was not yet a member of the Company so that after 1838 the Company did not again take part in the Lord Mayor's ceremonies until 1898 when Sir John Voce Moore took up that office and was supported by the Company on both 8 and 9 November. On 8 November Master F. V. Nicholls, together with Past Masters Bohm, Dowden, Durrant, Paddon and Ward and Assistants Pringle, Terry and Crisp 'all habited in their proper furred Gowns and the Clerk in his silk gown' assembled at the Mansion House for a City luncheon, and then proceeded to the Guildhall for the installation ceremony. The following day the same members of the Company, with the addition of Liveryman J. A. Corah, assembled at the Albion Tavern for breakfast where they entertained the Master and several members of the Loriners' Company and the Senior Warden of the Cordwainers' Company. In the ensuing Lord Mayor's procession the Company's Beadle, 'wearing his Gown and Scarf and carrying his Silver Staff', rode on the box with the coachman of the first of the Company's carriages, while the second carriage had the Assistant Beadle on the box with the coachman. In the third of the

Company's carriages was Master Nicholls, Wardens H. Pocock and G. J. Woodman and Liveryman Corah. 'All the Past Masters wore their Past Masters Jewels and all the Members of the Company wore their furred Robes, except the Clerk who wore his Silk Robe, and in this order preceded by their Banners and Brass and Drum and Fife Bands they took up their place in Basinghall Street. From whence they in due course joined in the procession with the other Companies through the appointed route to the Royal Courts of Justice where leaving their Carriages they went into the Great Hall attending the Lord Mayor who waited upon Her Majesty's Judges and invited them to dinner. The Master and Wardens with his Past Masters, Assistants and Clerk having again taken their places in the Carriages the procession was reformed and proceeded through the Strand returning by the Embankment to Guildhall where the procession broke up. The Company then returned to the Albion Tavern and having taken off their robes dined with the Members of the Loriners' and Cordwainers'. 'The Past Master Sotheran of the Loriners' Company faced by Past Master Bohm of this Company presided and all the parties being seated according to their Seniority in their Companys. Lieut. Col. Sewell the Clerk of the Loriners' Company taking one end of the table and the Clerk of this Company the other with Mr. Garrard Clarke the Clerk of the Cordwainers' Company on his right. This was the first recorded time of these Companys dining together and the Entente Cordiale was most pronounced'. While the rest of the Court was feasting in the Albion Tavern the Master attended the Banquet at Guildhall, together with Junior Warden Woodman and Past Master Cooper who were personal friends of the new Lord Mayor. It was noted that 'this Company had handsome Banners, Bands whose Music was as sonorous and popular as any other, fine Horses and Carriages better than the other Companies . . . and that it did not suffer by comparison with the other Companys'.[42]

On 20 April 1899 Lord Mayor Moore and Sheriffs dined with the Livery of the Company and later that same year Past Master Alderman A. J. Newton was elected Lord Mayor of London. For the second year running the Company proposed 'to the utmost of its power (to) support the honour and dignity of the Lord Mayor Elect through his office of Mayor'. As reported by Liveryman J. A. Corah to the Court the Company's presence on the two days 'was carried out in a manner in every way worthy of the Company by the Master and Wardens who had undertaken the duties. The installation at Guildhall was attended by 18 Members of the Court including Senior Past Masters Kingdom and Bohm. . . . Judging from my experience of the previous year I may say that the Company more than equalled its former efforts. The Bands of Music, the Banners, Horses and Carriages were in no way inferior in appearance to the other Companies taking part'. The Lord Mayor, who had been created a Baronet by the Queen early in his year of office, and Sheriffs dined with the Company in June 1900.[43]

Although by the 1890s no barge had to be hired, as the Thames had ceased to be used for processions in 1856, the other expenses of having a member of the Company as Lord Mayor were borne by the Company or its officials and not by the member concerned. In 1898 the cost to the Company was about £80; carriages for the Court were hired from Wolfe & Sons for £12 15s. 6d., gowns came from Messrs Ede for £5, and for £25 a brass band, drums and fifes, totalling about fifty musicians, was hired from the First Tower Hamlets Rifle Brigade. In 1899 Master Henry Pocock and Wardens G. J. Woodman and E. Terry bore the Company's costs.[44]

The Hall and the Company's possessions

The sale of the Red Cross Street estate comprising the Hind public house, the block of stables, and property fronting White Cross Street, in addition to the Company's Hall, was ordered by the Court of Chancery to increase the size of the planned debtors' prison on White Cross Street, the first stone of which was laid by Alderman Matthew Wood in July 1813 and housed only debtors from London and Middlesex. Negotiations for the site, valued at £2,100, (two thousand guineas) were started in 1811 and on 4 February 1812 the Company entered into a agreement for alternative land in Moorfields, but this was later rescinded when preemptions for both the Framework Knitters' and Fishmongers' Companies were cancelled by the Corporation of London in favour of the Catholic Congregation. Negotiations continued, however, and the City took over Calvert the brewer's lease in 1819. The site was finally compulsory purchased on 24 June 1821 for £3,628 10s. 3d. and the prison extension was duly built, only to be demolished with the rest of the prison, about 1855, to become a railway yard. The site is now part of the Barbican Centre.[45]

Master's Chair
During the nineteenth century the Company's Chair continued its peripatetic existence. Starting in the custody of Past Master John Pugh, it was later deposited with the Company's Clerks and spent much of its time in whichever inn the Company's courts were being held, most especially from 1844 the London Tavern. In 1878 it was loaned to the Bethnal Green Museum where it formed an exhibition with the Masters' Chairs of the Carpenters' and Ironmongers' Companies, and in 1884 graced the Company's stand at the International Health Exhibition. Repairs were frequently made to the Chair during the century; in 1838 it was given new castors at a cost of 7s. 6d. and in 1854 it was repaired, cleaned and revarnished to put it into 'a suitable condition for comfortable occupation' at the expense of Past Master R. H. Manning.[46]

Plate
Although inspected and signed for annually by the Master and Wardens the plate seems to have experienced the same sort of treatment as the Master's Chair. For many years at the beginning of the century it was kept by the landlord of the Kings Head Tavern in the Poultry, and then from 1844 was in the London Tavern, Bishopsgate. Whenever a meeting was held in a different place the Beadle arranged for its transportation by porters.[47]

By the nineteenth century the plate was, probably, regarded by the Court as old fashioned and was certainly regarded as a nuisance, for from 1836, when it was first proposed by Alderman Thomas Wood, then Under Warden, there were a number of motions to sell it. In 1843 James Capel proposed that both the plate and the State Chair should be sold and repeated this proposal in 1861, although by the time he, seconded by Robert Romanis, put the resolution to the Court in October that year, when it was passed unanimously, it only referred to the plate.

At this time the plate was listed as:

Large silver cup with the arms of the Framework Knitters' Company
Large silver cup with cover, the gift of John Carwarden

Two handled silver cup and cover, the gift of Robert Summer
Two handled silver cup and cover, the gift of Mr. Richardson in 1664
Large two handled silver cup and cover weighing 35 ozs. and 10 dwts., the gift of a well wisher
Silver tankard and cover, the gift of J. Margrave
Large silver plate with the arms of the Company and large silver chain
Twelve silver salts
Three table spoons with buttons at end
Eight old fashioned table spoons
Six modern table spoons
Beadle's staff with silver ornaments[48]

On first comparison this list differs considerably from that of 13 October 1769, but as there is almost the same number of items in each list and presumably items such as the 'tankard' of 1861 can be equated with the 'flagon' of 1769, this difference would seem to be more in the description than in actual fact; although, however it is added up, at least three more silver spoons are missing by 1861.

The plate, most articles of which dated from the late seventeenth or early eighteenth centuries and whose simplicity was out of fashion in the Victorian age, was sold in 1861 for £79 15s. 1d. The money raised was put towards repairs at the Almshouses.[49]

The Company was without any silver for only just over twenty years because, on its revival at the end of the nineteenth century, members, realising that some tangible evidence was needed to emphasise the Company's renewed prestige, began to buy plate and other items. The first of the new cups was presented by Past Master William Creasey in 1884, followed in 1887 by the Jubilee Loving Cup presented by Past Masters Capel, Kingdom, Bohm, Worthington and Dowden, and Assistants R. Birkin, T. Bell, J. Cooper, A Durrant and J. Paddon to commemorate the fiftieth year of Queen Victoria's reign. Then, just before he became Lord Mayor in 1889, Sir Alfred Newton presented the Company with a new Beadle's staff with a head depicting the Company's Arms in solid silver for, extraordinary though it may seem, the Beadle's previous staff seems to have been mislaid.

By the end of the century the Company's plate consisted of:

Beadle's mace
Creasey and Jubilee Loving Cups
Silver Guilt cup, presented by J. Paddon (1893)
Silver Cup, presented by George Reid (1893)
Silver cup, presented by Richard Birkin (1894)[50]

Company's other possessions
The fate of the other articles, previously in the Company's Hall and for which there was no inventory, are unrecorded. Some were in the Company's possession until at least 1787–9, as in the former year a warehouse room was rented at a cost of 5s. for the pictures and in 1789 a porter was paid 4s. to move the Chair and other, unspecified, articles to one of the Company's meetings. Then from about 1787 until 1824 some items were in the care of Clerk Thomas Lodington. However their subsequent deposition was not known to Company members for when in 1851

Prince Albert requested the Balderton painting of William Lee to start a gallery of British inventors of machinery no trace of any possessions, other than the plate, could be found, so that not only the pictures, but also the pewter, furniture, banners, flags and linens had over the years just disappeared.[51]

Corporate finances

Until 1821 the only guaranteed annual income of the corporate fund of the Company was the £79 15s. rent of the Hall. This increased to £109 17s. 2d when in 1821 the £3,628 10s. 3d. received for the Hall site was invested in 3 per cent Consols held for the Company by the Paymaster General of the Chancery Division. The income from these Consols, together with the income from the various fines, formed the fund. However, the Company seems to have been no more efficient in collecting the annual fees in the early nineteenth century than it had been in the eighteenth, for in 1826 quarterage was again backdated, this time for five years.[52]

The impression obtained from the few details available is that, although the Company no longer had countrywide expenses and was able to continue to provide the Court dinners and the annual Livery dinner, some, sometimes trivial, economies had to be practised at various times as a consequence of the decline in membership, and consequently of income. Between 1827 and the 1840s there were no payments for special Courts and in October 1829 it was decided that 'no dinner in future (be) ordered for the Court unless there are sufficient funds to pay the Tavern bill'. In 1870 no cigars were to be supplied at the Company's expense at dinners.[53]

It was only with the revival of the Company in the 1880s that dinners again became opulent (see Plate 38). The sixty-seven diners at the Albion in 1895 cost the Company £105 13s. 6d.; eighty-seven cigars were smoked, and forty-eight bottles of champagne, thirteen port vintage 1868, eleven claret vintage 1878, plus a single bottle of Beaune were drunk.[54]

The result of the frugality was, however, that in 1879 cash in hand amounted to £516 1s. 10s. and a further £400 was invested in Consuls. In 1880 the corporate account amounted to £4,378 10s. 3d. Consols. Although it was proposed to bring the capital up to £4,628 10s. 3d., even the increased amount was estimated to bring in only an income of about £170, while it was reckoned that the Company's expenditure was about £200. One proposed solution was to apply for an increase of the Livery, which was impractical as numbers had not yet reached sixty, and the solution eventually accepted was to reinvest the £3 per cent stock in 4 per cent Debenture Stock.[55]

However, in 1882 the corporate investment policy was changed for in August the Company began to invest in property and bought eighteen freehold ground rents of houses on Regina Road, Holloway, Middlesex, at a cost of £3,074 8s., each of which brought in a yearly rent of six guineas, except for two which produced seven guineas. In 1890 the Company bought the further freehold ground rent of 91 Tulse Hill, in 1893 that of 48 Arodene Road and in 1894 that of 29 Helix Road and later 10 Arodene Road (formerly 53 Helix Gardens). Although the returns on these properties, together with the vastly increased fees and fines, greatly improved the corporate account of the Company, they increased the work load of the Court and the Clerk as they were held on repairing leases, and the Minutes frequently refer to the difficulties and the time necessary to collect rents and enforce repairs (see Plate 39).[56]

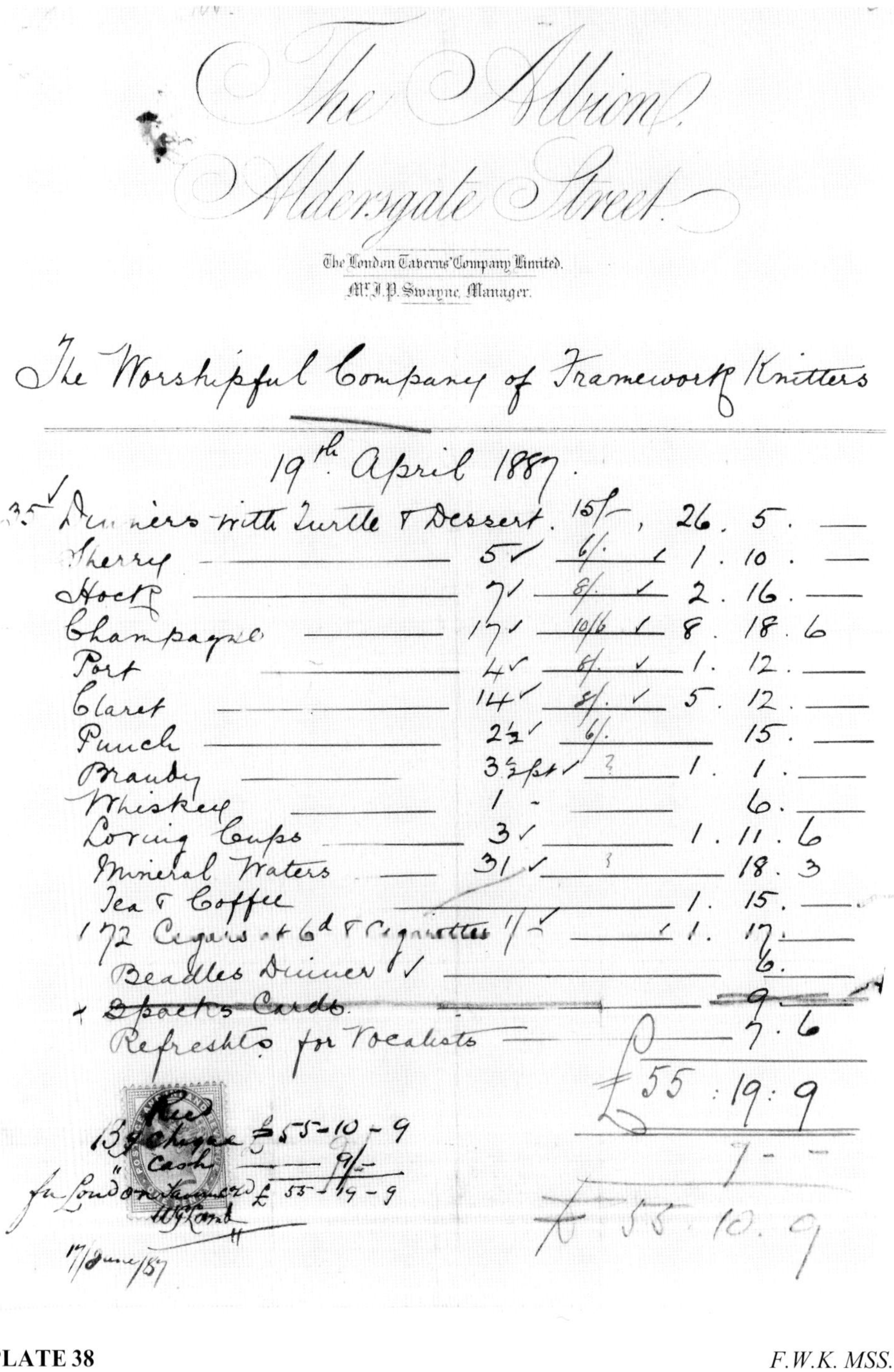

The Albion, Aldersgate Street.

The London Taverns' Company Limited.

Mr. J. P. Swayne, Manager.

The Worshipful Company of Framework Knitters

19th April 1887.

35 Dinners with Turtle & Dessert.		15/-	26.	5.	—
Sherry	5	6/-	1.	10.	—
Hock	7	8/-	2.	16.	—
Champagne	17	10/6	8.	18.	6
Port	4	8/-	1.	12.	—
Claret	14	8/-	5.	12.	—
Punch	2½	6/-		15.	—
Brandy	3½ pts		1.	1.	—
Whiskey	1			6.	—
Loving Cups	3		1.	11.	6
Mineral Waters	31			18.	3
Tea & Coffee			1.	15.	—
72 Cigars at 6d & Cigarettes	1/-		1.	17.	—
Beadles Dinner				6.	—
+ ~~3 packs Cards~~				~~9.~~	
Refreshts. for Vocalists				7.	6
			£55 :	19 :	9
				1 -	
			£55.	10.	9

Recd Cheque £55-10-9
" Cash 9/-
for London Taverns Co Ltd £55-19-9
W. G. Lamb
17/June/87

PLATE 38 *F.W.K. MSS.*

A DINNER BILL OF 1887

A convivial evening was obviously had by the thirty-five members attending this dinner, as in addition to the dinners, alcohol and 72 cigars the Company provided three packs of cards.

PLATE 39

REGINA ROAD, LONDON

These houses formed part of the Worshipful Company of Framework Knitters Corporate property from 1882 until the remaining ones were sold in 1944.

lent by S. A. Mason

Almshouses

During the century further monies were given to the Company's charitable trust. By his will of 28 March 1810 Thomas Cook bequeathed £2,100 £3 per Cent Consols, the interest from which was to be used for the benefit of the residents by increasing pensions. Then in February 1854 Thomas Taylor gave the Company £100; this too was invested in Consols, and the dividend distributed annually at Christmas among the residents.[57]

The twelve Almshouses in Kingsland Road absorbed all the interest received in the charitable account during the nineteenth century and, although pensions continued to be paid to residents who were Freemen or Widows of Freemen, no pecuniary assistance was available for Freemen outside the Almshouses. Six bags of coal were also supplied to the Company's pensioners within the Almshouses, although in 1835, and again in 1848, the recipients petitioned, unsuccessfully, for a larger allowance. Not until October 1878 was the coal allowance extended to all inmates, irrespective of their status, because it was felt that poorly heated houses were deteriorating in the winter. In addition to the pension and the supply of coal the Master and other members of the Company gave Christmas gifts, such as tea, and from 1886 the Duke of Portland provided their Christmas fowl. On the occasion of her Majesty's Jubilee in 1887 all residents were presented with a new sovereign.[58]

Until 1873 the key holder of each Almshouse continued to be either a Freemen or the Widow of a Freemen, first preference being given to those with connections to the Livery. Into the 1840s three pensioners of the Company were surnamed Lee – Mary, Sarah, and a daughter Emma – although it is unrecorded if any of these ladies were descendants of either William Lee or his brothers. Vacancies were advertised in *The Morning Advertiser*, although, as the century advanced, it became progressively more difficult to find qualified applicants and often houses were empty for years. In January 1855 it was noted that House Number 2 had been vacant since 1843 and Number 12 since 1850; these were occupied in January 1865 by which time House Number 4 had been empty since March 1863. In 1873 when Elizabeth Page, the widow of a Freeman, died the Court permitted her daughters Mary and Ann to occupy Almshouse Number 11, without pensions or coals, until such time as a properly qualified person should apply. No qualified person came forward to displace the Pages, or replace other deceased tenants, and by 1885 only three out of the thirteen inmates qualified for pensions – a Freeman, Alexander Dufy, a Free Sister, Isabella Stephenson, and one widow of a Freeman, Mary Corner – although there were also in residence three daughters of Freemen – the two Pages and Mary Archer – and one niece of a Freeman – Mary Simmons; the other five female residents, aged between sixty-seven and seventy-five, were 'strangers' to the Company. As since 1875, after the case of Isabelle Stephenson, (see below), women had not been admitted to the Freedom of the Company without the approval of the Court, to enable additional residents to receive the Company pension in 1886 Mary Archer, Mary and Ann Page and Mary Simmons were admitted to the Freedom of the Company by Patrimony, and one of the 'strangers', Susannah Dover, was admitted by Redemption. Two years later Elizabeth Smith of Almshouse Number 8, and Mary Dawes, of Number 6, both widows, were also admitted to the Freedom.[59]

Occupancy of the Almshouses was not confined to the elderly. In 1836 the widows of both a Liveryman and a Freeman applied for the single vacancy. The former, Elizabeth Archer, together with her three children aged eleven, nine and six, were appointed by the Court to the empty house after having been cautioned that she was 'not to allow her children to become troublesome to the other Inmates'. In 1865 one of Elizabeth's children, Mary Ann, became a key holder until 1868 when a suitable applicant was finally found, although she was re-admitted as an unpensioned inmate on the death of her mother in 1870. Children were not the only unexpected residents of the Almshouses for some inmates took in lodgers. In 1844 Mrs. Cross was admonished 'on the impropriety of her conduct' for having admitted a young woman into her Almshouse 'who was then ill of the Typhus Fever of which she afterwards died in her house'; the Minutes do not make clear, however, whether the objection was to lodgers in general or to one who subsequently died of an infectious disease.[60] Even after being interviewed by the Master and any other members present at the appropriate Court tenants chosen for the Almshouses did not always turn out to be suitable. In the early 1800s Mrs. Muskett was given warning by Master John Pugh that if she continued 'her course of inebriety', she would be thrown out, and the Company went to a lot of trouble to pay her pension weekly instead of quarterly, while in 1848 the Treasurer, John Norbury, was requested to inquire into the 'alleged misconduct', again it would seem of drunkenness, of Betty Clements and was 'empowered to remove her if he should consider it necessary.[61]

In the days before universal social security some were so desperate to qualify for an Almshouse and a pension that they bought their Freedom of the Company very late in life and often when they could not really afford it. George Clements, son of a Freeman of the Company, was admitted a Freeman at a cost to himself of £2 4s. 6d. in June 1851 and then, in October that year, requested to be admitted to a vacant Almshouse; this he received the following January. Another who used this method of getting into a home was Isabelle Stephenson who paid her £2 4s. 6d. on 25 November 1873. On 14 April the following year she tried for, and was refused, an Almshouse place on the grounds that 'persons in distressed circumstances should (not) join the Company for the express purpose of receiving the benefits of the Charitable funds', but that decision was overturned in June and she was admitted 'without the emoluments'; only in 1881 was she finally allowed a pension. For another female marriage to an elderly inhabitant probably seemed to solve the problem of a roof over her head and a pension, but the Company was having none of this, and in 1843 when eighty seven year old John Thurman died leaving a widow of fifty whom he had only married eighteen months before, she was required to give up possession of his Almshouse.[62]

The Almshouses were one hundred years old before the middle of the century and had become a continual drain on the charitable, and sometimes on the corporate, funds of the Company, as well as on individual members. References to repairs and improvement occur in almost all Minutes during the nineteenth century. In 1845, for example, because of burglaries grape vines against the walls had to be removed and the windows at the back of Mrs. Archer's house 'be so far closed as to prevent ingress or egress'.[63]

There was no 'fabrick fund' and the yearly income just about covered ordinary expenses – minor repairs, pensions, insurance and the such like – but by 1854, the year in which Thomas Taylor donated £100, major repairs totalling £390 11s. 3d. were needed, including an estimated £358 16s. for the roof. Only £277 14s. 1d. had been saved in the charitable account and the income from investments was £144 5s. 10d. If the charitable fund was to meet future commitments the cost of these repairs had to be found from elsewhere and twenty two members of the Court, led by James Capel and John Norbury, contributed £1,222 17s. from their own pockets to fund this and other repairs.[64]

The £79 obtained from the sale of the Company's silver in 1861 went to 'the expense of painting and repairs' of the Almshouses and gave scant relief to the charitable funds. Vandalism at the Almshouses grew worse as the area became built up and in 1881 one persistent young breaker of windows had to be taken a to court, where he was fined 4s. 6d., as a deterrent to others. Another expense was updating the Homes and in the spring of 1882 water was finally supplied to the outside toilets. Another recurring problem was the garden and in 1896 the cost of taming the wilderness that this had now become was paid for by Senior Warden Wolf Harris.[65] The Almshouses had been built in a semi-rural position (see Plate 31), but, as the surrounding area was developed, from the middle of the century there were a stream of offers for the whole site, or for all or part of the garden. In 1864 the Vestry of St. Leonard, Shoreditch made three proposals to the Company; to buy one half of the site and rebuild the Almshouses at a cost of £2,000 with another £500 for an endowment, to purchase the whole site and build twelve new Almshouses for the Company on a new freehold site, or else to purchase the whole site for £4,500, leaving the Company to rebuild its Almshouses elsewhere. The Court rejected the first and second proposals and asked for £7,000 for the whole Kingsland Road site but, although the Vestry increased its offer to £6,000, this sum was considered too low by the Company and declined. Another offer for the site from the Metropolitan Free Hospital in April 1882 was also turned down.[66]

By the end of the nineteenth century the Court was actively seeking a solution to the problem of the London Almshouses, but no final decision about their future was taken until the next century.

Education

Although it continued to enrol apprentices after 1809 the Company showed little interest in either their education, or in that of the hosiery trade in general, until the end of the nineteenth century. In 1873 it replied to a request from the Chamberlain of London about the establishment of the body that was eventually to become the City and Guilds of London Institute that 'this Company cannot take any action to promote Technical Education', and followed this in 1877 by reiterating that it was not justified in contributing to the national scheme for technical education then proposed and supported by Companies such as the Mercers' because 'the majority of City Guilds were for the protection of Handicrafts' while the Framework Knitters' 'had for its object the protection of Labourers by a Machinery requiring little education or handicraft skill', adding also that there was 'no application from the Masters or Workmen in the Trade for assistance in Education'.[67]

It was only after its renaissance in 1882 that the Company finally decided to support education for the knitting industry. Past Master Bohm and Junior Warden T. Loveridge represented the Company at the official opening of the Technical

School for Hosiery at Leicester on 20 November 1882, and William Bohm, delivering one of the opening addresses, announced that the Company was presenting a scholarship of £20, which was divided into a top prize of £5, plus three prizes each of £3 and £2. Past Master Bohm became the first of a number of members of the Company who were appointed to the governing body of the Technical School, to which he presented on behalf of the Framework Knitters' Company the frame making silk hose which had formed part of the Company's exhibit at the 1884 International Health Exhibition. From this time the Company took an active interest in both this school and the soon-to-be-formed College of Art; usually the Master attended the schools' prizegiving, as did Mr. Loveridge in 1887. Liverymen of the Company, such as William Rowlett of Leicester, gave lectures to the students, while many members of the Company, among them J. G. Ward, J. H. Cooper and William Rowlett were on the Colleges of Art and Technology Textile Trades Advisory Committees and on the Colleges' management committees. If a prize was unawarded one year the Company advised on its allocation the following year; in 1890 it advised that 'the balance of last gift unawarded' might be used for 'lace', which probably explains why Leicester, and not Nottingham, has specialised in the design and manufacture of women's foundation garments, for which the principal textiles used are lace and elastic net. The Company kept a careful eye on proceedings in the Technical School and in 1895, dissatisfied with the result of the training at Leicester, reduced its subscription to five guineas; although things obviously soon improved for two years later the Leicester members of the Court won a motion that £50 was to be contributed for equipment for the Hosiery Section of the Technical School when the London members had wanted to settle for £25.[68]

Also in 1882 the Company joined a number of textile and other Livery Companies in the supporting the City and Guilds of London Institute founded in 1878, and became one of that body's most enthusiastic and continuing supporters of technical education for the knitting trade, sponsoring from its inauguration in 1886 the Guild's silver medal, the first one of which was won by the J. H. Quilter. In 1889 the Company began to contribute an annual £20 to the prize fund of the City and Guilds of London Institute.[69]

Summary

The Worshipful Company of Framework Knitters weathered its eclipse at the beginning of the nineteenth century as a Society completely involved in the industry whose name it bore and ended the century in a position strong enough to advance the involvement of its members in all aspects of the hosiery trade and its education and able to build on its strong charitable foundations.

References

1 *Report of the Commissioners into Framework Knitters*: 1845 609 (XV); *Appendix to the Report of the Commissioners appointed to inquire into the Condition of the Framework Knitters*: Part I Leicestershire: 1845 618 (XV); Part II Nottinghamshire and Derbyshire: 1845 641 (XV); Wells, p. 94.
2 Mason, pp. 68–81.
3 MSS, 3451/2 p 308, 24 September 1894; 3452/1, Certificate of Thomas Wood, 10 July 1827;

R(ecord) O(ffice of) L(eicester,) L(eicestershire and) R(utland), MSS, 9D52/2; *R(ecords of the) B(orough of) N(ottingham)*, VIII, p. 141, II.115, pp. 143–4, I.64.

4 MSS. 3444; NAO, MSS. CA 4040, RBN, VIII, p 147, I.97, p. 151, I.119; VIII, p. 139; *Leicester Hall Books*, folio 1456, 28 March 1820, folio 1473, 11 April 1821; The Brandreths (Brandrith) had been involved in framework knitting since the seventeenth century and in 1720 a family member was a Warden of the Company and one of the Joint Stock Committee. Jeremiah Brandreth, was one of the journeymen disadvantaged by the rise of the entrepreneurial hosiers and in 1818 led the abortive Pentrich Rebellion. *Biographical Dictionary of Modern British Radicals: I: 1770–1830*. The connections between the former families involved in the hierarchy of the Framework Knitters' Company in London and the East Midlands and the radicals/ revolutionaries such as the Luddites in Nottinghamshire is a subject that requires a more detailed study than can be provided here, but it is surely no coincidence that many whose ancestors had been prominent in the Company were at the forefront of the disturbances of the nineteenth century.

5 MSS, 3452/1.

6 MSS. 3452/1, printed notice from E. Simmons, Beadle, 4 January 1827, 24 June 1843; W. Booth, *In Darkest England and Way Out* (London: Salvation Army, 1890), Preface.

7 *Report of the commissioners into the Framework Knitters: 1845.*

8 MSS, 3451/1, pp. 153–4.

9 MSS, 3452/2, Thomas B. Pugh's accounts for 1845; 3451/1, pp. 153–6.

10 MSS, 3451/1, pp. 174–5.

11 MSS, 3451/1, pp. 194–5.

12 MSS, 3451/1, 24 June 1865, Act 6 Geo: 3 c. 29; repealed in Statute Law Revision Act 1867; 3451/1, p. 353, letter 15 March 187 Act Geo. 3 c. 55 protection of Stocking Frames; Felkin, 1845. p. 3.

13 MSS, 3451/2, pp. 4, 45; 3452/2, p. 29.

14 *Daily Telegraph*, 14 July 1884.

15 MSS, 3451/2, pp. 57, 463; 3451/2, p. 2. Originally it had been hoped that the jewel would not cost more than £25.

16 MSS, 3451/2, 24 September 1894, 24 June 1897, 10 January 1899.

17 MSS, 3447; Funston, 1901, p. 15.

18 MSS, 3451/1, pp. 4, 14, 17, 33, 34, 42, 51, 134, 136, 137, 151, 160, 212, 241, 328, 348, 414, 416, 431, 434, etc.; 3447; Moy Thomas, pp. 17, 23.

19 MSS, 3451/2.

20 MSS, 3451/1, pp. 440–41; 3447; Funston, 1901, p. 16.

21 MSS, 3451/2, pp. 147, 262; CLRO, MSS, *Sir James Whitehead*; *CP*, 26 September 1894.

22 MSS, 3453; 3451/2, pp. 152, 244.

23 MSS, 3452/1, p. 220; 3453.

24 MSS, 3451/1, p. 72, 9 January, 10 April 1877; 3451/2, p. 3.

25 MSS, 3451/1, p. 465; 3451/2, pp. 79–83, 101; 3452/4, 12 January 1915; 3450, *Accounts 1883–4*; Felkin, p. 461.

26 Funston, 1901, p. 17; *The Lady's Magazine*, May 1811, p. 238.

27 MSS, 3453; 3451/1, p. 414.

28 MSS, 3450, 14 April 1812; 3451/1, pp. 326–30.

29 MSS. 3451/1.

30 NRO, MSS, DD 65/10; Thoroton, p. 296.

31 MSS. 3451/2, pp. 386–8; *The Worshipful Company of Frame-Work Knitters: A List of Masters: 1726–1929*, authorship unrecorded, but probably James Funston.

32 MSS, 3451/2, p. 301.

33 MSS, 3451/2, p. 302; *CP*, 26 September 1894.

34 MSS, 3451/2, pp. 302, 308–13.

35 MSS, 3451/1, p. 56; 3450, 1810; 3446/3.

36 MSS, 3451/1, pp. 365; 3451/2, pp. 363, 396–7; 3451/2, p. 227; Funston, 1901, p. 20.

37 Baylen and Grossman, pp. 504–6; Beavan, p. 321; Robert Waithman, *War proved to be the real cause of the present scarcity*, pub. 1800.

38 MSS, 3451/1, pp. 181, 184; 3451/2, pp. 218, 347; 3452, 1849; Funston, 1901, p. 19.

39 MSS, 3452/1, extracts of Minutes of 15, 28, 30 September 1820; 3450, 1824–25.

40 MSS, 3451/1, pp. 5, 92, 94, 120, 121, 123; 3452/16.
41 MSS, 3451/2, p. 288.
42 MSS, 3451/2, pp. 368, 370–77.
43 MSS, 3451/2, pp. 395, 400–1, 407–8.
44 MSS, 3451/22, pp. 390, 395; 3450, October 1898–99; Melling, p. 18.
45 MSS, 3452/14, Clerk's letter 26 November 1931; 3452/1, James Montague Office of Works, Guildhall, to Clerk Thomas Lodington, 30 October 1811, Jos. Busman Comptroller to the Master, 10 January 1815, indenture of 24 June 1817; 3450, 1819–20; John Timbs, *Curiosities of London* (London: Virtue, 1877), p. 704; Charles Knight, *London* (London, Virtue & Co, u.d. c.1875–7), V, p. 326.
46 MSS, 3452/2, accounts for 1838, 1871–72; 3451/1, 8 October 1878.
47 MSS, 3451/1, 18 September 1829, p. 124; 3452/2, 4 January 1845, Beadle's bill of £5 15s 6d includes 6d. for porter to carry the plate.
48 MSS, 3451/1, p. 49, 103, 157, 288, 290 and endpapers.
49 MSS, 3451/1, p. 293; 3452/3.
50 3451/2, pp. 187, 190, 291; 3452/3.
51 MSS, 3450, accounts for 1787 and 1789; Funston, 1901, pp. 8–9.
52 MSS, 3451/1, p. 12.
53 MSS, 3451/1, p. 50; 3452, Clerk's accounts 1870–71.
54 MSS, 3452/4, 24 June 1895 accounts.
55 MSS, 3451/1, pp. 433, 448–450, 459.
56 MSS, 3451/1 p. 42; 3451/2, pp. 54, 239, 333; 3450, accounts 1881–82; 3452/5; 3452/9.
57 MSS, 3452/1; 3451/2, pp. 132–4.
58 MSS, 3451/1, pp. 97, 126, 157, 197, 215, 224, 419.
59 MSS, 3452/2, 23 March, 1837, 24 December 1840, 23 September 1843, 14 January 1845; 3452/4; 3450, 1885, 1886; Funston, Charitable Fund Report, 1886, pp. 4–7.
60 MSS, 3451/1, pp. 99, 160, 312, 333–4.
61 MSS, 3451/1, p. 192.
62 MSS, 3451/1, pp. 149, 212, 214, 215, 369, 370, 374; 3451/2, p. 34.
63 MSS, 3451/1, pp. 172, 351.
64 MSS, 3451/1, pp. 234, 236, 238–240, 290; 3450, 1853–54.
65 MSS, 3451/1, pp. 165, 290; 3451/2, pp. 34, 41, 335.
66 MSS, 3451/1, pp. 49, 165, 302–6; 3451/2, pp. 42, 44.
67 MSS, 3451/1, pp. 364, 404–5.
68 MSS, 3451/2, pp.103–4, 108, 118, 150, 188, 323, 347, 352; CLGL, MSS, 21871/29; *Centenary History of the School of Textiles* (Leicester: Leicester Polytechnic Press, 1983), p. 3.
69 MSS, 33451/2, p. 217; Minutes, 20 January 1978; *Centenary History*, p. 12.

VIII

The twentieth century

The functions of the Worshipful Company of Framework Knitters in the twentieth century were summed up by one Master as 'education, charity, good cheer and fellowship', and it has achieved this combination extremely successfully. It has supported education for the hosiery trade, greatly increasing its involvement in the last quarter of the century. It has expanded its charity throughout the century and at the beginning of the century replaced the eighteenth century Almshouses in north London with expanded, purpose-built Cottage Homes on the outskirts of Leicester which have since been continually upgraded. At the same time it has remained fully committed to its position as a Livery Company of the City of London and taken a full part in City affairs, providing three Lord Mayors and four Sheriffs during the century, as well as liaising with other Livery Companies.[1]

Composition of the Company

Hosiery, with its centre of production in the East Midlands, is one of the most successful industries in Britain during the twentieth century with a gross output rising nearly every year between 1907 and 1970, from 9.1 million pounds value in 1907 to 563.5 million pounds in 1970, and throughout the century persons connected with the hosiery trade have held dominant positions in the Worshipful Company of Framework Knitters, with those from Leicestershire predominating.

The strength of the Leicestershire hosiery members was emphasised early in the century when, after a lapse of twelve years, the Court made a three night visit to Leicester in June 1906 during the Mastership of John Corah. On Friday, 22 June, a visit to the St. Margaret Works of Cooper, Corah and Sons, was followed by a Court meeting at John Corah's house at Oadby Hill which aimed 'to further extend the Company's usefulness and bring it into closer association with the craft with which it is identified and . . . also to commemorate the establishment of the Scheme for the consolidation of the Company's Charities and their adaption to modern requirements'. After a lunch for 125 at the Master's house the Court 'proceeded to inspect a suggested site for the proposed new Almshouses at Stoughton Road, Oadby'. Additional entertainment for Court members was provided by Junior Warden Rowley and Alfred Corah on the Saturday and Assistant Reynolds on the Sunday. Another Court meeting which emphasised further the important role that

Leicester played in the Company was held in Leicester Town Hall on 30 September 1907 when the Mayor of Leicester, Sir Edward Wood, was on the Court of the Company. This involvement with the hosiery trade and the influence of members from Leicestershire continued. Between 1905 and 1930 all but six Masters came from Leicestershire. A number of the leading Leicester hosiery families, most notably Rowley, Corah, and Lorrimer, provided more than one Master and in 1914–15 five members of the Corah family, Alfred, John Arthur, John Harold, John Reginald and Leslie, were Freemen. In 1935 83 per cent of the Company were still directly connected with hosiery and its allied trades, most of them from Leicestershire for, although the slump of the 1920s and 1930s had badly affected the industry, Nottinghamshire, Derbyshire and Leicestershire contained about 56 per cent of the firms, 64 per cent of the workforce and accounted for 71 per cent of total production, and about 35 per cent of this production was manufactured in Leicestershire.[2] This percentage increased after the Second World War for in 1949 at least 90 per cent of Court and Livery were actively connected with textile trades, most with knitting, and still came mainly from Leicester and Nottingham. In 1985, when several of the Livery who rarely, if ever, took part in Company affairs resigned, twelve of the thirteen new Liverymen were either directly or indirectly involved in the hosiery industry. Even when a member did not come from the East Midlands he was still usually engaged in the trade; Leslie Hayman, the Master in 1954, had been a merchant in the knitwear trade for fifty years and his firm had been in existence in the Cripplegate/Aldersgate area of London for 150 years, while the Master of 1976, W. K. Lowe, was the son of a Liveryman who had founded a knitwear company in Congleton, Cheshire.[3]

The continuing dominance of the East Midlands, and Leicester in particular, in the Society's affairs would not seem to have been deliberate. In the first quarter of the century there was no lack of applicants for the Livery and of the sixty-nine who joined between 1900 and 1920, twenty one were from outside the East Midlands. Liverymen were invited in order of seniority to become Assistants but in the slump of the 1920s and 1930s vacancies proved difficult to fill, with many of those next in seniority declining to serve. In 1923 three Liverymen, including the son of Past Master Baddeley, refused and in 1932 and 1933 nineteen more declined, while others wrote stalling their decision. The only two Liverymen who accepted outright were Alfred Roe of Nottingham and Harry Baker of Leicester. Few gave detailed reasons like those offered by Harry Howe of the Curzon Works at Leicester who stated that he would have liked to follow in his father's footsteps but felt unable to do so owing to 'increased business responsibilities and heavy charges that have resulted from my Father's death'.[4]

This pattern of reluctance continued and it is noticeable that although Liverymen of the 1940s continued to come from outside the conurbation of Leicester few went onto the Court, presumably because the offices of Wardens and Master were time consuming and also required a large financial commitment to the Company. By the 1950s the Company found itself not only with Liverymen who did not want to proceed onto the Court of Assistants, but also with at least nine Assistants who felt unable to proceed to the offices of Wardens and Master. It was decided by a special committee that, as the persons concerned had been informed when they became Assistants that they could expect to take office in turn, they should all, with the exception of Assistant S. F. Peshall, be requested, if they felt that there was no possibility of their being able to accept office, to resign thus making room for those willing to proceed to office. In 1960 a Selection Committee was formed to sound out and select Liverymen, no longer always by seniority, who wished to serve as Assistants, but the difficulty of appointing Court members continued. In 1969 the chosen candidates, two each from Nottinghamshire and Leicestershire, refused and in the following year all seven candidates declined to become Assistants, the expense of Mastership being one of the reasons given for the refusal. Although it would also seem that the Company did not know its Livery very well because, at the same time as it was experiencing difficulty in filling Court vacancies, there was a waiting list for admittance to the Company and some Liverymen felt that they had to wait too long to become Assistants.[5] Once on the Court, however, promotion continued to be by seniority.

Company committees

Apart from the permanent committees appertaining to the Oadby Cottage Homes most Company affairs were, until the Second World War, run by the complete Court, with separate committees formed only for a short time and for a specific purpose, such as reorganisation of finances. However, after the Second World War more permanent, annually appointed, committees were set up and run by active members of the Court of Assistants, as well as a number of the Livery. In 1985 there were eight committees – Bursary Appeals, Bursary Awards, Livery Selection, Finance, Records, Residents of the Cottage Homes Selection, Executive Committee of the Cottage Homes and the Committee of Managers for the Cottage Homes. The Records Committee was disbanded in 1991, and by mid-1999 the main committees were those for Nominations and General Purposes, Finance, Charities Appeals, Education, and Management of the Cottage Homes. In addition more short-term committees were formed, many, such as that set up in 1984 consisting of Rolf Noskwith, Howard Russell Ellis, Peter Ward, G. N. Corah and the Company Treasurer, to consider the Company's future.[6]

One committee formed for a single purpose was established in 1986 to co-ordinate the Company's celebrations of the quatercentenary anniversary of the invention of the stocking frame by William Lee in 1589 and comprised Assistants Russell Kempton, H. P. Corah, J. P. Polito, J. A. Ridge and S. C. Wegerif. A limited edition commemorative plate was commissioned from Royal Doulton and the main event organised for 1989 was a banquet attended by 556 people in the Guild-hall in London which was graced by the Princess Royal. One of the four bursary winners of that year, Leonie Gate of Leicestershire Polytechnic, also became the William Lee Award winner, and was presented with this special honour by the Princess at the Guildhall. On 18 June the annual Livery Service was held in Leicester Cathedral, instead of its usual venue of St Peter's Church, Oadby, and was followed by a champagne luncheon in the grounds of the Cottage Homes to which all residents were invited. Members of this committee and other members of the Company were also involved in other commemorative events for William Lee and the Master, Michael Martin, represented the Company at a banquet organised by the William Lee Quatercentenary Committee at Christ's College, Cambridge.[7]

Company Newsletter

In the second half of the century it was felt that the Livery needed to be kept in closer touch with Company affairs and Master Alan Bent suggested that a News-letter should be started. Between 1962 and 1980 this was edited by Past Master Roger Foister after which it became the responsibility of the Clerk, although with clerical changes it lapsed in 1993, and was only re-established under Clerk H. W. H. Ellis in 1999.[8]

Corporate finances

In the opening decades of the twentieth century the Company's corporate income was finely balanced at about £300. Just over half – about £180 – came from the ground rents of the Company's properties, in Regina Road and elsewhere, and the dividend from London and South Western Railway shares, with the remainder from Company fees and fines. The management of the corporate properties continued to cause a great deal of work for few were kept in good repair by the tenants and in 1909 Schedules of Dilapidations had to be served on sixteen tenants. Not all rents were paid on time, and in 1926 a writ for forfeiture of the lease was issued to one occupant who had apparently for years 'given trouble'.[9] Some of the properties seem to have been disposed of in the 1920s and 1930s and in 1944 a Finance Committee composed of the Master, Wardens and Treasurer, plus Past Masters Whitehead, Gledhill and Ward and Assistant F. T. Carmichael recom-mended in a report dated 30 November the sale of the ground rents of the remaining Regina Road properties valued at £2,770. Just over a year later all remaining ground rents were finally sold for £2,562 8s.; the delay being partially caused by the neces-sity to establish ownership after the destruction of the deeds by enemy action.[10]

Steps had been taken to put the Company's corporate finances on a sounder footing just after the First World War. From 1921 the Master and Wardens were required to pay fines on election to office – £42 and £21 respectively – and at the same time a number of other proposals were put forward, including the suggestions that the cost of Court dinners be defrayed by the members attending, that the privileges of Past Master and Court members inviting guests at the cost of the Company and the fee of 10s. paid to members attending punctually at Court be suspended, and that an application be made to the Court of Aldermen to increase both the size of the Livery and Livery fees. It was decided to pursue the latter course and also suspend the privilege of Court members, other than the Master and Wardens, for inviting guests at the cost of the Company. In 1923, in the hope that it would boost finances and allow the greater part of the Livery and Admission fees to be invested, it was decided to increase the fees to join the Court from £75 to £105, and Court members, except for the Master, were encouraged to subscribe five guineas per annum towards general funds.[11]

The Company's Second World War damage claim, settled at £184 8s. 5d., hardly paid for replacements for items destroyed in the Clerk's office during the Blitz and finances soon had to be re-examined. In 1943 the balance of the corporate fund had been £800 12s. 2d. but by 1947 ordinary expenditure exceeded income by £609. A general increase in fines followed and, although the total continued to fluctuate, this measure momentarily corrected the financial position so that by the end of 1948 there was a surplus of £1,059 4s. 3d. However, further adjustments had to be made in 1956 when the surplus of income over expenditure had declined to £27. Subscriptions paid by the Court were increased by £7 and the fine on admission to the Livery increased from £63 to £80; a year later it was raised to £100, which included the cost of the Livery dinner. The cost of Court dinners continued to be met from the corporate fund, although the cost for guests to this dinner increased to £3 5s., and to the Ladies' dinner to £3 13s. 6d. as the Master was no longer expected to pay for the lady guest of each member of the Court. One financial burden had always been members who habitually paid late – these had come both from Court and Livery, although the latter were the worst offenders – but with twenty five Liverymen in arrears by 1990, it was decided that everyone had to bring their payments up-to-date if they wanted to stay in the Company; eventually all but one did so.[12]

Company functions

As is appropriate to a City of London Livery Company most meetings of the Court and Court dinners continue to be held in various venues in London. For many years the Company had met in the Albion Tavern, Aldersgate Street, but in 1905, when the accounts became of an 'excessive nature', it was decided to change. In April that year the Court was held at the Savoy Hotel in the Strand, with subsequent meetings held in the Clerk's office on Ludgate Hill with dinners at the Hotel Metropole, Northumberland Avenue, or in the Halls of other Livery Companies. In 1907 both the Sadlers' and Haberdashers' Halls were used, and in following years the Leathersellers' and the Grocers' Halls were added to the list. Dinners were suspended during World War I but immediately after its cessation the venues included the Savoy and the Hotel Victoria in Northumberland Avenue (see Plates 40 and 41).[13]

It is mainly unrecorded where the Company met between 1927 and 1941, but during the rest of World War II Courts were, in spite of enemy action and the risk of bombing, and with the exception of a Court at Leicester in August 1944, held in various venues in London – the Mayfair and Wardorf Hotels and the Livery Halls of the Vintners', Innholders', Tallow Chandlers' and Grocers' Companies being used – although the traditional dinners were mostly replaced by luncheons. Post-war Court dinners continued to be held in one of the Livery Halls, most usually the Tallow Chandlers', although in January 1951, when Sir Cyril Osborne M.P. had succeeded Sir Bracewell Smith as Master, the post-Court dinner for about 130 was in the Members' Dining Room of the House of Commons. Indeed London remained the venue for nearly all functions until 1974 when the January Court and a luncheon were held in the Corah Hall at Oadby. From 1977 inflation, and the falling numbers attending the various functions, caused a radical alteration in the Company's arrangements. It was agreed that any change must bear in mind the traditions and dignity of a City Livery Company and the constraints of the City Aldermen but should increase contact between the Court and the Livery. It was decided that from 1977 the January Court meeting and lunch were to be held at Oadby, but no admissions would be taken. The Installation Court meeting was to be held in London, initially at the Tallow Chandlers' Hall, where admissions would be made to Court and Livery; the Court and their Ladies, plus such members of the Livery and their Ladies or guests as accommodation would allow, would then dine. A further Court meeting was to be held at the Oadby Almshouses on a Saturday in the middle of June to be followed by a garden party. Then the October Court meeting, at which admissions to the Court and Livery were to be made, was to be held in London followed by the Livery Dinner at the Mansion House. From 1978 participants at the dinners were given the choice of full evening dress or dinner jacket.[14]

Ladies' evenings
From 1909 a dinner for Ladies of Court members became a more frequent, although to begin with not annual, event held in April. These were initially held at the Hotel Metropole in London. In 1911 the dinner during the Mastership of Alexander Lorrimer was attended by fifty-one ladies for whom souvenirs were commissioned from Stewart Dawson & Company. In May 1919 Ladies of Assistants were invited to a dinner at the Trocadero, London, by Past Masters T. S. Rowley, Ernest Walker and Frank Moore, then there was a gap until 1923 after which it would appear that these dinners were held on a more regular basis. At the Ladies' banquet held in London in 1933 each lady present received a silver cream jug engraved with the arms of the Company as a gift from the Master. The Ladies' dinner was confined to the guests of members of the Court until 1972, after which date six of the Livery and their wives were also invited; invitations being issued by rota starting with senior Liverymen. When females began to be invited to the annual Livery dinner in 1976, the same year as they were admitted to the Livery, the Installation dinner reverted for a time to being an all male affair.[15]

Dinner with the Lord Mayor
During the early 1900s the Lord Mayor and Sheriffs of the City of London had frequently dined with the Company, but the first recorded Company dinner at the Mansion House was on 9 March 1922 when the Past Master of the Company and Lord Mayor, Sir John Baddeley, entertained the Court and their Ladies. After the Second World War the Livery dinner of 1947, attended by the Lord Mayor and Sheriffs, was held in the Mansion House on 31 October and from that date the Company's Livery dinner has traditionally been held in this venue, except for a break between 1984 and 1986.[16]

The Company and the City of London

Although the majority of its members were based outside London the Company has nevertheless throughout the twentieth century taken a full and active role in the affairs of the City of London. At the very beginning of the century it received the South African War Medal in 'commemoration of the spontaneous and patriotic liberality shown . . . in assisting to raise and equip the City of London Imperial Volunteers for active service in South Africa'.[17]

By the middle of the century the Company was so successful in recruiting and retaining members that in 1942, when the Livery Committee to Common Hall, established in 1864, was expanded from twelve to sixteen, the Worshipful Company of Framework Knitters was acknowledged as one of the four companies possessing the greatest numerical strength not already represented on this

F.W.K. MSS.

THE WORSHIPFUL COMPANY OF FRAMEWORK KNITTERS.
Dinner at the Hotel Victoria, London, October 10th, 1933.
Master: Arthur Stannage Whitehead, Esq.
Wardens: Julian Ronem, Esq., John Harold Cooper, Esq.   Clerk: Ernest Arthur Ebblewhite, Esq., J.P., LL.D.

PLATES 40 and 41

1933 LIVERY DINNER AND SEATING PLAN

THE WORSHIPFUL COMPANY OF FRAMEWORK KNITTERS.

Livery Banquet.

10th OCTOBER, 1933.

PLAN OF TABLES.

The Master:

A. S. WHITEHEAD, ESQ.

committee and was asked to nominate a member; Past Master Gledhill becoming its representative. In 1962 Past Master Henderson represented the Company, and in the 1980s Past Master Kershaw. As membership of the Livery Committee is now rotated the Worshipful Company of Framework Knitters will provide its next committee member in 2002.[18] The Company also aided the City in its battles with the government. In 1917 it made a five guineas donation and supported the committee opposing the deprivation of Liverymen of the franchise to vote for the Members of Parliament representing the City of London. In 1947 the Company actively supported the opposition by Common Council to the provisions in the Town and Country Planning Bill which sought to deprive the City of its planning powers.[19]

Company members also acted as advisors on various City of London Committees. After the First World War the Framework Knitters Frank Moore and Ernest Walker sat on the committee formed by the City of London Livery Companies to assist the Ministry of Reconstruction and after the Second World War the Company advised the City on the textile trade. For many years Assistant Cyril Hurd was its representative on the City's textile committee, and on his death his place was taken for a short period by Liveryman Professor Munden and then by Past Master John Whitehead. Past Master Whitehead also advised the Lord Mayor on the creation of a clothing and fashion centre in Brixton and in 1986, together with Liverymen Munden and Millington, was on the Livery Companies' Colouration and Craft Committee. In addition to giving advice the Company also took part in City Exhibitions and in 1989 mounted an exhibition in the Guildhall in commemoration of the 800 years of the Mayoralty.[20]

Masters of the Company participated fully in the events of the City, most years attending the United Guilds service in St Paul's Cathedral, as well as the Lord Mayors' functions and briefings for Livery Company Masters, the Buckingham Palace garden parties, and other such events. In 1953 the children of Clive Henderson remember attending the Lord Mayor's Children's Fancy Dress Party in the Mansion House during his Mastership.[21]

During the twentieth century the Society again provided both Sheriffs and Lord Mayors of the City of London, as well as a Mayor of Cape Town. In 1904 Liveryman William Thorne, who was later knighted, became Mayor of Cape Town, while the Master of 1900, George Woodman, was elected Sheriff of the City of London at a ceremony and breakfast attended by the Framework Knitters' Master and Court members. For the Lord Mayor's procession in November that year the Master, Frederick Dyer, Past Masters Pocock and Crisp, Assistant Rowley and the Clerk hired two landaus, plus two postillions and footmen, from Thomas Tilling of Peckham for a total cost of seven guineas 'to do honour to Mr. Deputy and Sheriff Woodman'. The Company's two carriages followed those of the Wheelwrights' Company and were followed by a band hired from the Third Middlesex Volunteer Artillery. In the evening the Master attended the Lord Mayor's banquet.[22]

In 1908 the Master of 1906, John James Baddeley, was elected Sheriff. The year 1909 was a busy one in the Company's involvement in City affairs as it took part in the Lord Mayor's procession in the November, Alderman Baddeley was knighted, George Woodman, by now also knighted, was elected Alderman for Wallbrook Ward and Frederick Painter, the Master in 1912, became Deputy Alderman for the Coleman Street Ward.[23] In 1913 when Frederick George Painter was elected unopposed to the Shrievalty the Company again hired two carriages for the November procession, and displayed the six feet by four feet six inches blue silk banner painted with the arms of the Company which had been hung in the Corah Hall in 1912. Master Francis Brice and Wardens John Woodhouse and Thomas Rowley, Past Masters John Corah and Robert Rowley and Assistants Frank Moore and Frank Wigley, plus the Clerk, met for breakfast at De Koysers Hotel before taking part in the procession. In the evening the Master, Wardens and Clerk attended the Lord Mayor's banquet.[24]

Sir John James Baddeley was elected Lord Mayor of London in 1921 and the Worshipful Company of Framework Knitters, as his Parent Company, 'held the place of honour among the Livery Companies . . . immediately before the Aldermen and Sheriffs, who preceded the Lord Mayor'. The Banner of the Company, carried by two Commissionaires, immediately preceded the two carriages containing Past Masters Brice, Moore and Wigley, and Assistants J. H. Corah, J. E. Ellis, Carryer and Hawkins. The Company's third carriage conveyed the Acting Master Colonel Oliver, Junior Warden Reginald Corah and the Clerk. On the box sat the Beadle carrying his Staff of Office. The fourth vehicle in the Company's procession was a dray drawn by a pair of horses containing an old, working, 16-gauge hand knitting frame. The Lord Mayor directed the lorry containing the knitting frame to draw up for an hour close to the pavement outside the Law Courts, where he and the Sheriffs were standing, so that all could inspect it working and speak to the framework knitter, Joseph Kimbrell, an employee of Corah's for more than forty years, who was assisted by his wife. The frame had been discovered in Bromley's hosiery factory in Leicester by Alderman Jabez Chaplin and George Bailey, Secretaries of the Leicester Amalgamated Hosiery Union, and was put into working order for the show at Corah's factory.[25]

In 1933, the year the Company received its Coat of Arms, it was invited to take part in the Lord Mayor's procession. The Company was allotted two cars, the first contained Past Masters Woodhouse and Ellis and Assistant Cooper, and the second Master William Moore, Upper Warden Whitehead, Deputy Clerk Price and the Acting Beadle with the Company's staff. Preceding the cars were two vehicles illustrating contrasting facets of the hosiery industry. The first, a horse dray, portrayed 'a framework knitting tableau with figures representing the Rev. William Lee . . . and his wife; and an old frame . . . accompanied by men in period costume, and preceded by a descriptive banner'. The second, on a lorry provided by G. Stibbe & Company of Leicester, contained a working 'underwear machine of the Stibbe-Interlock type, with a machine for women's silk hose, with cuban heel of the well-known Maxim make, both being built in the finest gauges of their class' (see Plate 42). In the evening both the Master and the Upper Warden attended the Lord Mayor's banquet.[26] In 1937 Sir Harry Twyford, who had been Master of the Framework Knitters' the previous year, and was also a Past Master of the Masons' and a Liveryman of the Loriners' Companies, was Lord Mayor of London. The Company was one of six Livery Companies who paraded in the Lord Mayor's Show, the theme of which was 'Empire Produce and Trade'.[27]

Alderman Bracewell Smith, the Master in 1949, became Sheriff in 1943, when there was no procession because of the War, and Lord Mayor in 1946. The theme of the first non-austerity Lord Mayor's Show was 'Work and Play', and only three Livery Companies, the Spectacle Makers' the Coach Makers' and the Merchant

PLATE 42   *F.W.K. MSS.*

1933 – THE WORSHIPFUL COMPANY OF FRAMEWORK KNITTERS FLOATS IN THE
LORD MAYOR'S PROCESSION

The two floats of the Framework Knitters' show contrasting facets of the Company's heritage.
(a) shows the foundations of framework knitting laid in 1589 with William Lee's invention of the frame.
(b) shows modern knitting machinery of the types used and supplied by members of the Company.

Taylors' took part, as most of the procession consisted of members of the armed forces.[28]

The Company has not provided any Lord Mayors or Sheriffs since the Second World War although Masters of the Company have frequently taken their place in the Lord Mayor's processions. In addition, in November 1955 when the theme was 'Wool through the Ages' the Worshipful Companies of Framework Knitters, Woolmen, and Weavers shared a float, towards which each contributed £75.[29]

Street processions were not the only events organised by the City in which the Company took part. In the Royal River Pageant on the Thames for the Coronation of Queen Elizabeth II the Company, represented by Master Henderson, Wardens Hayman and Spencer and Past Masters Gledhill and Ellis, together with the Clerk and the Beadle, shared the 'Maid of Kent' with the Companies of the Gold and Silver Wyre Drawers, Gunmakers, Masons, Master Mariners, Painter Stainers, Pattern Makers, Paviours, Stationers & Newspaper Makers, and Upholders. The launch, decorated with the Companies' shields, processed from Greenwich to the Pleasure Gardens at Battersea where lunch was served. The Company's cere-monial shield was displayed again in Cheapside on the occasion of the Queen's Silver Jubilee in 1977 and in Ludgate Hill for Prince Charles's marriage in 1981.[30]

In addition to attending City events the Company has supported a number of City schemes. In 1954, in consultation with the City of London Territorial and Auxiliary Forces Association, it agreed to adopt one of the City-based Territorial Army regiments, but, on being instructed to sponsor 326 (City of London) Battalion of the Womens Royal Army Corps, regrettably pulled out of the scheme feeling that an all-male Livery Company could not in all seriousness adopt an all-female corps. The Company has also made a large number of donations to charities nominated by the City and has usually supported the Lord Mayor and Lady Mayoress's annual charities. In 1907 £250 was given to the Lord Mayor's Fund for Crippled Children. During the Second World War the Company made a donation of over fifty pounds to the Lady Mayoress's Comforts League, and a smaller donation towards H.M.S. Anson, the ship adopted by the Lord Mayors and the City of London.[31] Since 1950 many other donations have been made, including twenty five guineas in 1956 towards the restoration of St. Mary-le-Bow Church, £100 in 1971 for St. Paul's restoration and £400 to the Queen's Silver Jubilee Appeal in 1977. In recent years the Company has usually contributed £100 to the various Lord Mayor of London's charity appeals, although in 1990, when the Lord Mayor supported three charities, it increased its donation to £150. In 1989 the Company gave £1,250 from its Guildhall Dinner to the Princess Royal's 'Save the Children Fund', as well as adding to its Corah House Development and Bursary Appeal Funds.[32]

The Company has continued to maintain connections with numerous Livery Companies. Members of the Worshipful Company of Framework Knitters were often members of other Livery Companies, as was Alderman Bracewell Smith in the 1940s whose parent company was the Spectacle Makers', and Robert Osborne in the 1990s who was Master of the Framework Knitters' in 1997 and of the Bakers' in 1999. In addition, the Company Clerk has since 1926 kept in contact with the other Companies through the Association of Clerks of Livery Companies. The Company also contributed to a number of appeals by other Livery Companies. During the century the Framework Knitters' frequently dined in the Tallow Chandlers' Hall and in 1969 £65 was enthusiastically donated towards the heraldic oriel window unveiled on 29 October 1969, which included the arms of the Tallow Chandlers', together with those of the Framework Knitters' and nineteen other Companies which regularly dined there. Four years later an interest was also expressed by the Company in donating a stained glass window for the new Livery Hall Suite in the reconstructed Guildhall and in 1984 £100 was given to the special appeal to commemorate the Mastership of Princess Anne at the Worshipful Company of Farriers.[33]

One item discussed intermittently during the century was the provision of a new Company Hall within the City, either in conjunction with other Companies or solely for the Framework Knitters'. A communal project had first been mooted in 1883 and in 1907 the Company supported the possible acquisition of Crosby Hall for this purpose. When nothing came of this idea the Company did not support a 1913 scheme for a joint Hall because by now it was considering building its own Hall. This dream of a new Company Hall lasted into the 1930s, for in October 1931 the Master, Clarence Kershaw, expressed the hope that a fund be opened so that 'in the not too distant future the Company . . . would even have a Hall of their own'. However, less than a year later this idea was already fading, for in March 1932 a meeting of the 'Hall-less' Livery Companies in the Guildhall included the Framework Knitters', and in 1933 the Company sent ten guineas to the scheme to provide a Great Hall for City Companies within the University of London. Again this scheme faded, as had the Company's hope of its own Hall, and in 1971 when the Shipwrights' Company investigated the possibility of incorporating a Companies' Hall in a new development in the City of London at an overall cost of £600,000, the Court simply noted the information.[34]

Relationships with other Livery Company are not all work however. During their year of office Masters usually entertained and were entertained by Masters of other Livery Companies and the Company also entered various inter-Livery competitions. From 1950 the Framework Knitters' entered a team for the Livery Companies' Prince Arthur Golfing Cup, early team members being Cyril Osborne, Eric Turner, Alan Bent and R. I. Bedingfield. In 1962 the Team captained by the Master, V. W. Coles, came ninth out of forty-five at Wentworth, and in 1966 came equal eighteenth of the forty-five teams taking part when represented by Timothy Bedingfield, John Fox, Howard Russell Ellis and John Simpson, quite an achievement when the Coachmans' Company was represented by the Bonallack family. In 1975, under the captaincy of Howard Russell Ellis, the Company again came eighteenth, only ten strokes behind the winners and in 1984, this time under the captaincy of Gordon Taylor, the Company's team were thirteenth, its second highest recorded position. Indeed, so popular has this activity proved that the inaugural meeting of the Company's own Golf Society, which is to be run by Liveryman Alan Shelton, was held at Luffenham Heath Golf Club on 14 October 1999, and members will annually play for 'The Howard Ellis Memorial Trophy'.[35] Bridge is another inter-Livery tournament in which the Company has participated since its inception in 1983. The first members representing the Company were C. Hamilton and P. Tahany. Past Master Peter Osborne has long been on the Company's bridge team and in recent years has been joined by his sister Baroness Hazel Byford.[36] In recent years numerous other members have represented the Company in the City's swimathon and other events.[37]

Moreover, in addition to its own and the City of London charities, the Company has contributed to a number of other causes. Although some were national, such as the support given to both to the National Relief Fund and the British Red Cross during the First World War, usually, however, its help went to projects more personal to the Company, such as the donation made in 1950 to the Appeal Fund raised by Oadby Parish Church for the widow of late Chaplain of the Cottage Homes, Canon Cooper. Until the Second World War the Company made an annual donation to the Oadby District Nursing Association, initially of five guineas, and then after 1925 of ten guineas. St. Peter's Church, Oadby, also received regular sums of money as did the Framework Knitters' Museum at Ruddington, Nottinghamshire, and, until it was taken over by Leicestershire County Council, the Master Hosier's House and Workshop at Wigston, whose meetings were attended by members of the Company. The Company also gave support, co-ordinated by Past Master Jeremy Ridge, when the Industrial Heritage Museum at Snibston, Leicestershire, was being established.[38]

Almshouses

London

Although the seventeenth century Almshouses in London were still almost fully occupied when a monetary gift was given to each resident by the Master, Edward Terry, and the Treasurer of the Almshouses, Henry Pocock, to celebrate the coronation of King Edward VII in 1902, the Company already realised that it was becoming increasingly difficult to find suitable tenants; framework knitting had long left London and most occupants had little connection with either the trade or the Company and, in addition, the Homes were now in a heavily built-up area instead of the earlier semi-rural setting. Although in 1904 seven applications were received for two vacant houses, it was decided to leave these empty until the future of the site had been decided, for, of the eleven persons occupying the Almshouses, only three, Mary Archer and Mary and Ann Page, were Free of the Company. All the occupants, except for Elizabeth Woods aged fifty-two and Anne Page aged sixty-nine, were in their seventies or eighties, and there was only one male occupant, John Snelling aged seventy.[39]

In 1905 the Master, John Corah, proposed that the Company's Almshouses be moved from London but, before these could be disposed of, the Company had first to regularise its position. In April 1905, when the Clerk began investigating all possible ramifications of the sale of the Kingsland Road site, he discovered that since 1745 the regular appointments of trustees, that the Company presumed had been correctly carried out, were in fact invalid as no legally executed Trust Deed existed. The case was submitted to Counsel Joseph Gatey to ascertain whether the Company had a good title to the Almshouses and, if not, in whom the property was vested. Counsel's opinion was that 'as matters stand a good title to the legal estate cannot be made out', and 'at present the Charity is being carried on in a manner . . . unauthorised and everyone concerned is liable to be proceeded against'. Gatey went on to suggest that 'the proper and only satisfactory course is to lay the matter before the Attorney General and with his sanction to apply to the Charity Commissioners to formulate a new scheme, bringing the Charity up to the modern state of affairs and getting the lands and funds vested in the Official Trustees'.[40]

The Company immediately established an Almshouse Committee consisting of the Master, John Corah, Wardens J. J. Baddeley and James McIntosh, and the

Clerk, and on 18 August 1905 authorised the Clerk to negotiate with the Charity Commissioners. The scheme submitted included the sale of the London Almshouses and the application of the proceeds in the acquisition of suitable land in or near Leicester or Nottingham for the erection of modern ones, and also the extension of the objects of the Company's charities to include poor framework knitters or hosiery workers and ex-framework knitters or hosiery workers, plus their widows, sons and daughters, whether or not Freemen of the Company.[41]

On 28 June 1906 the Charity Commission published its approved scheme for the regulation of The Framework Knitters' Company Almshouse Charities. Although the Framework Knitters' Company of the City of London continued to be the trustee, money not needed for immediate working purposes had to be invested in the name of the Official Custodian for Charities. The Charity Commission not only laid down rules for the administration of the charities, it required to be consulted on most aspects of this work, which was to lead to decisions taking a considerable length of time. It made provision for the payment of out-pensions to the inhabitants of the London Almshouses, but allowed the trustees to purchase 'a suitable site', in either Leicester or Nottingham, for 'new Almshouse buildings to be erected . . . with a view to the ultimate accommodation therein of 40 Almspeople, a married couple for this purpose being counted as one Almsperson'. 'The Almshouses and Persons shall be administered, by a body of not less than nine or more than fifteen Managers . . . appointed by the Trustees . . . majority of the Managers shall be members of the said Company . . . remaining Managers shall be appointed from operative Framework Knitters or Hosiery Workers . . . not less than one-third of the whole body of Managers for the time being shall be such operative Framework Knitters or Hosiery Workers . . .'.[42]

Although work could now began on Almshouses in the East Midlands those in London still had to be disposed of. They were put up for auction on 19 July 1906, but proved difficult to sell, and at Christmas 1906 six were still occupied (see Plate 43). The Company wanted £6,000 for the whole Kingsland Road site and £3,500 for half the site, and it was not until April the following year that an offer of £3,250 for the northern half was accepted from E. Carwardine & Company Limited. In spite of the Clerk's efforts no firm offer had been received for the southern moiety by mid-1908 when the Clerk had to deal with vandalism to several windows. In mid-1909 the Company thought it had sold this southern half to Nathaniel Fortescue for £3,000, but after this contract fell through it was not until 11 December that J. J. Chapman bought the site.[43]

Four females – Mary and Ann Page, E. and M. J. Woods – remained in the Almshouses until the sale was finalised, after which the Company was required to pay each a pension of five shillings per week in lieu of residence for the rest of their lives. In view of the ages of these ladies it must have been hoped that the pensions would only be required for a short time, but three were still being paid in 1922. The surviving Miss Page only died in 1932, by which time she was well into her nineties. The cost of her funeral and a wreath were paid for by the Company.[44]

Oadby

Long before a site in the East Midlands was purchased John Corah inaugurated an appeal fund for the new Almshouses, for in July 1905 a fund-raising committee with himself as Secretary and consisting of Sir Edward Wood and Assistants

By order of The Worshipful Company of Frame Work Knitters.

KINGSLAND ROAD

Particulars, with Plan & Conditions of Sale

OF

·A VALUABLE

FREEHOLD SITE

OF

Building Land

HAVING AN IMPORTANT

FRONTAGE OF 200 FEET TO KINGSLAND ROAD

AND A RETURN

Frontage of 87ft. 6in. to Pearson Street,

AND CONTAINING AN AREA OF

17,400 Superficial Feet

(LITTLE MORE OR LESS).

Tne Site is about 600 yards North of Shoreditch Station on the North London Railway, within a mile and-a-half of the Bank of England, and is suitable **for the**

Erection of large Manufacturing Premises,

Warehouses, Shops, or an Institution.

For Sale by Auction by Messrs.

S. WALKER & SON

At the Mart, Tokenhouse Yard, E.C.,

On THURSDAY, the ~~14th~~ day of ~~JUNE,~~ 1906

At TWO o'clock precisely, IN ONE LOT.

Particulars with Plan and Conditions of Sale may be had of JOHN WOODHOUSE, Esq. (Messrs. Stanley, Woodhouse & Hedderwick), Clerk to the Company, Bank Chambers, 45, Ludgate Hill, E.C.; at the Mart; and at the Auctioneers' Offices,

22, MOORGATE STREET. E.C.

" Estates Gazette," Ltd., 6, St. Bride Street, E.C.

PLATE 43   *F.W.K. MSS.*

1906 AUCTION NOTICE FOR THE KINGSLAND ROAD ALMSHOUSE SITE

Rowley, Brice, Donisthorpe, Lorrimer, Hawley, Oliver, Alfred Corah and W. G. Waterhouse Reynolds, was set up. By February 1907 £3,000 had already been promised.[45]

The original suggestion of moving the Company's Almshouses from London to either the Nottingham or Leicester areas was probably always a non-starter, for it would seem that John Corah was always determined that the development should be in the immediate vicinity of the city in which his great hosiery works were situated and which he regarded as the centre of hosiery manufacture. There is no record that sites other than the one on Stoughton Road in Oadby, Leicestershire, situated 'in the midst of some pretty pastoral country', was ever considered, and members of the Court were shown around this site as early as July 1905.[46]

The Oadby site of approximately four acres was finally purchased from Harry Leycester Powys-Keck, the owner of the Stoughton Estate on 24 June 1907 for £1,000. Draper & Walker were appointed architects and plans were speedily drawn up. The first pair of cottages and the archway entrance were built by Bradshaw Brothers of Leicester for £787 8s. 6d.[47]

The foundation stone in the entrance archway of the Worshipful Company of Framework Knitters' Oadby Cottage Homes was laid on Monday, 30 September 1907, by the Lord Mayor of London, Sir William P. Treloar, with a silver trowel presented to him by the Company (see Plate 44). This ceremony was both a prestigious occasion for the Company and a unique one for Leicester, because although the town had been visited previously by a Lord Mayor of London, it was the first time such a visit was 'in State'. The Clerk's sonorous seven page report to the Court and various newspaper articles describe vividly the state visit of the Lord Mayor and Sheriffs of London to Leicester for the inauguration of the Oadby Homes in a day of ceremony which was also attended by the Lord Mayor of Sheffield and the Mayors of Leicester, Derby, Nottingham, Loughborough and Northampton. The state coaches of the City of London together with horses, coachmen and grooms were sent to Leicester in advance and were waiting at the station for the arrival of London's civic dignitaries. 'Many of the factories were closed' and the routes from the station to the town hall and from the town hall to Oadby 'were lined by many thousands of people', to watch the processions of eight carriages escorted by mounted police in what was described by the press as 'an almost Royal Welcome', and by the Company as 'a distinct success'. 'Hearty cheers were given as the State coaches passed, their artistic appearance and the magnificent uniforms of the attendants exciting general admiration. A perfect furore of applause greeted a brake load of old framework knitters'. 'On arrival at the Site at Oadby to the accompaniment of Music from the Oadby Brass Band, the Master, Robert Rowley, conducted the Lord Mayor of London and the Sheriffs to a raised platform or staging erected over the Archway or Entrance to the Site and after some introductory remarks to the assembled Company, handed to the Lord Mayor a silver trowel . . . and requested him to perform the ceremony of laying the stone. The Lord Mayor having performed the Ceremony, addressed the assembled Company, expressing the great pleasure it had afforded him to be present that day . . . Past Master J. A. Corah proposed a vote of thanks to the Lord Mayor in felicitous terms to which his Lordship suitably replied. The Master requested the Vicar of Oadby (Rev. J. Raine) to pronounce the Benediction. The Vicar thereupon offered a prayer in very impressive terms which he had specially composed for the

PLATE 44

repr. with permission from the Record Office of Leicestershire, Leicester and Rutland

A POSTCARD ISSUED ON THE OCCASION OF THE LORD MAYOR OF LONDON'S STATE VISIT TO LAY THE FOUNDATION STONE OF THE COTTAGE HOMES AT OADBY, LEICESTERSHIRE, ON 30 SEPTEMBER, 1907.

occasion . . .The Band played the National Anthem and the procession reformed and returned to the Mayor's Rooms at the Museum Buildings, Leicester, where some 230 guests assembled' for a luncheon in the Art Gallery which 'was a repast in every way worthy of the occasion'. The cost of bringing the Lord Mayor and Sheriff's State coaches to Leicester, £55 18s. 6d., and the cost of stabling and accommodation for the horses and servants, £7 16s. 4d., was met by the Company.[48]

In October 1907 a committee consisting of the Master and Wardens of that year, plus Past Master J. A. Corah and Assistants Wood, Brice, Lorrimer, Donnisthorpe and Ward, approved further buildings. The Lodge, costing £285, two blocks of three cottages costing £600 each, and two houses costing £200 each were approved, and the Company also paid £100 to Blaby Union towards the cost of the necessary sewer. On 29 August 1908 200 people, mostly manufacturers and workers in the hosiery trade, were shown the site and the eleven dwellings already completed.[49]

Two months later, before an audience which included the Mayor of Leicester, Past Master Baddeley, the Master, Wardens and other Past Masters and Assistants of the Company and 'several local gentlemen connected with or interested in the Hosiery Industry and a number of ladies' the Cottage Homes were formally opened on Monday, 26 October 1908 by their initiator, Past Master John Corah, with a 'handsome gold key', 'with which he unlocked the gates of the complex. (This key is now housed in the Corah Hall on the site.) The many people present admired the homes already built before proceeding to the Museum Buildings in Leicester for a luncheon.[50]

In 1909 the Charity Commissioners permitted the erection of a further six Almshouses. The offers of W. Raven, a Leicester family firm long connected with hosiery manufacture and the Company, to erect two dwellings – 'The Raven Cottages' – and of the employees of Corah & Sons to build a further two dwellings – 'The Corah Cottages' – were accepted. By the end of the year the firms of R. Walker & Son and Donisthorpe & Company, both of Leicester, had each also made substantial donations towards the scheme. Donisthorpe's pair of semi-detached cottages, each with two bedrooms, cost £394 and the cottages gifted by Theodore, Ralph, Ernest and Kenneth Walker to accommodate four men in separate rooms, with a communal sitting room, cost £389. John and Alfred Corah paid for the erection of the communal hall given the family name, which was formally opened on 25 July 1910; the piano for this being given by Past Master Wolf Harris (see Plates C5a and 45a). By mid-1913 fourteen cottages had been built and no further building was to take place until the 1920s. In 1916 a pair of cottages were proposed by the employees of Corah & Sons and endowed by the company with £1,000 in memory of Liveryman Captain Leslie Corah who had been killed in the Great War, but these were not finished until 1925. In 1926 a further cottage was donated by Wolsey Limited.[51]

The Cottage Homes had been further honoured by a visit from a Lord Mayor of London in 1922 when the Past Master of the Company, Colonel Sir John Baddeley, and his wife paid a visit to what were described as Homes 'unrivalled in England'. As well as talking and dining with the Court and the Almspeople Sir John also unveiled in the Corah Hall the hand knitting frame featured in the Lord Mayor's procession of that year, which had been given to the Company by T. Bromley &

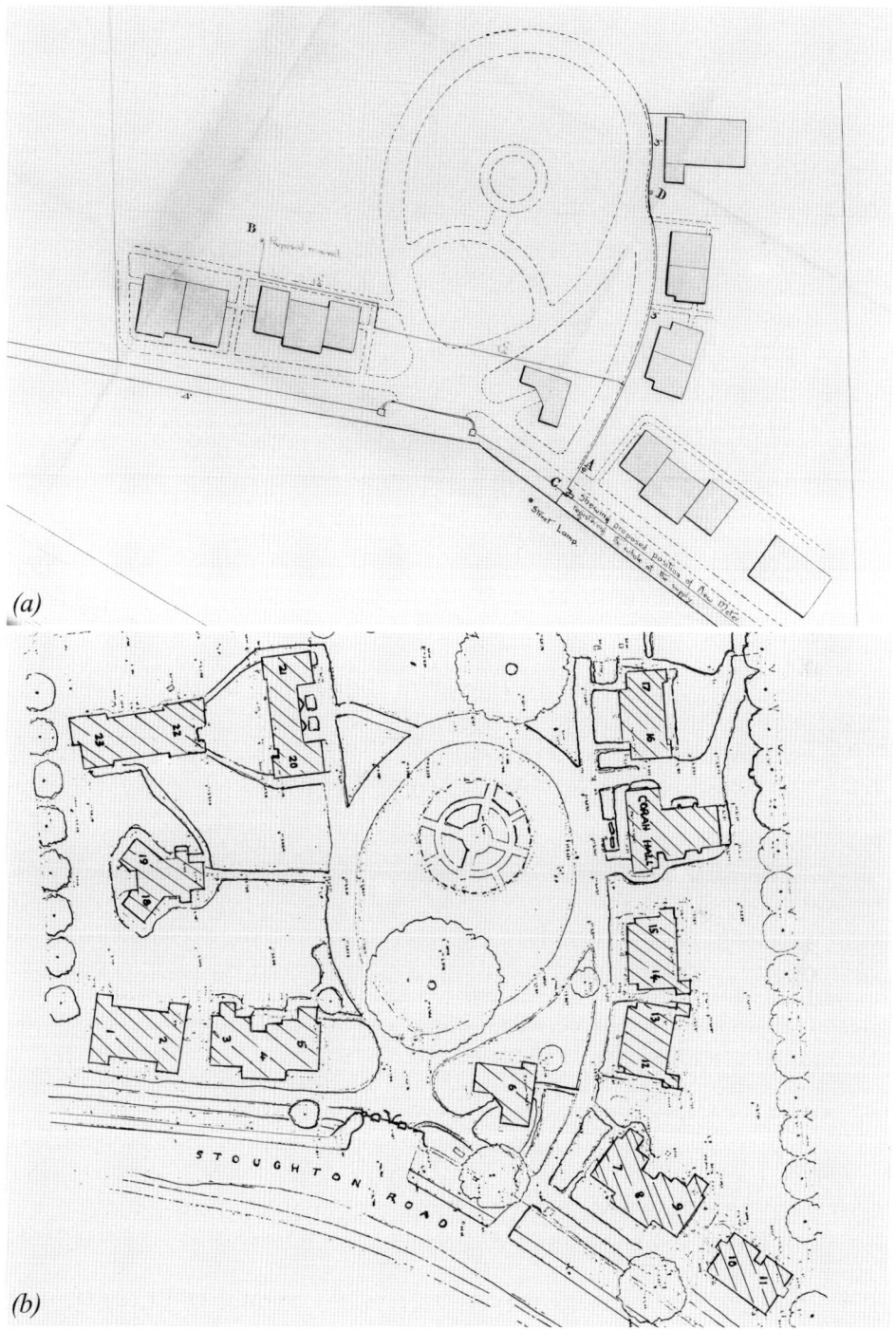

PLATE 45   *F.W.K. MSS.*

COTTAGE HOMES, OADBY

(a) in 1911, when gas lamps were installed; *(b)* in 1977.

Sons, and at the same time presented to the Company a portrait of himself.[52] Such was the prestige of the Society's Homes at Oadby in the first quarter of the twentieth century that on 10 March 1927 they were visited by Prince of Wales (see Plate 46). He was met at the gates of the Homes by the Master, George Ellis, and the Wardens, Charles Carryer and Edward Ellis, and planted the oak tree which still features at the entrance to the complex. All members of the Company and their ladies were invited to the ceremony and a visitor's book specially made for the occasion, and now in the Corah Hall, was signed by the Prince. Eleven Past Masters and the Treasurer of the Company, Sidney Pears, were presented to the Prince and he also talked to a number of the residents, including Mr. Goddard aged eighty-six and Mr. Ashby aged eighty-four, and inspected the cottage erected in memory of Captain Leslie Corah which was occupied by Mrs. Storer. The Company presented to the Prince, as a souvenir of his visit, a hunting cup made of whalebone covered with kangaroo skin and mounted with a gold band on which the Prince's feathers and the date were engraved, enclosed in a blue morocco case inscribed with the Coat of Arms of the Company in silver gilt on enamel. During the visit a bunch of flowers and refreshments were taken to every resident.[53]

After the Prince's visit new building work was less frequent. In 1953 'anonymous' donors presented two additional cottages to the Oadby complex at a cost of £5,000, although as these were opened by Assistant Cecil and Mrs. Coleman it is presumed that this couple were the benefactors. By 1964 the Homes were for forty elderly people, about half of them married couples, and the twenty-three cottages were usually fully occupied.[54]

By 1975 the Cottage Homes were nearly seventy years old and it was recognised that it was now necessary to 'provide standards of amenity, safety and insulation, in keeping with today's requirements'. A special committee under the Chairmanship of Past Master Clive Henderson, together with the Company's Chaplain and Past Masters G. Kershaw, W. Lowe and P. Morley and Assistant J. Whitehead, was set up to consider a scheme of modernisation of the buildings and the possible development of the allotments. By this time forty-two persons were in occupation, and one suggestion was to reduce this number to twenty-eight by reducing the occupancy from two persons to one in cottages numbered 3, 4, 5, 7, 8, 9, 10, 11, 12, 13, 14, 15, 18, 19. However these, and other radical proposals, were not adopted for in 1977 there were still thirty-three residents, eleven of whom were married couples (see Plate 45b).[55]

A continuing scheme of improvements was begun in 1980. Cottages 16, 17, 22 and 23 were altered, the Warden's cottage, number 6, extended and a new cottage built, to create twenty-five dwellings – twelve large doubles, five small doubles and eight singles. As well as the improved internal layout and total redecoration, most kitchen and bathrooms were replaced, gas central heating was fitted, wiring and other electrical equipment renewed, and street lighting and driveways were improved. The renovated buildings were soon fully occupied. The official opening of the modernised cottages, in summer 1983, was performed by Eric Devenport, the Bishop of Dunwich and Chaplain to the Company; the £3,000 that this event cost being met by the Fund Raising Committee. Four years later a further £25,000 was spent on more essential maintenance in which the kitchen and lavatories at the Corah Hall were extended and altered at a cost of £9,500 and up to £10,000 spent on replacing the alarm system. However, this was not the end of the improvements.

PLATE 46

1926 ROYAL VISIT

Edward, Prince of Wales visited the Cottage Homes during the Mastership of George Ellis, when he planted an oak tree and visited a number of Cottages.

In 1985 the notice boards in the Corah Hall, detailing the Company's officers, were extended and refurbished at cost of £1,600 and the Cottages were painted externally at a cost of £5,136.[56]

In 1988 it was decided, eventually, to rebuild Cottages 18 and 19, to demolish the two blocks of three single Cottages near the road and replace them with two-bedroomed Cottages for couples, and refurbish Cottages numbered 14, 15, 16 and 17, and finally to alter the double Cottages for single occupation. The following year it was also decided to build at the cost of about £200,000 a new four-bedroomed complex with communal area. The resulting Corah House was opened on 22 June 1991 by the Lord Lieutenant of Leicestershire, Timothy Brooks (see Plates C5b and C6).[57]

One matter which caused the Court concern during the eighties was the pro-posed designation in 1987 of the Framework Knitters' Cottage Homes complex, together with the North Memorial Homes on the opposite side of Stoughton Road, as a Conservation Area.[58] It caused a great deal of aggravation and expense for expert advice to obtain a description of the Homes in the Conservation document that did not preclude future alterations and expansion.

The future of the allotment site also occupied the attentions of the Court from the end of the 1980s. Discussions first with the University and later with the developers of the adjacent playing fields continued until the end of the century. Originally it was proposed that the Company should develop this land itself as an extension to the Cottage Homes, either with more Almshouses or for a nursing home, and in 1989 it tried to obtain road access to the site from the University Playing Fields. Although for a time in the early 1990s matters were halted when the university's planning application was turned down by the Oadby and Wigston plan-ning authority discussions were soon resumed. On 26 January 1996 the Company commissioned a feasibility study into a possible partnership between the Company and a specialist 'care operator' to build and operate a forty-bed nursing home on the site of the allotment garden, and the redevelopment of Corah House into a ten person residential unit with the aim that the three services provided on the site – sheltered housing, residential social care, and residential nursing care – should be separate but interdependent, but this scheme proved impossible. By 1999 it was hoped to sell the site to the adjacent developers Bryant Homes East Midlands Limited.[59]

Originally the Company provided the Almshouses free of rent, rates, insurance and repairs, and in addition paid a pension to the Almspersons for the Company's permission from the Charity Commissioners in 1909 to erect six additional Almshouses was conditional on funds being 'forthcoming . . . to provide stipends . . . of not less than six shillings for each single inmate or seven shillings and sixpence for each married couple'. By 1913 it was accepted that the total of stipend and old age pensions should not exceed twelve shillings for a married couple and ten shillings for a single person, although if residents had to leave the Homes, as did Mrs. Astill in 1925, then an allowance was paid in lieu of residence. From 1916, until it was merged with the charitable fund in 1961, the Company made grants to deserving cases which were not authorised under the Company's charitable scheme from a 'maintenance fund' created from the donation of £330 2s. 5d. from Past Master T. S. Rowley. Rowley's fund covered cases where a resident became ill and had to be moved to hospital, and was also used in 1945 to give a daughter of a Past Master who had fallen on hard times a donation of £25.[60]

As in the London Almshouses both the number and amount of Company pensions fluctuated. During 1929–30 forty-seven persons received payments ranging from five shillings a week for many of the single people to twenty-four shillings a week to the married warden(s), Mr. and Mrs. Payne. Pensions were later standardised and in 1962 the Company's pension of six shillings per week was raised to ten shillings. However, inflation and the universal state pension later reduced this to the status of pocket money and it was stopped at the end of October 1974, saving about £1,000 a year. Inflation hit the Company's funds heavily in the 1970s and from 1 January 1976 'the benefits of coal, gas, electricity, laundry and television repairs' had to be withdrawn and their cost met by the occupants. A few years later, from 1 January 1980, the residents, with the agreement of the Charity Commissioners, were required to make weekly maintenance payments. From 1 July 1981 these charges were fixed for the modernised dwellings at £11 for a single and £11.75p. for a double and for the unmodernised dwellings at £8 for a single, £8.65p. for a double and £9.85p. for a two-bedded one. From 1987 the applicants were means tested and by 1990 the rent was £26 for a single and £27.50p. for a double and £40 for a flat in Corah House.[61]

The Cottages Homes are run by a Board of Management approved by the Charity Commission. After 1941 it was decided that if managers had not attended a meeting for over a year they automatically ceased to be on the Board.[62] Selection to the Homes is made by a committee following a set of rules agreed with the Charity Commissioners which, except for periodic modernisation, have changed little over the years. The earliest rules stated that:

1. Candidates must not be less than 60 years of age.
2. They must be operative Framework Knitters or Hosiery Workers or the widows, sons or daughters of Framework Knitters or Hosiery Workers.
3. They must not have been in receipt of Poor Law Relief within two years prior to the date of application.
4. They must be able to furnish their cottage.
5. They must, if single, be prepared to share a cottage with another person of the same sex.

The wording of the advertisement for the Cottage Homes approved by the Charity Commissioners gave notice

'that a vacancy exists for an almsperson of these (Framework Knitters' Company Almshouse) Charities' for which 'poor persons of good character of not less than 60 years of age . . . are eligible . . . Every applicant . . . must be prepared to produce sufficient testimonials and other evidence of his or her qualification for appointment and unless physically disabled to attend in person'.

Initially vacancies were advertised in the *Leicester Mercury* and the *Nottingham Journal*, although there appear to have been very few applicants from Nottinghamshire, and none were allotted places. In 1926 it was decided to suspend the advertisements and arrange for printed notices to be displayed in the factories of firms who subscribed to the charitable funds. Details about the Oadby Homes were also distributed with the *Bulletin of The National Hosiery Manufacturers' Federation*.[63]

From the beginning there was a strong demand from the Leicester area for places in the Almshouses with forty applications in 1908, all but four of them male, of whom thirty-six came from Leicester and one each from Loughborough, Countesthorpe, New Queniborough and Dunton Bassett. The gender of the occupants of the Cottage Homes changed considerably between the early 1900s, when the Walker cottages were built for single men and most applicants were male, and 1977, when there was only one male resident living on his own, and most occupants were female. In 1985 there was a waiting list of seven single ladies and one couple, and no single males (see Plates 47 and 48).[64]

In addition to those for entry, further regulations governed the conduction of accepted Almspersons. The original rules from about 1907 are displayed in the vestibule of the Corah Hall, although these rules too have been modernised 'to take account of the changed circumstances of present day living'. Not until 1968 were Almspeople allowed to bring in their own television sets, and then from 1970 the Company provided these from money raised by members of the Court. By the 1980s the in-house rules numbered eighteen.[65]

Fourteen rules were also drawn up for allotment holders. An annual agreement allowed for three months notice on either side except that 'the Managers should have power to expel, on giving fourteen days' notice and without paying any compensation, any tenant who persistently breaks any of the conditions'.[66]

The first doctor for the Cottage Homes was Dr. Barnsley of Wigston who was employed at the rate of five shillings per visit, while Mrs. Bennett was employed as the first nurse at eight shillings a week. The day-to-day running of the Homes was carried out by a Warden, in the early days assisted by a Matron, who was responsible for the well-being of the residents and lived on the premises (see Table 8.1) This practice only ceased in 1994 with the appointment of Anne Brown as Assistant Clerk with an office at Oadby. In contrast to the second half of the century the first Wardens were men. Mrs. Daly was the longest serving Warden and when she retired on 31 March 1972 in her seventies, she was allowed to stay on in her cottage – as had the widow of A. Pembleton – and members of the Court contributed £3 each to her retirement present.

The inflationary pressures on the Company during the middle decades of the century are clearly shown by the increase in the Warden's salary from the

Table 8.1 **Wardens of the Oadby Cottage Homes**

Years	Warden's name
1905–1911	Mr. Venn
1911–1925	Mr. J. Palmer
1925–	Mr. Alfred Payne
–1945	Mr. A. J. Pembleton
1945–1947	Miss Coe
1947–1972	Mrs. Daly
1972–1978	Mrs. B. Ames
1978–1983	Mrs. D. Grant
1983–1986	Mrs. Anne Towers
1986–	Mrs. J. M. Duff
1987–1994	Mrs. Enid Greenwood

The Worshipful Company of Framework Knitters.

Application for Appointment to one of the Cottage Homes at Oadby, near Leicester.

SPECIAL NOTES TO CANDIDATES.

(1) Candidates must be over 60 to be eligible for election.

(2) Must be able to furnish his or her own cottage.

(3) Must be approved by the Board of Managers.

Candidates after their election will be duly informed of same, but cannot take up their residence in the Homes until notified, and then only by rotation in order following date of election.

PLEASE NOTE.—*The questions must be fully and distinctly answered, and this form, when filled up, and duly signed by the Applicant, should be returned to the Clerk,* J. WOODHOUSE, Esq., *18 Essex Street, Strand, London, W.C.*

QUESTIONS.	ANSWERS.
1. Write Name in full.	*Thomas Haines*
2. Age and date of birth ?	*68 Jan 22/1840*
3. Present address.	*Albion Street Oadby nr Leicester*
4. Are you— (A) A Member of the Company ?	(A) *no*
(B) An operative Framework Knitter or Hosiery Worker ?	(B) *Yes F.W.K*
(C) The widow, son or daughter of a Framework Knitter or Hosiery Worker ?	(C) *Son of F.W.K.*
5. Have you at any time, and if so when, been in receipt of Poor Law Relief ?	*no*

PLATE 47   *F.W.K. MSS.*

ONE OF THE FIRST APPLICATIONS FOR THE COTTAGE HOMES

All applicants had to fill in these forms.

(a)

(b)

beginning of the sixties to the mid-seventies. Mrs. Daly's salary in 1965 was raised to £624 per year, from less than £460, while Mrs. Ames's salary was over £2,000 when she retired in 1978. By 1987 the advertised warden's salary was £3,700.[67] There is also a gardener/handyman for the upkeep of the extensive grounds. From the 1960s the gardener/handyman position was occupied by Mr. Wilshaw and he, and Mrs. Wilshaw who assisted the Warden, lived in Cottage No. 2. In 1966 Wilshaw's wage was £15 per week; ten years later it had been increased to £1,794 per annum, while that of his wife, who was still acting as Assistant to the Warden, was £208 based on one day's work a week.[68]

Similar problems to those encountered in the London Almshouses did not take long to surface at Oadby and there was the occasional poor behaviour by the tenants which had to be dealt with. In 1910 a resident of Raven Cottages had to be reprimanded for his intemperate habits, and as a mark of the Company's annoyance his pension was reduced temporarily to three shillings, and in 1924 one female resident was instructed to keep her home in better order, while another had to be removed from her cottage, although whether this was due to infirmity or bad behaviour is unrecorded. Two years later the Master and Wardens had to deal with what were described as 'differences between the old women at the Homes'.[69]

From its opening the Company has taken immense pride in, and care of, the Oadby complex. It is visited weekly by either the Master or Wardens and social events are arranged for the residents who meet regularly in either the Corah Hall or House. The annual custom of the Master giving the residents a tea and entertainment in the Corah Hall at Christmas seems to have started at the end of the First World War, and in addition frequent concerts and other entertainments are provided by individuals, firms and other organisations. In 1924 six firms – Corah, Rowley, Wolsey, Donisthorpe, Moore Eady & Murcott Goode, and Downing – provided these; in the following year, in addition to the festivities provided by firms, a tea and concert were provided by the Executive Committee of the Hosiery Trade Union. By 1927 tea and a concert were being provided every other Saturday by various firms connected with the hosiery trade. In 1975/76 entertainments

◀ **PLATE 48**

RESIDENTS OF THE COTTAGE HOMES, OADBY

(a) in about 1912   *F.W.K. MSS.*

(b) 12 April, 2000   *repr. with permission of Neville Chadwick Photography, Wigston, Leics.*

Back row, left to right: Mr. John Morley; Mr. Fred Norman; Mr. Frank Walker; Mr. Cliff Russell; Mr. Cyril Maud; Mr. Tom Duckworth; Mr. John McConnell.
Middle row, left to right: Mrs. Joyce Whitehead; Mrs. Olive Johnson; Mrs. Joyce Morley; Mrs. Hilda Wakefield; Mrs. Gladys Walker; Mrs. Ann Russell; Mrs. Hazel Littlewood; Mrs. Peggy Duckworth; Mrs. June McConnell; Mrs. Doreen Smith; Mrs. Enid Hubbard.
Seated front row, left to right: Mr. Roger Marshall (Gardener); Mrs. Enid Walton; Mrs Rene Jordan; Mrs. Eileen Hiercock; Miss Evelyn Clarke; Mrs. Doris Tilley; Mrs. Alma Grocock; Mrs. Margaret Whiston; Mrs. Joan Craythorne; Mrs. Amy Goodman; Mr. Norman Goodman.
Unable to appear in the photograph: Mrs. Barbara Penny; Mr. Bill and Mrs. Essie Turner; Mrs. Nancy Beach; Mrs. Iris Coleman. Cottages 22 and 23 were vacant prior to refurbishment.

were provided at least once a month for the residents by various firms including Gwilliam Enterprises, Klynton Davies, Albert Martin, Towles, Wolsey, Corah and Cherub, and similar events have continued into the twenty-first century.[70]

The residents were also included in many royal visits to Leicester. When the King and Queen visited the city on 10 June 1919 Corah & Sons provided viewing seats for all the Almspersons and entertained them at their works, and when King George VI and Queen Elizabeth came in 1946 the pensioners had a front row view from the office of the Master, Edward Stibbe. To commemorate Queen Elizabeth's Silver Jubilee the residents of the Cottage Homes produced the carpet bearing the Company's Coat of Arms which now hangs in Corah House, and this communal effort was so successful that the first of the now annual bazaars was held at the end of 1977; the initial venture raising about £280 to sponsor a guide dog for the blind.[71]

Christmas gifts continued to be given to Almspeople of the Company after the move to Oadby and the individual parcels of groceries given by the Master often had added to them extra gifts from other members of the Company. In 1910 there was a pork pie from Maurice Lorrimer, two shillings from Senior Warden Russell Donisthorpe, a plum pudding from Deputy Painter, three pairs of stockings from Past Master John Corah and a pot of ginger from Past Master Reynolds. In 1979 the Christmas hampers were discontinued for a short time in favour of cash, but later reinstated. The Duke of Portland continued to present a fowl to each resident until 1915 after which, for a time, this was a gift from the Company or unnamed donors; then from about the 1960s until his retirement in 1990 the fowls became the gift of Assistant Richard Humphreys. There were also gifts to commemorate special occasions; a coronation mug, as well as a celebration at the Homes, was provided for each pensioner on the crowning of George V.[72]

Since at least the building of the Corah Hall there has been a monthly service at the Cottage Homes, usually led by the clergy of St. Peter's Oadby; the Vicar of Oadby usually being the Honorary Chaplain of the Company. However, on 30 November 1998 this service was conducted by Bishop Mort. Residents accompanied by the Master, Peter Ward, and the Upper Warden also attended the service of thanksgiving at Westminster Abbey in commemoration of 1,000 years of almshouses and the fortieth anniversary of the National Association of Almshouses.[73]

Financing their Almshouses has always been at the forefront of the Company's concerns. As it was felt that 'the object of the Company should be to secure a permanent endowment', in May 1908 the Master, Robert Rowley, Wardens Alfred Corah and W. G. Waterhouse Reynolds, Past Masters Sir George Woodman, Frederick Dyer, John Corah, John Baddeley and Assistants Lorrimer, Donisthorpe and Brice, plus James Holmes, Secretary of the Leicester and Leicestershire Amalgamated Hosiery Union, formed an Almshouse and Pensions Managers Committee which aimed to increase the return on the Company's charitable investments. The Consuls, in which the Charitable Funds were formerly lodged, were sold and the £4,000 plus return invested in various, mostly 3° per cent, dated redeemable stocks, issued mainly by local authorities and railways. In 1910 the balance of the purchase money for the Kingsland Road site was invested in similar stocks. However, this fund was never large enough to provide both for the expanded number of Almshouses and for their running costs.[74]

At first sight it might seem that the Company could be criticised for not maximising its investments, but it should not be forgotten that any changes had to meet the stringent rules laid down by the Charity Commissioners. Income could only be invested in securities authorised by this Commission, and from 1925 action was further limited by the Trustee Act. In 1955 the Finance Committee, under the leadership of Under Warden Rouse, tried to break out of the imposed straight jacket and invest in equities and other non-trustee investments, but as the Charity Commission required that any such investments were restricted to a quarter or less of a charity's investments, and required a 'finance committee in more or less continuous session', it was decided to continue juggling with the type of investments already held.[75]

Various methods of raising money were tried over the years. For a period in the 1940s even the Corah Hall was rented out for 7s. 6d. a session to the local Townswomen's Guild Choral Society of which five of the pensioners were members. For most of the century, however, the main source of charitable revenue was successive Masters' subscription lists for donations to the Cottages Homes during their year of office, a practice which had started with John Corah in 1905/6. Although at first consideration this might appear to be a crude method of fund raising, it in fact only put the burden on an individual for a single year and, because each Master was usually a leader in his own employment area, had the added advantage of annually opening up new sources of revenue as during their year of office Masters approached companies with which their businesses were particularly associated, including many abroad; just before the First World War, for example, a number of firms in Chemnitz contributed. This subscription list continued during the two World Wars; between 1913 and 1914 it amounted to £82 7s. 3d., while in 1943 Master E. J. Ward collected £866 12s. 9d. and in 1945 Master Donald Byford reported that he had raised £1,170 9s. 6d. The scope of the annual appeal was widened in 1955 to provide a continuation of pensions to Almspeople who had to leave the Homes, so that increased sums were required. By the 1950s and 1960s the amount being raised annually by the Masters had increased to thousand of pounds – under Master Cyril Osborne in 1950/51 it was £2,716 1s., £3,500 during the Mastership of G. H. Spencer and up to £5,500 in the Mastership of William Bentley in 1959.[76]

It had been hoped that the Company could have built up funds in the charitable fund and obviated the annual 'whip round', but such a large amount was spent on the Cottage Homes each year that by 1957 there was a deficit of £582.[77] This over-spending perturbed many members, including Past Master Pears, senior partner in the London firm of accountants Cooper Brothers and a former Treasurer of the Company, nevertheless the annual subscription list was continued, although in addition the Finance Committee tried others ways of increasing income.

At the beginning of 1964 an Appeals Sub-Committee was established to review the Company's charitable finances. The report of 1 May, presented by Assistant R. L. Wessel, proposed that a capital sum of £60,000 be raised to give an annual return of £3,000 and that the Masters' Appeal should be discontinued. Much to the disapproval of some Court members this Appeal was much more broadly based than hitherto, with donations being solicited not only from hosiery firms but also from suppliers. Most donations were covenanted, although a few were single payments from such special gifts as that of Mrs. J. M. Edwards of London in memory of her son who had been Toller & Lankester's London agent. By 1967 the fund stood at £27,000 of which 64 per cent was invested in equities and the remainder in fixed interest securities. In addition to the Corah Foundation's seven year covenant to give £1,500 per annum, other notable donations were from D. Byford & Company and the Byford Benevolent Fund, Wolsey Limited, G. Stibbe & Company, and also from the National Union of Hosiery Workers.[78]

In 1972 the Charity Commissioners put forward a new scheme for the administration of the Almshouse and pension charities and this was accepted with only a few amendments and sealed by the Company in December that year. The charity income now derived mainly from investments bought from the monies received from the special appeal of 1964, plus comparatively small amounts of annual donations and allotment rents. By January 1977 the cost of running the Oadby complex was about £10,000 a year, which included repairs, salaries, administration and an annual payment of £460 towards an accumulating repair reserve fund for extraordinary repairs. Although, from 1 January 1976, residents had begun paying towards some of the services previously provided by the Company their payments could not cover the whole cost because the Charity Commissioners decreed that expendable income must be used before maintenance contributions from residents could be increased.[79]

However, inflation, as already shown by the wardens' salary increases, badly affected the Company's charities and by the end of the 1970s funds were again seriously depleted. This inflation occurred at a time when occupancy of the Cottage Homes was less attractive than previously; there were no applicants in 1978 for the four that were empty because they needed modernising. The Court decided that funds to renovate some Homes would have to be found and an appeal for £150,000 was launched in January 1979. Master J. Whitehead and Assistants C. B. Byford and H. R. Ellis, who was appointed Chairman, formed an Appeal Committee to raise the money for a modernisation scheme, and Past Master Peter Morley was appointed chairman of the Works Committee, while Liveryman John Strange remained Secretary of the Executive Committee until 1987. Many considered that this was an over ambitious scheme but, in spite of the recession, after two years £152,000 had been raised from the industry, in particular from the Corah Foundation and Marks & Spencer which gave £7,500 over three years, and Liveryman Derek Tiney who raised £4,000 from an auction. In addition £41,000 came from grants from Oadby and Wigston Council and there were two loans from Help the Aged.[80]

Following this special Appeals Committee a committee was set up in 1981 under the chairmanship of Assistant Michael Martin to look at more permanent methods of raising money. Previously most donations had come from companies, now it was suggested that individual Liverymen should covenant £15 per annum. A Livery luncheon at the Grand Hotel, Leicester, was also started at the beginning of 1983 to raise funds for the Cottage Homes. Costs continued to rise, however, and by 1987 at least £1,000 was needed annually to meet even the cost of the residents' Christmas dinner and presents. In 1988 a committee chaired by Under Warden Patrick Corah was set up to consider the future of the Homes as well as set up a further appeal. It was decided that in order to bring the Cottages up-to-date some needed to be rebuilt or altered, while others were in urgent need of refurbishment. The following year a Development Committee, with Patrick Corah in the chair and Nicholas Corah, John Whitehead and Michael Turnbull as members, was established to arrange the construction of a new four-bedroomed complex with communal area, Corah House, at an estimated cost of about £200,00; it was funded by three charities of which the Corah Benevolent Fund was the main contributor.[81]

During the twentieth century, in addition to the many covenants and donations made by firms connected with the hosiery industry, a large number of individual bequests, mostly legacies, benefitted the Company's charitable funds. The largest recorded individual legacy was that of Past Master William Bentley who in 1986 gifted £15,000, but there were many others of smaller amounts, such as the £100 left by Assistant William F. Stuttaford in 1910. Different generations of a number of families benefited the Homes, as did the Corah, Donisthorpe, Ellis and Coleman families; Miss Mary Ann Coleman left £619 17s. 5d. in 1909, Mrs. Coleman, wife of Assistant Cecil Coleman £1,000 in 1959, while in 1975 there was a £1,000 legacy from Cecil. Some Almspeople too showed their appreciation and in 1961 the Company was the beneficiary of the estate of Mrs. Ellen Garner.[82]

A variety of trade functions also benefited the Cottages Homes. The £600 profits from two dances organised by the Underwear and Stockings division of the Hosiery Manufacturers' Association in 1953 and 1954, and £200 raised by a golf match between the Hosiery Industry and *Drapers' Record* in 1988 were donated to Oadby. The charitable funds were further boosted by the donations of £162 11s. 9d. by the South of England Knitting Industries Association in 1969 and £128 3s. from the National Union of Hosiery and Knitwear Workers in 1975.[83]

Education

In addition to its expanding Almshouse and charity fund the Company also increased its commitment to education throughout the twentieth century. As a founder member the Society continued its involvement with the City and Guilds of London Institute – its annual subscription in 1999 amounting to £250 – and members of the Company continued on the Institute's various councils and advisory boards. From the 1920s Past Master John Cooper served first as the Company's representative on the Advisory Committee for Hosiery Training and continued on the Advisory Committee on the Manufacture of Hosiery and Knitted Goods created in 1943. J. E. Johnson followed Assistant Roe on to this advisory committee in 1951 and on his death at the end of the 1950s was succeeded by Assistant William Bentley. No successor was appointed on Past Master Bentley's retirement in 1968 until 1991 when Liveryman Paul Bethel was appointed in an advisory capacity, a position he still retains.[84]

The Company made annual awards to the students of the Institute. Between 1889 and 1928 contributions for cash prizes for the framework knitting examinations totalled more than £125, with the medals being awarded by the Institute. From 1929 the Worshipful Company of Framework Knitters' gold, silver and bronze medals replaced the monetary award and were given to the students obtaining the highest marks in the knitting examinations. Sometimes, if examination results warranted it, joint medals were provided. In other years, such as 1933, when no-one reached the required standard, no medals were presented. During the Second World War certificates replaced the medals and for about the next thirty years recipients were presented with both medals and certificates, the medals for the war years being presented in retrospect. In 1947 the Master Edward

Stibbe gave £500 in memory of his friend and colleague Past Master A. S. Whitehead to be used towards the cost of the gold medals.[85]

The Company took a keen interest in their City and Guilds of London Institute prizes. Many awards were won by students at Leicester College of Technology, where it became the custom for the current Master to present the prizes at the annual awards ceremony (see Plate 49). However, these prizes were not confined to Leicester, or even to British-based students, for some winners came from associated institutions in overseas countries, and in 1975 Edward Browne of the Auckland Technical Institute in New Zealand was awarded a silver medal. Until Jane Clark Honeyman won both the gold and silver medals in 1974 all recipients had been male. A number of people later distinguished in the Company and the hosiery trade won Company awards while students, as did two academics in hosiery. In 1905 James Henry Quilter, who was to become the Principal of the Knitting Department of Leicester Technical School, was awarded the silver award sponsored by the Company and in 1935 the Company's gold medal was awarded to Harry Wignall. Thirty years later Mr. Wignall became the Head of the School of Textiles at the Leicester Regional College of Art and Technology and continued to be Head of Textile Technology after 1969 when the Leicester Regional College of Technology was incorporated into the new Leicester Polytechnic (see Appendix 9).[86]

PLATE 49   *repr. with permission of the* Leicester Mercury

22 NOVEMBER 1938, THE MASTER OF THE WORSHIPFUL COMPANY OF FRAME-WORK KNITTERS PRESENTING THE PRIZES AT THE LEICESTER COLLEGE OF TEXTILES

Master George Moore presents a medal to Charles Carter, who was later a staff member of the School of Textiles. Other members of the Company in the photograph are Mr. P. A. Bentley, Mr. T. G. Hirst, who was also Chairman of the Textile Trades Advisory Committee, and Lawrence Kershaw, who became Principal of the College of Technology from August 1928.

As early as 1944 some members of the Company were expressing misgivings about the City and Guilds examinations and a sub-committee, later converted into a standing committee, was formed to keep a watching brief on and consider matters relating to the education of young people engaged in hosiery and allied trades. The initial members were Wardens Byford and Bussens, and Assistants Bromley and Hirst, to whom were later added Past Masters Walker and Whitehead and Assistant Peshall. In 1967 Master David Foister informed the Court about examinations of a higher standard than those of the City and Guilds, but after investigation it was concluded that, as by far the largest number of students still sat City and Guilds, the Company's awards continued to fulfil a useful need. However, some in the Company still harboured doubts about the scheme when, owing to the escalation of university degree courses in knitting technology in the 1970s, the City and Guilds examinations continued to lose their pre-eminence as the highest level of scholastic attainment. In 1971 the Company's representatives, William Bentley and David Foister, recommended that silver medals only should be awarded at distinction level in five sections of the final certificate and gold should only be awarded if a student had gained a distinction in two sections, so that from this date the Company restricted its medals to gold and silver. Ten years later it was suggested that a gold plated plaque incorporating the heraldic emblem of the Worshipful Company of Framework Knitters would be more acceptable and in 1982 the medals were replaced by plaques donated by Liveryman Russell Kempton. One, plus a cheque for £50, was presented to the best student of knitting technology at degree level – a subject then only offered at Leicester – and the second was presented to the best student of knitting technology in the TEC Higher Diploma which was offered by a number of colleges.[87]

The Company has continued to work with the City and Guilds of London Institute, as well as expanding its involvement in education for the hosiery trade into the universities. One result of this expansion was that at the end of the 1980s the Company began closer links with The City University, London. Assistant Michael Chapman was the Company's representative on the Court of the University until 1991 when he was succeeded by Assistant J. Lewis.[88]

In 1984, due to the rise of hosiery courses in universities, discussions began under the chairmanship of Howard Russell Ellis to establish awards to encourage students with degree projects of practical use to hosiery. The Worshipful Company of Framework Knitters' Educational Bursary Scheme, open to British nationals permanently resident in the United Kingdom, was introduced in 1985 to 'encourage interest in, and contribution to, the knitting industry'. In the first year the scheme was confined to students from three institutions, Leicester and Trent Polytechnics and the University of Bradford, but was soon extended nationwide. In only its second year applications were also received from Leeds and Galashiels and by 1988 entries came from seven separate institutions.[89]

Two committees were established, the Bursary Appeals Committee and the Bursary Awards Committee. The first Chairman of the Appeals Committee was Assistant John Dean who was succeeded by Liveryman Andrew Winkler, while the first Treasurer was Assistant R. A. Wessell. A general appeal for money to establish the Bursary Fund was made to both the Livery and firms in the hosiery industry; one of the first donations being £500 from Marks & Spencer. In 1989 four bursaries were awarded and a further invitation for sponsorship saw the inauguration of the

International Wool Secretariat Bursary, initially for £1,000, which was to run for seven years from 1991 to support a student and/or a project in designing woollen knitwear. In 1991 the bursaries were increased to £1,500 and the scope of the scheme was widened to include candidates from courses with hosiery connections in management, technology and science, in addition to design. Also in 1991 the Company contributed £250 to the Texprint Prize of £500 and was represented on the prize committee by Liveryman Winkler. In 1994 the Rouse Award was established from a legacy given by Mrs. Olga Wynnes, the daughter of a former Master, and it was followed a year later by the Benson Turner Bursary set up for five years. The Howard Russell Ellis Education Award was established in 1997 by his legacy of £5,000. By 1998, in addition to its own three bursaries of £1,500 each, the Company also administered and chose the winners of the £1,500 International Wool Secretariat Bursary, the INSTEP Award and the Benson Turner Bursary, and in 1999 the Howard Russell Ellis Education Award presented its first £500 to Kirsty Robertson of Heriot-Watt University (see Appendix 9).[90]

The Bursary Awards Committee has only had three active chairmen since its inception, Past Masters Barrie Byford and Gordon Taylor, and Assistant Dr. David Bethel. As the aims of the Company's Educational Trust and that of the Leicester Textile Society were similar Past Master Byford was also appointed to that Society's Educational Trust in 1987. All applications are discussed and most candidates are visited and interviewed in their educational establishments by members of the Bursary Committee of the Company, with winners being invited at the Company's expense to the annual Livery Dinner. Mentors from the knitting and knitwear industry are now assigned to work with each bursary awardee. In addition it is felt that the 'visits to the institutions by members of the Bursary Awards Committee are vital in providing an up-to-date appraisal of relevant departments, and discussions with teaching staff help to identify problems in up-dating courses to meet the changing needs of industry'.[91]

The Company's property and gifts

Until 1911 the Company's deeds, cups and other portable property, with the exception of the gowns, were kept at the Princes Street Branch of the Union of London and Smith's Bank, after which they were deposited in Bank's branch at 66 Charing Cross, while the Company's stocks and shares and the oil painting of Alderman Waithman were kept at the Clerk's office; later this portrait was moved to the Corah Hall. Many of the Company's documents were deposited in the City of London Guildhall Library in 1939, although the Charters remained in the Bank's vaults until 1977, after which date and to prevent further deterioration, they were transferred to the Guildhall. In 1978 a Records Committee consisting of Assistant J. C. Hurd and Liveryman J. A. Ridge was created, and within months other historical items had been deposited in the Guildhall and the Corah Hall at Oadby. The Company's gowns, made in 1896, were kept by Ede & Ravenscroft of Chancery Lane and when new ones were ordered in 1911 Ede, Son & Ravenscroft took care of these initially for an inclusive charge of 7s. 6d. By 1969 the gowns had become decidedly bedraggled and renovations costing £231 6s. 9d. were carried out with new fur and various repairs for the Masters', Wardens', Livery and Beadle's gowns and a completely new one for the Clerk; later in the year another new gown bearing the Company's colours was made for the Chaplain. In 1978 Ede & Ravenscroft were no longer able to store the gowns and the Master, Wardens and the Honorary Chaplain became responsible for their own while the Clerk undertook responsibility for his and the Livery gowns.[92]

Many gifts were made to the Company during the twentieth century and the presentation of silver begun in the 1880s continued. In the first three years of the new century immediate Past Masters gave the Company cigar and cigarette boxes, a silver rose water dish and a ramshorn mounted as a silver snuff box. In 1912 the Company acquired from Crichton Brothers for about £1,500 a silver loving cup of 1656, which had been the one of the treasures sold in 1861 and is presumably the first item on that list. (It would seem that the fifth item on the 1861 list surfaced at the same time, for also in 1912 the Goldsmiths' Company bought a Caudle Cup of about 1660 of 'ogee outline, embossed with daffodils, tulips, a stag and boar' inscribed 'This Cupp and Cover is given for the use of the Wor. Companie of fframework Knitters London by a well wiser to that Society'.) By 1955 the Society had, in addition to the Victorian silver cups known by the names of their donors and the seventeenth century cup, a silver replica made by Edward Barnard of a cup of 1611 in the Victoria and Albert Museum donated by Past Master Sir Frederic Painter, a silver gilt ewer, the rosebowl, cigar, cigarette and snuff boxes mentioned above, a set of four Sheffield plate candlesticks, a candelabra, a silver trowel, as well as the badges of office of the Master, Treasurer and Wardens, and the Beadle's tipstaff and head.[93]

At the beginning of 1959 the former Master and Lord Mayor of London Sir Bracewell Smith offered the Company up to £250 to buy silver gilt wine goblets for the use of the Master, Wardens and members of the Court at Court dinners. This initial purchase was followed in succeeding years by gifts of similar goblets from other officers of the Company, mostly immediate Past Masters, but also families such as the widow and son of Alexander Hamilton who had been Under Warden at his death in 1972. By 1981 when the Company had fifty goblets, forty eight for members of the Court and two for the Master's personal use, it was decided that the presentation of goblets should be discontinued. In 1967 Assistant Norman Goodman, who regretted being unable to carry on to become Warden, presented a silver punch bowl and ladle crafted by Alex Styles, and in 1976 Master Geoffrey Kershaw gave to the Company the silver medallion presented to him by Fra. Angelo de Mojana di Cologna, the Prince and Grand Master of the Sovereign and Hospitaller Order of St. John of Jerusalem, Rhodes and Malta, at the Livery Dinner at the Mansion House on 8 October 1975.[94]

From the resurgence of the Company in the late 1800s until the present day Past Masters of the Company have been presented with an enamelled badge to commemorate their year in office. Until 1958 these were made by H. E. Lamb, with a design change in 1933 after the grant of Arms to the Company. In 1958 the Company ordered six spare badges at a cost of only £22 each, but by 1964 the £1,000 plus cost of new jewels was considered a serious drain on the corporate account. In 1953 the Past Masters' jewels of Edward Cooper and Ernest Walker had been given back to the Company and by 1978 four Past Masters' badges had been returned, including one of 1887 of Thomas Loveridge. In 1986 Master Howard Russell Ellis donated two of his own family's badges to be used again, hoping that his example would be followed by others. With the permission of their families those of Ernest Walker and Thomas Toller, then hanging in the Corah Hall, were also refurbished and since that date a number of other Past Masters' jewels have been represented. In addition to the Masters' jewel, the Master's lady wears a brooch during her husband's year in office which was presented to the Company by Michael Martin during his Mastership.[95]

Following a suggestion from Past Master Donald Byford, from 1964 the Company's silver was again inspected annually, and in 1966 a register illustrated with photographs was made by Hicklenton & Phillips when they revalued the Company's plate. Hicklenton & Phillips also advised that the Company's cups should receive a silicone coating, and this process started with the Painter cup and continued with the Paddon and Creasey cups. In 1989 it was suggested that some of the plate should be sold, but this idea was later shelved, only to reappear in the second half of the 1990s, when it was again rejected.[96]

Not all gifts made to the Company were, however, of silver or jewels, and most of these other gifts, plus the Company's painted banner, have all been housed at Oadby. An interesting painting of an old stockinger's cottage and a working model of an old frame were given by J. F. Heggs Bates in 1925 and in 1984 Sir John Peel gave a drawing of the Company's Almshouses in London. Written matter too has been presented to the Company. In 1947 Liveryman S. A. Welch arranged for the Company to receive the original indenture of Apprenticeship to the Company in 1719 of Robert Middleton. In 1974 Past Master Henderson and Assistant Clarkson presented copies of the limited edition of the 1819 Framework Knitters' Petition and a year later, and in addition to a silver-gilt goblet, Colonel Ward gave a Treatise, dated about 1780, on silk, wool, worsted, cotton and thread, while in 1968 A. F. E. Poley's tome on St. Paul's Cathedral had been given to the Company. Two books on the history of hosiery were donated in memory of Past Master Trotman in 1984 by his son, Liveryman Peter Trotman, and son-in-law, Liveryman R. Eberlin. More recently a large number of volumes of the *Hosiery Trade Journal*, the *Jersey Magazine* and *Textile Monthly*, dating from the 1950s to the 1980s, were gifted to the Company by Liveryman Derek Tiney. In 1943 Master Sidney Pears presented to the Company the 'Proclamation prohibiting the transportation of frames for knitting and making of silk stockings and other wearing necessities – 24 October 1686', which would seem to have been housed in the Guildhall Library (see Plates 26 and 32b).[97]

Several times during the century the Company's treasures have been lent out for exhibition. In June 1911 the Company's plate went to the Mansion House for the Lady Mayoress's exhibition in aid of the Women's Hostel in Soho Square, and the State Chair, Beadle's staff and Company's Banner were chosen for an exhibition at the Victoria and Albert Museum in 1926. The punch bowl and ladle crafted by Alex Styles were considered such important examples of modern silver that they were shown by the Crown jewellers Garrards in an exhibition entitled 'Five Centuries of English Silver' in 1968 and were shown at the exhibition, 'Alex Styles: a retrospective', in Goldsmiths' Hall in the summer of 1988. So neglectful at times has been the Company's custody of some of its treasures that it is surprising that most still survive. In particular the Master's Chair, given by Thomas Carwarden (see Plate C2a and Appendix 11), has at times received the most casual treatment. Past Master James Capel had argued in 1844 that if not sold it should be given away and, although it did not suffer this fate, for much of the twentieth century, as in the nineteenth, it would seem to have again been either in the custody of the various Clerks or whichever place the Court last met; in 1919 this was recorded as the Savoy Hotel, where it had probably been throughout the Great War. During the Second World War the Company's treasures were dispersed among Past Masters, and E. T. Walker took the Chair home to Launde Abbey in Leicestershire. When this building was requisitioned by the military the Chair was sent to the removal contractors, Timson & Sons of Leicester, for storage. It is uncertain whether it was returned to Launde Abbey after the war but by 1947 it was lodged and being used by all the Livery companies who dined at the Tallow Chandlers' Hall. In 1955 it was sent to the Victoria and Albert Museum for repair but returned to the Tallow Chandlers' Hall, leaving there two years later when the Tallow Chandlers' obtained their own chair. A home was found for it in 1958 in the Guildhall Museum, now renamed the London Museum, where it still resides; although, even when lodged in the Museum, its wanderings were not yet over, as in 1958 it was exhibited at Ghent, Belgium in 'L'Age d'Or des Grandes Cités', and for two months in the summer of 1982 was loaned to Selfridges for an exhibition on London's Guilds and Livery Companies.[98]

As well as being the recipient, the Company also presented gifts, those given to Past Masters in the first half of the century being particularly splendid. On the occasion of his marriage in 1914 Past Master Alexander Lorrimer was presented with a silver tea tray and coffee pot and on his marriage in 1923 Past Master David Haes received a silver tea service engraved with the Company's Arms. In 1926 Master Ellis was presented with a silver rose bowl and two silver fruit dishes on the occasion of his silver wedding and Past Master Rowley with a silver Armada bowl on the occasion of his marriage. In 1901 the Company presented the retiring Clerk, James Funston, who had been involved with the Company since the middle of the 1800s, with a suitably inscribed silver salver and a velvet purse containing 105 sovereigns, in addition to an illuminated testimonial.[99]

Summary

The twentieth century has been one of both consolidation and growth for the Worshipful Company of Framework Knitters which leaves it in good shape and heart to meet the twenty-first century.

References

1   MSS,. 3452/14 – speech by Senior Warden William Moore, 16 October, 1931.
2   *Historical Record of the Census of Production 1907 to 1970* (London: Government Statistical Service, 1970); H. A. Silverman, 'The Hosiery Industry' in *Studies in Industrial Organisation*, ed. H. A. Silverman, (London: Methuen & Co, 1946), p. 6.
3   MSS, 3451/3, 22 June 1906, 30 September 1907; 3451/9, 1914–15; 3452; *L(eicester) M(ercury)*, 7 October 1933; *CP*, 25 Nov. 1949; *WCFK Newsletter*, 23, 1985; CLGL, MSS. L37.21871/29
4   MSS, 3451/4, 16 January 1923; 3452/15, J. Boswell Brown, 1931, Frank Wrigley 28 September 1932, 12 September 1932; *CP*, 25 November 1949; Silverman, 1946, pp. 10–12.
5   MSS, 3451/5, 25 January, 17 May, 28 August 1946, 27 June 1950 – S.F. Peshall had been invited to join the Company in recognition of his services to the trade during the war, and in the New Year's Honours List of 1951 was made a CBE (3451/4, 26 January 1951); 3451/6, 29 June 1960, 26 June 1969, 23 October 1969, 14 April 1970.

6   MSS, *Minutes*, 4 April 1984, 19 April 1985, 18 April 1991; Agenda for the Court Meeting 25 June 1999.

7   MSS, *Minutes*, 20 October, 1986, 2 April, 6 November 1987, 22 April 1988, 19 April, 16 June 1989.

8   MSS, *Minutes*, 25 April 1980.

9   MSS, 3451/3, 1 November 1904, 5 April, 24 June 1909; 3451/4, 19 April 1926.

10 MSS, 3451/5, 27 October 1944; 3451/5, 30 November 1944, 30 May 1945, 25 January 1946.

11 MSS, 3451/4, 20 April, 29 June, 11 October 1921, 29 October 1923.

12 MSS, 3451/5 15 October 1943, Cooper Bros. letter 6 January 1947, 15 October 1948; 3451/6, 21 January 1954, 24 June 1955, 26 October, 20 November 1956, 22 January 1957; *Minutes*, 23 October 1990, 18 April 1991.

13 MSS, 3451/3, 10 January, 11 April, 18 August 1905, 15 April, 14 October 1907, 17 October 1913; 3451/4, 29 April 1920, 21 July 1920, 18 January 1921; *The City of London Observer*, 19 October 1908.

14 MSS, 3451/5, 22 April 1941, 30 March, 15 October 1943, 1 August, 27 October 1944, 25 October 1945, 13 October 1950; *Minutes*, 8 January 1974, 29 June 1976, 20 January, 28 April 1978.

15 MSS, 3451/3, 13 April 1909; 3451/4, 3 April 1919, 16 January 1923; 3452/9, 25 April 1911; *Minutes*, 11 January 1972; *LM*, 2 May 1933.

16 MSS, 3451/3, 11 October 1910, 25 June 1912; 3451/4, 8 October 1920, 27 June 1922; 3451/5, 25 April 1947; *Minutes*, 12 January, 12 April 1984; *CP*, 17 October 1908.

17 MSS, 3451/2, 8 October 1901.

18 MSS, 3451/5, Corporation of London, 8, 30 June 1942; 3451/6, 4 May 1962; *Minutes*, 22 April 1982, 20 July 1990.

19 MSS, 3451/4, 5 July 1917, 10 January 1918; 3451/5, 25 April 1947; 3451/6, 21 January 1955.

20 MSS, 3451/4, 16 April 1918; *Minutes*, 21 June, 28 October 1983, 16 January 1986, 19 April 1989.

21 MSS, 3451/6, 21 January, 29 October 1954.

22 MSS, 3451/3, 12 January, 1 November 1904, 10 January 1905; 3452/6, 6 October 1904.

23 MSS, 3451/3, 15 October 1908, 12 October 1909, 23 April 1912.

24 MSS, 3451/3, 24 June, 17 October 1913, 13 January 1914; 3452/8 1913; 3452/9 1911–1912. (The banner cost nine guineas.)

25 MSS, 3451/4.

26 *Hosiery Trade Journal*, December 1932, *Leicester Evening Mail*, 7 November 1932 and other papers in MSS 3452.

27 MSS, 3451/6, 10 January 1967; *CP*, 5 November 1937.

28 MSS, 3451/5, 15 October 1943, 25 October 1946; *CP*, 1 November 1946.

29 MSS, 3451/6, 26 October 1955.

30 MSS, 3451/6, 24 April, 24 June 1953; *Minutes*, 22 April 1977, 29 July 1981.

31 MSS, 3451/5, 3 November 1942, 30 May 1945; 3451/6, 7 May 1954; 3452/3, 9 April 1907.

32 MSS, 3451/5, 13 October 1950, 3451/6, 20 April 1956; *Minutes*, 20 April 1971, 18 June 1977,18 October 1985, 26 January, 23 May 1990; *CP*, 5 October 1907.

33 MSS, 3451/4, 19 January 1926; 3451/6, 14 January, 26 June, 23 October 1969; *Minutes*, 9 January 1973, 26 October 1984.

34 MSS, 3451/2, 9 October 1883; 3451/3, 18 July 1907, 17 October 1913; 3452/14, newscutting of 16 Oct. 1931; *Minutes*, 20 April 1971.

35 MSS, 3451/5, 5 May 1950; 3451/6, 24 April 1953, 29 October 1954, 26 June 1962, 28 June 1966, 27 June 1967; *Minutes*, 24 June 1975, 19 June 1977; *WCFK Newsletter*, 8, November 1999.

36 MSS, *Minutes*, 21 January 1983, 4 April 1984.

37 MSS, Master's Report July 1998.

38 MSS, 3452, Abstract of Corporate Accounts, year ending 24 June 1915; 3451/4, 21 January 1925; 3451/5 28 January 1942, 6 April 1951; *Minutes*, 10 January, 21 June 1985, 16 January, 20 October 1986, 15 January 1987, 2 April 1987.

39 MSS, 3451/3, 24 June 1902, 1 November 1904, 10 January, 24 June 1905.

40 MSS, 3451/3, Report on Bourne's Charity, 24 June 1905.

41 MSS, 3451/3, Bourne's Charity 1905, 18 August 1905, 21 June 1906.

42 MSS. 3451/3, Charity Commission Report, 28 June 1906.
43 MSS, 3451/3, 25 July 1906, 10 January, 9 April 1907, 24 June, 15 October 1908, 24 June, 10 November 1909, 11 January 1910.
44 MSS, 3452/11, 21 September 1921; 3452/14, 17 January 1932.
45 MSS, 3451/3, 6 February 1907.
46 *Leicester Chronicle*, 5 October 1907.
47 MSS, 'Framework Knitters – Cottages, Stoughton Road, Oadby, the Legal Title and its Implications for Development'; 3451/3, 9 April, 18 July 1907.
48 MSS, 3451/3, 30 September, 14 October 1907.
49 MSS, 3451/3. 24 October 1907, 29 August, 15 October 1908; *Leicester Daily Post*, 27 October 1908.
50 MSS, 3451/3, 26 October 1908.
51 MSS, 3451/3, 12 January 1909 (Joseph Raven was bound to John Evans at the court in Nottingham on 5 June 1705 – MSS, 3446), 12 October, 10 November 1909, 24 June 1910, 17 January 1911, 23 January 1912; 3451/4 18 January 1916, 8 October 1925, 19 April 1926; 3452/8, 23 January 1912.
52 *CP*, 15 July 1922.
53 MSS, 3451/4, pp. 341–8.
54 MSS, 3451/5, 13 October 1953.
55 WCFK, 'Cottages Homes Appeal brochure', 1979; L. C. Cavendish, 'Recommendations for the Improvement of the Cottage Homes, August 1976; WCFK Leaflet, January 1977.
56 MSS, *Minutes*, 22 January 1980, 21 June, 28 October 1983, 29 June 1984, 21 June, 18 October 1985, 20 June 1986, 2 April, 6 November 1987, 15 January 1988.
57 MSS, *Minutes*, 6 June, 30 October 1989.
58 MSS, *Minutes*, 2 April 1987.
59 MSS, *Minutes*, 19 April, 16 October 1989, 18 April, 23 October 1991; *Minutes of Finance Committee*, 4 June 1999.
60 MSS, 3451/3, 12 January 1909, 25 April 1913; 3451/4, 27 June 1916, 5 July 1917, 21 January 1925; 3451/5, 17 January 1945; 3451/6, 2 November 1951, 29 October 1953, 21 April 1961.
61 MSS, 3452/14, 17 July 1930; 3451/6, 26 June 1962; *Minutes*, 9 October 1974, 8 October 1975, 23 October 1979, 30 April 1981, 2 April 1987, 23 October 1990.
62 MSS, 3451/5, 8 October 1941, 16 January 1948.
63 MSS, Charity Commission, 'In the matter of the Charities called the Framework Knitters Company Almshouse and Pension Charities . . . of 28th June 1906', 12 December 1972, p. 8; 3451/4, 19 January 1926; 3451/6, 12 April 1952.
64 MSS, 3452/6, 1909; Leaflet, January 1977; *Minutes*, 18 October 1985.
65 *WCFK Newsletter*, 20, 1982–83; MSS, 3451/6, 22 April 1969, 14 April 1970.
66 MSS, 'Conditions under which tenants hold their allotments in the grounds of the Cottage Homes at Oadby', December 1983.
67 MSS, 3451/3, 12 January, 5 April 1909; 3451/4, 8 October 1925; 3451/5, 11 January 1949; 3451/6, 22 January 1952 – (Female Wardens were initially called Matrons) – 1 July 1965, 26 June 1969; Minutes, 30 January 1963, 11 January, 14 April 1972, 15 October 1976, 28 April 1978, 14 April 1983, 16 January 1986, 19 June 1987; *The Lady*, 12 February 1987.
68 MSS, 3451/3, 23 January 1912; 3451/4, 19 April 1926; 3451/6, 21 January 1966; *Minutes*, 15 October 1976.
69 MSS, 3451/3, 17 January 1911; 3451/4, 29 April 1924, 19 April 1926.
70 Leaflet, January 1977; MSS, 3451/4, 22 October 1918, 24 June 1924, 8 October 1925, 27 April 1927; 3452/14.
71 MSS, 3451/5, 25 October 1946; *Minutes*, 18 June 1977, 20 January 1978.
72 MSS, 3451/3, 17 January, 27 June 1911; 3451/4, 12 January 1915, 18 January 1916; *Minutes*, 22 January 1980, 23 October 1990.
73 MSS, *Minutes*, 20 October 1986, 16 June 1989.
74 MSS, 3451/3, 28 May, 20 August 1908, 12 January 1909, 19 April 1910.
75 MSS, 3451/6, 21 January, 29 April, 26 October 1955.
76 MSS, 3451/5, 1 August 1944, 19 July, 25 October 1945, 29 June 1951; 3451/6, 26 June 1956, 16 October 1959, 29 June 1960; 3452/8.
77 MSS, 3451/6, l8 October 1957.

78 MSS, 3451/6, 30 June 1964, 21 January 1965, 21 January 1966, 27 June 1967, 25 June 1968; *Minutes*, 11 January, 14 April, 16 October 1972, 7 January 1975, 22 April, 18 June, 7 October 1977, 20 January, 6 October 1978, 24 April 1979.

79 MSS, *Minutes*, 16 October 1972, 6 April 1973, 24 April 1988; Leaflet, January 1977.

80 MSS, *Minutes*, 13 September 1978, 23 January 1979, 30 April, 7 July 1981, 2 April 1987.

81 MSS, *Minutes*, 20 January, 24 April 1981, 14 April 1983, 19 June 1987, 22 April, 30 October 1988, 6 June, 6 October 1989, 26 January, 23 May 1990, 25 January 1991.

82 MSS, 3451/3, 12 October 1909, 17 January 1911; 3451/4, 12 January 1915; 3451/5, 15 October 1948, 11 January 1949; 3451/6, 26 October 1956, 24 June, 16 October 1959, 27 October 1961; *Minutes*, 25 April 1975, 1 July 1980, 20 October 1986, 31 January 1991, and many others.

83 MSS, 3451/6, 24 June, 13 October 1953, 7 May 1954, 21 January 1955, 14 January 1969; *Minutes*, 8 October 1975, 22 April 1988.

84 MSS, 3451/5, 25 January 1944, 16 March 1951; 3451/6, 31 October 1958, 21 January 1964; *Minutes*, 21 June 1991; *Minutes of the Finance Committee*, 6 March 1998; CLGL, MSS. 21871/29.

85 MSS, 3451/3, 24 June 1904; 3451/5, 3 November 1942, 31 January, 25 April 1947, 26 October 1949, 20 January 1950; 3451/6, 17 October 1952, 14 October 1958; CLGL, MSS. 21871/29, *Leicester Evening Mail*, 12 July 1933.

86 MSS, 3451/5, 16 April 1948, 29 April 1949; 3451/6, 21 January 1965; Minutes, 25 April 1975, 20 January 1978; *Centenary History of Leicester Technical School*, p. 52.

87 MSS, 3451/5, 11 May 1944; 3451/6, 11 April, 27 June 1967; Minutes, 14 April 1972, Letter from Liveryman J. C. H. Hurd, to Clerk Weale, December 1981, 15 October 1982, 4 April 1984.

88 MSS, *Minutes*, 6 October 1989, 31 January 1991.

89 MSS, *Minutes*, 29 June, 26 October 1984, 21 June 1985; David Bethel, Chairman of the Bursary Awards Committee, 'Educational Bursary Scheme; A Review', December 1991, p. 1.

90 MSS, *Minutes*, 18 October 1985, 18 April 1986, 13 January, 19 April 1989; 16 June 1989, 20 July, 23 October 1990, 21 June, 23 October 1991, 31 January 1992; *WCFK Newsletter*, 30, 1993/94.

91 MSS, *Minutes*, 15 January 1987, 24 October 1988; Bethel, 'Review, 1991, p. 3. The president of the Leicester Textile Society in 1987 was Past Master John Whitehead. Names and educational establishments of bursary winners are given in Appendix 9.

92 MSS,. 3451/3, 17 January 1911, 25 June 1912; 3451/6, 22 April, 26 June 1969, 13 January 1970; *Minutes*, 22 April 1977, 20 January, 28 April 1978; 3452/9, 1911.

93 MSS, 3451/2, 9 October 1900, 24 June 1901, 14 January 1902; 3451/3, 23 April 1912; 3451/4, 18 January, 27 April 1927; 3451/6, 29 October 1954, letter from Harman & Lambert, 18 January 1956, 24 January 1956.

94 MSS, 3451/6, 18 October 1957, 21 January, 24 June 1959, 11 April 1967; *Minutes*, 14 April 1972, 13 January 1976, 30 April 1981.

95 MSS, 3451/5, 1 July 1949; 3451/6, 29 October 1953, 25 June, 31 October 1958, 25 June 1968; *Minutes*, 16 January 1986, 28 April 1978, 22 April 1988.

96 MSS, 3451/6, 30 June 1964, 2 March 1966, 10 January 1967; *Minutes*, 6 October 1989, 25 January 1991.

97 MSS, 3451/3, 23 April 1912; 3451/4, 7 July 1925; 3451/5, 14 January 1943, 31 October 1947; 3451/6, 25 June 1968; *Minutes*, 9 October 1974, 24 June 1975, 26 October 198; *Minutes, Nominations and General Purposes Committee*, 4 June 1999; *Victoria County History of Leicester*, p.7. Robert Middleton and brother Joseph were farmers and frame work knitters of Long Whatton.

98 MSS, 3451/1, 9 April 1844; 3451/3, 27 June 1911; 3451/4, 13 January 1919, 19 April 1926, 27 April 1927 (The Clerk reported that he had purchased an illustrated catalogue of the 1927 exhibition to be placed in the Company's papers.); 3451/5, 22 April 1941, 30 March 1943, 25 April 1947; 3451/6 21 January, 29 April 1955, 2 May 1957, 17 January, 18 April 1958, 8 October 1968; *Minutes*, 22 April 1982, 15 January, 24 October 1988.

99 MSS, 3451/2, 24 June 1901; 3451/4, 21 April 1914, 29 October 1923, 7 October 1926.

IX

The future for the Company

Michael D. P. Turnbull, Immediate Past Master
of the Worshipful Company of Framework Knitters
and Chairman of the Millennium Book Committee,
May 2000

The future is simply a continuation of the past and present, for tradition is a strong element for any living institution. The members of the Worshipful Company of Framework Knitters, particularly from the late nineteenth century, were almost all connected with the knitting/knitwear industries in the Midland counties of Leicester, Nottingham and Derby, and today this is still largely true so that the Company, a London Livery Company, has often been referred to in London Livery circles as *the Midlands Livery*. There is no evidence to suggest that this tradition will change even though the knitting/knitwear manufacturing base has largely moved overseas.

Unlike most Livery Companies, the Framework Knitters admitted women into membership, particularly the widows of Liverymen who inherited and carried on their late husband's work. The Company now welcomes female members and has three lady Assistants on the Court. The number of lady members is likely to increase in future not least because so many buyers and others in the retail industries are of their gender. So far, no lady has been elected Master, but this will almost certainly change in the next decade and the erroneous conception that the Livery is 'all male' will be demonstrated to be false.

What is changing and will continue to change is the direct connection of each Liveryman to the knitting/knitwear industry. The Company prides itself that, unlike most other Companies, around 75 per cent of its members are, or have been, drawn from its parent industry. To ensure that some of this valued tradition shall continue, the Freedom of the Livery is offered to all students who have gained one of its Bursaries or Awards. This ensures that there is a group of young, fresh people associated with the Company ensuring its future.

Membership of the Court has traditionally been by seniority in the Livery, this being considered a great honour. As the Company becomes in need of careful, imaginative and time-consuming management, Court membership is now subject to a wider selection criteria and this will continue to develop when the time of those in full-employment becomes less available for charitable and social activities. Court members must be free to give time and energy to the various committees – Education, Almshouses, Finance, Residents' social life, etc. The nature of the Court is therefore likely to change.

Various Lord Mayors of the City of London (not to be confused with the elected Mayor of Greater London), have exhorted the Livery Companies to take an active

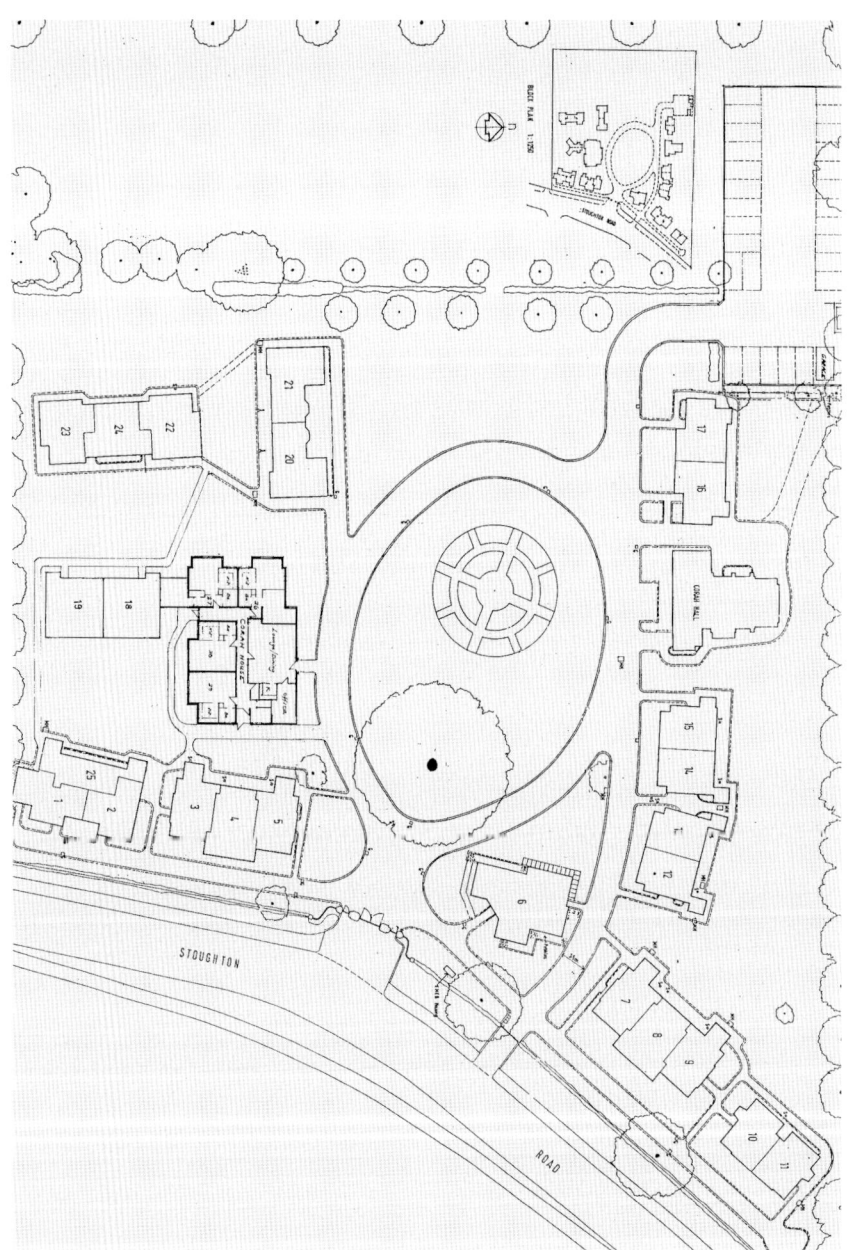

PLATE 50

F.W.K. MSS.

COTTAGE HOMES, OADBY, IN 2000

role in the City's affairs and life. The 'Square Mile' is still the World's leading financial centre and, increasingly, seeks to help the less affluent in and around the City. To survive with a purpose in the modern world, each Livery Company must look beyond the very pleasurable dinners at the Mansion House and Livery Halls, and be seen to be active in charitable and social matters.

Almost from its foundation, the Company has provided accommodation for those from the industry in need. The Cottage Homes at Oadby provide sheltered accommodation in very attractive surroundings for retired employees from the industry. Each cottage requires updating from time-to-time, sometimes involving demolition and re-building, and this expensive process will continue into the future (see Plate 50). As the numbers in the knitting/knitwear industries diminish, the Company will have to formulate new criteria for the selection of residents which may break a long-standing tradition.

From its early days, the Company provided education, training and supervision for apprentices. Since 1985 the focus on education has switched to final year undergraduates and post-graduates in universities who are eligible to apply for a Bursary or Award by developing a project or a research topic which, if successful, could benefit the industry. The Bursary Awards Committee provides Mentors for each successful student to help and guide the student through his/her project and offer technical information. It seeks to assist the academic staff in the universities with information and advice on curriculum development and research needs. In the future the Company plans to administer more educational funds and be able to help more students to be effective in their studies and to introduce them to career structures. The UK will continue to need highly trained technical and computer literate designers able to inter-act with overseas clients and provide for the needs of home and export consumers.

Clearly, in the future, the Worshipful Company of Framework Knitters can have a very important role to play in education, in helping to re-shape the knitting/knitwear industry and to continue to provide sheltered accommodation for those in need. It will take its full share in the life of the City of London whilst remembering its Midlands origins.

X

Summary

The knitting frame was invented by William Lee in Calverton, Nottinghamshire, in 1589. The Worshipful Company of Framework Knitters was incorporated sixty-eight years later to control the increasingly successful industry that had grown up around this invention. Although in the succeeding years its functions and format adapted to political whims and prevailing fashions in economics, education and the City of London, since Incorporation the Company's central core has remained constant and it has always carried out its commitments both to the industry from which it took its name and to the City of London to the best of its ability.

William Lee invented and improved his knitting machine with the help of family and friends drawn from the ranks of the minor gentry and more prominent artisans from the area around Calverton to the north east of Nottingham, and from the county town itself. These same family and friends and their descendants then formed the Association of Framework Knitters in the first quarter of the seventeenth century so as to control the progressively important industry into which knitting by machine was developing. This Association was converted by the Charters and Ordinances of 1657 and 1663 into a Society which was the sole, and legal, arbiter of the burgeoning industry, and whose absolute power was recognised by the City of London whose customs it adopted.

The incorporated Society of Framework Knitters established a sophisticated organisation to control its monopoly, much of which has been transferred to the Livery Company of the twenty first century. Moreover, in addition to the legally enforceable rules established by the Charters and Bye-laws, further licit regulations governing many facets of the trade, from the width of women's and men's hose to the prohibition of the transportation of frames, were drawn up. Overall control was vested in a London Court, housed for a time in the Company's Hall between Red Cross and White Cross Streets, and supplemented for the first two centuries by a permanent provincial Court in Nottingham, and the temporary establishment of subsidiary Courts wherever they were required. The Court in London was, and is, chosen from Liverymen who are elected Assistants for life, thus creating an oligarchy, and was originally composed mainly of either Lee's friends and family or their immediate descendants. The three chief officers of the Company, the Master and two Wardens, were, and still are, elected annually from the Assistants. The subsidiary Court established in Nottingham, also initially, consisted of other friends and family of the initiators of the Company and the

provincial Deputies not only policed the growing trade, but also tried to set themselves up as the sole marketing agents for knitting from the provinces.

However, to draw up rules to control a countrywide industry was one thing, to
police it when the horse or carrier pigeon were the quickest means of communi-
cation was another. The increasingly widespread success of the industry meant that
it proved impossible for the Company to exercise complete control, and from the
beginning there were always other astute entrepreneurs wanting a share of this
prosperous trade without the restraints of the Company. A long, and often bitter,
battle, of which the journeymen were ultimately the greatest losers, was fought by
the unregulated hosier-entrepreneurs, aided and abetted by the local government
hierarchy, to wrest control of framework knitting from the hands of the Company.

Moreover, the Company did not help its own cause by failing so abysmally to
confirm its monopoly with the Joint Stock Company of 1721, and the loss of
accumulated monies from the fees and fines meant that it was subsequently
permanently short of money. Public and government opinion turned increasingly
against monopolies during the eighteenth century and the 1753 declaration that the
Bye-laws were 'injurious and vexatious' undermined the power of the Company.
Although the Company retained an intimate interest in framework knitting for
the next half century, and remained the legal controller of the industry, the Court
no longer actively sought to alter most new working practices and recognised
privately that many were entering the industry illegally.

The Company's total control of framework knitting was finally severely curtailed
when, after being pushed by East Midland's journeymen to prosecute William
Payne of Hinckley for breaking the Bye-laws, the Company was nonsuited in 1809
and its monopoly broken. Although the Bye-laws were never declared illegal, they
were ruled to apply only to members, and as most engaged in machine knitting
no longer joined the Company, its absolute control of framework knitting was
finished.

During much of the nineteenth century the Company stepped back completely
from any involvement in the industry from which it took its name, so that at the
time of its greatest upheaval framework knitting was no longer subject to the influence, often benign, of the Company of Framework Knitters. It is not a coincidence
that the appalling conditions and low wages in this section of textiles, which were
the subject of so many government enquiries in the nineteenth century, occurred
after the authority of the Worshipful Company of Framework Knitters had been
broken by the very people who stood to gain from its eclipse. Even though its
influence lingered, especially in the East Midlands where it was significant that
many of the leaders of the unions and rebellions against the power of the new breed
of hosier came from families who had formerly held positions of authority and
helped manage the Company of Framework Knitters, from 1809 the Worshipful
Company of Framework Knitters had to reorganise its role.

For the next sixty years the Company concentrated on its own affairs and
those of the City of London and gradually metamorphosed into a modern Livery
Company.

It re-emerged from the 1880s reconnected with the hosiery trade – although now
it no longer controlled the industry – and it was the entrepreneurs of that trade, not
the journeymen, who voluntarily joined the Company.

The Company's beneficial influence in the efficient training of the craftsmen for the industry, which was originally by compulsory apprenticeship, was transformed in the nineteenth and twentieth centuries; first into donations to the Leicester Technical School and to the City and Guilds of London Institute exams in framework knitting and hosiery, and later by its substantial bursaries. This bursary scheme has been well received by universities and colleges and 'now encompasses students of science, technology, management, marketing and design who propose a research topic or undergraduate final year project which, if successful, could benefit the knitting/knitwear industry'. The national press and *Knitting International* have made a number of complimentary reports on some past Bursary winners, thus proving that the Company's investment in education for its industry is paying dividends and contributing to the national economy.

The Company's Almshouses have been in continuous occupation since 1734, first of all in London and then, from 1907 at Oadby in Leicestershire. The Cottage Homes at Oadby have been expanded and continually updated since their opening and the programme of upgrading will continue well into the twenty-first century.

The Worshipful Company of Framework Knitters may have lost its original function of acting as the regulator for the whole of the hosiery trade but it has entered the twenty first century in a strong position to meet the functions of a modern Livery Company, harnessing both new and old ideas to meet its needs. It has joined the technology revolution by establishing its own website, yet reinstated the class of membership limited to the Freedom of the Company, thus broadening the appeal of the Company and making it more accessible to a wider range of applicant. Improved communications between the Court and the Livery are being established and in order to promote increased social contact within the Company a golfing society has been formed. The opening of the extensions to Corah House on 4 March 2000 by Sheriff Pauline Halliday cemented further the relationship between the Company and the City of London, as well as continuing the improvements to the Company's Almshouses (see Plate C7). The bursaries of the Company are continuing to gain in prestige and strength and these, together with the other financial awards administered by the Company, such as the Peshal, Hurst, Gwilliam and The Textile Distribution Association Funds, will prove an important source of funding for the hosiery students of the future, and the Company has also provided mentors for students awarded the City and Guilds of London Institute Centenary Bursaries.

Appendix 1

An Address or Petition to the Protector Cromwell, of the Framework-Knitters

Taken from Charles Deering, *Nottinghamia Vetus et Nova*
(Nottingham: George Aysccugh & Tomas Willington,
MDCCLI, pp. 301–308)

To his Highness the Lord Protector of the Commonwealth of England, Scotland and Ireland, etc.

The humble representation of the promoters and inventors of the art and mystery or trade of Frame-work-knitting, or making of Silk-Stockings, or other work in a frame or engine: Petitioners to your Highness, that they may be united and incorporated by Charter under the Great-Seal of England, whereby their just right to the Invention may be preserved from Foreigners, the Trade advanced, Abuses therein suppressed, the benefit of the Commonwealth by importation and exportation, and otherwise increased, and hundreds of poor Families comfortably relieved by their several Imployments about the same, who will otherwise be exposed to Ruin, having no other calling to live of.

May it please your Highness.

Among the civil ways of improvement of a Common-wealth (next to agriculture) in all ages and times, have been, and are most securely beneficial and prosperous during their cherishment and retention: . . . the experience whereof has anciently and generally made it a principal maxim in state, to encourage by all favourable means requisite, the erectors and practisers of trading: and has notified for one of the greatest errors in state-government, the discountenancing and disordering thereof.

Whence in succession of time (from the antiquity of all records) the great variety and multitude of incorporations, overspreading the face of all eminent parts of the civilly governed world, flourishing under the favour and protection of the several princes and estates thereof, each province striving to exceed its neighbours in numerosity of them, and enlargement of all convenient privileges, and powers grantable unto them, and reaping innumerable benefits at the cheap rate of countenance, encouragement, and protection of the industrious labours of the natives: who in retribution unto the state for licence and privilege to earn their own subsistances, do disburthen the common-wealth (by employment or maintenance) of many poor, keep themselves in closer order and less circumference then others in ready ability for publick service, pay all publick charges and impositions: draw commerce into their country with profit unto the state by importation and exportation, and furnish their own all others necessities with useful commodities. So (and in many ways much more) profitable is encouraged and well governed industry, which if discouraged, and denied order in the practice, prosecution and

209

exercise thereof: it sometimes has (and ever will) most certainly become a disadvantage, weakening, and impoverishment to the common-wealth, and an advancement, strength, and enrichment of the neighbours who are, or may prove, enemies.

In prevention whereof, all nations who live not in absolute slavery to their sovereigns, but enjoy a propriety in their estates and goods, by claiming also a right of propriety in the fruits of their own endeavours (which was never yet denied but to the great prejudice of the contradictors) have provided and do allow, that as they severally and successively arrive to any assured profit, they are included within their own territories and appropriated unto the particular deservers, with grants in perpetuity of the regulation of affairs in trade, meerly as matter of power, or the immediate ministers thereof, unless for justice against infringers and invaders of such establishments as have been to that purpose obtained. And it has been (and remaineth) a great part of the felicity of England, that by the grave advice and appropriation of the state, it abounds with indulgend presidents and provisions of this kind, to the great encouragement and comfort of present and future industries.

Whereby the petitions are emboldened (now at length) to offer to your Highness consideration and grave judgement, the fulness of capacity they humbly conceive themselves to have been in, to receive the like grant of favour, trust, and protection, which many other companies have (upon fewer and less weighty inducements) obtained: and whereof there is apparent necessity, their trade being no longer manageable by them, nor securable unto the profit of this common-wealth, without it.

Which trade is properly stiled framework-knitting, because it is direct and absolute knitwork in the stitches thereof, nothing different therein from the common way of knitting (not much more ancient for publick use practised in this nation than this) but only in the numbers of needles, at an instant working in this, more than in the other by a hundred for one, set in an engine or frame composed of above 2000 pieces of smith, joyners and turners work, after so artificial and exact a manner, that by the judgement of all beholden, it far excels in the ingenuity, curiosity and subtility of the invention and contexture, all other frames or instruments of manu facture in use in any known part of the world. And for the skill requisite to the use and manage thereof, it well deserves (without usurpation as some others impertinently have) the title of mystery and art, by reason of the great difficulty of learning, and length of time necessary, to attain a dexterous habit of right, true and exquisite workmanship therein, which has preserved it hitherto (from the hands of foreigners) peculiar to the English nation, from whence it has extraction, growth, and breeding unto that perfection it is now arrived at. Not only able to serve your Highness dominions with the commodities it mercantably workes, but also the neighbouring countries round about, where it has gained so good repute, that the vent thereof is now more foreign than domestick, and has drawn covetous eyes upon it, to undermine it here, and to transport it beyond the Seas. Of whose sinister workings to that pernicious end, these petitioners (as most interested) standing in the nearest sent, think themselves in the common duty of well-affected persons to your Highness and their country, (besides their own case of necessity) bound to make address unto the wisdom, protection and care of your Highness (as predecessors in former times have done to the rulers of this nation) speedily to restrain and suppress all attempts, to bring so great a detriment and inconveniency upon the common-wealth.

Now so it is, and may it please your Highness

That the trade of frame-work knitting was never know or practised either here in England, or in any other place in the world, before it was (above 50 years past) invented and found out by one William Lea of Calverton in the county of Nottingham, gent. who by himself and such of his kindred and countrymen as he took unto him for servants, practised the same many years, (somewhat imperfectly in comparison of the exactness it is sithence brought unto, by the endeavours of some of these petitioners. Yet even in the infancy thereof, it gathered sufficient estimation of a business of so extraordinary a national profit and advantage, as to be invited over in to France, upon allurements of great rewards, privilege and honour; not long before the suddain murther of the late French King Henry IV. unsuccessfully accepted by the said Mr. Lea, (at that time wanting due encouragement at home). And transporting himself with nine workmen, his servants (with some frames) unto Roan [Rouen]; there wrought to so great applause of the French, that the trade was in all likelihood to have been settled in that country for ever, had not the decease of the said King disappointed Mr. Lea of his expected grant of privilege, and the succeeding troubles of that kingdom delay'd his renew'd suit to that purpose, into discontentment and death at Paris, leaving his workmen at Roan to provide for themselves, seven of which returned back again into England with their frames, and here practised and improved their trade; under whom, (or the master-workmen since risen under them) most of the petitioners had their breeding and served their apprenticeships. Of the other two which remained in France only one is yet surviving: but since so far short of the perfection of his trade (as is used here) that of him, or what can be done by him, or his means, these petitioners are in non apprehension of fear, nor have not been (since then) endangered in foreign countries by any that have served out their full time of apprentiship here.

But near about that time a venetian ambassodor gave 500l. for a remnant of time of one Henry Mead, then an apprentice to this trade, and convey'd him with his frame from London to Venice, where altho' his work and the manner of it was for a while admired, and endeavoured to be imitated: yet as soon as necessity of reparation of his frame and instruments happened, for want of artificers experienced in such work there, and of ability in him to direct them, the work prospered not in him managing: so that (his bought time of service being expired) affection to his native country brought him home again into England. After his departure the Venetians grew disheartened, and impatient of making vain trials, they sent his disordered frame and some of their own imitation to be sold in London at very low valuation

And within a few years afterwards the trade was greatly endangered by one Abraham Jones, who having by underhand courses and insinuations (and not by servitude as an apprentice) gotten both the mystery and skillful practice thereof, did (contrary to the articles with the rest of the company that had taken some jealous notice of him) pass himself with some more unto Amsterdam, and there taking some Dutch unto him as servants, erected frames, and wrought for the space of two or three years, until the infection of the plague seized on him and his whole family and carried them all to the grave. His frames also (as things unprofitable to them that could not find out their right use without an able teacher) were sent to London for sale at slight rates.

These preservations and escapes of this trade from transplantation into foreign countries, these petitioners do with thankfulness acknowledge, and ascribe to have been brought to pass by the divine providence, limiting his bounties and administration whither he has been pleased to direct them. For it may well seem marvellous in human judgment, how otherwise this trade should remain (nothwithstanding all the covetous and envious attempts to the contrary practised for the space of 40 years past) an art peculiar to only this our nation: And to the nimble spirits of the French, the fertile wits of the Italian, and industrious inclination of the Dutch, a concealed mystery unto this day.

Yet a continued negligence in presumption thereupon, would ill beseem the receivers of so many damageless warnings and may soon prove of hard consequence unto these petitioners who without intermission are environed with the like or greater dangers. For there are by other means than the way of apprenticeship so many intruders crept into this trade, that ill work and ill ware is everywhere offered to sale; and the ignominy and disparagement thereof, commonly imputed to the whole manufactury, not without much loss, hinderance and interruption of the true and allowable artisans, and tending to their utter impoverishment who in continual workmanship produce the best, finest, and most approvedly merchantable and useful wares ever sold and bought in the memory of men, otherwise the petitioners could not have driven their trade through many oppositions and difficulties, up unto the height it is now brought, and into fair expectations and open way of large increase, if intrusion were barred, and transportation and teaching of the mystery unto foreigners restrained, and none of this our nation, either artisan, apprentice or intruder, be permitted so mischiviously to seek for gain.

As one here in London makes his profession and custom to do; exposing himself as a teacher of this art and trade for any inconsiderable parcel of money, unto all manner of people without distinction, whether native or not, hitherto uncontroulably: nor to inveigle and corrupt apprentices from their masters, to discover and teach unto them the whole trade; (and having gotten it) pretend upon scruples of conscience in matters of religion, or some other occasion, to depart your Highness dominions, and set it up in practice in a foreign country; as one not long since has done, whom these petitioners are labouring all day they may to reduce, and are not hopeless to find prevalent means to recover him back again time enough, if they receive encouragement in this their humble suit. Wherein they farther shew:

That altho' this manufacture may be wrought in any other materials that are usually made up (or can possibly be made up) into the form of knitwork: Yet has it chosen to be practised in Silk, the best and richest of all others in use and wearing, and most crediting the artisans, and of greatest advantage unto this State and Commonwealth, yielding several payments to the use of the state before it passes out of the hands of the traders therein, and increasing merchandise by both the ways of importation and exportation of the self-same material, imported raw at cheap rates, exported ready wrought at the utmost extent of value: so that the distance of those valuations is totally clear gain to this Commonwealth, and esteemed upwards of six parts in seven of the whole quantity of this material in the highest value thereof, wrought up by this manufacture; which has vindicated that old proverbial aspersion: – 'The stranger buys of the Englishman the case of the Fox for a groat, and sells him the tail again for a shilling.' And may now invert and retort upon them: 'The Englishman buys silk of the stranger for twenty marks, and sells him the same again for one hundred pounds.'

That this trade encourages and sets on work other artificers also; as smiths, joyners and turners, for the making erecting and repairing of frames, and other necessary instruments thereunto belonging, and has bred up many excellent workmen among them for farther publick service.

That the artisans of this trade, do moreover employ a multitude of hands besides their own about the preparation and finishing of materials and ware they work: On which do compleatly subsist and thrive: The winders, throwers, sizers, seamers and trimmers thereof: And also the needlemakers totally depend thereon.

That altho' these petitions seem in the eyes of the world, to be present under a cloud and every moment ready to be undone by intruders and foreigners, so that many people fear and forbear to bind their children apprentices unto a trade of such instant hazard and irregularity, until a settlement thereof, under a corporation to the great retarding and increase of able artisans, who are therefore but few in number, in comparison of the knitters the way common to other nations; yet do they subsist by the labours in a more substantial and serviceable degree to the Commonwealth disburthening it of many poor of both sexes. Whereas the common tedious way multiplies needy persons here, rather because the people of other nations, outwork those of this therein, than by any hinderance they receive from the best artisans of this manufactury that bend their endeavours all they can to the foreign vent in general, as well as, in their own particulars most profitable to this nation, leaving the home sale in great part to the common knitters, uninterrupted, unless by the intruders into this art, whose multiplications (if not restrained) will be equally pernicious and destructive unto them as unto the petitioners; who only (and not the common-knitters) have shewed unto this Commonwealth, that it is able abundantly to serve itself and ultra with all commodities of knitwork, as stockings, calceoons, waistcoats, and many other things, with the help, or rather inconveniency it formerly had of importation of the same in quantities ready wrought from foreign parts.

That this trade is in no kind impertinent or damageable to the Commonwealth, nor driven in trifling, base, and unnecessary stuff or ware, seeing all the world (where habits are worn) is in general and permanent use thereof: But to the contrary, it works on the principle of stuffs, and makes commodious and decent ware for the cover of the whole body of men, perpetually unchangeable in fashion, endeavouring (as much as in the artisan lies) to found an unexhaustible mine within this nation already prepared to become, (if it shall please your Highness to establish it) henceforth the place of sole resort, as to a special mart, of the rich and staple commodities wrought by this manufacture, for the general service of all the great, honourable and better sorts of inhabitants of the whole communicable world.

That the petitioners have made a large and competent probation of the worth of this manufacture in itself, and merit thereof to the Common-wealth, (for the proportion of its growth) far exceeding any other that trades with foreigners in their own materials, extracting from them (to the use of the Commonwealth) and the maintainance of the people of this land, at foreign charge) upwards of fourscore in every hundred de claro of the whole value now, or that may be hereafter, upon a regular way of trading, dealt in, and defraying out of the other parcel of the hundred, being less then twenty current, all customs, imposts, and freights, both homeward and outwards, and also reserving the remainder of the twenty, to the manage of the merchant for as much unwrought material. Which eighty, in quick passages and returns of home trade, (by the way twice accounted for unto the officers of excise) suddenly and insensibly diffuses and disperses itself through very many hands, either totally maintaining, or otherwise adding to the subsistences of many other severally (in part) before enumerated trades and professions, besides this manufacture, the prime wheel, gathering only thereby an ordinary ability, to make the rest move: *viz* merchants, owners of ships, hosiers, dyers, winders, throwsters, sizers, seamers, trimmers, wire-drawers, needle-makers, smiths, joyners, turners, with many other assistants, all having their sufficient contents and inablements to live out of the clear product of the foreign vent, raised and furnished by the labours of the petitioners and their servants; who have voluntarily among themselves kept order in their trading, according to the duty of probationers (hitherto) without making any request unto the state for particular countenance and protection, until they found themselves now risen into a number not incapable of incorporation; and their trade into foreign parts of so great and growing increase (were the momentary dangers of utter ruin, for want of regulating power diverted) that it may well be esteemed the most improveable way of benefit and advantage of this kind, apparent to this present age, and (within some late hundreds of years past) offered unto this nation, and presented unto the state, (as this now is unto your Highness) for an inclosure within the boundary of its native soil, where it may receive its proper husbandry.

That if the petitioners had no other inducement to offer, but what every other trade which is (common also to foreigners) in fear to be over-wrought and out-sold by them, has heretofore presented, as motives, and means to obtain charters and privileges, and consequent provisions by statute, upon reasons, drawn from conveniences accrewing by civil education of some youth of the land, employment of persons, serving this Commonwealth with commodities better wrought here, than those transported hither from beyond the seas, and maintaining many of our people at home with the same money which foreigners did get away from hence for the maintenance of theirs: Yet might the petitioners (in confidence of the right of subjects) sue for power subordinately (according to the laws and constitutions of this land) to regulate their own endeavours in a company and fraternity among themselves. But these petitioners stand not in the same sole capacity, that the pin-makers, and others did at the times of their incorporation. For these have (additionally thereunto) an higher merit towards the Common-wealth, who's interest in all the fore mentioned extraordinary advantages and benefits, and in the further uses of them is annexed unto the prosperity of this manufacture, and wholly depending thereon. Insomuch that the petitioners (in their humble suit) do plead unto your Highness, a general cause of the Commonwealth in gross, for an inestimable concernment to all posterity, and crave in their own to be but barely to be preserved, as their lawful endeavours have qualified them, the temporary instruments and servitours to that public use. Which they may reasonably hope, shall not now (first of all sorts of men, ever petitioning semblable favour) begin to be refused unto them, who have not been wanting to the Common-wealth in the main service thereof, during its late extremities of danger[?], but have all been faithful to their country in every thing according to their utmost abilities, and have many of them undergone much loss of worldly goods, and peril of life, by and against the common enemy, and some of them continue in military office to this day.

And seeing the mistress of knowlege, experience, has taught that the some proprietary of a generally desired commodity, has a master key to command the lock of trading; which whosoever can prudently manage, has no small mastery over the wealth of the universe; and feeling that this art of frame-work-knitting here in England (as Printing formerly in Germany out-wrought all the manual writers in the world) is likewise able to out-work all the common-knitters among all nations, and make the commodity (without divulging of the mystery) generally desirable and entertained (as that other was here) with grace and privilege of importation (by provision of statute, 1st of Richard III, cap.9) and feeling this is much more capable of secreting, than that, by reason of the great difficulty to attain this with long practice, and the facility of the other to be conceived at first sight. This arising in an entire dominion, and that other in a region full of divided principalities. This is endued with a quality retentive, to continue for many ages, if not ever, (altho' the other could not so in Germany) a peculiar in propriety unto this nation of England. Therefore it is fit to be owned as a native (by the hand of your Highness) established in the rank, as a nonpareil of handicrafts, to be taken into your possession inclusively within your power of command and special protection, who is herein not slightly concerned, because intrusted to husband the Common-wealth, and is the balance of reason to distinguish between the allegations and aims of good and bad patriots. Some striving to scatter abroad (about all the earth) that harvest, whereof others desire the storing in a magazine; and some urging the same exploded clamours against the use of engines in trading, which the file and hammer workers of a single pin did heretofore, to divert or retard the privileging the company of pin-makers, in opposition to those that now sue and refer themselves to be considered according to discretion at home, for what they might write their own conditions every where abroad; if piety to their native country, as strongly restrained not them, as they implore the coercive power of your Highness to restrain their ill willers from unravelling the entrails of the Common-wealth, and giving or yielding opportunity unto strangers, to gather them up, and make that common to all the world, which is naturally particular in sole propriety to this nation, and prepared for the management of your Highness in such manner, as in your Highness's wisdom and great favour shall be thought expedient for the best advantage of this Common-wealth, ever in thriving condition and flourishing by exportation of commodities, as well artificially as naturally appropriated unto this island not unknown to your Highness to have suffered some late decay in the main support of its foreign trading, which may receive a great supply and increase by means of good encouragement of this manufacture, only in present necessity of the like protection and privileges, that have been granted, confirmed, and are enjoyed by many others, tho' of foreign invention and use, and never in possibility of becoming, as this is solely from hence impartable unto all other nations:

As which is humbly submitted to your Highness's pleasure, with great hopes that you will graciously patronise and cherish the honest endeavours of such as aim at the public good, as well as their own private interest,

And your Petitions shall ever Pray

Anciently

Appendix 2

Version in modern spelling of the Charter of the Company of Framework Knitters, 1657

Guildhall Manuscripts Department reference no: 16,865

(This Charter of 1657 was 'translated' for the
Worshipful Company of Framework Knitters by
Mrs. Hilary Marshall of the Society of Genealogists)

Oliver Lord Protector of the Commonwealth of England Scotland and the Dominions thereto belonging **To all to whom these presents shall come Greeting Whereas** we are informed by the humble petition of divers persons in and near our City of London using the Art Mystery or Trade of Framework Knitting that sundry persons using the said Art and Mystery in several places of this Commonwealth have therein for many years past and still do use and practice much deceit in that Trade in making much bad and deceitful work to the great abuse of the people of this Commonwealth and the scandal of the said Art or Mystery of Framework Knitting And likewise that it is endeavoured by divers persons wholly to remove and carry the said Art Trade or Mystery out of this Commonwealth into foreign parts to the impoverishing and undoing of the contrivers promoters and inventors of the said Art and Mystery of Framework Knitting and to the great discouragement of other ingenious persons of this Commonwealth to exercise their arts within the same and likewise to the undoing of many poor people in and near our Cities of London and Westminster for the better upholding of which said Art and Mystery of Framework Knitting within this Commonwealth the said petitioners have humbly besought us to incorporate them into a Body Politic and to invest them with such grants powers and privileges as may be meet and necessary for the well ordering and regulating the said Art and Mystery And we having taken into our consideration their said humble request and of how good use and benefit it may be as well to the people of this Commonwealth as to the artificers therein to uphold the said Art and Mystery and being willing to continue and maintain the same within this Commonwealth and to advance it (if it may be) for the good and benefit of the artists using the same Art and Mystery of Framework Knitting and for the general service and advantage of the people of this Commonwealth And forasmuch as the Framework Knitters are now dispersed amongst divers Companies of London and elsewhere by reason whereof they have not that form of government as is necessary and advantageous to the said Art and Mystery of Framework Knitting Know ye therefore that we being graciously inclined to the humble petition of the Framework Knitters in the premises and for the better reformation of the abuses now frequently used and practised in the said Art and Mystery to the common damage of the people of this Commonwealth and for the better government and regulation of the said Art and Mystery and the persons using and exercising the same in a just and orderly way of our especial grace certain knowledge and mere motion **have** willed ordained granted constituted and appointed and by these presents for us and our successors do will ordain grant constitute and appoint that all persons as well freemen as foreigners who now do or hereafter shall use or exercise the Art Trade or Mystery of Framework Knitting within the said City of London and four miles compass of the same forever hereafter be and shall be by virtue of these presents one Body Corporate and Politic in deed and in name and shall have continuance forever by the name of Master Wardens Assistants and Society of the Art or Mystery of Framework Knitters of the City of London and them by the name of Master Wardens Assistants and Society of the Art or Mystery of Framework Knitters of the City of London We do for us and our successors fully and really create erect make ordain establish constitute declare and appoint to be one Body Corporate and Politic to have continuance for ever to them and their successors And that by the same name they shall and may have perpetual succession And that they by the name of Master Wardens Assistants and Society of the Art or Mystery of Framework Knitters of the City of London be for ever hereafter persons able and capable in law to purchase have receive and enjoy messuages lands tenements liberties privileges jurisdictions and hereditaments whatsoever of what kind quality or nature soever they be to them and their successors in fee and perpetuity or for term of life lives or years or otherwise in what sort soever as the same exceed not the clear yearly value of one hundred pounds the statute for not putting lands or tenements in mortmain or anything therein contained or any other act or statute to the contrary notwithstanding And also all manner of goods chattels and things whatsoever of what name nature or quality soever they be And also to give and grant let assign alien and dispose of any the said messuages lands tenements or hereditaments goods or chattels and likewise to do perform and execute all and singular other acts and things whatsoever by the name of Master Wardens Assistants and Society of the Art or Mystery of Framework Knitters of the City of London and that they and their successors by that name shall and may be persons able and in law capable to plead and be impleaded answer and be answered unto defend and be defended in what court or courts soever and before any judges or justices and other persons and officers of us and our successors whatsoever in all and singular actions pleas suits plaints matters and demands of what kind nature or quality soever they shall be in the same and in as ample manner and form as any other the people of this Commonwealth may or can do being able and capable in law or as any other body corporate and politic within this Commonwealth may or can have purchase receive possess enjoy retain give grant let alien dispose and assign plead and be impleaded answer or be answered unto defend or be defended do perform or execute And that they the said Master Wardens Assistants and Society of the Art or Mystery of Framework Knitters of the City of London and their successors shall and may forever hereafter have a Common Seal to serve and use for all causes things matters and affairs whatsoever of them and their successors and that it shall and may be lawful to and for them and their successors to alter and make new the said Seal from time to time at their wills and pleasures as they shall think fit   **And** further we will and ordain and by these presents for us and our successors do give and grant unto the said Master Wardens Assistants and Society of the Art or Mystery of Framework Knitters of the said City of London and their successors for the time being full power and lawful authority to assemble themselves and meet together from time to time in some convenient place within the City of London where they shall think most meet and then and there they shall and may elect and choose one of the said Art or Mystery of Framework Knitting in manner and form hereafter in these presents mentioned and expressed who shall be and shall be called the Master of the said Company of Framework Knitters of the City of London and also that then and there they shall and may elect and choose two meet persons of the said Society in manner and form hereafter in these presents mentioned and expressed who shall be and shall be called the Wardens of the said Company of Framework Knitters of the City of London And also then and there they shall and may nominate elect and choose thirteen meet persons of the said Society in manner and form hereafter in these presents mentioned and expressed who shall be and shall be called the Assistants of the said Company of Framework Knitters of the City of London who from time to time shall be aiding and assisting to the Master and Wardens of the said Company of Framework Knitters of the City of London for the time being in all causes matters and things touching or concerning the said Company   And also that there shall be elected and chosen two or more of the said Society from time to time by the Master Wardens and Assistants of the said Company or the greater part of them for the time being who shall have power and authority by writing under the Common Seal of the said Society as Deputies of the said Master Wardens and Assistants to make search in the presence of a constable or other lawful officer in all or any place or places within this Commonwealth as well in places privileged as unprivileged and there to prove try and see whether all stockings tops waistcoats trouches or any other things whatsoever made or wrought by the said frame or engine be workmanlike wrought And if upon such search either of the Master Wardens and Assistants or of the sworn Deputies of the said Company for the time being as aforesaid they shall find any stockings tops waistcoats trouches or other things whatsoever made and wrought by the said frame or engine to be unworkmanlike wrought or unartificially made or to be made of bad and deceitful stuff that then and so often they cause the same to be cut in pieces and defaced and the persons in whose hands any of the goods so deceitfully wrought and made shall be found to punish by reasonable fines and penalties according to the ordinances orders and bye-laws in that behalf to be made by the said Master Wardens and Assistants or the greater part of them for the time being and their successors   **And** further we will and by these presents for us and our successors do give and grant unto the Master Wardens and Assistants of the said Company of Framework Knitters of the City of London and their successors power and authority to administer meet and convenient oaths unto their Deputies before they be admitted to the execution of their said offices well rightly and faithfully with diligence according to their best skill and power to execute the same   **And** further we do by these presents for us and our successors give and grant power and authority to the said Master Wardens and Assistants of the said Company of Framework Knitters of the City of London or the greater part of them for the time being to elect and choose unto the said office of Deputies meet persons yearly and every year or oftener as they case shall require And the said Deputies for just and reasonable causes to remove and other or others in his or their places so removed to elect and choose unto the said office of Deputies   And that from time to time the said Master Wardens and Assistants or the greater part of them for the time being and their successors (whereof the Master and one of the Wardens of the said Society for the time being we will to be two) shall and may give and administer unto all and every such person and persons so chosen into the office of Deputies as aforesaid meet and convenient oaths for the due and faithful execution of their said office   **And** we do hereby for us and our successors further grant unto the Master Wardens Assistants and Society of the said Art or Mystery of Framework Knitters of the City of London and their successors that the Master Wardens and Assistants of the said Company for the time being or the greater part of them (whereof the Master and one of the Wardens of the said Company for the time being we will to be two)   shall and may have full power and authority by virtue of these presents to make ordain constitute and appoint and set down from time to time such reasonable acts orders ordinances and constitutions in writing which to them or the greater part of them (whereof the Master and one of the Wardens of the said Company for the time being we will to be two)   shall seem fit good wholesome profitable honest necessary and convenient according to their discretions as well for and concerning such oaths as shall be fit to be administered to the Master Wardens and Assistants and their Deputies and all others of the said Society   And also for touching and concerning the said Art or Mystery of Framework Knitting within the said City of London and within four miles' compass thereof And also for the punishment and reformation of such deceits and abuses as shall be from time to time found to be committed either in uttering or making of bad and deceitful work within the City of London and four miles' compass of the same And also for the support of the said Company and for the good rule and government of the said Master Wardens Assistants and Society of the Art or Mystery of Framework Knitters of the said City of London and all and every the person or persons now using or which hereafter shall use or exercise the Art or Mystery aforesaid within the said city suburbs and liberties or within four miles' compass thereof in all matters and things touching and concerning the same   And for declaration after what manner order and form the said Master Wardens and Assistants and all and every other person and persons using and exercising the said Art or Mystery within the limits aforesaid shall behave demean and carry him and themselves in their said Art Trade and Mystery for the public good as well of the people of this Commonwealth in general as of the said Master Wardens Assistants and Society and their successors   And for all other matters things and causes touching and concerning the said Art or Mystery and to provide and limit reasonable pains penalties and punishments either by fines and amercements or otherwise to be inflicted upon all offenders or breakers of such acts orders ordinances and constitutions   And that they the said Master Wardens Assistants and Society of Framework Knitters of the City of London and their successors shall and may have levy and take by distress or action of debt or by any other lawful ways or means the said fines and amercements to their own use without the let or hindrance of us or our successors and without giving or rendering any account or other thing to us or our successors for the same   All which acts orders ordinances and constitutions fines and amercements we will shall be reasonable and not repugnant to the laws and statutes of this Commonwealth nor to the customs or usages of the City of London   **And** further for the better execution of this our grant we have assigned named constituted and made and by these presents for us and our successors do assign name constitute and make George Ashton the first and present Master of the said Company of Framework Knitters of the City of London who shall continue in the said office from the date of these presents until the four and twentieth day of June which shall be in the year of Our Lord one thousand six hundred fifty eight if he shall so long live and shall well behave himself in the said office of Master and from thenceforth until another shall be chosen and sworn unto the said office of Master of the said Company in due manner according to the ordinances and provisions hereafter in these presents mentioned and expressed   he the said George Ashton first taking his corporal oath before the Wardens and Assistants of the said Company for the time being or the greater part of them for the due and faithful execution of the said office or place of Master of the said Company   To which Wardens and Assistants or the greater part of them we do hereby for us and our successors give full power and lawful authority to administer the said oath to the said George Ashton the present Master of the said Company according to the true intent and meaning of these presents **And** also we have assigned named ordained constituted and made and by these presents for us and our successors do assign name ordain constitute and make Thomas Phillips and Humphrey Jamson to be the first and present Wardens of the said Company of Framework Knitters of the City of London who shall respectively continue in their said offices of Wardens of the said Company from the date of these presents until the four and twentieth day of June which shah be in the year of Our Lord one thousand six hundred fifty eight if the said Thomas Phillips and Humphrey Jamson or either of them shall so long live and shall well demean themselves in their said offices or places respectively and from thenceforth until two others be chosen and sworn unto the said offices of Wardens of the said Company of Framework Knitters according to the ordinances and provisions hereinafter expressed and declared they the said Thomas Phillips and Humphrey Jamson first taking their corporal oaths well rightly and faithfully to execute the said office of Wardens before the Master and Assistants of the said Company or the greater part of them for the time being whom we do hereby authorise to administer the said oaths accordingly   **And** we have assigned named constituted appointed and made and by these presents for us and our successors do assign name constitute appoint and make Henry Womball John Lee John Crosen Lawrence Pomfrett Gregory Fishborne Jonathan Gramar Richard Bumby Joseph Tomlinson Gabriel Brewer Richard Read George Balderstoun Anthony Bennett and Samuel Knight all freemen of London to be the first and present Assistants of the said Company of Framework Knitters of the City of London who shall continue in their said offices of Assistants during their natural lives unless they or any of them shall be removed from his or their said offices for misbehaving him or themselves in their said offices or for some other just or reasonable cause (they taking their corporal oaths before the said Master and Wardens beforenamed for the due and faithful execution of their said places of Assistants) to which said Master and Wardens we do hereby give full power and lawful authority to administer the same oaths accordingly   **And** we will and by these presents for us and our successors do give and grant unto the said Master Wardens Assistants and Society of the Art or Mystery of Framework Knitters of the City of London and their successors that the Master Wardens and Assistants of the said Company for the time being or the greater part of them (whereof we will that the Master and one of the Wardens for the time being be two) from time to time for ever hereafter shall have full power and authority by virtue of these presents yearly and every year at or upon the four and twentieth day of June to elect and nominate one of the Wardens or Assistants of the said Company for the time being to be Master of the said Company for one whole year from thence next ensuing and from thenceforth until one other of the Wardens or Assistants of the said Company shall be nominated chosen and sworn unto the said office of Master according to the ordinances and provisions mentioned and declared in these presents   And he that shall be so chosen and named unto the said office of Master of the said Company before he be admitted to the execution of the said office shall take his corporal oath before the last Master and Wardens of the said Company or any two of them and before the Assistants of the said Company for the time being or the greater part of them to execute the said office rightly well and faithfully in all things touching the same and that after such oath so as aforesaid taken he shall have and exercise the said office for one whole year from thence next ensuing and from thenceforth until another fit person shall be duly chosen and sworn into his place   To which last Master and Wardens or any two of them and the Assistants for the time being or the greater part of them we do by these presents for us and our successors give and grant full power and lawful authority from time to time to administer the said oath accordingly and likewise that at the same time of electing the said Master as aforesaid they shall and may also elect choose and nominate two other of the Assistants of the said Society of Framework Knitters of the City of London who shall be Wardens of the said Company for one whole year from thence next ensuing and from thenceforth until two others of the Assistants shall be chosen unto the said office of Wardens of the said Company of Framework Knitters of the City of London according to the ordinances and provisions in these presents expressed and declared And that they who shall be so chosen and named to the office of Wardens of the said Company of Framework Knitters of the City of London before they be admitted to execute the said office of Wardens shall likewise take their corporate oaths before the last Master and Wardens of the said Company or any two of them and before the Assistants for the time being or the greater part of them to execute their said offices well rightly and faithfully in all things touching the same and that after such oaths so as aforesaid taken they shall and may execute their said offices for one whole year from thence next ensuing   To which last Master and Wardens or any two of them and the Assistants for the time being or the greater part of them we do by these presents for us and our successors give and grant full power and authority from time to time to administer the said oaths accordingly   **And** further we will and by these presents for us and our successors do give and grant unto the aforesaid Master Wardens Assistants and Society of the Art or Mystery of Framework Knitters of the City of London and their successors that if it shall happen that the Master Wardens or Assistants of the said Company for the time being or any of them at any time after they shall be elected and chosen into his or their office or offices to die or be removed from his or their said office or offices (which said Master Wardens and Assistants and every of them for evil government or for any other just and reasonable cause we will from time to time shall be removed by the greater part of the Master Wardens and Assistants of the Company aforesaid for the time being) that then and so often it shall and may be lawful to and for the said Master Wardens and Assistants for the time being or the greater part of them at their wills and pleasures to elect and choose one other or others of the Assistants of the said Company to be Master Warden or Wardens in the place or places of him or them so dead or being removed) according to the orders and provisions before in these presents expressed and declared to execute and exercise the office of Master Warden or Wardens of the said Company until the four and twentieth day of June then next ensuing after such election and from thenceforth until some other or others meet person or persons shall be elected and sworn to be Master and Wardens of the said Company of Framework Knitters of the City of London according to the ordinances and provisions before in these presents expressed   **Nevertheless** we will that every Master Warden or Wardens of the said Society of the Art or Mystery aforesaid to be nominated and elected in the place or places of him or them so dead or removed as aforesaid before he or they be admitted to the execution of his or their said office or place shall take his and their corporal oath before the Master Wardens and Assistants of the said Company for the time being or the greater part of them well rightly and faithfully to execute the said office and place in and by all things respectively touching and concerning the same (to which said Master Wardens and Assistants for the time being or the greater part of them we do by these presents for us and our successors give and grant full power and authority to administer such oaths from time to time as often as the case shall so happen)   **And** further we will and by these presents for us and our successors do give and grant unto the said Master Wardens Assistants and Society of the Art or Mystery of Framework Knitters of the City of London and their successors that whensoever it shall happen that any of the Assistants of the said Company to die or be removed from his or their said office or place of Assistant (which said Assistants and every of them for evil government or for any other just or reasonable cause we will from time to time shall be removed by the greater part of the Master Wardens and Assistants of the said Society of the Art or Mystery aforesaid for the time being) that then and so often it shall and may be lawful to and for the said Master Wardens and Assistants of the said Company for the time being or the greater part of them at their wills and pleasures to elect and choose other meet person or persons out of the Society aforesaid to be Assistant or Assistants in the place or places of him or them so deceased or removed according to the ordinances and provisions before in these presents mentioned and expressed who shall execute and exercise the said office of Assistant or Assistants of the said Company during his and their natural life and lives in manner and form aforesaid   **Nevertheless** we will that every Assistant of the said Society of the Art or Mystery aforesaid so to be nominated and elected in the place or places of him or them so dead or being removed before he be admitted to the execution of his said office of Assistant shall take his corporal oath before the Master Wardens and Assistants of the said Company for the time being or the greater part of them (to whom by these presents we give power and authority to administer the said oath) well rightly and faithfully to execute the said office and so as often as the case shall so happen   **And** also we will and by these presents for us and our successors do grant unto the said Master Wardens Assistants and Society and their successors full power and authority that the Master Wardens and Assistants of the said Company for the time being or the greater part of them shall and may from time to time nominate elect and choose one meet person to be Clerk of the said Company to serve for the affairs of the said Society and one other fit and meet person to be Beadle of the said Company to be serviceable to and attendant on the Master Wardens and Assistants of the said Company for the time being in all matters touching and concerning the said Company wherein he shall be employed and the said Clerk and Beadle or either of them for reasonable and just cause to displace and remove out of their said place or places and other persons in their places at the pleasure and discretion of the Master Wardens and Assistants of the said Company for the time being or the greater part of them to choose and elect Which said Clerk and Beadle so elected and chosen before he or they be admitted to the execution of his or their said office or offices shall take his and their corporal oaths before the Master Wardens and Assistants of the said Society of the Art or Mystery of Framework Knitters of the City of London for the time being well faithfully and honestly to demean and behave themselves in the execution of their said respective offices   (to which said Master Wardens and Assistants or the greater part of them for the time being we do hereby for us and our successors give power and lawful authority to administer necessary and convenient oaths as well to the Clerk and Beadle of the said Company as to all other persons who shall be from time to time admitted into the said Society   **And** forasmuch as we are informed that divers persons as well of the people of this Commonwealth as also divers strangers have by secret means and indirect ways sought to carry the said Art and Mystery of Framework Knitting into foreign parts to the great damage of the people of this Commonwealth and to the detriment and impoverishing of such of the people whose livelihood depends thereon (it being an English invention) which would prove to be of evil consequence to this Commonwealth and a means to discourage the industrious people thereof   **We** therefore intending a speedy and effectual prevention and reformation of the aforesaid abuses do hereby for us and our successors charge and command that from henceforth after the date of these presents no person or persons freemen or foreigners denizens or strangers do presume to carry or cause to be carried beyond the seas any frame or frames or any engines used for making of silk stockings or other things appertaining to the manufacture of Framework Knitting or any part or parcel thereof or anything thereunto belonging upon no colour or pretence whatsoever under the pain loss and forfeiture of ten pounds of lawful English money for every such offence to be levied from time to time to and for the only use and benefit of the said Society   **And** furthermore we do by these presents for us and our successors give and grant unto the said Master Wardens Assistants and Society of the Art or Mystery of Framework Knitters of the City of London and to their successors that the Master Wardens and Assistants of the said Society for the time being or any two or more of them with two or more of the said Society from time to time for ever when and as often as to them shall seem meet shall have full power and lawful authority to oversee search and view govern correct and punish all and singular person and persons of the said Corporation using and exercising and which shall use or exercise the said Art Trade or Mystery of Framework Knitting or that shall make or sell any manufactures which shall be knit or in any wise wrought or made with the said frames or engines within the City of London and four miles' compass of the same as well in places privileged as not privileged   **And** we do by these presents for us and our successors give and grant full power and lawful authority unto the Master Wardens and Assistants of the said Company for the time being or any of them and to their sworn Deputies or any of them in the day-time with the assistance and in the presence of a constable or other lawful officer to enter and go into all manner of houses shops warehouses chambers yards orchards gardens cellars and backsides and into all and all manner of other places whatsoever as well privileged as not privileged within the City of London and four miles' compass thereof where there shall be any suspicion of any such frames or deceitful manufactures of what person or persons soever   And whatsoever frame or frames or parts of frame or frames or anything thereunto belonging or appertaining they shall find upon such search to be of bad work or of bad stuff and materials or to be deceitfully or unworkmanlike wrought or made the same frame or frames & deceitful manufacturers so found to break or deface   And to correct and punish the makers sellers and delinquents in the premises by fines and amercements or any other lawful way   **And** we do by these presents for us and our successors owe and grant unto the Master Wardens and Assistants of the said Company and their successors that they or any of them or any one or more of their sworn Deputies in manner as aforesaid may search within the limits of their jurisdiction for all and all sorts of frames or part or parcel thereof and whatsoever frame or frames or part or parcel thereof they shall find upon such search to be prepared or endeavoured to be transported or carried beyond the seas they shall and may deface and break and the offender or offenders therein shall be punished as contemners of our commands and shall also undergo the penalty before in these presents expressed   **And** further we do by these presents for us and our successors give full power and authority to the Master Wardens and Assistants of the said Society of the Art or Mystery of Framework Knitters of the City of London and their successors from time to time either by themselves or any of them or by their or any of their sworn deputies to enter into all or any place or places within the limits of their jurisdiction in such manner as aforesaid to search for all and all manner of stockings tops waistcoats troushes or any other things whatsoever made or wrought by any Framework Knitters and in their hands and possessions by the use of the said frame or engine and the same to view prove and try and all such stockings tops waistcoats troushes and other things aforesaid which upon such search and view shall be found to be unworkmanlike wrought or made of bad and deceitful stuff and materials to break and deface in whose hands and custody soever any such false and deceitful manufactures shall be found   And that all such persons as shall transport or provide to transport any of the said frame or frames or any part or parcel thereof or anything thereunto belonging contrary to the true intent and meaning of these presents shall undergo the aforesaid pain and penalty of forfeiture of ten pounds of lawful money of England for every of such their offences and shall be looked upon as contemners of our commands which said forfeiture or penalty ten pounds shall be levied by distress or action of debt or by any other lawful way or means whatsoever and being so levied shall be and remain to the only use and benefit of the said Society   **And further** we well weighing and considering the great prejudice and damage that will redound to the said Society and the members thereof and others as aforesaid by the transporting or carrying out of this Commonwealth the aforesaid frames to prevent such exportation of the same do for us and our successors give and grant full power and lawful authority to the Master Wardens and Assistants of the said Company and their successors either by themselves or their sworn Deputies to search within the limits of their Corporation where they shall hear and receive information of any person or persons endeavouring and contriving to transport or export any parts of frames or whole frames and whatsoever frames or part of frames shall be found upon such search to deface and break the same and the offenders therein shall be punished as is before mentioned declared and expressed   **And** further we do hereby for us and our successors will ordain and declare that no person or persons shall be hereafter admitted to the place of Master Warden or Wardens or Assistant or Assistants or Deputies of the said Company of Framework Knitters of the City of London or to the execution of the office or offices aforesaid unless he or they shall be a freeman or freemen of the said City of London before his or their election to the said office or offices or any of them respectively And further we do by these presents for us and our successors give and grant unto the Master Wardens Assistants and Society of the said Art or Mystery of Framework Knitters of the City of London and their successors that the Master Wardens and Assistants of the said Company for the time being or the greater part of them (whereof the Master and one of the Wardens of the said Company for the time being we will to be two) shall forever hereafter have full power and lawful authority from time to time to assess upon all and every person and persons free of the said Company or using or exercising or which hereafter shall use or exercise the said Art Trade or Mystery of Framework Knitting within the said City of London or four miles' compass of the same as well freemen as foreigners the sum of twelve pence every quarter of a year for his and their quarterage respectively and also all such other reasonable sum and sums of money as the Master Wardens and Assistants of the said Company for the time being or the greater part of them shall think fit for defraying other the necessary charges and expenses of the said Society and that the Master and Wardens of the said Society for the time being may from time to time collect and receive the aforesaid several quarterages and sums of money so as aforesaid to be assessed of the persons aforesaid and from time to time dispose and apply the same to the use and benefit of the said Society without accompt or or any other thing to be rendered paid or done to us or our successors for the same   And we will that every person and persons so as aforesaid to be assessed to such quarterage and other sums of money as aforesaid shall pay or cause to be paid the said quarterage and other sums of money to be assessed as aforesaid in due manner and according to the tenor and true intent and meaning of these presents as is before expressed and declared   **And** for the better discovery of the frauds and deceits now frequently used and practised in the said Art Trade and Mystery of Framework Knitting and for the encouragement of true workmanship in the said Art and for upholding the same within this Commonwealth we will and by these presents for us and our successors do declare ordain and appoint that no person or persons whatsoever from henceforth shall use or exercise the said Art Trade or Mystery of a Framework Knitter unless he or they shall have served as apprentice or apprentices for the term or space of seven years at least by covenant of indenture unto some person lawfully using and exercising the same trade or mystery under pain of our high displeasure and of being punished for his or their contempts in the premises according to the laws and statutes made in that behalf and according to the customs of the City of London   **And** furthermore that no person or persons whatsoever that now do or hereafter shall use or exercise the said Art Trade or Mystery of Framework Knitting within this Commonwealth shall take any apprentice or other person to instruct and teach the said Art or Mystery being an alien or stranger born out of the obedience to us or our successors or being the son or daughter of an alien or stranger born upon pain of our high displeasure and contempt of our commandment herein and to be further punished by such reasonable fines and penalties as shall be limited and appointed by the Master Wardens and Assistants of the said Company or the greater part of them for the time being and according to the custom of the City of London   **And** forasmuch as we are informed that divers persons do use and exercise the Art or Mystery aforesaid within the Commonwealth who have been partly contrivers of the said Art or Mystery and who are not in or under any form of government   **It** is therefore our will and pleasure that all persons within this Commonwealth that at the date of these presents do use the said Art Trade or Mystery of Framework Knitting within convenient and reasonable time may enter themselves before the Master Wardens and Assistants of the said Society or the greater part of them for the time being that so they may become known members of the said Society and shall take such meet and fit oaths as shall be administered unto other members of the said Society and that all such person and persons using and exercising the Art or Mystery aforesaid within this Commonwealth who shall not make such his and their personal appearance as aforesaid within such convenient and reasonable time as shall be limited by the Master Wardens and Assistants of the said Company for the time being shall be dealt with as contemners of our commandment and as persons disobedient thereunto   **And** we do by these presents for us and our successors give and grant unto the Master Wardens and Assistants of the said Company or the greater part of them for the time being and their successors full power and lawful authority to administer the said oaths accordingly   **And** for the better regulation of the said Art or Mystery and of all and singular the persons now using or exercising or which hereafter shall use or exercise the said Art Trade or Mystery of Framework Knitting within the place and limits aforesaid we do hereby for us and our successors will command declare and appoint that all and every such person and persons whatsoever as are freemen and members of any other Society guild brotherhood fraternity or body politic shall bind such of his her or their apprentice or apprentices as he she or they at any time or times hereafter shall take unto some member or freeman of the said Society of Framework Knitters of the City of London to the intent they may become free of the said Society and that upon pain of our high displeasure and of their due punishment for their contempt or neglect of our commandment in that behalf   **And** moreover we will and by these presents for us and our successors do give and grant full power and authority unto the said Master Wardens and Assistants of the said Society of the Art or Mystery of Framework Knitters of the City of London for the time being and their successors that they or the greater part of them (whereof we will that the Master and one of the Wardens for the time being shall be two) shall and may make establish and appoint such lawful orders ordinances and constitutions as they shall conceive necessary for the good rule and government of the said Art or Mystery within the City of London and four miles' compass thereof and of all persons using or exercising or which shall use or exercise the said Art Trade or Mystery of Framework Knitting within the limits aforesaid and to impose and assess reasonable fines and amercements for disobeying or not fulfilling the same ordinances or for not paying the duties to the aforesaid Society to be paid or for any other evil behaviour and to recover and levy those fines and amercements or any of them by distress or action of debt or in any other lawful manner to the use and benefit of the said Society and their successors so as the said orders ordinances fines and amercements be not contrary nor repugnant to the laws and statutes of this Commonwealth **And** further for the well ordering of the said Society of the Art or Mystery of Framework Knitters and of the members thereof under the government of the City of London and that the offenders in the said trade may be the more effectually dealt with and punished according to their demerits and those that duly and honestly exercise the same as they ought to do may the better be encouraged we do hereby declare our will and pleasure to be that the Lord Mayor and Aldermen of the City of London for the time being do cause admit and allow these our letters patents to be enrolled within the Common Chamber of the said City amongst the records thereof to the intent that those which are and shall be Freemen of London and Members of the said Society of Framework Knitters of the City of London may be subject to the government of the said City and may enjoy the benefit thereof **And** furthermore we will ordain and grant for us and our successors by these presents to the said Master Wardens Assistants and Society and their successors that it shall and may be lawful to and for the Master Wardens and Assistants of the said Company or the greater part of them for the time being to take and admit into the same Society such persons as they shall from time to time think fit and as shall desire to become members or free of the said Society and to administer such oaths to them and to the Members or Freemen of the said Society Which said persons so to be admitted (together with the Master Wardens and Assistants and the rest of the Company of Framework Knitters of the City of London shall be and shall be reputed taken and known by the name of the Master Wardens Assistants and Society of the Art or Mystery of Framework Knitters of the City of London **And** further we do by these presents for us and our successors give and grant full power and authority to the said Master Wardens and Assistants of the said Society for the time being and their successors to cause the Statute made in the fifth year of the reign of Queen Elizabeth and all other statutes concerning trades mysteries and manual occupations to be put in execution upon all persons offending in the premises as firmly fully and effectually as if the said Master Wardens Assistants and Society had been one body politic and corporate before the making of such laws and as fully as any other body politic and corporate within the Commonwealth may or can do **And further** we will and by these presents for us and our successors do firmly require charge and command all and singular justices of the peace mayors sheriffs bailiffs and constables and all other officers and ministers of us and our successors to whom it shall or may appertain that from time to time as the case shall require they be and shall be aiding and assisting unto the aforesaid Master Wardens and Assistants of the said Company and their successors and to their sworn Deputies of the said Art or Mystery of Framework Knitting in the due and lawful execucion of these our Letters Patents in and by all things according to the true intent and meaning thereof **And lastly** we will and by these presents for us and our successors do grant unto the said Masters Wardens Assistants and Society and their successors that these our Letters Patents or the enrolment of the same and all and singular matters and things in the same contained shall be from time to time good sufficient and effectual in law in and by all things according to the true intent and meaning thereof and shall be construed adjudged and taken in all our courts of record and elsewhere most beneficially and largely for the advantage of the said

Master Wardens Assistants and Society and their successors   **Although** express mention of the true yearly value or certainty of the premises or any of them or of any other gift or grant of us or of any King or Queen of England to the said Master Wardens Assistants and Society heretofore made in these presents is not made or any statute act ordinance provision proclamation or restraint to the contrary heretofore made ordained or provided or any other thing cause or matter whatsoever in any wise notwithstanding   **In witness** whereof we have caused these our letters to be made patents   **Witness** ourself at Westminster the thirteenth day of June in the year or Our Lord one thousand six hundred fifty seven

By writ of Privy Seal   **Beale**

Appendix 3

Abridged version of 1663
Charter of Charles II

Taken from *Second Report of the Commissioners*
(Trades and Manufactures); 1843, 430 (XIII), pp. 5–7

1. I, Charles, by the grace of God, &c., having taken into consideration the petition of the Frame-work Knitters of London, Westminster, England and Wales, that many deceits and abuses are made, to the ruin of their families, by strangers and others, think it necessary to uphold the trade, for the general benefit of my subjects, as well as the Frame-work Knitters; and as the Frame-work Knitters are dispersed among other trade companies in London, and have not proper government for the management of their affairs:

2. Being desirous of encouraging the manufacture, all persons having served seven years' apprenticeship, and apprentices who shall hereafter serve seven years, and all others who may be admitted as follows, shall be one fellowship and body corporate and politic, by the name of master, wardens, assistants, and society of the art or mystery of Frame-work Knitters of the Kingdom of England and dominion of Wales, and shall have power to govern the said trade in the said kingdom as herein directed; and they shall have in that name perpetual succession.

3. The society shall have full right to that name to hold any property not exceeding 100l. yearly.

4. And shall have power in that name to sue, and be sued at law.

5. The said Society shall have a common seal, which they may alter at their pleasure.

6. The Society or Company shall consists of one master, two wardens and fifteen or more assistants.

7. John Croson shall be the first master, and shall continue in office until the nativity of St. John the Baptist (June 24) 1664, upon taking the oath before a Master in Chancery; and the master shall be chosen annually from the two wardens.

8. Jonathan Gramer and George Balderston shall be the first wardens, who shall continue in office until St. John's day, when the wardens shall be chosen annually from the assistants.

9. John Lee, Thomas Philips, Joseph Tomlinson, Richard Read, William Rigson, William Gramer, Gabriel Brewer, Samuel Knight, Francis East, J. Patiger, jun., Samuel Yomon, Owen Lavender, John Bennet, jun., F. Armstead, Thomas Stevenson, George Massie, Osmond Smith, William Pickerne, and Thomas Ladd, shall be assistants for life.

10. The wardens and assistants shall choose a master on the feast-day of St. John the Baptist, in the room of John Croson, who shall continue one year.

11.   The master, warden and assistants, shall choose two wardens at the same feast, to continue in office one year, but shall remain as assistants when out of office.

12.   Master or warden dying, there shall be a new election within 15 days.

13.   Upon the death of an assistant, the master, wardens, and assistants shall supply the vacancy from the society.

14.   Any person of the Society who shall be so nominated, and refuse to serve, shall be fined any sum, not exceeding 10l., to be enforced by distress and sale of his goods.

15.   The society shall appoint a clerk of the Company.

16.   John Hennis, Gent., shall be clerk for life; all other clerks after his decease may be removed at the pleasure of the Company.

17.   The master, wardens, and assistants, may make such laws and regulations as they think proper for the government of the Society, for the reformation of abuses, or preventing fraudulent work, and many inflict and levy fines by distress and sale, or otherwise.

18.   Such laws, ordinances, &c., not to be repugnant to the laws of the realm, nor prejudicial to the customs of the city of London.

19.   The master, wardens, and assistants, shall choose a beadle; but William Patrick shall be the first beadle, to serve only during pleasure, under the seal of the Company, and shall have the power to levy all fines, by distress or otherwise.

20.   All mayors, sheriffs, bailiffs, constables, and officers, are commanded to assist the Company, according to the laws of the realm.

21.   The master, wardens, and assistants, shall from time to time appoint two deputies from the Society, under their common seal, to search in the day-time, in the presence of a constable, any place, whether privileged or not, to try and prove whether all stockings or frame-work knitted goods be workmanlike wrought, and if found made bad, or of deceitful stuff, to cut the same in pieces, and to fine the parties making them, according to the bye-laws of the Company.

22.   The master and wardens shall administer an oath to the deputies that they will rightfully and faithfully perform their office as searchers.

23.   Such deputies shall be chosen yearly, or oftener, and may be removed on just cause.

24.   The invention being purely English (natural-born subjects, as well as aliens, having by secret means endeavoured to take the art to foreign states, to the discouraging of the industrious subjects), no person, whether freeman or foreigner, denizen or alien, shall presume to carry, or cause to be carried, any frames used for making silk stockings, or used in Frame-work Knitting, beyond the seas, upon any pretence whatever.

25.   The master, wardens, assistants, or deputies, or any two of them, may seize such frames going to be exported, and may deposit the same in the custody of a lawful officer, until due proof be made thereof, before a justice of the peace, when it shall be forfeited. Such conviction and judgment shall be within forty days if within twenty miles of London, and six months if further distant.

26.   One-half the value of such forfeitures shall go to the Company, and the other to the Exchequer.

27.   Master, wardens &c., may search for fraudulent frames, fraudulent machines, and fraudulent goods.

28.   No person shall follow or use the trade of Frame work Knitting, unless they shall have served seven years' apprenticeship, according to the custom of London.

29.   Every person using the art of Frame-work Knitting within twenty miles of London must enter the society in three months, and beyond twenty miles in six months, and take the necessary oaths, or forfeit 5l. for every week they may neglect.

30.   Persons who are freemen of the City of London, or any other company, are commanded to bind their children, who are Frame-work Knitters, to the members of the Frame-work Knitters' Company.

31.   The Lord Mayor of London is commanded to enrol this Charter in the records of the Common Chamber of London, that they become freemen.

32.   The master, wardens, and assistants may receive any person they think fit, upon taking the oaths, into their body.

33.   The master shall enforce the statute of the 5th Elizabeth, or any other statute, as respects apprentices and the occupations of the trade.

34.   Master, wardens, and assistants may appoint deputies in the districts where the manufacture is carried on, who shall have the same power in their districts as to the enforcing the bye-laws and statutes.

35.   Such deputies shall report, under their hand and seal, an account of their transactions as to money, &c., from time to time to the Company, and must render an account and pay the money yearly.

36.   The Society shall pay yearly to the Exchequer four nobles on the feast of our Lord God (25th December), and if not paid in forty days shall forfeit twenty shillings.

37.   All justices, Custom-house officers, &c., are enjoined to assist the Company.

38.   This Charter shall be taken in all Courts of Record, and construed most largely.

39.   The master, wardens &c. must take the oath of supremacy and allegiance.

40.   If the master, wardens, and assistants do not enrol this said Charter before the clerk of the peace within six months they shall forfeit 10l., and so for every six months default.

By the King
H O W A R D
Fine twenty marks

Signed, 19 August, 15th King.

Appendix 4

Table of Orders, Rules and Ordinances – 4 July 1664

The full ordinances are to be found in the City of London
Guildhall Library and the Nottinghamshire Archives

		Fines
1.	The Election of the Master and Wardens	£5.00.00
2.	The Election of Auditors	
3.	To choose others in the place of officers dead or removed	£2.00.00
4.	For swearing of the Master and Wardens	£0.05.00
5.	The Election of the Assistants	£2.00.00
6.	The Election of the Livery with their Fines and Officers Fee	£20.00.00
7.	The Choice of Deputies	
8.	The Choice of Stewards	
9.	The appointing of Deputies in the Master or Wardens Absence	
10.	The Choice of Clerk	
11.	The Choice of Beadle	
12.	The Company to have a Chest with Three Locks	
13.	Keeping of the Quarter Days and payment of Quarterage	£0.06.08
14.	The Order of Search for Bad Work	£1.00.00
15.	The Search to be made quarterly	
16.	The Search for the Frame	
17.	Against hiring Frames of Strangers	£0.01.00 p.w.
18.	Against teaching the Trade to any other than Apprentices	£50.00.00
19.	No person to take an Apprentice until he has his Masterpiece approved and allowed (to be) a Workhouse Keeper	£5.00.00
20.	Every freeman to give a Spoon at their Admittance and for their refusing Admittance	£1 10.00
21.	How many apprentices every man shall keep	£5.00.00 per month
22.	Against concealing of foreigners	£40.00.00
23.	Touching the timely presenting of Apprentices	£2.00.00
24.	No person of the Company shall bind his Apprentices otherwise than as followeth	£2.00.00
25.	Touching the turning over of Apprentices or the buying or selling of Apprentices	£3.00.00
26.	Against the frequent abuse in turning over Apprentices	£50.00.00
27.	Touching the making of Indentures	£1.00.00
28.	No journeyman to depart his service without a months warning	£5.00.00
29.	Against enticing of Apprentices out of their service	£3.00.00

Fines

30. No journeyman or others to work with any person but such as
    are members and sworn and admitted of the said company £3.00.00
31. An Ordnance for the Master and Wardens to bring in their
    accounts £1 a day
32. An Ordnance for the recovery of Fines
33. An Ordnance that none shall set any at work but such as are
    Members of the Company £5
34. No man to despise the Master, Wardens, Assistants or Deputies
    during their office 6s. 8d.
35. No person to rebuke or otherwise another before the Master
    and Wardens 1s.
36. To make proportional contributions towards the defraying
    of necessary charges Double the sum
37. To enroll Apprentices within one year £1
38. Widows to be admitted and exercise the trade only during widowhood
39. To recover fines according to the law
40. The Oath of every freeman and person at his first admittance
41. The Oath of the Master
42. The Oath of the Wardens
43. The Oath of the Assistants
44. The Oath of the Deputies
45. The Oath of the Clerk
46. The Oath of the Beadle

signed Edward Clarendon, Lord High Chancellor
        Sir Robert Hyde, Lord Chief Justice
        Sir Orlando Bridgemen, Knight and Baronet, Lord Chief Justice of the
                                                        Common Pleas
Ratified 4 July 1664

Appendix 5

Table of Orders, Rules, and Ordinances – 1745

Taken from *Report of the Commissioners appointed to inquire into the Condition of the Framework Knitters*; 1845 609 (XV), pp. 8–10 and Nottinghamshire Archives: MSS. CA 4041/8

The full Ordinances are to be found in the City of London Guildhall Library and the Nottinghamshire Archives.

Fines

1. The Court of Assistants shall yearly, on Midsummer-day, choose out of the assistants one master and two wardens.
2. The Court shall, at the same time, choose three persons to audit the master and wardens' accounts.
3. The Court may choose others to fill the office of master and wardens, on their dying or being displaced within the year.
4. The master and wardens shall, within one week, be sworn into their offices.
5. The Court shall, as often as they think fit, admit such members as are free of the city and of the livery to be assistants; upon refusing to serve forfeit   £10.00.00
6. The Court may admit into the livery so many members of the Company as they may think fit, and every person so admitted refusing to come into the clothing (unless upon showing a reasonable excuse before the lord mayor or one of the aldermen) forfeit   £20.00.00
7. The Court may elect two or more members to be their deputies, to rule and govern all persons exercising the trade of frame-work knitting, according to the powers of the charter, within such district as may be assigned them from their habitations.
8. The Court may elect yearly, on the second Tuesday in April, two members as stewards, within 40 miles of London, who shall provide a dinner on Midsummer-day for the master, wardens and assistants, at their own charge or forfeit such dinner not to exceed the value of £12.   £6.00.00
9. The Court may elect three members to be stewards on the lord mayor's day, who shall provide a dinner of the value of £21, according to the bill-of-fare to be presented to them, or shall pay their share of £7, or be fined £10. No person to be chosen steward who has served the office before.
10. The Court may choose a clerk.

11.   The Court may choose a person, being a member, to be their beadle.
12.   The Company shall have a chest, with three locks, for the custody
      of their treasure, the keys of which shall be kept by the master
      and two wardens.
13.   Four quarterly Courts shall be kept every year, for every member
      that will attend to hear the ordinances read. The Court of Assistants
      shall attend as often as required by the master and wardens, to
      transact the affairs of the Company; every member neglecting
      to appear, to forfeit,   first offence £0.01.00
                                                                second offence £0.02.06
                                                        for every other default £0.05.00
14.   It shall be lawful for the master and wardens, or any two of them,
      with two or more assistants, and also for their sworn deputies,
      four times in every year, or oftener, in the presence of a constable,
      to enter into shops, &., to view, search, and prove all frame-work
      knitted goods, frames, &., and if found defective to seize the
      same, and produce them at their hall of meeting on their next
      Court day, to be fined at the discretion of the Court not exceeding   £0.10.00
      every person obstructing the master, &.,   £5.00.00
      The master upon searching any house may demand   £0.00.04
      any person refusing to pay to forfeit   £0.03.04
15.   No member shall hire frames but of such as are members, on pain
      of paying per frame   £0.01.00 per week
16.   No member shall teach and instruct any person in the art of
      frame-work knitting other than his male child or children,
      apprentice or apprentices, unless bound according to the
      ordinances of the Company, upon forfeiture for every offence   £50.00.00
17.   No member shall retain an apprentice until, for trial of his skill,
      he shall have wrought in the presence of the master and wardens,
      or some persons appointed by them, a pair of silk stockings, &.,
      upon finishing thereof, if approved, he shall be allowed as a
      work-house keeper, upon pain of forfeiting   £5.00.00
18.   No person shall exercise the trade of frame-work knitting unless
      he shall have served seven years' apprenticeship, and shall first
      be admitted a member of the Company; and neglecting to be a
      member for three months, to forfeit for every neglect   £1.10.00
19.   No person shall employ an alien or foreigner, under penalty for
      every offence   £10.00.00
20.   Every member residing within 40 miles of London who shall be
      minded to take an apprentice, shall present him within one month
      at the hall, or, if at a greater distance, to the deputies, to be bound
      by the clerk of the Company, on pain of forfeiting   £2.00.00
      Any member free of the city of London who shall cause an
      intended apprentice to be bound to a freeman of any other
      Company shall forfeit   £5.00.00
21.   No member shall turn over his apprentice without license of the
      master and wardens, on pain of forfeiting for every offence   £2.00.00

22. No journeyman shall depart his service without a month's warning, except for non-payment of wages, or by mutual agreement; no master to turn away such journeyman without the like warning, and paying him what shall be due to him, under penalty of £5.00.00

23. No journeyman shall work with any but such as are members of the Company, under a penalty of £1.00.00

24. No master shall set any person on work but such as are members, except his male children or apprentices, under penalty of £5.00.00

25. The master and wardens, within 40 days after quitting office, to bring in their accounts to the auditors.

26. The master and wardens, or any person appointed by them, shall
    receive of every member using the trade as a master per quarter £0.00.06
    and from every journeyman per quarter £0.00.03
    and from every member not of the trade £0.00.06
    every member refusing to pay when demanded to forfeit £0.06.08

27. Every member shall contribute proportionally to the necessary expenses of the Company, what he shall be rated for that purpose upon pain of paying double

28. Every member free of the City of London who shall neglect to enrol his apprentice before the Chamberlain, within one year after binding shall pay £1.00.00

29. widows, upon being admitted members, may exercise the trade during their widowhood.

30. The Court of Assistants may moderate or wholly remit any penalties, provided such persons pay such sum without suit at law.

31. All fines and penalties to be sued for in the name of the Company, by action of debt, in any of His Majesty's Courts of Record

Fees paid to the Company
Every person at admittance £0.15.00
(10s. admittance, 2s. to clerk, 1s. to beadle and 2s. stamp)
Each apprentice binding £0.09.00
(3s. apprentice binding, 2s. to clerk, 1s. to beadle, 3s. stamp)
Workhouse keeper £0.13.00
(10s. for proof piece, 2s. to clerk, 1s. to beadle)
Turning over an apprentice £0.03.06
(3s. for turning over, 1s. to clerk, 6d. to beadle)

Signed 22 May 1745
by Lord Chancellor
    Chief Justice of Court of King's Bench
    Chief Justice of Court of Common Pleas

Appendix 6

Masters, Clerks, and Honorary Officers of the Worshipful Company of Framework Knitters

Masters

1657	George Ashton
1658	? either of 1657 Wardens, Humphrey Jamson or Thomas Phillips
1663	John Croson, (John Cros(s)in)
1664	? either of 1663 Wardens, Jonathan Gram(ma)r or George Balder(s)ton
1668	Warden, John Pargiter
1669	Henry Wombell; Wardens, William Gram(m)er and John Pa(r)git(t)er
1670	Warden, William Rixon (Rigson)
1676	Francis East
1677	Senior Warden, Thomas Carwarden (Carwardine)
1678	Treasurer, Thomas Carwarden
1678	Carwarden, (? Thomas)
1681	Carwarden, (Thomas or John)
1694	Warden, Ralph T(h)ompson
1696	Anthony Ruslye, (?Russell or Rossell), Wardens, Thomas Pilkington and Sampson Colcough
1720	Capt. William Portress, Wardens, Hart, Edgloy or Brandreth
1722	Thomas Littler
1723	Thomas Littler
1724	Capt. Roger Broome
1725	William Burch, (Birch)
1726	Thomas Bourne
1727	William Hubbald
1728	Michael Mitchell
1729	Joseph Rossell
1730	Joseph Rossell
1731	John T(h)ompson
1734	John Crofts
1743	John Duffield
1744	Charles Cole
1745	John Bradshaw

1746	Thomas Robinson
1747	Charles Cole
1748	Nathaniel Mayes
1749	William Spencer
1750	Richard West
1751	John Moore
1752	George Alcock
1753	George Alcock
1754	Stephen Flower
1755	Thomas Barnfather
1756	Hugh Jones
1757	Edward Needham
1758	John Bradshaw
1759	Westfield King
1760	Benjamin Cole
1761	John Page
1762	William Jepson
1763	Charles Tyrell
1764	George Field
1765	William Robinson
1766	Thomas Grimes
1767	Jonathan Bradley
1768	Thomas Hodgson
1769	John Hollingworth
1770	Ald. John Sawbridge, M.P.
1771	Thomas Birch
1772	Thomas Lever
1773	John Masters
1774	Jude Day
1775	Richard Kemp
1776	Philip Jones
1777	Thomas Clarke
1778	Robert Thompson
1779	John Everard
1780	James Aslatt
1781	William Robinson
1782	Robert Bicknell
1783	Robert Morrell
1784	Ald. Luke Staveley
1885	Thomas Beresford
1786	Robert Bicknell
1787	Charles Barron
1788	Heaton Wilkes
1789	Thomas Hayward
1790	James King
1791	Henry Hardy
1792	William Beckley
1793	Matthew Hilback

1794	Peter Delaport
1795	John Styles
1796	Henry Crosley
1797	Henry Goldfinch
1798	Joseph Wilson
1799	John Pugh
1800	Thomas Swaine
1801	Ald. Sir Charles Flower
1802	Ald. Sir Charles Flower
1803	James Haygate
1804	John Duffield
1805	John Patton
1806	Richard Ovey
1807	Thomas Harrison
1808	Joseph Bowcock
1809	Richard Noble
1810	John Tyrell
1811	William Plestow
1812	Robert Morrell
1813	Richard Gouldsmith
1814	Jonathan Stirtevant
1815	Ald. Robert Waithman, M.P.
1816	John Garton
1817	Richard Gosling
1818	Richard Manning
1819	John Lloyd
1820	Thomas Dawson
1821	John Stirtevant
1822	Thomas Richardson
1823	Samuel Arthur Vardon
1824	William Sampson
1825	John Waithman
1826	Robert Stevenson
1827	William Smallbone
1828	James Capel
1829	John Norbury
1830	Robert Pugh
1831	Henry Smith Cafe
1832	John Lloyd
1833	Henry Bradshaw Fearon
1834	Thomas Francis Noble
1835	Stephen Cundy
1836	Henry Capel
1837	Ald. Thomas Wood
1838	William Nicholson
1839	Henry Lloyd
1840	Robert Henry Manning
1841	Thomas Capel

1842	Robert Romanis
1843	William Morris
1844	Arthur Vardon
1845	Robert Alexander Strachan
1846	John Edwards
1847	Joseph Hannah
1848	Sidney Vardon
1849	Arthur Risdon Capel
1850	Joseph Withers
1851	Robert Manning
1852	John Waithman
1853	William Smallbone
1854	James Capel
1855	James Simon Ewart
1856	John Norbury
1857	Robert Pugh
1858	Frederick W. Cosens
1859	John Lloyd
1860	Henry Capel
1861	Charles Lloyd
1862	Robert Henry Manning
1863	Thomas Capel
1864	Robert Romanis
1865	Arthur Vardon
1866	Robert Alexander Strachan
1867	John Stephen Banning
1868	Joseph Hannah
1869	Sidney Vardon
1870	Arthur Risdon Capel
1871	Joseph Withers
1872	Frederick W. Cosens
1873	John Stephen Banning
1874	Joseph William Hannah
1875	James Smith Kingdom
1876	John King
1877	Robert H. Manning
1878	Thomas Capel
1879	Sidney Vardon
1880	Arthur Risdon Capel
1881	William Bohm
1882	Richard Worthington
1883	Henry Joseph Dowden
1884	William Creasey
1885	James Boyes
1886	Thomas Loveridge
1887	David Wellesley Bell
1888	Lieut.-Col. William A. LeMottee
1889	Thomas Bell

1890	W. H. Whiteway Wilkinson
1891	George Reid
1892	John Paddon
1893	Lieut.-Col. Alfred Durrant
1894	John Harris Cooper
1895	Ald. Sir. Alfred James Newton, Bt.
1896	Wolf Harris
1897	Joseph Griffin Ward, J.P.
1898	Frederick Valentine Nicholls
1899	Henry Pocock
1900	Ald. Sir George J. Woodman, J.P.
1901	Edward Terry
1902	Frederick Crisp, J.P.
1903	Capt. Thomas Blashill
1904	Frederick Dyer
1905	John Arthur Corah, J.P.
1906	Ald. Sir John J. Baddeley, Bt.
1907	Robert Rowley, J.P.
1908	Alfred Corah
1909	William George W. Reynolds
1910	Alexander Lorrimer, J.P.
1911	Frederick Russell Donisthorpe
1912	Ald. Sir Frederick G. Painter
1913	Francis Strange Brice, J.P.
1914	John Woodhouse, J.P.
1915	Thomas Stirk Rowley. J.P.
1916	Ernest Theodore Walker, J.P.
1917	Frank Moore, J.P.
1918	John Lipson Ward, J.P.
1919	Frank Gardiner Wigley
1920	Lieut.-Col. Sir Charles Frederick Oliver
1921	Maurice Lorrimer
1922	David Haes
1923	John Reginald Corah
1924	John Harold Corah, J.P.
1925	Henry Howe, J.P.
1926	George Ernest Ellis, J.P.
1927	Charles Barrowdale Carryer
1928	John Edward Ellis
1929	Sir Arthur Wheeler, Bt., J.P.
1930	Sidney Pears
1931	Clarence Ross Kershaw
1932	William Moore, J.P.
1933	Arthur Stannage Whitehead
1934	Julian Roney
1935	John Harold Cooper
1936	Ald. Sir Harry E. A. Twyford, K.B.E
1937	Henry Gledhill

1938	George Harold Murray Moore
1939	Col. Sir Arthur Hazlerigg
1940	Archibald Edward Gordon Ellis
1941	Reginald Victor Rodwell, F.C.A.
1942	Sidney John Pears, F.C.A.
1943	Ernest John Ward
1944	Donald Byford
1945	Percy Bussens
1946	Edward Victor Stibbe
1947	Thomas George Hirst, J.P.
1948	Shirley Russell Ellis
1949	Ald. Sir Bracewell Smith, Bt., K.C.V.O.
1950	Cyril Osborne, J.P., M.P.
1951	Brig. Cecil B. S. Morley, C.B.E., T.D., A.D.C., D.L.
1952	Walter Lea
1953	Roland Clive Henderson, M.A., B.C.L.(Oxon.).
1954	Leslie Crease Ridd Hayman, C.C.
1955	George Hooton Spencer, J.P.
1956	Harold Linsay Rouse, C.C.
1957	John Eric Foister
1958	Ralph Langford Wing Bedingfield, J.P.
1959	William Bentley, M.B.E, M.I.Mech.E.
1960	Benjamin Hugh Armstrong Russell, M.A.
1961	Vincent Coles
1962	Alan Bent
1963	Thomas Eric Toller
1964	Ernest Henry Westnidge
1965	Gerald William Leigh Holland
1966	David Neil Foister, T.D.
1967	Roger Charles Foister, B.A.
1968	George Fenwick McDonald
1969	Robert Leslie Wessel, O.B.E.
1970	Edward Russell Trotman, M.B.E., Ph.D.
1971	Robert Park Guild
1972	Ronald Dennis Lea, F.C.A
1973	William Munro Fraser
1974	Lieut.-Col. Richard E. Harding Ward, M.C., T.D.
1975	Geoffrey Ross Kershaw, M.A., M.R.C.S., L.R.C.S.
1976	William Kenneth Lowe
1977	Peter Morley
1978	John Michael Stannnage Whithead, J.P., F.R.S.A.
1979	Frederick Arthur Moody
1980	Charles Barrie Byford, O.B.E., A.T.I.
1981	Roger Francis Stevenson, J.P.
1982	Gordon Maurice Taylor
1983	Sir John Peel, M.A.(Cantab.).
1984	Rolf Noskwith, M.A.
1985	Howard Russell Ellis, J.P., A.T.I.

1986   Peter Lipson Ward, M.A., LL.B.(Cantab.).
1987   Ernest George Harding, L.T.I.
1988   Michael Charles Martin, C.Eng., C.B.I.M.
1989   Hugh Patrick Corah
1990   George Nicholas Corah, D.L.
1991   Alfred Michael Chapman
1992   Jeremy Austen Ridge
1993   Robert Anthony Wessel, O.B.E.
1994   Peter Charles Osborne
1995   Arthur James Winterbotham Lewis, O.B.E.
1996   Thomas Munro Fraser, L.T.I.
1997   Robert Brian Osborne
1998   David John Goodenday, J.P.
1999   Michael David Patterson Turnbull
2000   Jonathan McAvoy Dean, M.C.I.M.

Clerks
1663–for life John Hannis (Hennis)
c.1688–1728 John Thurlby
1728–1745   Henry Matthews
1745–1746   Thomas Green
1747–1749   Peter Roberts
1750–1786   John Reynolds
1787–1824   Thomas Lodington
1825–1833   Thomas Wood
1834–1846   Thomas Bless Pugh
1847–1873   Robert Anderson
1874–1902   James Funston
1903–1911   John Woodhouse, J.P.
1912–1923   Philip Hedderwick
1924–1930   Norman Stanley Hedderwick
1931–1937   Dr. Ernest Arthur Ebblewhite, J.P., LL.D., F.S.A.
1937–1961   Cecil John Poley Price
1962–1964   Keith Mountfort
1964–1968   Michael Tynan
1968–1978   Harry Curson Weale
1978–1979   Ian Gordon Williamson
1980–1987   Harry Curson Weale
1988–1992   Colin James Eldridge, LL.B.
1992–1995   David Tate
1996–   Howard Ellis, F.C.A.

Assistant Clerks
1980–1990   A. Gilbert Scrimshaw, F.C.A.
1990–1994   Derek J. Tranter, A.C.I.B.
1994–   Mrs. Anne Brown

Beadles (where known)

1663	William Patrick
1696	John Heminge
c.1720–30s	William Paine
late 1700s/ early 1800s	George and Edward Simmons
c.1860–74	James Funston
in 1894	Mr. Lovell
1902–c.1910	Edwin Clark
–1952	John W. Houghton
1952–1979	John Barker
1979	Arthur Seaman
present	James Wallis

Honorary Treasurers

1966–1987	Roland Clive Henderson, M.A., B.C.L. (Oxon.)
1987–1994	Peter Lipson Ward, M.A., LL.B.
1995–	Hugh Colin Stevenson

Honorary Chaplins

1925–1950	The Revd. Canon B. R. Cooper, B.A.
1951–1963	The Rev. Canon I. D. Powell-Hughes, M.A.
1964–1980	The Rev. Canon E. N. Devenport, B.A.
1980–1984	The Rev. Canon R. J. Tonkin, B.D.
1985–	The Rev. David H. Clark, B.A.

Honorary Surveyors

1908–1917	Arthur T. Draper
1917–1952	J. Stockdale Harrison, F.R.I.B.A.
1952–1964	Maurice W. Pike, F.R.I.B.A.
1964–1985	Laurie C. Candlish, F.R.I.B.A.
1985–	S. R. G. Anderson, Dip.Arch., R.I.B.A.

Honorary Medical Officers

1965–1979	Dr. G. L.Ward, D.S.C., V.R.D., M.A., M.B., B. Chir., F.R.C.G.P.
1979–199	Dr. G. H. Sullivan, M.B., B.S.
1990–	Dr. N. G. Dadge, M.B., Ch.B., B.R.C.O.G.

Appendix 7

The Livery and Apprentices of the Worshipful Company of Framework Knitters

As at April 2000

Mr. C. L. Arundale
Mrs. A. L. V. Ashe
Mr. A. C. Ashton
Mrs. A. M. Ashton
Mr. J. Ashton
Mr. S. M. Ashton
Mr. P. G. Austen
Mr. P. Bailey
Mr. J. W. Baker
Professor K. Barker
Miss C. L. Beachell
Mr. J. G. Beachell
Mr. P. A. Beachell
Mr. J. Bennett
Mr. J. Bennett
Dr. D. P. Bethel
Eur. Ing. P. D. Bethel
Mrs. J. M. Birchall
Mrs. F. R. Bluck
Mr. J. Bluck
Mr. E. B. Bowler
Prof. P. J. Boylan
Mr. C. D. Brewin
Mrs. A. Brown
Mr. D. A. Bryars
Miss V. S. Bryars
Mr. P. Buckland Large
Mrs. M. D. S. Burrows
Mr. S. J. M. Burrows
Mr. A. P. Buswell
Mr. D. A. Buswell
Mr. C. B. Byford
Mr. D. C. K. Byford
Mrs. S. J. Cameron

Mr. L. C. Candlish
Mr. P. A. Carr
Mr. T. J. Caven
Mr. A. M. Chapman
Mr. J. K. Chell
Mr. K. B. Chell
Mr. W. Clayton
The Hon. R. H. Coles
Mrs. P. J. Colvin
Mr. M. J. Condon
Mr. T. C. Constable
Mr. C. M. Cook
Mr. G. S. Cope
Mr. B. N. Corah
Mr. D. P. Corah
Mr. G. N. Corah
Mr. M. B. Corah
Mrs. B. L. Dabbs
Mr. J. A. Davenport
Mr. J. A. Davis
Mr. J. B. Dean
Mr. J. M. Dean
Mr. J. W. Dearden
The Rt. Revd. E. N. Devenport
Mr. F. C. L. Dobson
Mr. J. S. Dobson
Mr. B. S. Durose
Mr. F. J. Ellis
Mr. M. R. Ellis
Mr. D. N. Foister
Mr. M. E. Foister
Mr. S. E. Foister
Ms. S. A. Fraser
Mr. T. M. Fraser

Mr. A. J. Glover
Mr. D. J. Goodenday
Mr. S. E. J. Goodman
Mr. J. R. Granger
Mr. M. Green
Mrs. M. E. Green
Mr. T. B. L. Green
Mrs. F. J. Greer
Mr. I. M. Grundy
Mr. D. E. J. Gwynne
Mr. D. S. Gwynne
Mr. H. Haddon
Mr. D. Hall
Mr. N. P. T. Hall
Mr. R. J. Hall
Mr. R. E. Hallam
Mr. J. N. D. Hancock
Mr. D. S. Harding
Mr. R. F. Harris
Mr. J. P. Harrison
Dr. R. J. Harwood
Mr. P. J. M. Hill
The Revd. W. G. B. Holland
Mr. B. J. Hollier
Mr. J. Houston
Mr. R. F. Humphreys
Mr. N. G. Humphries
Mr. J. T. P. Hurd
Mr. H. E. G. Hurt
Mr. G. D. Johnson
Mr. D. P. St. J. Johnson
Mr. D. L. Jones
Mrs. L. R. Jones
Mr. P. L. Jones
Mr. J. Kapasi
Mr. R. T. S. Kempton
Mr. D. R. Kershaw
Dr. G. R. Kershaw
Mr. W. Kiley
Mr. L. A. W. Lappin
Mr. A. J. W. Lewis
Mrs. J. J. Ling
Mr. D. W. J. Little
Mr. J. T. Littleton
Mr. G. B. Lodge
Mr. J. M. Lowe
Mr. W. A. Lowe
Mr. W. K. Lowe

Mr. C. T. Martin
Mr. M. C. Martin
Mr. C. J. B. Mason
Mr. J. B. Mason
Mr. J. T. Millington
Mr. G. H. Moore
Mr. P. M. M. Moore
Mr. W. K. Moore
Mrs. E. L. Moorhead
Mrs. D. M. Morley
Mrs. J. S. Morse
Mrs. S. K. Murray
Mrs. C. Neville-McCarthy
Mr. J. L. G. Newmark
Prof. E. W. Newton
Mr. R. Noskwith
Mr. M. G. O'Brien
Mrs. H. A. Ogundele
Mr. P. C. Osborne
Mr. M. Parker
Mr. A. W. Pears
Mr. J. J. Pears
Sir John Peel
Mr. N. F. Pettit
Mr. J. P. Polito
Mr. P. M. Preston
Mr. W. J. Proctor
Mr. R. W. Rawlinson
Mrs. A. K. Read-Ward
Mr. A. J. Richards
Mr. I. M. Richards
Mrs. S. F. Richards
Mr. J. A. Ridge
Mr. F. Robinson
Mr. J. S. Robinson
Mr. P. Robinson
Mr. A. C. Roche
Mr. M. J. Rook
Mrs. P. M. Rose
Mr. W. M. Ross-Wilson
Mr. F. W. Rosser
The Rt. Hon. The Lord Sanderson
   of Bowden
Mr. R. D. Sands
Mr. A. G. Scrimshaw
Mr. A. C. Seneant
Mr. J. E. Sharp
Mr. W. E. A. Shelton

Mr. J. R. Simpson
Mr. R. J. Simpson
Mr. T. J. Smalley
Mr. B. Smallman
Mr. B. A. F. Smith
Mr. G. A. F. Smith
Mr. R. B. Start
Mr. F. J. Stevenson
Mr. H. C. Stevenson
Mr. M. F. Stevenson
Mr. R. F. Stevenson
Mr. W. R. Stevenson
Mr. J. A. Stocks
Mr. E. A. Strange
Mr. J. C. Strange
Mr. C. W. D. Sutcliffe
Mr. M. P. Tahany
Miss C. E. Tasker
Miss C. J. Tasker
Mr. P. W. Tasker
Mr. G. M. Taylor
Mr. D. J. Tiney
Mr. D. J. Tranter
Miss E. G. C. Turnbull
Mr. M. D. P. Turnbull

Mrs. V. M. Turnbull
Mr. A. H. B. Turner
Mr. G. F. C. Turner
Mr. S. J. Turner
Mr. D. W. Wall
Mr. R. E. Walton
Dr. G. L. Ward
Mr. P. L. Ward
Mr. M. Watson
Mr. S. C. Wegerif
Mrs. G. R. Welch
Mr. B. C. Weldon
Mr. L. A. Weldon
Mr. C. A. Wessel
Miss L. J. Wessel
Mr. R. A. Wessel
Miss S. C. Wessel
Mrs. A. T. White
Mr. J. M. S. Whitehead
Mr. M. J. S. Whitehead
Mr. L. B. Whittaker
Mr. R. H. Whowell
Mr. D. J. Wilson
Mr. J. R. Wilson
Mr. A. Winkler

LIST OF APPRENTICES – As at 1st March 2000

Apprenticeship entered into/ completed	Admitted to the Freedom of the City of London and the Livery	Apprentice's Name *(Principal's name is stated in brackets)*
Completed 1937	–	Olga Lindsay Rouse *(J. Roney)*
Completed 1939	–	John Hubert Wildt *(E. Wildt)*
Completed 1948	–	Barbara June Carmichael *(F. T. Carmichael)*
Completed 1974	–	Diana Margaret Heginbotham *(D. N. Foister)*
Completed 1976	–	Nigel George Dunn *(J. S. Dunn)*
Completed 1982	1992	Rowton Jeremy Simpson *(J. R. Simpson)*
Completed 1985		Ann Kathleen Pettit *(N. F. Pettit)*

Apprenticeship entered into/completed	Admitted to the Freedom of the City of London and the Livery	Apprentice's Name *(Principal's name is stated in brackets)*
Completed 1987	1998	Joanna Jane Taylor *(G. M. Taylor)* now Mrs. Ling
Completed 1987	–	Amanda June Taylor *(G. M. Taylor)*
Completed 1987	1992	Matthew Robert Simpson *(J. R. Simpson)* Resigned from the Livery
Completed 1990	1994	David Paul St. John Johnson *(G. D. Johnson)*
Completed 1991	1994	Lucy Roxanne Simpson *(J. R. Simpson)* Now Mrs. Jones

Current Apprentices

Entered into 1999 To be completed 2003	Richard Thomas Corah *(D. P. Corah)*
Entered into 1999 To be completed 2004	Deborah Anne Brown *(Mrs. A. Brown)*
Entered into 2000 To be completed 2004	Phillipa Rosemary Hall *(N. P. T Hall)*
Entered into 2000 To be completed 2004	Justin Alistair Hall *(N. P. T Hall)*

All apprentices are entitled to take up the Freedom of the Company on reaching the age of 21 years, provided they have completed the term of their individual Indenture agreement.

Appendix 8

Masters, Wardens and Assistants of the Worshipful Company of Framework Knitters in 1657 and 1663

Francis Armstead (63)
George Ashton (Master – 57)
George Balderstoun (57), George Balderston (Warden – 63)
Anthony Bennett (57)
John Bennett jun. (63)
Gabriel Brewer (57) and (63)
Richard Burnby (57)
John Crossin (57), John Croson (Master – 63)
Francis East (63)
Gregory Fishborne (57)
Jonathan Gram(m)er (57) and (Warden – 63)
William Gramer ([63)
Humphrey Jamson (Warden – 57)
Samuel Knight (57) and (63)
Thomas Ladd (63)
Owen Lavender (63)
John Lee (57) and (63)
George Massie (63)
John Pargiter jun (63)
William Pargiter, (Pagiter), (Patiger), (63)
Thomas Phillips (Warden – 57) and (63)
William Pickerne (63)
Lawrence Pomfret (57)
Richard Read (57) and (63)
William Rigson (63)
Osmond Smith (63)
Thomas Stevenson (63)
Joseph Tomlinson (57) and (63)
Henry Womball (57)
Samuel Yomon, (Tomon), (63)

Appendix 9

Medals, Awards and Bursaries
of the Worshipful Company
# of Framework Knitters

CITY AND GUILDS OF LONDON INSTITUTE

Winners of the WCFK Medals

The medals have been awarded by the Company on the results of the examinations in the Manufacture of Hosiery and Knitted Goods held by the City and Guilds of London Institute.

1929	(*Gold*)	Walter Bennett
	(*Silver*)	John William Galloway
	(*Bronze*)	Donald Charles Gwillim
1930	(*Gold*)	John Gibson Healey
	(*Silver*)	Collis Bernard Good
	(*Bronze*)	Francis Henry Colson Brook
1931	(*Gold*)	William Albert Dutton
	(*Silver*)	Richard Cecil Boyce
	(*Bronze*)	John Worthington Polito
1932	(*Gold*)	Ernest Henry Darral Sugden
	(*Silver*)	John Archibald Campbell Murray
	(*Bronze*)	Arthur Richard Hambly
1933	(*None awarded*)	
1934	(*Gold*)	Arthur Thomas Cole
	(*Silver*)	John Johnstone Duncan
	(*Bronze*)	John Anderson Bell
1935	(*Gold*)	Harry Wignall
	(*Silver*)	Arthur Thomas Cole
	(*Bronze*)	None awarded
1936	(*Gold*)	John Pitt Moffatt
	(*Silver*)	James Thomson Galloway
	(*Bronze*)	Leslie Booth
1937	(*Gold*)	Naum Grodenski
	(*Silver*)	Elsie May Fordham
	(*Bronze*)	Andrew John Horsburgh Burrell
1938	(*Gold*)	Charles Robert Carter
	(*Silver*)	Benjamin Goldman
	(*Bronze*)	None awarded

1939	(*Gold*)	Gertrud Muller
	(*Silver*)	Gordon A. Baxendall
	(*Bronze*)	Frank Smith
1940	(*Gold*)	Denis Frederick Paling
	(*Silver*)	Alfred William Marvin
	(*Bronze*)	George Miller Smith
1941	(*Gold*)	Robert Howden
	(*Silver*)	Ivor Rolfe Thornton
	(*Bronze*)	None awarded
1942	(*Gold*)	Harry Haddon
	(*Silver*)	Kenneth Harold Osborne
	(*Bronze*)	None awarded
1943	(*Gold*)	Walter C. Nivet
	(*Silver*)	Frank Bradshaw
	(*Bronze*)	None awarded
1944	(*Gold*)	Herbert Nichol Aitken
	(*Silver*)	Frank Ronald Jones
	(*Bronze*)	None awarded
1945	(*Gold*)	Walter I. Braun
	(*Silver*)	George A. S. Bell
	(*Bronze*)	F. A. B. Goldschmidt
1946	(*Gold*)	Percival Norman Milne
	(*Silver*)	Alan Bernard Ashwell
	(*Bronze*)	Eric Spira
1947	(*Gold*)	Peter Fernyhaugh Wilks
	(*Silver*)	Frank Morton Bruckshaw
	(*Bronze*)	Derek Bradley
1948	(*Gold*)	F. K. Hill
	(*Silver*)	John M. L. Jacobson
	(*Bronze*)	M. Pitchers
1949	(*Gold*)	Noel Ralph Charles Prior
	(*Silver*)	{ Benjamin William Ball / Alex George Hughan
	(*Bronze*)	Marvis Lassman
1950	(*Gold*)	Jack Hardy
	(*Silver*)	John Balmer Harrison
	(*Bronze*)	Frank Anthony William Clowes
1951	(*Gold*)	John William Beardsworth
	(*Silver*)	Michel Gabriel Billon
	(*Bronze*)	Nicolas Molnar
1952	(*Gold*)	George Scott
	(*Silver*)	John Murray Ralston
	(*Bronze*)	{ Adolf Zukowski / David Haynes Warsop
1953	(*Gold*)	Ralph Gunther Bauer
	(*Silver*)	Graham Everard Pollard
	(*Bronze*)	Richard Maurice Toeman

1954	(*Gold*)	Walter Bruce Arnold Attenborough
	(*Silver*)	John Stuart Forrester
	(*Bronze*)	Ian Scott Rorrison
1955	(*Gold*)	Douglas Bryan Field
	(*Silver*)	John Colin Forsyth
	(*Bronze*)	John Bennett
1956	(*Gold*)	William John Getgood
	(*Silver*)	Brian Beverley Herbert
	(*Bronze*)	Martin Schneider
1957	(*Gold*)	Alexander Maxwell Mann
	(*Silver*)	Richard Osborne Rawson
	(*Bronze*)	John Hadfield
1958	(*Gold*)	Henry Stewart Clarefield
	(*Silver*)	{ Harvey Oliver Hutchinson / Penti J. K. Toivonen
	(*Bronze*)	None awarded
1959	(*Gold*)	Thomas George Whitmore
	(*Silver*)	Lewis William Wood
	(*Bronze*)	None awarded
1960	(*Gold*)	Peter Graham Sangan
	(*Silver*)	Peter Mountfort Johnson Jnr.
	(*Bronze*)	David Robert Hanney
1961	(*Gold*)	Frank Nicholas Tarratt
	(*Silver*)	David Ramsden
	(*Bronze*)	James Colin Watson
1962	(*Gold*)	Angela Barrett
	(*Silver*)	John Bell
	(*Bronze*)	David Graham Smith
1963	(*Gold*)	Dermot Christopher MacShane
	(*Silver*)	John Ewart Sharp
	(*Bronze*)	Thomas Richard Hammond
1964	(*Gold*)	Arthur Elliott Bell
	(*Silver*)	Peter Eric Samwell
	(*Bronze*)	Andreas Jacobsen
1965	(*Gold*)	Richard John Law
	(*Silver*)	Ronnie Hodkins
	(*Bronze*)	Saki Passweg
1966	(*Gold*)	Philip John Johnson
	(*Silver*)	Roberto Bernardo Mandelik
	(*Bronze*)	Anthony Garth Howell Bayliss
1967	(*Gold*)	William Douglas Thorpe
	(*Silver*)	Chun Kiu Cheung
	(*Bronze*)	Tore Tidemann
1968	(*Gold*)	Peter Walter Pasold
	(*Silver*)	George T. Tothill
	(*Bronze*)	Donald Rowland Gleave
1969	(*Gold*)	Howard John Price
	(*Silver*)	Ignatius Michael Hunter
	(*Bronze*)	None awarded

1970	(*None awarded and from 1970 on no further bronze awarded*)		
1971	(*Gold*)	Norman Henderson Taylor	
	(*Silver*)	Kalidas Jayanthkumar	
1972	(*None awarded*)		
1973	(*Gold*)	Murray J. Nancekivell	
	(*Silver*)	{ Murray J. Nancekivell Jean-Michel Guyomar	
1974	(*Gold*)	Jane Clark Honeyman	
	(*Silver*)	{ Jane Clark Honeyman Michael Gregory Wilson	
1975	(*Silver*)	{ Edward John Browne Mahendrakumar Liladhar Sampat	
1976	(*Silver*)	{ Hugh David McTavish Trevor Stanley Ainge	
1977	(*Gold*)	Stephen John Prentice	
	(*Silver*)	Malcolm Simpson	
1978	(*Silver*)	Graham John Mann	
1979	(*Silver*)	David Alistair Thorpe	
1980	(*Silver*)	{ Elizabeth Mary Foulkes George Stylios	

BURSARY AWARD SCHEME AWARDEES

Year	*Award*	*Awardee*	*University*
1985/86		Joan Cotterill	Leicester Polytechnic
		Caroline Harvey	Trent (Notts.) Polytechnic
1986/87		Alison Banister	Leicester Polytechnic
		Ann Neilson	Galashiels
		Yvonne d' Souza	Trent (Notts.) Polytechnic
1987/88		Jaquine Oliver	Trent (Notts.) Polytechnic
		KarenStorie	Galashiels
		Joanna Taylor	Royal College of Arts
1988/89		Amber Rowe	Textile Conservation Centre
		Elizabeth Sterland	UMIST Manchester
		Sandra Hopkins	UMIST Manchester
		Theodore Lantitis	Leicester Polytechnic
1989/90		Leonie Gale	Leicester Polytechnic
		Serena Gavin	Trent (Notts.) Polytechnic
		Lynn Hamilton	Galashiels
		Ingrid Tait	Royal College of Arts
1990/91		Louise Allen	Royal College of Arts
		Caroline Randolfi	Royal College of Arts
		Sonia Mann	Birmingham Polytechnic
1991/92		Claire Nicklin	Birmingham Polytechnic
		Laura Thomson	Leicester Polytechnic
		Lesley Bryden	Galashiels
		Paul Moody	Nottingham Polytechnic

Year	*Award*	*Awardee*	*University*
1992/93	Company Bursary	Alison Slater	Leeds University
	Company Bursary	Belinda Sosinowicz	Nottingham Polytechnic
	Company Bursary	Marion Williams	Leicester Polytechnic
	IWS Bursary	Louise Hill	UMIST Manchester
1993/94	Company Bursary	Louise West nee Snell	UMIST Manchester
	Company Bursary	Jonathan Fisher	UMIST Manchester
1993/94	Company Bursary	Judith Harris	Royal College of Arts
	IWS Bursary	Marco Rebora	Kingston University
1994/95	Company Bursary	Barrie McPherson	Royal College of Arts
	Company Bursary	Annette Reilly	St. Martins School of Art
	Company Bursary	Deborah Wells	UMIST Manchester
	IWS Bursary	Laura Watson	Royal College of Arts
1995/96	Company Bursary	Julien Macdonald	Royal College of Arts
	Benson Turner	Kate Berry	Manchester Metropolitan Univ.
	IWS Bursary	Adrienne Fulton	Royal College of Arts
	Rouse Award	Jessica Payne	Royal College of Arts
	Rouse Award	Rachel Ross	Galashiels
	Rouse Award	Ainsley Sullivan	UCE Birmingham
	Rouse Award	Verity Concannon	University of Derby
1996/97	Company Bursary	Georgia McKie	Royal College of Arts
	Company Bursary	John Arbon	De Montfort University
	Benson Turner	Tracey Hunt	Royal College of Arts
	Willey & Pearson	Kate Wheeler Award	Royal College of Arts
	Rouse Award	Jane Miller	De Montfort University
	Rouse Award	Sharon Bell	Nottingham Trent University
1997/98	Company Bursary	Caroline Connor	Galashiels
	Company Bursary	Louise Greenall	De Montfort University
	Company Bursary	Helen Taylor	De Montfort University
	Benson Turner	Douglas Stuart	Galashiels
	IWS Bursary	Jessica Payne	Royal College of Arts
	INSTEP Bursary	Laura Hill	De Montfort University
	Rouse Award	Helen Jones	Manchester Metropolitan Univ.
	Willey-Pearson	Claire-Yvette Munsey	Manchester Metropolitan Univ.
1998/99	Company Bursary	Kirsty Brown	Bolton Institute
	Company Bursary	Caroline Greenwood	Bolton Institute
	INSTEP Bursary	Andrea Middleton	De Montfort University
	Benson Turner	Hayley Rivers	UMIST Manchester
	Howard Ellis	Kirsty Robertson	Heriot-Watt University
1999/2000	Company Bursary	Joanna Cattanach	Heriot-Watt University
	Company Bursary	Tammy Kane	Heriot-Watt University
	Company Bursary	Alison Coward	The University of Derby
	Company Bursary	Karen Honour	Royal College of Art
	Willey-Pearson	Judith Mundell	Heriot-Watt University
	Howard Ellis	Gabrielle Allen	The University of Derby

Appendix 10

Inventory of the Worshipful Company of Framework Knitters' Plate

1 Baluster Stem Cup engraved with the Company's Arms and the inscription 'The Framework Knitters Company London. Maker's Mark: Orb and Star; Hallmarked: London 1656.

2 Silver Gilt Cup and Cover engraved with the Company's Arms and an inscription identifying the donor as William Creasy.
Maker: Chas. S. Harris; Hallmarked: London 1884.

3 Silver Loving Cup and Cover engraved with the Company's Arms and an inscription commemorating the Jubilee Year of Queen Victoria and identifying the donors as D. W. Bell, John Chappell, Lieut. Col. Le Mottee, A. R. Capel, J. S. Kingdon, W. D. Bohm, R. Worthington, H. J. Dowden, R. Birkin, T. Bell, J. H. Cooper, Major A. Durrant, J. Paddon, George Reid.
Maker: SM; Hallmarked: London 1887.

4 Silver Gilt Loving Cup and Cover engraved with the Company's Arms and an inscription identifying the donor as George Reid.
Maker: W. J. Barnard; Hallmarked: London 1897.

5 Silver Gilt Cup and Cover engraved with the donor's Arms and an inscription identifying the donor as John Paddon.
Maker: W. J. Barnard; Hallmarked: London 1892.

6 Silver Gilt Cup and Cover engraved with the Company's Arms and donor's crest and an inscription identifying the donor as R. Birkin.
Maker: JNN; Hallmarked: London 1892.

7 Silver Gilt Standing Cup and Cover engraved with the badge of the Guildhall Lodge and an inscription identifying the donor as Sir Harry Twyford.
Maker: Hicklenton and Phillips; Hallmarked: London 1938.

8 Gilt Loving Cup with green onyx plinth engraved with an inscription identifying the donor as Sir Frederick George Painter.
Maker: EBS Ltd.; Hallmarked: London 1927.

9   Silver Gilt Rosewater Dish engraved with the Arms of the Company and of the City of London with an inscription identifying the donor as C. J. Woodman. Maker: Martin Hall & Co.; Hallmarked: Sheffield 1900.

10 Silver Gilt Ewer engraved with an inscription commemorating the Silver Jubilee of King George V and Queen Mary and identifying the donors as Frederick Russell Donisthorpe and George Ernest Ellis. Maker: G&S Co Ltd; Hallmarked: London 1932.

11 Silver Gilt Rose Bowl with wooden plinth engraved with the Company's Arms and an inscription identifying the donor as T. B. Cartwright. Maker: G&S Co Ltd; Hallmarked: London 1922.

12 Silver Gilt Box engraved with the Company's Arms and an inscription identifying the donor as Henry Pocock. Maker: A&JZ; Hallmarked: Birmingham 1900.

13 Silver Cigarette Box engraved with the Company's Arms and an inscription identifying the donor as Henry Pocock. Maker: A&JZ; Hallmarked: Birmingham 1899.

14 Silver Cigarette Box engraved with the Company's Arms in chased silver gilt and an inscription identifying the donors as George and Ivan Tarratt of Leicester. Maker: Padgett & Braham; Hallmarked: London 1951.

15 Snuff Box with Silver Plated Mounts on Ramshorn engraved with an inscription identifying the donor as W. H. Whiteway Wilkinson.

16 Four Sheffield Plate Candlesticks by Padley Perkin & Co. circa 1850. The gift of Thomas Eric Toller.

17 Three Light Silver Plated Candelabrum.

18 Silver Trowel with Ivory Handle presented to Sir Arthur Wheeler when he laid the foundation stone of the Oadby Parochial Buildings on 13 July, 1929.

19 Silver Punch Bowl with silver gilt Arms of the Company on the inner centre of the bowl and an inscription identifying the donor as Norman E. Goodman. Silver Punch Ladle with gilt finial engraved with the Company Crest. (Also donated by Norman E. Goodman.) Designer: A. C. Styles; Hallmarked: London 1966.

20 2 Silver Gilt Goblets engraved with the Company's Coat of Arms.

21 48 Silver Gilt Goblets each engraved with the Company's Coat of Arms and inscribed at the base with the donor's name.
Hallmarked: various dates.
Donors: Sir John Corah, S. John Pears, Ernest John Ward, Donald Byford, Edward Victor Stibbe, Mrs. W. G. Fox for T. G. Hirst, Ald. Sir Bracewell Smith, Cyril Osborne, Brig. C. B. S. Morley, Walter Lea, Roland Clive Henderson, Lesley Hayman, George Hooton Spencer, John Eric Foister, R. W. L. Bedingfield, William Bentley, Benjamin Hugh Armstrong Russell, Vincent Walter Coles, Alan Bent, Thomas Eric Toller, Ernest H. Westnidge, G. W. L. Holland, David Neil Foister, George F. McDonald, Robert L. Wessel, Alexander Ian McPherson Hamilton by his wife and son, E. Russell Trotman, Robert Park Guild, R. Dennis Lea, William Munro Fraser, Lieut. Col. R. E. H. Ward, Dr. G. R. Kershaw, William Kenneth Lowe, Peter Morley, John Michael Stannage Whitehead, Frederick Arthur Moody.

Appendix 11

The Master's Chair of the Worshipful Company of Framework Knitters

Report and description of the Master's Chair on display in the department of Early London History and Collections at the Museum of London. Curator Cheryl Smith.

A large masters chair, partly gilded and with painted decoration. Raised on a platform base with the centre removed. The front legs in the form of cherubs and the rear legs and front arm supports of barley twist design. With 'dolphin' arms, carved panel in back and cresting with coat of arms over bearing the motto '**Honi soie qui mal y pense**'. In the centre of the cresting are the words, in gilt script, '**THE GIFT of Mr. THO's. CARWARDEN**' contained in an oval, slightly raised, cartouche. At the base of the carved panel in the back are the words, in black, '**JUNE 4th 1618**'. The leather covered seat is set into the part original seat frame. The stiles and mouldings with carved decoration. Probably constructed mostly of oak but because of the painted decoration identification of all the timber is not possible.

To more accurately date the chair would require further and more detailed examination in a conservation/restoration workshop because of alteration, additions and repair over the years. Research into the history, or some of the history of the chair, would also be useful in helping to establish when the chair was made.

Initial examination of the chair suggests it dates from the third quarter of the 17th century. However, parts of the chair could possibly be from earlier in the 17th century and subsequently used in the construction of this chair at a later date.

Assuming the chair (basically) dates from the third quarter of the 17th century, the cresting appears to be a later addition, the seat and part of the base structure has been altered and new timber introduced to either strengthen the construction or adapt the area in question. The leathered seat is an adaptation. Mouldings have been cut and altered. None of the gilded and painted decoration appears to be original and was probably applied in the 19th century. There are inconsistencies between the different areas of carving but the later painting and gilding masks both definition and style.

The origin of the coat of arms (superficially suggesting Royal connections) requires proper investigation. It is suggested that the College of Arms is asked to give an informed opinion.

The chair was exhibited at 'An Exhibition of Works of Art belonging to the Livery Companies of the City of London' at the Victoria and Albert Museum, possibly sometime during the 1950's. In the catalogue it was described under the heading 'The Worshipful Company of Framework Knitters' as exhibit 600: 'Master's Chair, carved and gilt wood. Period of Charles II. The gift of Thomas Carwarden. Plate XLII'. Under the illustration it was dated 'About 1670'.

Stephen Jarrett – February 1999

Organised by Liveryman David Little.

Appendix 12

Equivalent contemporary values of the pound as at June 1999

These are taken from figures supplied by the
Office for National Statistics

It should not be forgotten that prior to decimalisation there were twelve pence (12d.), in one shilling (1s.), and twenty shillings (20s.) in £1.

£1 in 1480 = £414.00
£1 in 1500 = £414.00
£1 in 1520 = £414.00
£1 in 1540 = £276.00
£1 in 1560 = £184.00
£1 in 1580 = £165.60
£1 in 1600 = £118.29
£1 in 1620 = £87.16
£1 in 1640 = £78.86
£1 in 1660 = £69.00
£1 in 1680 = £75.27
£1 in 1700 = £72.00
£1 in 1720 − £72.27
£1 in 1740 = £78.86
£1 in 1760 = £69.00
£1 in 1780 = £57.10
£1 in 1800 = £29.05
£1 in 1820 = £33.80
£1 in 1840 = £36.00
£1 in 1860 = £42.46
£1 in 1880 = £43.58
£1 in 1900 = £53.42
£1 in 1920 = £18.40
£1 in 1940 = £25.09
£1 in 1960 = £13.35
£1 in 1980 =   £2.48
£1 in 1990 =   £1.31

Glossary

Bag hosiers	Middlemen, between hosier and journeyman.
colt	Person who started framework knitting without having served an apprenticeship.
course	Row of loops.
cut-up	Stocking, or other knitted item, cut from a flat piece of knitted fabric and with no selvage, instead of being shaped on the machine with a selvage. It was less costly and against the rules of the Framework Knitters' Company.
mystery	Handicraft or trade, especially when indentured.
putters out	First mentioned 1727 in letter from hosiers to the Framework Knitters' Company. For Deering (p. 101), these were essentially independent entrepreneurs since they all traded directly with London. For Wells (p. 61) after 1750, this term came to signify a person engaged by the hosier to distribute work.
worsted	A smooth wool yarn produced by keeping the wool fibres parallel during spinning.

Bibliography

Official Documents – Government

The Report from the Trustees of the South Sea Company to the Honourable House of Commons January 25th 1722 (London: Jacob Tomon, Bernard Lintot, William Taylor, 1724).

Report from the Select Committee appointed to take into consideration the several Petitions which have been presented in this Session of Parliament by the Persons employed in Framework-knitting: 1812 247 (II)

Minutes of evidence to the Report of the Select Committee appointed to inquire into the Grievances . . . of Hosiers and Framework Knitters in the Woollen Manufactory of the town and county of Leicester, House of Commons, 1 April 1819.

Second Report of the Commissioners appointed to inquire into the Municipal Corporations in England and Wales, House of Commons, 25 April 1837.

Report of the Royal Commission on the Condition of Framework Knitters: 1845 (609) XV.

Report of the Royal Commission on the Condition of Framework Knitters: 1845 (618) XV (641).

Appendix to the Report of the Commissioners appointed to inquire into the Condition of the Framework Knitters: *Part I Leicestershire*: 1845 618 (XV).

City of London Livery Companies' Commission, Report and Appendix, III (London: Eyre and Spottiswoode, 1884).

Historical Record of the Census of Production 1907 to 1970 (London: Government Statistical Service, 1970).

Receuil des Anciennes et Nouvelles Statuts, Lettres Patentes, Divers Arrest du Conseil, et de la Cour du Parlement, Sentence et Ordonnance du Police concernant l'État du Corps des Marchands Bonnetiers de la Ville, Fauxbourg et Banlieuë de Rouen (Rouen: Imprimerie de Prevost, 1736).

Published Sources – Books

Baddeley, John James, *The Aldermen of Cripplegate Ward* (London: Baddeley, 1900).

Baylen, Joseph O. and Norbert J. Grossman (eds), *Biographical Dictionary of Modern British Radicals: I: 1770–1830* (Sussex: Harvester Press, 1979).

Beavan, Alfred B, *The Aldermen of the City of London*, II (London: Eden, Fisher, 1913).

Bevan, G. Phillips (ed.), *British Manufacturing Industries* (London: Edward Stanford, 1876). 'Hosiery and Lace,' by the late W. Felkin.

Blackner, John, *The History of Nottingham* (Nottingham: Sutton and Son, 1815).

Bonduis, Paul-M., *Colbert et la fabrication du bas: 1655–1683: La transformation d'une industrie par le méchinisme au XVII siècle* (Paris: Librarie des Sciences Economique et Socials, 1929).

W. Booth, *In Darkest England and Way Out* (London: Salvation Army, 1890).

Chamberlain, John, *Manufacture of Knitted Footwear* (Leicester: Alfred Tacey, 1930).

Chinnery, G. A. (ed.), *Records of the Borough of Leicester*, V (Leicester: Leicester University Press, 1965).

Cobbing, Beryl, *William Lee and the Stocking Frame* (Calverton Preservation Society, 1991).

Dale, T. C, *The Inhabitants of London: 1638* (London: Society of Genealogists).

Deering, Charles, *The History of Nottingham*, first published Nottingham 1751 (Nottingham: S. R. Publishers, 1970).

Denton, Rev. W., *Records of St. Giles' Cripplegate Without* (London: George Bell & Sons, 1883).

Ditchfield, P. H., *The City Companies of London* (London: J. M. Dent, 1904).

Earle, Peter, *The Making of the English Middle Class: Business, Society and Family Life in London: 1660–1730* (London: Metheun, 1989).

Ellis, Collin, *History in Leicester*: 55BC–AD1976 (Leicester: Information Bureau, 1976).

Evelyn, John, FRS., Diary and Correspondence of, ed. William Bray Esq., 1854.

Felkin, W., *An Account of the machine-wrought hosiery trade* (London: W. Strange, 1845).

Felkin, William, *A History of the Machine-Wrought Hosiery and Lace Manufactures* (London: Longmans, Green, and Co., 1867).

Grass, Milton and Grass, Anna, *Stockings for a Queen* (London: Heinemann, 1967).

Gurnham, Richard, *A History of the Trade Union Movement in the Hosiery and Knitwear Industry*: 1776–1976 (Leicester: National Union of Hosiery and Knitwear Workers, 1976).

Hartopp, Henry, *Register of the Freemen of Leicester*: 1196–1770 (Leicester: Corporation of Leicester, 1927).

Hazlitt, W. Carew, *The Livery Companies of the City of London* (Benjamin Blom: New York/London, 1969).

Henson's History of the Framework Knitters (David & Charles Reprints: Newton Abbot, 1970).

Holford, Christopher, *A Chat about the Broderers Company*, 1910.

Howes, Edmund (ed.), John Stow's, *The Annuals of England*, 1615.

Johnson, T. Fielding, *Glimpses of Leicester* (Leicester: Clarke and Satchell, 1906).

Kahl, William F, *The Development of London Livery Companies* (Boston: Baker Library, 1960).

Knight, Charles, *London* (London: Virtue & Co, u.d. c.1875–7).

Lee, Sidney (ed.), *Dictionary of National Biography*, XXXII (London: Smith Elder & Co., 1892).

Leicester Polytechnic, *Centenary History of the School of Textiles* (Leicester: Leicester Polytechnic Press, 1983).

Leicestershire Museum Services, Discovery Park, Snibston, pamphlet on 'Framework Knitting'.

Mason, S. A., *Nottingham Lace*: 1760s–1950s (Ilkeston: Cluny Lace Co. Ltd., 1994).

Mason, S. G. (ed.), *British Hosiery and Knitwear* (London: The Hosiery and Knitwear Export Group, ?post 1950).

Melling, John Kennedy, *Discovering London's Guilds and Liveries* (Princes Risborough: Shire Publications , 1988).

Nichols, John, *The History and Antiquities of Leicester: 1811* (Leicester: Leicestershire County Council/S.R. Publishers, republished 1971).

Nichols, John Gough, *London Pageants* (London: Nichols, 1831).

Orange, J., *History of Nottinghamshire*, 1840.

Palmer, Kenneth Nicholls, *Ceremonial Barges on the River Thames* (London: Unicorn Press, 1997).

Palmer, Marilyn, *Framework Knitting* (Princes Risborough: Shire Publications, 1990).

Pavord, Anna, *The Tulip* (London: Bloomsbury Publishing plc., 1999).

Plummer, Alfred, *The London Weavers' Company*: 1600–1970 (London: Routledge & Kegan Paul, 1972).

Prideaux, Sir Walter Sherburne, *Memorials of the Goldsmiths' Company* (London: Eyre & Spottiswoode, 1896).

Saxton, Henry B., *A History of Arnold* (Nottingham: Saxton, 1913).

Tawney, R. H., and Eileen Power (eds), *Tudor Economic Documents* (London: Longmans, Green, 1924).

Silverman, H. A., 'The Hosiery Industry' in *Studies in Industrial Organisation*, H. A. Silverman (ed.) (London: Methuen & Co., 1946).

Skinner, Martin, *The Proper Care of Parrots* (Neptune City, New Jersey: T. F. H. Publications, Inc., 1992).

Sutherland, Lucy S., *The City of London and the opposition to Government* 1768–1774, The Creighton Lecture in History 1958 (London: Athlone Press, 1959).

Thirsk, Joan, 'The Fantastical Folly of Fashion', *Textile History and Economic History: Essays in Honour of Julia de Lacy Mann*, N. R. Harte and K. G. Ponting (eds) (Manchester: Manchester University Press, 1973).

Thirsk, Joan, and J. P. Cooper (eds), *Seventeenth-Century Economic Documents* (Oxford: Clarendon Press, 1972).

Thoroton, Robert, *The Antiquities of Nottinghamshire* (London: Robert White for Henry Mortlock, 1677).

Timbs, John, *Curiosities of London* (London: Virtue, 1877).

Throsby, John , *Thoroton's History of Nottinghamshire*, II (London: B. & J. White, 1797).

Trevor-Roper, H. R., 'Oliver Cromwell and his Parliaments', in *Essays presented to Sir Lewis Namier*, Richard Pares and A. J. P. Taylor (eds) (London: Macmillan & Co. Ltd., 1956).

Unwin, George, *The Gilds and Companies of London* (London: Methuen & Co., 1925).

Victoria County Histories of Leicestershire, Derbyshire, and Nottinghamshire.

Waithman, Robert, *War proved to be the real cause of cause of the present scarcity*, pub. 1800.

Watkins, Susan, *In Public and in Private: Elizabeth I and her World* (London: Thames and Hudson, 1998).

Wells, F. A., *The British Hosiery and Knitwear Industry: Its History and Organisation* (Newton Abbot: David & Charles, 1970).

Wheatley, Henry B., *London Past and Present* (London: John Murray, 1891).

Whitmore, Major J. B., *London Aldermen* (Typescript for the Society of Genealogists, 1961).

Journals

Belfanti, Carlo Marco, 'Fashion and Innovation: The Origins of the Italian Hosiery Industry in the Sixteenth and Seventeenth Centuries,' *Textile History*, 27, 1996.

Bethel, Slingsby, *The World's Mistake in Oliver Cromwell* (tract pub. 1668, details supplied by Assistant Dr. David Bethel).

Kahl, William F., 'Apprenticeship and the Freedom of the London Livery Companies, 1690–1750', *Guildhall Miscellany*, VII, August 1956.

Knight, Mark, 'A City Revolution: The Remodelling of the London Livery Companies in the 1680s', *English Historical Review*, 112, November 1997.

Lewis, Peta, 'William Lee's Stocking Frame: Technical Evolution and Economic Viability 1589–1750', *Textile History*, 17, 1986.

Marshall, 'Nottinghamshire Subsidies 1689', *Nottinghamshire Family History Society Records Series*, XXIV, Part I.

'Nottinghamshire Marriage Index up to 1699', Part I, *Nottinghamshire Family History Society Record Series*, 84.

Pasold, E. W., 'In Search of William Lee', *Textile History*, 1975.

Ponting, K. G., 'In Search of William Lee' *Textile History*, 9, 1978.

Webb, Cliff, 'City of London apprenticeship and livery company records', *Genealogists' Magazine*, XXVI, March 1998, pp. 1–4.

Webb, W. H., F.R.Hist.S., 'The Genesis and History of the Hosier or machine-knitting trade', *The Textile Recorder*, 15 November 1913.

Webster, W. F. (ed.), 'Nottinghamshire Hearth Tax, 1664: 1674', *Thoroton Society Record Series*, Vol XXXVII.

Wykes, David L., 'The Origins and Development of the Leicestershire Hosiery Trade', *Textile History*, 23, 1992, pp. 23–54.

Newspapers

City of London Observer
City Press
Hosiery Trade Journal
Lady (The)
Leicester and Nottingham Journal
Leicester Chronicle
Leicester Daily Post
Leicester Evening Mail
Leicester Mercury
London Gazette
Nottingham Journal
The Times

Index

(Neither the Appendices nor the names on Plates C8, 41, 42 and 48 have been indexed. The page numbers in *italics* refer to Plates).

267

THE BOY IN THE MONKEY